Circle in the Darkness

"As our circle of knowledge expands, so does the circumference of darkness surrounding it."

—Albert Einstein

Circle in the Darkness

Memoir of a World Watcher

Diana Johnstone

Clarity Press, Inc.

ISBN: 978-1-949762-13-6
EBOOK ISBN: 978-1-949762-14-3

In-house editor: Diana G. Collier
Cover design: R. Jordan Santos

Library of Congress Control Number 2019952337

Clarity Press, Inc.
2625 Piedmont Rd. NE, Ste. 56
Atlanta, GA 30324, USA
https://www.claritypress.com

Table of Contents

Table of Contents
(continued)

To Jean Bricmont,
who persuaded me to write this book,
and provided me with his encouragement
and good cooking all the way.

PART I

Looking for the World

1.

Memories of Memories

What one calls childhood memories are really memories of memories. Moments or incidents that one recalled, and later recalled having recalled, and that became part of a limited repertoire of the tiny spots of light in a very long darkness of forgetfulness. To what extent is the adult really the same person as the child?

My very earliest memorized memory is a dim recollection of a family picnic in the woods and seeing a man with a dog walking along the edge of a nearby cliff. I was afraid that the dog would fall off. When much later I asked my grandmother when that could have been, she was able to date the picnic; I was eighteen months old at the time. That was an early indication of my lifelong fear of falling—or more precisely, my fear of seeing others fall. Animals and fear of falling: basic baby attention-getters. And I was already worrying.

The first lesson in life that I can recall came from my maternal grandmother, whom I called Ooma. It must have been when I was three or four, staying with my grandparents in Saint Paul as my mother went to work for the New Deal in Washington. When going to bed at night, I must have been afraid of the dark. Ooma intervened decisively. "When you're afraid of the dark, say 'boo' to the dark, and the dark will be afraid of you." That advice stayed with me all my life.

Early memories are mostly atmospheric: the sunshine and clouds in the garden, and the large threatening hollyhocks. Or the much bigger garden, practically a farm, of my paternal grandparents in Excelsior, Minnesota, where grandfather Bruff tried to chase birds out of the fruit trees and the neighbor's turkeys out of the vegetable patch. I picked strawberries and was encouraged to go into the hen house and steal eggs from the hens, who hardly seemed to mind. And the lakes, the Minnesota lakes, so peaceful, and sky so blue.

But what concerns me mainly is to evoke the Zeitgeist, glimpsed even at an early age, whose changes, and the awareness of how much they change, are the main treasure of old age. This is not nostalgia, although it may sound like that. Rather it is the lived experience of the transitory nature not merely of things (which have been drastically transformed in my lifetime) but especially of the moral environment.

The period called "the Depression" was a moral environment, and I was born into it. Or it was around us, as we were safe and secure in the home of grandfather Elmer Bonnell, whom I called Boopa, as he was principal of Harding High School. All was calm, and walks were taken between the spaced trees on the campus of neighboring Macalester College. Only one adventure was known to have intruded into this middle-class paradise. In the dark eternity before I was born, a family up Vernon Avenue had rented their house for the summer to an uncertain number of persons who kept the window shades down and were almost never seen. It turned out they were Chicago gangsters hiding out either from the police or from competitors. It ended badly, but I don't recall the details. People on Princeton Avenue still talked about it, but the adventure dated from an earlier era, the era of prohibition, which had been ended by the god of my childhood, Franklin Delano Roosevelt.

The Bonnells had no economic worries but shared a general concern over the fact that so many people were out of work, hungry, desperate. The magazines showed color photos of big dinners and the radio broadcast lots of jokes and laughter, but the poor people were all out there, dressed in their shabby best, looking for work.

My paternal grandparents had a harder time since my grandfather Bruff had lost his job, but they ate well from their gardens, and my grandmother Maude earned money for playing organ in church and piano in the Sunshine Home on Lake Minnetonka, where she took me to see the old people sitting in deep chairs on the wide white porches. For a while, she took in a foster child called Glen. Everybody worked on odd jobs. My father worked for a while in the local amusement park, and even as a professional baseball player. Their problems were more psychological than material. They were all too aware of being poorer than Maude's stock broker cousin Roy Howard, who lived on the top of the hill in a house with a lily pad pond. The feeling of failure haunted Bruff, whereas Maude expressed her indignation (as I learned much later) by voting Socialist in the 1932 election, as did my father.

Until 1932, the ideological divide in Minnesota had been essentially between Republicans and socialists—whether the Socialist Party or the local Farmer-Labor party, which in 1930 won the governorship. Both attitudes were a pretty fair, rational reflection of the differing attitudes between business people and workers in a state which blended New England Yankees with hard-working Germans and Scandinavians, all pretty much united against Eastern Banks but at the same time rather internationalist in outlook. But in the 1932 presidential election, the political landscape altered when Franklin D. Roosevelt defeated the Republican incumbent, Herbert Hoover, by three to one. Just as Germany was acquiring its demon, Adolf Hitler, the United States was acquiring its first Great Man since Abraham Lincoln, but a Democrat this time—a party known for its Southern white segregationists who ran most Senate committees and its northern city political machines that juggled ethnic clans, both of whom tended in their contrasting ways to get in power and stay there until late retirement. The ambiguity of the multi-faceted Democratic Party required a leader who was Above It All—because there was too much questionable stuff down below. Part of being above it all was to create his own "brain trust," to bring people into government on the basis of ability and conviction rather than the spoils system.

The New Deal

Considering how totally FDR dominated the United States during his dozen years as President, it is somewhat surprising how quickly he was forgotten—much more quickly than John F. Kennedy, who was stopped from completing his four-year term. JFK was more romantic and left behind him the disappointed hopes for what might have been. FDR took America in and (almost) out of World War II and died exhausted in April 1945. There was not much more to expect.

Early in the New Deal, in 1934, while my father was completing his doctoral thesis in Minnesota, my mother Dorothy took her Phi Beta Kappa key to Washington and went to work for the Social Security Administration. In the fall of 1936, the little family was united in an apartment just behind the Supreme Court building in Washington. My father was doing research in the neighboring Library of Congress, and it was there that I encountered my first deity, known as "the mosaic Minerva." I was hugely impressed. An even more pagan divinity, next to the Folger Shakespearean Library, was the statue of Puck from Midsummer Night's Dream, with the inscription "Lord, what fools these mortals be," which was the first sacred text I ever memorized.

An only child is particularly attentive to parents, since they are all that is around. To be close to parents, one must try to understand what they are saying at the dinner table and see the world as they speak of it. Since their world was very political, that was the world I glimpsed in little fragments.

I was taken to watch the inaugural parade for FDR's inevitable second term. It was a grey and rainy day, but important, I understood.

Around that time, in early 1937, there was great excitement in our world over conflict between the Great Man and the Supreme Court, which had been blocking New Deal legislation. One Saturday afternoon, some of my mother's friends were visiting our Capitol Hill apartment when a Supreme Court Justice was spotted being driven out of the back exit. "Resign!" a lively little friend shouted out our window in the direction of the Justice. I was surprised that adults could act like that.

I remembered that by myself, but not an incident that my mother repeated to me long afterwards. My parents had taken me to some patriotic event with speakers and fireworks. As a politician was making a long speech, I piped up, "Papa, is all that *true?"* This was repeated as an early sign of my eternal naiveté, a Candide looking for truth. Surrounded by so much political talk, I suppose the question "is all that true?" was natural and remains so forever.

In the spring of 1937 I was taken by my grandmother, Maude, to a strange ceremony called an Easter Egg Roll on the White House lawn, where kids milled about making a mess with boiled eggs. The story goes that the White House lawn, cluttered with eggs, was where I must have caught a very bad case of measles. This illness inspired my mother to get me my first pet, a small turtle that lived in a bowl, with "Simple Simon" painted on its back, and then to send me back to St Paul to be fed and cared for by Ooma. Thus I started first grade in Ramsey elementary school in St Paul, with a teacher named Miss Wunn. Minnesota was so neat and orderly that I could have expected my second grade teacher to be named Miss Two. But before that, I was send back to Washington, where my father, his thesis completed, was henceforth working at Henry Wallace's Department of Agriculture as agricultural historian. Between social security and Henry Wallace, my environment could not have been more heavily New Deal.

Life was simple for children in those days, without all the obligatory cultural activities of later periods. I got exercise walking a mile or so back and forth to school, exploring detours. I liked to read what they called the funny papers, re-read Winnie the Pooh and the Oz Books over and over, play with dolls, draw faces, ride my bicycle, climb trees and write. Once I wrote a story while sitting in a tree and showed it to my father. It was a story about some sort of magical voyage. My father did not exactly disapprove, but advised me that a writer should write about real things she knows. That advice made a deep impression on me.

War in Other Places

War was something that was happening in other places that my father knew about. At first I was afraid of it. It might have been the late summer of 1939 when I first heard that war was coming. The radio had been broadcasting some declarations of Hitler, who sounded quite angry, and my father announced to us that war was inevitable. I burst into tears, because in my mind, war meant men in uniform lining up in opposing rows and shooting each other dead. Since he was a declared enemy of Hitler, war meant that Papa would be put in one of those lines to shoot at others and be shot at.

But the fall of France raised personal hopes. My parents spoke of taking in for the duration the daughter of a French colleague my father knew when he was in Paris, a little girl my age. As an only child, the war was a stroke of luck if it would provide me with a French sister. I dreamed of my life with Michèle, but she never came.

I greatly admired both my parents, but one incident raised my admiration to new heights. On Sundays, we usually drove to a place on the Chesapeake called Scientists Cliffs where we went fishing for croakers and walked along the beach collecting sharks' teeth. One Sunday, for a change, we drove to a place called Rehobeth Beach where you had to pay to get in. At the entrance was a sign reading "Gentiles Only." My father went into a righteous rage. He demanded to see the manager. I just understood him saying, "Why don't you hang out your Nazi flag?" We drove away in a glow of heroism. In retrospect, he may have welcomed the chance to go fishing instead of to a beach.

My parents were so far into the war in Europe that Pearl Harbor was no surprise. It brought new fantasies. In expectation of a German invasion, I eyed all the surrounding woods as potential hiding places for my fight against the invading Nazis. Meanwhile the adults also played imaginary games, covering windows at night so that the Luftwaffe wouldn't see us, while the husbands of the neighborhood were obliged to relay each other at the overnight air raid watch. This was slightly closer to reality than my war, but the participants were more skeptical, writing wry comments in the log book. At school, we had to duck during air raid drills, and with my head down, I always rather wished for a bombing in order to escape from the boredom—perhaps to my favorite woods. From all this, I conclude that children are not as sensitive to mere talk of dangerous threats as they are sometimes made out to be. They are waiting for something to happen.

Living safely in a well-to-do Maryland suburb of Washington, where all the men and my mother were working overtime to defeat the Nazis and the Japs, the war was a constant preoccupation. I remember historic moments. Getting up early to go fetch the *Washington Post* from the doorstep in order to read the latest episode of *Terry and the Pirates,* I saw the headline: Germany invades the Soviet Union. My father actually welcomed that as good news, since it meant that Hitler would be defeated.

Thursday was the maid's night off, so I would go into Washington to watch the war at the Newsreel theater before meeting my parents to go to Hogate's for a seafood dinner. That gave me a more comforting view of the war than my earlier notion of soldiers lined up to shoot at each other. There were lots of inspiring shots of the Star Spangled Banner and happy pilots about to take off to go kill Japs while the optimistic commentator insisted on the obvious fact that America was the greatest thing that ever happened and was sure to win. Actually, I found all this almost as boring as Westerns, since I much preferred romantic films with beautiful actresses I would like to turn into. I never liked to watch violence, but they didn't show us much of it.

Lessons of Life

When I was ten years old, my Bonnell grandparents came to stay with us in Rock Creek Hills, just between Rock Creek and Kensington, Maryland. In earlier times, after my grandfather was retired, we drove during winter holidays through the poor South, with its shacks and Burma Shave signs along the two-lane roads, to visit them in their winter cabin in Melbourne, Florida, where we could admire the flamingos, flee the mosquitos and buy crates of citrus fruits to bring home. But now, they came to stay with us because something was going very wrong, and Ooma could no longer handle her much adored husband.

Tall, slender, still handsome with his ivory-white hair and mustache, Elmer N. Bonnell, my Boopa, was losing it. Nobody spoke of Alzheimer's in those days, and this trouble was diagnosed as hardening of the arteries, which made sense considering the way it affected him.

He could be very confused about where and when. Sometimes he was back coaching the baseball team. At such moments, as a child I most easily went along with his fantasies and we were both happy. My mother was sometimes in tears, lamenting that I was getting such a wrong impression of my grandfather. She was mistaken. I had known my grandfather before I could read and remembered the story books he read to me, his gentleness and kindness. If I could play along with his disrupted imagination, I was happy to be with him.

But this malady went in cycles. The theory was that the cycles were related to how much blood was flowing regularly through his arteries. At times he would be somewhere else, in fantasy land, and then he would come back, and for a day or two seem almost normal. We could play some simple board game, talk about things. But then would come the day when the blood flowed truly normally in his brain and his awareness of reality was suddenly sharp and clear. And then he would sit and weep.

That has remained my deepest lesson of human life. Lucidity can bring suffering in a world of madness.

There is only one other incident from my elementary school days that I preserved over the years by thinking back on it. After we moved to Rock Creek Hills, posh enough to house a few lobbyists and even a Senator from Texas, I walked every day back and forth to Kensington Elementary School. Since then, Kensington has been greatly gentrified, but at the time, a large proportion of the kids came from economically and culturally poor homes. I remember visiting the home of a schoolmate where the only printed literature were the pornographic comics she had found by rooting around in her parents' closet. Among these "poor whites," as the stereotype had it, the boys tended to be racist and use "nigger-lover" as their top insult—although colored people were totally absent from Kensington in those days of segregation. The girls could be mean, but when the boys were mean it was even worse. They had chosen as their victim a tall, gentle, intelligent redhead named Roscoe Reeves, Jr. For these little savages, the name "Roscoe" was the ultimate in ridicule, and anyone with such a name had no right to live in their company. The teasing could turn violent. The incident I recall happened at the end of the school day as we prepared to walk home (kids weren't driven all over by their parents as they are now). The chief bully found some pretext to pick a fight with Roscoe, who although bigger, was not the belligerent type and scarcely defended himself. The bully rounded up his followers and formed a pack, to torment Roscoe all the way home. Roscoe lived in the same direction as my home, but even farther away. I took an alternative route and hid in a wooded area near my home, watching horrified as the little monsters harassed Roscoe, shouting insults and even throwing things at him. I was too aware of the unfavorable relationship of forces to intervene, considering that I was already on the edge of pariah status myself. I am sure Roscoe Reeves Jr. grew up to be a distinguished gentleman while the little bully probably had no future. That was the class struggle as I saw it in Kensington Elementary School.

Otherwise, the "home front" was an easy place to be. Certainly, there was the grief of Americans who lost their sons, fathers, brothers, husbands and fiancés in the actual battles. But such bereavement can scarcely be compared to what the civilians went through in China, Japan, Russia, Germany and other places on whose territories the war had really taken place. I mention all this only to stress the notorious fact that two horrible world wars failed to immunize Americans against yet another. There are few Americans still alive who remember World War II even as little as I do. At D-Day, we were let out of school in order to go pray in church. I had no church to go pray in and instead I wandered around trying to feel as solemn as they expected me to feel when they let me off school.

Sometime when I was around 12 or 13 years old, the world suddenly moved away. This had nothing to do with my eyesight, which was excellent. But suddenly, everything seemed at a greater distance than before. I have never read about this phenomenon, but if it happened to me, it must happen to others. Perhaps this loss of proximity marks a passage from childhood to early adolescence.

At that age, I was dissatisfied with whatever I had just done and imagined that the movie must start all over. That indicates that I must not have been very happy, but it was not believed then that a child must be happy. I wanted to change and get better.

On Saturdays, my parents kept working but I was free to do as I liked. Ostensibly I went to the movies, but without telling anyone, I took the bus and the trolley car into downtown Washington and explored. I particularly liked Southwest Washington, the wharfs along the Potomac, the only natural border of the District of Columbia, cutting it off from the state of Virginia. There, behind the seafood restaurants, was a real port with real ships, delivering fish and softshell crabs to the restaurants. Inland was a residential neighborhood, with houses and trees, a few shops and churches, where everybody was black. I would buy a bag of chocolates and walk around everywhere, exploring. People didn't pay much attention to me, but if they did, it was friendly. That was my secret. I know no other child who did that.

That peaceful neighborhood vanished years ago to make way for condos.

Uncle Bruce was a junior officer on some ship in the Pacific, my father was in India as chief of East Asian intelligence in the Bureau of Economic Warfare, but no one in our family was killed or injured. The only casualty was my parents' marriage.

My mother was working at the Office of War Information, using her clever writing skills for propaganda, I assume. For the summer vacation of 1944, she sent me off to a camp in Pennsylvania, supposedly for my own good, although I suspected otherwise. I was too tall and too thin and dreaded sports. The only thing I was good at was "music appreciation." But I was able to sneak away and wander alone in the adjacent forest where I came upon a cabin inhabited by an extremely old woman, just like a good witch in a fairy tale. This was the adventure that made summer camp worthwhile. The ancient lady perked up at seeing me and as we got to know each other, she told me that she had lost her land to the camp owners who had reduced her to this little cabin all alone in the midst of a forest. I was very indignant about this, and even wrote home that we should adopt her. I snuck away repeatedly to visit her, and also went even farther to a place where I discovered a beautiful view of Pennsylvania countryside. These were the only pleasures of summer camp.

Shortly before Christmas of 1944, I was lying in front of the fire, reading, and my mother said she had something to tell me. My heart sank and I was paralysed. I knew what she was going to say. My personal magic was always to expect the worst so it wouldn't happen, but the magic failed this time and the worst happened. Dorothy was leaving with her great love, Drummond, a fellow OWI writer, whom she was sure I would like (she couldn't have been more wrong), but meanwhile I was to stay home with our maid and be nice to my father who was due to arrive in the next couple of days.

I never spoke to anyone about the divorce and nobody said anything to me. I stayed with my father, of course, who brought his mother, Maude, to stay with us until he remarried—rather too quickly, to a woman he scarcely knew. All my parents' friends became my father's friends.

Neither of my parents ever spoke to me critically of the other, but they never spoke to each other again either. My father's only derogatory remark was to liken Dorothy to Madame Bovary.

But they had no contact, except meeting in court in a fight for my custody. This came about in a rather strange way. My father had taken me to California, but I visited my mother and Drummond during the summer vacation in their apartment in downtown Washington, where I became close friends with his angelic daughter, Candace, three years younger, who normally lived with her mother, Drummond's previous wife. We were in some sense allied against the man who had broken up both our parents' marriages.

At some point, the pressure grew intense: stay with my mother or with my father? There was a big white Church at Thomas Circle, and when I couldn't handle things any more, I went into that church and told the pastor all about it. I had never seen him before and we were perfect strangers. Somehow he took over and this led to my dilemma being transferred to the courts. I do not have to believe in the Christian religion to be grateful that I was able to take my problem to a Christian minister rather than to a psychologist. A psychologist might have started prodding around my unconscious, looking for stereotypes, but the minister was very discreet, factual and practical. He took emotions as what they were, and not as the expression of something hidden that had to be dug up, treating the person in trouble as a soul, whatever that is, rather than as a case.

My father won the custody battle.

Since there was absolutely no affinity between me and the southern woman he rapidly married in order to provide me with a mother, I went through adolescence essentially motherless.

My stepmother, as befits a southern lady, was a practicing Presbyterian, leaning to the punishing more than the rewarding side of Christianity. Largely in an attempt to please her, at the age of fifteen, I became a passionate admirer of Jesus. But two incidents shook my faith. One was the lecture on Christian morality delivered to Sunday school by a deacon or some such luminary. He illustrated Christian duty by recounting the following incident. He was walking with a friend when the friend had a heart attack. He helped the friend into a nearby bar in order to get a glass of water and call for help. But on reflection, he considered this a bad action. Some passerby might have seen him go into a bar and concluded that he was not a good Christian after all.

I was silently appalled, but figured this had nothing to do with Jesus, who retained my affection.

One morning the three of us were having breakfast, and I was extolling Jesus. My father remarked wryly that this was a phase I was going through, and I would go through other phases—agnostic, atheist... At that point, Polly exploded: "She won't live in this house if she's an atheist!"

He looked pained but neither he nor I said anything. He was perhaps thinking that women are strange and often incomprehensible, so one had to accept what they said even when it made no sense. I was thinking that Polly's desire to get rid of me had burst out. She baffled me. It's true that for a while, I truly hated my stepfather, not only because he was responsible for separating my parents but for his behavior afterwards. As for Polly, she was too strange to hate, and it was not her fault. She had a Manichean side I found a bit crazy. A person she disliked would not be foolish, or mistaken, or even just mean, but "evil!"

Since my stepmother would clearly jump at the chance to throw me out, and my mother had undergone a metamorphosis from being the super-liberated woman of her time into starry-eyed obedience to her possessive lover, I did not feel very much at home anywhere. Indeed, my stepfather forbade Dorothy from speaking with me in his absence. Feeling in the way naturally made me more independent than I might otherwise have been. Also, perhaps, more naïve. The only thing my stepmother ever said to me about the opposite sex was a vague, "Watch out for the boys." My mother's only advice was an impassioned, "Don't marry a man unless you can't live without him." That did not strike me as very helpful.

The advantage of not feeling at home at home is that you feel no less at home anywhere else.

When I was just able to walk and talk, my father went to Europe to work on his thesis in Paris and Heidelberg. Very early in life, France was *the other place,* the place with houses and people but not the same as here, gentler somehow, with buildings like lace and small courtyards instead of lawns. I don't know where I got these impressions, but there they were. In some way, France seemed more real than where I was, as a dream is more real than reality just before you wake up.

In 1948, my father was sent to Shanghai as U.S. economic advisor to the collapsing nationalist government. I desperately wanted to go with him. But since my stepmother refused to go so far from her mother, and my father considered that he could not take me all by himself, he left me with my mother after all, promising that I could come after graduation to attend the University of Shanghai.

I was sent back to my mother in Washington to finish 12th grade in Central High School, whose most famous alumnus was J. Edgar Hoover. Still dreaming of living in China, when I learned that Emily Hahn, who wrote about China for my adored magazine, *The New Yorker,* was in town, I managed to meet her and ask for advice about life in

China. She received me in a very friendly way, and I started preparing for life as an old China hand. That of course was not to be.

Politics and Militarism

My interest in Asia was reinforced by a young Korean whom I met in my senior year in high school in Washington, D.C. A war orphan, he had been brought to the United States by some government agency and obliged to earn a U.S. high school degree in order to enroll at a university, although he was already far better educated than any of us. He was very lonely and miserable, and I was the only classmate Kim was able to talk to. He stressed to me that the Americans had come to Korea with the fixed idea of supporting a political "third force," neither fascist nor communist, which, in the wake of World War II, simply did not exist. As a result of their search for this imaginary "third force," the Americans demonized the Left and idealized the rightist politicians who made a great show of being pro-American, in order to gain power.

As I was feature editor of the school paper, I turned my conversations into an article which won me a prize. But this was soon followed by disgrace.

One day we were all summoned to the auditorium for a patriotic rally. The theme was the Reserve Officers Training Corps (ROTC) which had chapters on campuses and even in high schools to encourage the military vocation. American flags were draped around the stage. The "boy most likely to succeed," Jack DeViney, was called upon to give a rousing speech about the merits of ROTC, culminating with a call for all patriotic young boys to come forward and sign up. At this, our star athletes (we had a winning football team, and our sportsmen were very popular) rushed up to join. The other guys, less sure of themselves, fearing condemnation and seeking approval, looked around, hesitated, then stood up and headed for the flags. The rally became a stampede. The meeting was a great success.

I soon found out that the rallying of our sports stars was just public relations, as they were automatically exempted and sent back to their playing fields. They were used as border collies to round up the sheep. I wrote an editorial criticizing the school authorities for exploiting the talents of our school orator and star athletes in service of a militaristic cause. This got me in quite a lot of trouble. My earlier prize was taken away on some pretext.

This was surely the start of my irregular journalistic career.

I had smoked a cigarette on school property. Just one. I don't know how they knew but I was called into the principal's office for a mental torture session. It lasted the whole school day. My journalism prize was retracted. Friends of mine relayed each other through the halls to try to see how I was doing. They made me take another IQ test, on grounds that "someone with that high an IQ wouldn't break school rules." The cold hostility of the school authorities made it clear that they knew about my ROTC editorial but never mentioned it. My nice journalism teacher, Mrs Kern, had warned me regretfully, "Diana, you'll come to a bad end." But this wasn't it.

I was left for a long time in the assistant principal's office to admire her African violets and wait for the axe to fall. With nothing else to do, I snuck a look at my school records, to see what they noted about me, theoretically a character assessment to pass on to future employers or institutions of higher learning. Only one detail stood out, which I considered significant. I had, the authorities judged, "no leadership qualities."

That told me nothing about myself but quite a lot about what such authorities meant by "leadership qualities." Essentially they meant "followship qualities," plus the ambition to use these qualities to gain approval and career advancement. The boy most likely to succeed, who exhorted the guys to join the ROTC, clearly had "leadership qualities." He adhered to the dominant ideology and its rules and would do whatever was asked of him to convince others to be as obedient as he was. It was like a military hierarchy—the good soldier obeys orders and if he exceeds, he will get to give orders. That is "leadership" in America.

2.

The Rest of the World

Life in the world begins with the first trip abroad. I couldn't wait to get started. If my family situation had been different, my experience with the rest of the world might have begun with a junior year abroad, coddled in a spacious bourgeois apartment in Paris, being coached in good food and good manners. It might have been in the neighborhood of Saint Sulpice, where my father stayed when he was researching for his thesis. That would have been a world of recognition, breathing the air of places inhabited by ghosts of characters from the novels of André Gide, strolling through the manicured paths of the Luxembourg gardens as they struggled with their inner conflicts of conscience, so unlike the aggressive moral dualism of America.

My voyage of initiation was not so predictable. Instead it was to a place whose novels I had not read, and which I experienced directly with no preconceptions to confirm or reject.

Nevertheless, disembarking in Le Havre from a frill-less Dutch liner, the first foreign country in my expanded world was indeed France. On the train to Paris, I marveled at the tidy landscape and was absolutely thrilled to see the Sacré Coeur on the horizon as we approached the Gare du Nord. I stayed up all night, walking through Paris, ecstatic with recognition: Notre Dame, the Seine, the Latin Quarter. In a café, I met a couple of nice young men of Arab origin who acted as guides on the rest of my overnight tour, with utmost courtesy, ending in the overnight cafés of Montmartre. In the morning, at the Gare de Lyon, I rejoined the group I had abandoned but who counted on my limited linguistic skills to get everybody safely aboard the Oriental Express, on our way to Belgrade.

The group was made up of half a dozen students plus Professor Thomas Magner, my Russian language professor at the University of Minnesota, on a program called SPAN, the Student Project for Amity among Nations. I doubt that that was really what it was all about. We seemed to have varying purposes in heading off to Yugoslavia. The ostensible aim of the mission was to offer students studying Russian or majoring in Russian Area Studies the experience of a Slavic country. This was 1953, just after the death of Stalin, at the very height of the Cold War. There was no possibility of carrying SPAN to Russia, or even to

Poland, Czechoslovakia or Bulgaria. The only Slavic country left outside the Soviet bloc was Yugoslavia, socialist in its own way but non-aligned and independent.

In reality, I was the only Russian area studies major in the group, as the others were all of Yugoslav origin who grew up in the northern Minnesota Iron Range and wanted to visit their ancestral homeland. Professor Magner was writing a book on the Serbo-Croatian language and wanted to perfect his command of its tonal nuances. He coached the group from a U.S. army handbook in the Croatian version of the language, and his keen interest in contacting Catholic priests made me wonder whether he had some other purpose—especially considering the political role of the Vatican in the Cold War.

As for me, my main purpose was simply to get out into the world. SPAN students had to pay their own way. As I had no family assistance, I earned money for the trip by working the night shift as a long-distance operator for the Bell Telephone Company. Operators were closely supervised, obliged to stick to standard phrases, so that any friendly remark to a customer waiting for his call to get through might incur a reprimand as being outside the manual. It was like *Modern Times* factory work but sitting down.

The very first lesson in Yugoslavia was not about Yugoslavia but about the way America officials interact with The Rest of the World. "Amity among nations" did not seem to be the main preoccupation.

Our group was immediately taken to the U.S. Embassy in Belgrade to be given instructions on how to treat the natives once we were settled in Belgrade University student dormitories. First rule: keep your suitcases locked. As these people are poor, they can be expected to steal whatever they can get. Second rule: beware of the local food. Especially the fresh food, which may be germ-ridden. Come to the Embassy commissary to stock up on healthy canned goods. Third rule: give trinkets to the natives. That is the way to make friends. We were supplied with ballpoint pens and chewing gun to hand around as signs of Amity among Nations.

Since others seemed ready to obey this idiotic advice, I succeeded in separating myself from the rest of the group, who went on to alienate everybody by doing as they had been told. Stories of the ballpoint pens and the chewing gum got around, making everyone wary of these arrogant Americans.

To my joy, I was assigned to a room with eight beds in the Studenski Dom, with seven genuine Yugoslav roommates. It was Spartan indeed, with just a bed and the open suitcase next to it holding my clothes and other possessions. The bathroom plumbing was foul. From the street below, you could hear the clip clop of horses pulling rickety carts full of vegetables.

At first, my roommates ignored me. In the evenings, they sang songs and ate together, dipping warm fresh white bread into a common bowl of cooked eggs and vegetables. It smelled good. And I would sit alone sniffing ostentatiously. This worked, and eventually the boldest among them, Shefika (a Bosnian Turk), had the nerve to ask if I would join them in their meal. I leapt at the chance, understanding instinctively that sharing food is what makes friends across borders. From then on we got to know each other.

Songs are an excellent way to learn a language, so I learned theirs and in turn taught them "Stormy Weather." Although Slavs are particularly good at learning languages, at that time, young Yugoslavs were less proficient in foreign languages than either before or after. Yugoslavia had broken with the Soviet Union, so Russian had gone out of style. English had not yet imposed itself as the universal lingua franca. This gap was fortunate, since it forced me to learn Serbian faster than if they had been using me to perfect their English.

I saw no sign of the market evaluation aspect of dating that prevails in the United States. I was impressed by the fervor of a young man, besotted with love, who from time to time stood below the window at all hours to bear witness to his adoration of the beautiful blond in the bed next to mine, named Angelka Doric. His gift to her of a Bible inscribed with a poem and their names in blood did nothing to overcome her solid indifference.

A healthy appetite is always helpful for making friends. Probably under Viennese influence, Belgrade features fancy little cakes totally unlike those in the United States. I took to frequenting a small pastry shop not far from the Skupstina (parliament) to indulge in these delicacies with a coffee. The proprietor had two handsome sons, and I developed a certain relationship with the younger. His name was Milosh, meaning "sweet," and his brother was named Dushan, meaning "soul"—common names in Serbian. He actually spoke fluent English and belonged to the middle class that had been demoted by communism. Before Tito took power at the end of World War II, the father had owned several pastry shops and was reduced to just this one. But he got along.

I also got to know a pair of elderly French-speaking sisters whose apartment was crammed with furnishings from the two larger flats they had been obliged to vacate due to their class origins, to make way for more modest tenants. But they insisted that Yugoslav communists were much nicer than those of other countries—notably the Red Army, whose temporary occupation had left bad memories. Reduction of property rather than confiscation seems to have been the Yugoslav communist means of dealing with the "bourgeoisie"—which was hardly a "bourgeoisie" in the Western sense of rich capitalists but was made up mostly of small businessmen and professional people. In the countryside, there was no collectivization of the small land-holding farmers who were still the backbone of the nation.

As far as I could tell, the measure most resented was limits on higher education for the privileged, although this was not systematic. This was counterbalanced by free university education for those who would not have been able to afford it.

Back in the dormitory, my open suitcase was greatly helpful in fostering Amity among Nations. As I recall, each of the girls possessed only one change of clothes, that is, two blouses each, and would exchange them for variety. I joined the exchanges, and my photo of the girls in Room 13 shows me wearing a blouse belonging, I believe, to Gordana, while Gordana was wearing something of mine.

Before long, my best friends were Angelka, Gordana and Gordana's sister, Ana. Angelka was a Serb from Croatia, who had escaped to northern Serbia after her parents were killed by the fascist Ustasha who ruled the "Independent State of Croatia" during the Nazi dismantling and occupation of Yugoslavia during World War II. She was in her final year of philosophy, with a seriousness rooted in her tragic past. Gordana, of Russian origin, was madly in love with a basketball player whom she called her "little bird," and would often refuse to go out, staying in out of self-imposed fidelity. Ana was a bit more frivolous. Sometimes we would play cards and they would gaily cheat, as that was apparently part of the game.

My open suitcase also held a treasure that became legendary in the *studentski dom.* It was an iron. In those days, clothes wrinkled, and wrinkles were more unseemly than they are today, when anything goes. News of my iron swept through the dormitory. The word for iron, *pegla,* sticks in my mind even when the rest of that beautiful but grammatically challenging language has slipped into the memory hole. Various schemes were devised to draw close enough to the *pegla* to be able to ask to borrow it. I accompanied my willingness to lend by explanations that

I had worked as a telephone operator to earn my trip, to avoid arousing jealousy at my presumed wealth.

The generosity went both ways. Not only did we share clothes on an equal basis. These young women, with scarcely enough money to feed themselves, pooled their money in order to take me to the theater. We all went together to see a Serbian production of "The Importance of Being Earnest" by Oscar Wilde. This was a great and happy occasion.

One of the *pegla* borrowers urged me to visit the province of Kosovo during the summer vacation. She was unable to invite me to stay with her, but urged me to come anyway, promising to introduce me to people.

So I took a train to Peć and stayed in a local hotel for a couple of weeks. Just as I was unaware of virtually everything about the country I was visiting, I knew absolutely nothing about the ancestral animosity between Serbs and Albanians living in Kosovo. I never saw signs of the animosity, only of the total separation of the two communities from each other.

The woman who invited me was Serb, and so, it seemed, were the vast majority of people in this ancient town at the foot of high mountains. Between the town and the mountains was the medieval Patriarchate of the Serbian Orthodox church—mysteriously closed. At least it was a mystery to me at the time. The reasons were certainly political.

The Albanian presence was visible from the slender minarets of a few mosques, and the occasional white-capped peasant leading his cow through the unpaved streets. Mira, the Serb who had urged me to visit Kosovo, was remarkably poor. A single lightbulb dangled from the ceiling of the room that filled most of her family's small dwelling. In the front yard, a cow grazed, and beyond the cow was an outhouse strategically placed above the gutter which carried sewage down the side of the street toward, I presume, the river.

The inevitable result was that the town was full of flies. Trying to write in my hotel room was the only time in my life that I have felt seriously tormented by flies.

One day a young Englishman arrived from the Montenegro side of the mountains on a bicycle. In his eyes, everything was delightful, and he raved about the local raspberry juice, *malina.* The rocky road, the flies, nothing fazed him. The British Empire was built by men like those, who can cross high mountains on a bicycle and find everything in the foreign land simply lovely. Americans clinging to their canned goods can never repeat the exploit.

The center of social life for young people in this town was the *corso,* an ancient custom which certainly disappeared rapidly in the following years, as Yugoslavia modernized. You would stroll with friends (usually girls with girls and boys with boys) along one side of the main street while others strolled in the opposite direction on the other side, in circular fashion. Obviously, boys and girls were checking each other out. I didn't think about it at the time, but they were all Serbs. Albanians kept to themselves.

There were also a couple of cafés where you could go to drink and sing in the evening. Just as it was during the centuries before music became a commercial commodity, people provided their own musical entertainment, which was jollier and more innocent.

A tall handsome boy named Atsa (short for Alexander) took me for walks past the closed patriarchate into the foothills of the mountains, where the views were magnificent. He also escorted me to the town swimming pool, which was actually a large irrigation ditch, running downhill, so one got in at the high end and got out at the lower. It was not exactly a swim, but it was cooling in the scorching summer heat.

The highlight of my friendship with Atsa was our trip to see the Decani monastery, one of the two most famous of the medieval Serbian Orthodox Christian monasteries (the other is Gracanitsa) in Kosovo, which together with the then closed patriarchate in Peć established Kosovo as the heart of historic Serbia. We admired the medieval frescoes before being invited by the Abbot to partake of the monastery's own red wine, traces of which could be observed on the white beard of this amiable cleric. The Abbot was fully aware of being barely tolerated by the communist regime but would only fleetingly allude to it with gentle irony. As we chatted on the terrace, we observed half a dozen Albanian men—recognizable by their white skullcaps—lounging among themselves on the monastery lawn drinking wine. The Abbot explained that the Albanians came to the monastery to drink since their Muslim religion forbade alcohol in their own milieu. That was the only time I saw Albanians in a group during my visit to Kosovo.

Atsa had a less tactful friend who one day when we were all together launched into praise of Queen Elizabeth of England and religion. After a bit I said that none of that interested me at all, neither the Queen of England nor religion. At that he triumphantly pulled out his Communist Party card, showing it to me and exclaiming, "That is my religion!" The naiveté of this exchange stuck in my mind. This young man, who appeared intelligent and educated, was provincial enough to imagine that political differences could be reduced to such simple expressions. It was rather touching, and just about the only "political discussion" throughout my summer travels through Kosovo, Macedonia, Montenegro, Bosnia and the gorgeous Adriatic coast.

Dubrovnik permitted my first sight of the Mediterranean, and at its best. Stunning sunsets over totally transparent blue waters, in a setting of Renaissance architecture and backed by high mountains. Dubrovnik was already a tourist magnet, but an incident illustrated that it was not only that. I was invited to leave the first hotel where I stayed in order to make way for a group of disabled war veterans, who had priority. I greatly admired this measure and easily found another place to stay. Prices were very low in those days.

The public night life in Dubrovnik was then more elegant than it has become. I waltzed in a seaside café with a young German who was touring Yugoslavia with his mother. They offered a ride in their BMW through Montenegro and Bosnia in return for the "cover" I provided. That is, not only could I act as interpreter with my rudimentary Serbian, but the fact that I was American could distract from their German identity, which they felt might arouse hostility. Perhaps they were visiting places where their father and husband had fought and been killed. I don't know. But they were uneasy about being German.

The rocky back roads of mountainous Yugoslavia nearly destroyed the Germans' BMW, but enabled me to visit places I could not have easily reached on my own. In Montenegro we were led through a cavern by a local villager who showed us everything with his lamp and refused any payment, although he invited me to sign the guestbook. "It is here, I am here, you are not from here, so I show it to you." Such old-fashioned hospitality would surely not last long.

Finally, the Germans invited me to stay with them in Augsburg, which provided my first glimpse of Germany, a country that was later to become very familiar.

At the end of the summer, I returned to the dormitory. The rest of the SPAN group had hurried home ahead of time, eager to quit this awful place and return to the comforts of Hibbing, Minnesota. Professor Magner was gone too. Feeling quite at home among my roommates, I decided to stay on to increase my knowledge of the language and also to write the paper I was vaguely supposed to write for SPAN based on my experiences of the country.

For me, the country's politics were simply one of its aspects to be observed, like the food or the scenery. I was not there to judge or to compare but to observe.

Of my seven roommates, two were members of the Communist Party: Gordana and Angelka. They were the best students in the lot, and also the most attractive personally, and it seemed evident that students were coopted into the party primarily on their merits. At least, that applied to my two friends. But there was a tough-looking, heavy-set young woman who was some sort of authority in the dormitory, and who would occasionally stop at the door of our room to see what if anything was going on. Her name was Draga—meaning "dear" in the custom of endearing Serbian first names, but I found nothing particularly endearing about her. What mattered was that I felt thoroughly accepted by my Yugoslav roommates, and indeed I never anywhere felt more that I belonged to a group than in room 13 of the Studentski Dom in Belgrade.

This idyll did not last very long.

The Theater of the Absurd

Early one autumn evening, I found my roommates in a state of great agitation. "We are going to demonstrate," they told me. "I want to come with you," I exclaimed, enthusiastic at the prospect of taking part in a demonstration—an event I had never seen before. So off we went, as I tried to find out what this was all about. When they told me it was about Trieste, I was not enlightened, as my ignorance of the part of the world where I found myself was so profound that I had scarcely ever heard of Trieste. We were soon in a crowd where people were shouting (in Serbo-Croatian of course) "We are Tito's, Tito is ours!" and "Trieste is ours!"

That was the problem, as I discovered for the first time. Italians thought it was theirs. Trieste, which had belonged to both the Venetian and Habsburg empires, had a mixed Italian and Slovenian population. At the end of World War II, it was scheduled to be an independent city state. The Italian government insisted that it must belong to Italy. Tito said no. The conflict had been going on for years, and the Italians were able to mobilize aggressive mobs to invade the city. British and American occupiers hesitated, but at this stage the Americans had pulled out in a move favorable to Italy. A compromise would be found several months later, giving the port city to Italy and surrounding areas to Slovenia, the northernmost part of Yugoslavia. But for the moment, Yugoslavs were mobilized primarily against the United States for giving in to Italian pressure.

I knew nothing about all that, but it was not my affair, and I thought light-heartedly that if my friends wanted Trieste, let them have it! So I went along in my first demonstration until I realized that we were getting dangerously close to the U.S. embassy, as the protests gained volume. My relations with the Embassy were already bad, and I didn't want them to see me in the company of a hostile crowd, so I bowed out and went to the Hotel Moskva in search of an American journalist who could brief me on what was happening. I didn't quite grasp it. Despite the confusion, back in the dormitory we all went to sleep satisfied at having done what we could.

It was only six o'clock the next morning when my roommates woke me up. They were clearly alarmed and worried. "Get dressed and come down to the office right away," Gordana told me. Three of my roommates went ahead of me, as I tried to wake up and figure out what was going on. As I arrived in the office, a stormy debate was going on, of which I understood only that it was about me, and the division was for or against. Nobody asked my opinion, which I was not prepared to express anyway, having no clear idea of what was the matter. I am not a morning person, and at 6:30 a.m. my perceptions can be foggy. Anyway, whatever the problem, I counted on my roommates to fix it.

Finally we left the office, and my first thought was that it was all settled. Then I noticed big posters on the walls of the entrance corridor announcing a trial to be held in the dining hall at three o'clock in the afternoon. The trial was of the American spy in their midst. That was me. How odd, I thought, especially since someone must have stayed up all night making those posters, which were in color. In this strange land I was used to surprises, so I took it calmly. My roommates did not see it that way. They were intensely worried. So, don't worry, I told them, I'll attend my trial, but don't say anything, any of you. You might get in trouble. But nothing can happen to me (which was true). Just stay silent.

Meanwhile, I got some rest, and went back to the Hotel Moskva to learn about events from the *New York Times* correspondent. Nothing very grave seemed to be happening.

At three o'clock I arrived promptly at my trial, surrounded by my roommates who insisted on sitting next to me. It was an amazing scene. The huge dining hall was full, and I noticed perhaps for the first time (as I rarely ate there, finding the food too heavy) the enormous photo of Tito staring over our heads.

The formidable Draga was there to lead the proceedings, starting off with a long indictment of the "spy in our midst." The one thing that was perfectly clear was that by attacking me, Draga was demonstrating her zeal in the defense of Trieste from the Americans who were giving it to Italy. But what did that have to do with me? Nothing of course. But I was the only "spy" at hand for her to denounce.

The charges were simple enough but developed rhetorically by several accusers. By asking questions of dormitory residents, I had committed espionage. Even worse, I had corrupted socialist Yugoslavia with capitalist values. How? "By bribing students with stockings and shoes." This was funny, since stockings and shoes had never been part of our exchanges in room 13. The stream of vituperation went on for what seemed rather a long time, as I prepared to answer as best I could. I kept cautioning my friends to stay out of this. But at one point, the bold Shefika broke in and announced forcefully, "No, Diana is a good person!" (*dobar chovek*). This brave defense nearly brought me to tears, whereas otherwise I was enjoying a sort of controlled indignation, knowing that this was ridiculous.

I was finally allowed to defend myself. The absurdity of anyone "spying" on a girls' dormitory was too obvious to go on and on about. It was after all perfectly normal to ask questions about a country one is visiting. My main line of defense was, I believe, both "politically correct" for the circumstances and totally sincere. Far from being "bribed by stockings and shoes," my roommates were introducing me to socialism. We shared food and clothes equally. They gave me more than I gave them. In reality, they were converting me to socialism. And now you paranoid fools are spoiling everything.

When people in the crowd made fun of my mistakes in Serbian grammar, I was emboldened by their unfairness. What could they expect?

As I feared, at some point Ana and Gordana also came to my defense. This made things much worse. The accusations shifted from me to them. The American had succeeded in corrupting room 13 because they were already corrupt. Gordana would rather see her boyfriend than attend a Party meeting. And on and on. Many of the girls who had been very friendly to me, especially with an eye to my *pegla,* raised their hands to add a touch of ignominy to the reputation of my comrades. When her "best friend" from another floor launched into a malicious denunciation of Ana's alleged morals, poor Ana burst into tears and fled the hall.

The whole proceeding lasted nearly three hours and culminated in a joint verdict and sentence: the spy and all the corrupted residents of room 13 were guilty and expelled from the dorm. Their expulsion from the university would follow.

We were devastated that night. We felt isolated and besieged in room 13. Angelka fell ill, running a high fever. As a lone orphan, she was hardest hit by the punitive measures.

Gordana tried to reassure her and the rest of us. She had good contacts in the Party, she explained, she would go to them and gain cancellation of these illegal, outrageous proceedings. We were encouraged. Gordana had a forceful personality and, as she said, contacts.

To no avail. Draga and her cohorts had got there first. There was no cancellation, but we were given a couple of weeks before the expulsions would take place.

My reaction at that time was defiance. Since I had been "convicted" of asking questions, well, I would just go on asking them! I made a questionnaire and took it to room after room, asking who would be so kind as to answer my questions. The main result is that I was actually spat on as I went down the corridor. That made me still more stubborn.

But I melted when a young woman from the third floor braved the mob to come to room 13 and apologize for the bad behavior of her compatriots. That one kindness was more important than all the foolish spite of others.

There was a remarkable lack of sympathy at the U.S. Embassy—so little that I began to have the suspicion that there was some sort of secret communication going on at my expense. The friendliest reaction was, "What is a nice girl like you doing in this hellhole?" Otherwise, I had asked for it by "going native." As I recall, there was only one person at the embassy who treated the natives as human beings, and that was the military attaché, of all people. He actually socialized with Yugoslavs, picnics and things like that. But it was clear that to advance in the diplomatic corps, one must not "go native." That is one reason that assignments to a particular country were usually short, no longer than two years. The embassy saw that I had "gone native" and darkly disapproved. That may have been the purpose of the initial ballpoint pens and chewing gum. Americans should remain aloof, as befits their superior civilization and hygiene.

When my friends saw me off on an evening train to Germany—I was accepting the invitation to Augsburg—we were intrusively observed by men in trench coats. Once on the train, I had to fight off the aggressive approaches of a man whom I took to be some sort of agent. Up until then, I had always found men in Yugoslavia to be totally correct and respectful—more so than in the United States, at least. It was an unpleasant way to leave.

Back to the Free World

In Augsburg, I stayed with the Germans I had met in Dubrovnik, who were working hard to recover their prewar standards. War-widowed Frau Werner ran a hat shop, and at least in those days all German ladies wore hats most of the time, so the business was doing well. Every evening they sat around the table adding up the day's receipts. I got used to hearing *vier und zwanzig, acht und dreisig.* The daughter, who was working in an office, wore the same rather elegant suit every day, obviously because she had no other. I was greatly impressed by the orderliness of everything, and *Ordnung muss ja sein* (we must have order!)—a line from my Assimil self-taught German book—became my slogan for Germany.

From Augsburg I went to Paris where the greyness of November was deepened by the blackened buildings (before Malraux enacted the obligation to clean façades and the city became cream-colored again). I shared a small hotel room in Montparnasse with my former university roommate, Joyce Mallinger, who had been traveling in Spain.

In Paris I received letters from my Yugoslav friends via touring athletes, mostly basketball or handball players. Although I had done nothing wrong, I still felt responsible and guilty for the misfortune my presence had caused others. I feared I had ruined people's lives. Fortunately, the results were not tragic. Punishment for political sins was mild in Yugoslavia. Angelka's home town found her a job in a hotel cloak room which allowed her to complete her degree. The others all managed, one way or another.

Angelka was by far the most distressed at the time. In addition to losing her lodging and her scholarship, she was deeply hurt at being expelled from the Party. And yet—at the Party meeting called to expel her, a tall dark handsome young man stood up and defended her brilliantly. The two later married and had two sons. That was Svetozar Stojanovic, then a graduate student but who went on to be one of the most prominent members of the Praxis group of critical philosophers, a regular at international meetings of Western socialists, with invitations to teach in Germany, Britain and the United States, where he spent some time as a Woodrow Wilson scholar. We stayed in touch for years and saw each other in the United States and in Belgrade.

My letter to Professor Magner recounting my misadventures never received an answer. As for my research paper, it now could only be about the trial, but I was blocked by the moral impossibility of exploiting my friends' misfortune for my own benefit. That would somehow have justified the accusations against me. I was not clever enough at the time to know how to fashion my little story in a way that would not feed the prevailing atmosphere of anticommunism, quite contrary to "amity among nations."

Yet to me, this incident had little to do with "communism" or "socialism" as a political system, and everything to do with human nature. The existence of an official ideology, whatever it may be, is an instrument of petty jealousies, a means to hurt rivals, to take revenge, or to seek praise and advancement by joining the mob. That is what I had witnessed at my "trial." The problem was not the content of the ideology, but the fact that it was "official." Any official ideology becomes a power tool that some can use against others. It was not that "the personal was political" but that the political was personal. Indeed, it seemed quite probable that the whole show had been engineered by Draga out of jealousy toward her far more attractive and intelligent fellow party members, Gordana and Angelka, even if she convinced herself it was for "the cause."

I had seen enough jealousy, meanness and herd instinct in the United States to recognize that such behavior could not be attributed to communist ideology. It was all too common in situations of rivalry. In fact, in Belgrade, I was more impressed by the small minority who boldly stood up to the mob than by the mob itself. I am not sure I would have seen such courage in the girls' dormitory at the University of Minnesota. The issues would have been different, but the conformism the same.

I had come of age in the heyday of McCarthyism, so this was just the other side of the coin.

All this put my future in doubt. I had majored in Russian area studies on the urging of my father, who was beginning his twenty years in the Pentagon and felt keenly the need for objective scholarship concerning the Soviet Union. But I had no strong vocation to pursue such a career, especially since I felt that doing so would in a sense "prove" the Belgrade accusations against me, in that I would become some sort of hostile agent. The embassy had given me a glimpse of what could be expected from a career in international relations: conformist adherence to official prejudice. I had absolutely no desire to become a foot soldier in the Cold War, as my inclinations were always toward reconciliation (probably a reason my father thought I might be helpful).

Still, in my short experience of Yugoslavia I had begun to understand the real basis of the communism of that period. I wrote a short story about it. The point was, that in the midst of a political argument in Belgrade, as often happened then, the lights went off. And that settled the argument in favor of socialism. At that time, I had no idea that in 1920 Lenin had said that "communism is Soviet power plus electrification of the whole country, since industry cannot be developed without electrification"—in fact, I had never read a word of Lenin—but I had seen that for myself. Except instead of "soviets," I would say that communism (of that period) was mass mobilization and electrification, on the way to industrialization. Mass mobilization was the substitute for capital where there was a grave shortage of capital, as in Yugoslavia emerging from the devastation of World War II. Students like my roommates had taken part in road-building. And in not so many years, such mobilization, along with much study of engineering (the favored subject even among women students), produced electrification, industrialization and a greatly improved standard of living. And it was because "communism" meant industrial development that it had such wide appeal in underdeveloped countries.

Deep down, my only ambition had always been "to be a writer," which meant something special in the first half of the twentieth century that it no longer means today. Jack London, Thomas Wolfe (the one who lived from 1900 to 1938), and Ernest Hemingway all nourished their writing from their experience of the world. This was more problematic for a woman, but it was my secret vocation. After World War II, all this changed, and novelists were mostly University English teachers, whose writing was nourished by introspection more than by encounter with the world out there. I wanted none of that. Besides, I was always bothered by the circumstance that novels were *not true,* and it made me uncomfortable to write something that was *not true.*

At Christmas I managed somehow to get to Venice. The splendor was a dream of icy grey, empty of tourists. Those were the days! There were so few foreigners that I was invited by local shopkeepers to join in wine and *panetone* celebrations. It was possible to *travel* and meet people before tourism erected its commercial wall. Today it is better to stay home and watch travelogues.

In the Milan railway station, I met my first communist outside Yugoslavia. Over coffee the young man professed his faith in communism and told me quite cheerfully, and in the most friendly way, that he would fight the Americans as hard as he could to defend communism in Italy.

This contrasted with my experience in a photo shop in Paris, where the clerk refused to serve me upon observing that I was American. Two ways of being a communist during the Cold War.

These travels were managed on surprisingly little money, due both to favorable exchange rates and a diet reduced to the minimum. At that age, I could go for a long time without eating or sleeping. As I recall, I only went to a real restaurant twice, once in Belgrade and once in Paris. I could eat out of bakeries. In Montparnasse, I did spend a lot of time over a single cup of coffee in La Coupole, reading and writing. Somehow, I connected with a network of Slavic exiles, who fed me pickles and showed me around.

After a month or two of being poor in Paris, Joyce and I went hitch-hiking through Germany. It was easy then to get rides and quite safe. We could sleep in railroad stations, without being bothered. In contrast to Augsburg, largely unscathed by the war, Cologne was still in ruins from Allied bombing. The Cathedral had been bombed but was too massive to have been destroyed. We passed through Brussels before taking a boat across the Channel. As we arrived in London, Joyce came down with a bad case of bronchitis, due to the heavy fog polluted by smoke from the stoves that kept homes not very far above freezing. England was colder and poorer than France. Luckily, the National Health Service took care of her.

Wherever we walked in Paris, we could find a café to sit down for coffee, but in London there were long stretches with nothing but closed tea shops and pubs for men only. Having friends there, we visited Oxford where our experience of "the young gentlemen" (as townspeople respectfully called them) sent us fleeing to Dublin where we stayed in the home of an Irish girl whom I had met when she visited the United States as an exchange student. It was a great distance from complex Oxford snobbery to the warm hospitality of an Irish family, where the mother told wild tales of her daily adventures while her grown children pretended to reproach her for exaggerating. As my money was gone, I had to return to Washington. The only thing I was sure of was that somehow I would return to Paris.

3.

An Educational Marriage

Back in Washington D.C., I soon got a job as librarian in the bureau of the Associated Press. I hoped this would be a stepping stone to a career as journalist, but it was more a stepping stone to male journalists.

The McCarthy Circus

In those days, Washington, and especially the Washington press corps, was completely absorbed in the twilight of the McCarthy moment.

For several years, Senator Joseph McCarthy and mainstream media had used each other with perfect cynicism. McCarthy knew that the press would gobble up his revelations of communist infiltration of everything, without bothering to find out whether they were true or false, because red-baiting was "a good story" and nobody wanted to be accused of aiding the enemy. Reporters who knew perfectly well that McCarthy's allegations were unfounded emanations of inebriated fantasies nevertheless wrote them up without comment. For years, almost the entire Washington press corps was active in this charade, treating McCarthy as a joke off duty and solemnly relaying his accusations to the public with straight faces.

All this was show, a spectacle based on hot air. The witch hunts designed to identify and eject communists from the U.S. government, Hollywood and trade unions really got underway in 1948, under the auspices of the House Un-American Activities Committee (HUAC), with significant participation of California congressman Richard Nixon, who used the new crusade to make a name for himself. But the decade of concentrated anti-communist denunciation is not called "HUACism," which would be more accurate, but is named after the whirlwind career of McCarthy, an alcoholic adventurer who came late to the witch hunt and captured the headlines for four years. As chairman of the Senate Committee on Government Operations, McCarthy simply rode the wave, heartily relishing both the attention and his bullying of witnesses.

Just about everybody in Washington, including President Eisenhower, detested Senator McCarthy, but it was his evil genius and chief counsel Roy Cohn who inadvertently set the stage for his ruin, thanks to Cohn's infatuation with a handsome hotel chain heir named David Schine. On the basis of an ignorant diatribe against "communism" which he had written to be distributed in the rooms of his father's hotels, Schine was brought by Cohn onto McCarthy's staff as a "chief consultant." In 1953, Cohn and Schine toured Europe looking for "soft on communism" books to be rooted out of U.S. Information Agency libraries. Things got even better when Schine was drafted and Cohn started harassing the Army to give Schine a commission and special privileges, threatening that otherwise he would "wreck the Army." McCarthy could wreck a lot of things in America, but wrecking the Army was going too far.

In the spring of 1954, the press was mobilized to cover the last act of the absurd McCarthy saga, in an epic confrontation between the McCarthy committee and the Army.

In the 1954 McCarthy-Army hearings, the flamboyant Wisconsin Senator was no longer the chair of the committee that undertook to investigate Army charges that McCarthy and his staff had improperly sought advantages for Private Schine. True to form, McCarthy tried to divert attention from the clear evidence against him by accusing the Army of harboring communists, and claiming to have a long list of communists in defense plants and even in the Army Signal Corps.

But the jig was up, as both the Republican government and the media had squeezed all they wanted out of the Senator, whose performance was getting stale. What the media had created, the media destroyed. A moment of drama, filmed by television and watched by millions, marked the fall of the charlatan. The new national hero was a Boston lawyer, Joseph Welch, who looked and spoke like the very embodiment of old-fashioned New England virtues. When Welch challenged McCarthy to reveal the names of the alleged subversives, McCarthy enacted one of his evasive moves by accusing a young lawyer in Welch's law firm of being a commie sympathizer, since he had once belonged to the left-leaning National Lawyers Guild. This gave Welch his opening, and in tones of regretful reproach, the elderly lawyer exclaimed, "Have you no sense of decency, sir? At long last, have you left no decency?"

This image of righteous indignation from a respectable old man was the coup de grace. To add the proper tone of piety, Welch added, "If there is a God in heaven, it will do neither you nor your cause any good!"

More than anything else, this theatrical exchange turned public opinion against McCarthy, who went on to be censored by the Senate before dying of hepatitis three years later, at the age of 48.

"McCarthyism" was just the fireworks at the end of the show, a show that dominated political life in America in the early post-war years. It is generally recognized that McCarthy never unearthed any authentic communist, and if he had, it would not have had any influence on the fate of the nation.

In reality, there indeed were genuine Communists in America, during the depression and the war years, when the Soviet Union was the ally that actually defeated Nazi Germany. There were members of the Communist Party active in the labor movement, in the civil rights movement, and in Hollywood. There were no doubt even a few in the Government, but McCarthy only pretended to find them.

The witch hunters claimed that "the Communists are plotting to overthrow the government of the United States by force and violence." This was totally absurd in view of the relationship of forces and represented a grotesque misunderstanding of what is meant by being in favor of "revolution." Anti-communism purged American labor unions of many principled organizers and prepared the AFL-CIO to play an international role opposing communist leadership of unions in other countries. Hollywood was a most significant target of the political purge. Blacklisting alleged communist writers, actors and directors prepared the film industry for its new Manichean propaganda war against the enemies of the Free World. Still, discreetly, American communists went on to play a very positive role in the civil rights movement for Black emancipation.

Communists were less and less identified as persons with radical social opinions and more and more as agents of a hostile foreign power. If the Kremlin was trying to take over America, it must be trying to take over the world.

In reality, the Soviet Union was recovering from massive war destruction, defensively determined to keep control of its glacis in Eastern Europe, but otherwise quite respectful of the agreements made at Yalta, refraining from coming to the aid of Communists in Greece and allowing Yugoslavia to leave the Soviet bloc, as Stalin had informally agreed with Churchill. All the leaders in Moscow wanted from Communist Parties in Western Europe was to promote peace, not to take power.

Such was the atmosphere in Washington when I was working for the Associated Press. The witch hunt was more tragic abroad. In

June 1954 the Dulles Brothers, John Foster as Secretary of State and Allen as head of the CIA, undertook to defend the interest of their client, the United Fruit Company, in Guatemala by overthrowing the democratically elected government of Jacobo Arbenz Gutman. The pretext for blocking orderly land reform was to stop "the communist octopus" (Senator Wiley). A CIA-managed invasion of Guatemala from Honduras was reported as a popular uprising. Journalists had no choice but to report the story as government spokesmen told it. The *New York Times* correspondent in Mexico, Sydney Gruson, was pulled off the story when the CIA expressed fears that he might prove too independent.

Life on Capitol Hill

In Washington, Joyce had no home to go to and I had two homes but felt unwelcome in both of them. So once again we shared an apartment, this time on Capitol Hill, behind the Library of Congress. We saw rather little of each other as we spent a lot of time with what she liked to call our "projects"—meaning men friends. I saw them mainly as conversations.

Joyce Mallinger was a native of the Red Lake Indian Reservation in Northern Minnesota. Her father was a German who had been more or less passing through. With her mixed background she still qualified as a "legal Indian," meaning at least one fourth Indian, making her eligible for a University of Minnesota scholarship if her high school grades were good enough, which indeed they were.

We met in French literature classes and became close friends after Joyce returned from a mysterious disappearance. She ran off to Little Rock and then came back without explanation. She attributed this mysterious escapade to her secretive Indian side, saying that Indians sometimes just took off without offering any explanation. When too much was too much, they just left. My suspicions focused on a male professor. Joyce was outgoing and fun, as well as extremely attractive, with dark eyes and black hair from the Ojibwa side of her ancestry. When she returned from Little Rock we shared an apartment in Minneapolis, met up again in Paris and finally shared an apartment on Capitol Hill.

At the University in the early 1950s, Joyce and I had in common a disrespectful attitude toward the Korean War, which we saw as another meat-grinder which young men should avoid at all cost. My G.I. Bill of Rights boyfriend, a veteran of the Pacific War, shared this judgment. Our favorite songs were those of Tom Lehrer.

Another thing we had in common was strong rejection of the reductionism of Freudian psychology as it prevailed in those days. The apoliticism of that conformist period was enforced by doctrinaire vulgar Freudianism, promoted by numerous psychology majors who needed a doctrine to help them understand anything. I hated Freudian psychology first of all because I didn't believe a word of it. Why should I envy a penis, of all things? And the Freudian analysis of dreams seemed even less convincing than those of a gypsy soothsayer. But the worst thing about the vulgar Freudian cult was its self-protective syllogism: all your desires stem from more or less repressed sexual drives, and if you say this isn't true, that is proof that you are repressing them. No way to detach yourself from that Tar Baby. Stop thinking about the world! Think about yourself! That was the constant message. Psychoanalysis was the fashion. As far as we could see, it meant concentrating on the subject that made you unhappy: yourself. Both of us agreed on the opposite strategy: think about something else. If you can afford an analyst, you can afford a trip abroad, which will do you more good. A simpler way to get out of a sad mood is to try teaching yourself a foreign language. Or playing a musical instrument. Or gardening. Or just about anything other than trying to dig up some hidden excuse for yourself.

Out of a spirit of contradiction, I let a number of budding shrinks who thought I was unusual give me psychological tests—they were a specialty at the University of Minnesota—hoping they might find something "abnormal" that they could fool around with. I always came out mentally healthy and crushingly normal, to their disappointment. Of course, one easily sees what those "personality test" questions are trying to get at and can give them what they want.

Joyce and I came from very different childhoods but were both relieved to be out of them. Joyce never talked about her childhood on the Indian reservation. I talked a lot about mine. My parents and their story were my founding myth. I chose to look on my parents' divorce as their tragedy, not mine, which is a healthy way to look at it. There was nothing I could do about feeling *de trop,* in the way, in either of my parents' homes—not unloved, just in the way. So I mostly got out of the way.

Still, independence causes anxiety when one doesn't know what to do with it. I wanted to "be a writer," but my family experience had warned me that just "being able to write" was not enough. There was the disquieting example of my mother's brother, Ben. Both he and my mother had skipped grades through high school, regarded in their milieu as little prodigies. While not yet twenty, Ben wrote a symphonic interpretation of Carl Sandberg's poems that won a prize and was performed by a local orchestra. That seemed to settle it, and instead of going to conservatory Ben went to New York, soon followed by my mother. Ben and Dorothy both dreamed of artistic careers. They didn't know anybody. Dorothy ended up writing advertising copy before returning to the University of Minnesota, where she met and married my father in a wedding that looks, from the photo I kept, like a musical comedy, with bridesmaids all in white satin dresses and shoes as in a chorus line. Ben went on to have a hectic but reasonably successful career in popular music, ending up as head music arranger for NBC in the age of the Big Bands. But meanwhile, alcohol made a shambles of his personal life.

Ben was a thin, soft-spoken man whose alcoholism was all the more devastating in that it was invisible. As a child, I loved his wry humor. He first took a showgirl away from her husband and brought her to staid St Paul where Ben's mother, Ooma, took care of her when Ben brutally threw her out. Then he married Betty, a former Miss Connecticut, who was a dancing teacher. Their lifestyle took its toll on their son, my cousin Alan, whom I adored. Things quietly went very, very wrong. At one point I wanted to move to New York to "save Alan" but my father quickly vetoed that idea. Shortly thereafter, Betty simply disappeared with Alan, probably with a more protective man. I was never able to find them.

I came to see my Uncle Ben as a victim of a common American notion that a "child prodigy" was sure to succeed without ever having acquired the discipline of a conservatory and years of training. Without a solid culture and discipline, there is a tendency to compensate by counting on stimulants, alcohol and drugs, to enhance creativity. Ben's personal shipwreck was a signal to me to beware of the bohemian life style that initially looked like fun but that I came to see as dangerous disorder.

At the same time, I did not know what to do to give myself the sort of serious preparation for life that I needed.

Meanwhile, Joyce's "legal Indian" origins brought her to the attention of the Cold War liberal wing of the Democratic Party close to Minnesota Senator Hubert Humphrey, co-founder of the anti-communist Americans for Democratic Action (ADA). They could not fail to see that her Indian background, language skills, delightful personality and good looks could be an asset in dealing with non-Europeans. I don't know exactly how this happened, but they soon had her working at the Mosque in Washington, doing I don't know what. She was soon being assigned to jobs abroad, notably North Africa. In short, she became some sort of agent, notably on missions for the U.S. Agency for International Development (AID), which were commonly linked to intelligence operations. I don't suppose any of this was particularly sinister, but it was remote from her original political outlook. The United States knows how to exploit its minorities to project an international image of progressive egalitarianism, even as it entails a sort of brain drain that leaves the minority in question no better off. Many years later, when Joyce was far away in another country, I called on her mother who lived in a trailer at the edge of the reservation, along with a niece and her baby. They owned a bruised automobile and a small television set. An extraordinary percentage of her family and neighbors died of cancer.

Bonn and Rome

Offering samples of my writing, I persuaded the chief of the Washington bureau to recommend taking me out of the library and letting me become a reporter. I was sent to New York to get the approval of the tyrannical boss of the Associated Press, Wes Gallagher. This was a huge failure. Gallagher gruffly declared that I "made a bad impression," without elaborating. I couldn't even know what it was about me that made that bad impression but my career was stopped before it started.

I lived in the news, both in the Associated Press library and in long evening conversations. France was much in the news: the defeat at Dien Bien Phu; Pierre Mendes-France, the only French leader admired in the United States, who pulled France out of Tunisia and Morocco and was favorable to Indochinese independence; and in August 1954, the French national assembly confirmed the national orneriness by refusing to accept Washington's plan for re-arming Germany, the "European Defense Community."

In the United States, the main news was the rise of the civil rights movement to end racial segregation in the South, marked by the refusal of Rosa Parks to sit in the back of the bus and by the eloquence of the Reverend Martin Luther King. They were aided by white militants from the north, many who were or had been members of the Communist Party, but all they were trying to "overthrow" was institutionalized racial discrimination, by standing up to the force and violence of its defenders.

By this time, my "projects" had narrowed to one. I remember Sunday mornings as Herb and I shared doing *The New York Times* Sunday crossword puzzle in a Capitol Hill café. Of all the conversationalists, he was the most fun and the most persistent. I felt blocked where I was and wanted to go back to Europe. I had saved money and could afford a long trip. To keep us together, Herb Altschull applied for a position as foreign correspondent and was immediately posted to Germany. He got to Europe before I did, and I saw him wave from the wharf as SS Cristoforo Colombo sailed into Venice.

Trans-Atlantic ocean liner trips were one of the great joys of that period. I took several, but that 1956 crossing was the most important because of the people I met. It was a long crossing, with stops at Lisbon, Gibraltar, Barcelona, Palermo and Patras, Greece, before arriving in Venice. This allowed time to meet a number of exuberant Italians, notably Liana Macellari, a young literary scholar specializing in Henry James, who almost instantly became my closest friend. After spending a visiting term at Mount Holyoke, which she had found very strange (she was amused by courses in "gracious living"), Liana was returning to her American lover in Rome, an intellectual Negro (that was the term used then) from Boston. Such ocean voyages were extraordinarily enriching life experiences. In comparison, a transatlantic flight by air today is as delightful as a session in a scanner.

The summer of 1956 was marked by the Suez crisis, when both the United States and the Soviet Union joined to stop the joint Franco-British-Israeli war against Egypt over control of the Suez Canal. At that point, Washington clearly considered that supporting Israeli aggression could only be harmful to U.S. interests, notably in the oil-producing Arab states. This attitude was reversed a decade later, but for the time being it kept the peace in the Middle East. The tacit agreement between Moscow and Washington made it clear that the old colonial powers, Britain and France, could no longer act without the backing of at least one of the "superpowers." This promise of better U.S.-USSR relations was rapidly shattered by the Hungarian uprising, which totally dominated the news toward the end of 1956. The violent military repression raised anti-Soviet feelings to new heights, taking a toll even among Western communist parties. U.S. propaganda focused on the tragedy with enthusiastic schadenfreude.

When refugees began streaming out of Hungary, Western reporters flocked to Vienna for interviews, or to Munich, or to other places where the fugitives were massed for relocation. I was in the crowd, taking photographs and talking to people, along with Herb and with Art Edson, an AP feature writer sent from Washington for his first and only time abroad. This was the Big Story. For me the high point was in the

German port of Bremerhaven, where a U.S. ship had docked and taken aboard young Hungarians, in order to sail them across the ocean to the Land of the Free. I was particularly interested in the relations between the military people organizing this much publicized exodus and the Hungarian refugees themselves. The refugees on route to America had been carefully selected. All were young, of good appearance, in perfect physical condition and well-educated. Still, many did not speak much English. After they had boarded, I wandered among them, taking pictures and chatting in whatever common language could be found, as the departure was delayed while officers checked the women to weed out those who were pregnant, so that none could sneakily give birth in the United States to a baby that would automatically be an American citizen. This made no sense to me, but that was the rule.

The military officers organizing all this were doing their job, with no visible sympathy for their charges. Rather, I heard comments such as, "Why don't they stay and fight in their own country?" There was surprisingly little human sympathy displayed.

Just before the ship set sail, an American army band installed itself on the wharf and attempted to play (apparently for the first time) something Hungarian, before settling into a mediocre rendition of "Anchors Away." The Hungarians, lining the decks above, looked down on the musicians with tears in their eyes. At some point, a bold soul gave the signal and a shout went up from the decks, "EEP, EEP, OURAH!" The musicians, puzzled and distrustful, looked at their instruments or at the ground. What could this mean? None were able to decipher the Hungarian version of "Hip Hip Hooray!" But the one black musician in the band didn't need language skills to understand, and alone among his sulking colleagues, raised his arm and replied to the cheering refugees with energetic waves and a big smile. And off they sailed to freedom.

My relationship with Herb was fun but problematic. I had no desire to be married, but in those days Americans could not live together as Liana and Ben lived in Rome. When Herb was named AP bureau chief in Bonn, he introduced me to people as "his wife," which made me quite uncomfortable. Feeling I had lost my independence, I ran away to Rome to stay with Liana and Ben in their big apartment in the Via Giulia. Ben was tall and thin as a Touareg, with a Bostonian reserve. He was compiling and translating a collection of Modern Italian Short Stories which was published by Modern Library. I rapidly was introduced to their limitless circle of writers. We dined evening after evening in nearby trattorias over half portions of spaghetti alla carbonara and carafes of

Frascati. From the first moment, this seemed to me to be paradise. I never spoke to anyone about my feelings, and when Herb came rushing down to get me back, Ben and Liana naturally assumed that this was just a lovers' quarrel and did all they could to get us together again. They arranged for a bunch of us to go stay in a farm on the island of Procida, in the bay of Naples, with vineyards and caged rabbits and a view of the sea. That had to be October 1957, because it was there on Procida that we learned that the Russians had successfully launched Sputnik, the first satellite fired into space. The Italians were rejoicing, not because they were all communists (although many were) but simply because the Americans, for once, hadn't got there first. More seriously, this suggested balance and balance suggested peace.

With nothing better to do, I let myself be taken back to Germany as the real wife of the Associated Press bureau chief in Bonn.

Herb and I found a charming apartment in the village of Muffendorf, as cute as its name, on the Rhine south of Bonn, from where you could see the spires of the Cologne cathedral on clear days. For that reason, the dead end street was called Am Domblick (on the Cathedral View). About our only neighbor was an Icelandic woman named Skulladottir, so I learned that Icelanders are all sons or dottirs. Our landlord was a charming retired man named Dr. Segelken who attempted in vain to instruct me on how to grow flowers in the Blumenfenster in our dining room, but I was too uncivilized and having too much fun.

Herb took me on all his assignments, and I would either take photos of where we were or of the person he was interviewing (Maria Callas, among others), or else wait for him in a nearby café, writing in my notebooks and eating elaborate German cakes. We traveled a lot, looking for feature stories to complement the political news in what was then the capital of the newly independent Federal Republic of Germany, governed by Chancellor Konrad Adenauer, "der Alte" (the old man), who resembled an aged Indian chief.

I remember particularly a trip to a camp for women refugees from East Germany. These were mostly girls from working class families, who would walk around in twos holding hands, as was customary in communist countries. The Irish priest who ran the camp, complaining that the West Germans provided no financial assistance, observed that these girls were not, strictly speaking, political refugees, but girls who ran away from home, for one reason or another. The camp was near Hamburg, and the priest's main concern was to prevent the girls from being snatched away to the heavy sex industry in that city, with its women wrestlers in mud and its streets lined with shop windows where available live women sat waiting for customers. That's where many of them ended up, he said.

We went to Berlin from time to time. At one Berlin film festival, we chatted with Rita Hayworth and David Niven, who—like many Westerners in those pre-Wall days—wanted to be taken on a tour of East Berlin. This was standard at the time, and most impressive for the view from atop what had been Hitler's bunker, with nothing but bombed-out buildings as far as one could see.

In Bonn, our evenings were full. Since, as a small university down, Bonn lacked all the important people habitually invited to embassy parties, journalists got more than their share of invitations to champagne receptions and formal dinners. We were thus able to chat with important diplomats from U.S. ambassador David K.E. Bruce to Dean Acheson (who was passing through), which doesn't mean that they told us anything of real importance. Rather, they liked to entertain us with diverting anecdotes. No secrets were shared but an atmosphere was created of being on the inside of power.

The only diplomat who really impressed me by his manner and intelligence was Maurice Couve de Murville, who was French ambassador to Bonn at that time. I recall chatting with him about the war in Algeria which was then raging, and asked whether France would finally withdraw, he replied in a meaningful way that "there is only one thing to do." Soon after, when De Gaulle came to power in France, Couve de Murville became his foreign minister and France did indeed grant independence to Algeria.

At one annual press ball, I had the honor of being seated to the right of the largely figurehead President of the Federal Republic of Germany, Theodor Heuss, a jovial old gentleman from southwestern Germany. He regaled me for over an hour with picturesque stories, as his protocol people attempted to drag him away before dancing started, since he was still in mourning for his late wife. I listened raptly, smiling and laughing when I could see it was appropriate, although my poor German and his strong Swabian accent meant that I understood almost not a word of what he was saying. Still, it was a lovely evening.

There was a large permanent press corps in Bonn in those days, before foreign news came to be covered mainly by itinerant television teams crashing in to cover a crisis. We often got together with journalists and their wives from McGraw-Hill, *Time, Life, The New York Times* and *Newsweek.* Our friend the *Newsweek* correspondent came straight out of the OSS (former CIA) and retained some spook habits, such as talking to strangers in fancy bars in search of some revelation. When not at some embassy affair, the Anglo-American journalists hung out at The Club or met in somebody's home to play bridge. We played a lot of bridge in those days. Herb was an excellent player, and I was just good enough to keep up. We even found time to play tournament bridge. I once went skiing in Davos with Flora Lewis, who was then the wife of *New York Times* correspondent Sydney Gruson. Flora was actually striving to be a journalist herself and became a regular *Times* columnist some years later. She was a unique case in that milieu. There were women journalists from other countries, such as the correspondent for the Paris daily *Le Soir,* but in those days the United States was behind most continental countries when it came to women in professions. In Italy and France, there were many more women professors than in the United States, not to mention lawyers, judges, journalists. In this as in so many things, America was not "the leader" as it perpetually proclaimed itself to be.

The Americans needn't notice how far behind they were in various matters because they all stuck together, along with their British counterparts, faithfully impregnated with the official Anglo-American attitude reinforced by encounters with information officers at the British and American embassies. We were sometimes also invited to the French embassy, but for the Anglo-Americans, such forays were slightly dangerous because of the risk of some communist scent in the air. As most daring, we had some Danish friends, who for their part were trying to be American.

Stories are always "framed," and in those days, the frame was the Cold War. Herb often tried to escape from the frame by interviewing some cultural figure, but the AP desk in New York was not enthusiastic. What was wanted were stories recounting how the United States had just won the latest match in the great global football game against the Soviet commies. I well recall one exemplary incident. There had been an election. It should be noted that the German Communist Party was, of course, banned. There were three parties, Adenauer's Christian Democrats, the Socialists (SPD) and the Liberals. Since Germany was an occupied country (and still is, although less blatantly) and had to conform to Western policies, politics was not very exciting. In this particular election, Adenauer's party won by a landslide. As a good reporter, Herb came up with an original but accurate angle, stressing that some considered the election a bit too one-sided for the country's beginnings as a multi-party state. In New York, editors changed his lead to: "The

German voters dealt a crushing defeat to the Kremlin tonight." Herb protested. The Kremlin had no candidates in this election. Maybe the New York editors didn't like his lead, he argued, but the one they came up with was fantasy. To no avail. Readers of all the many papers that print AP reports learned that the Kremlin had been defeated in a German election, score one for our side!

In the evenings at the Club, American journalists would gather at the bar to complain of their editors and brag of some slight hint at the truth that they had managed to sneak past the rewrite desk. But who wants to complain too loudly? This was a great life, and dozens of people were eager to get the job. Why rock the boat?

I did rock the boat very seriously one evening, but I was only a young wife, so maybe it didn't matter. A couple of U.S. Senators were passing through, and Anglo-American journalists were invited to share their wisdom at the residence of the U.S. information officer. Senator Thomas Dodd of Connecticut, the unquestioned star of the evening, was seated in the middle of a long plush divan between two wives, placed there for decorative purposes. I was one of them. Senator Dodd launched into an interminable rant on the need for the free world to roll back godless communism from Eastern Europe. All means should be used, he declared, even nuclear weapons. All that was lacking was the will to fight for freedom. I saw American journalists, my friends, standing around smiling as if they agreed with him—a bit as I had smiled at President Heuss. But I knew that they did understand and did not agree. Still, the tirade continued without the slightest question. "We should send in tanks rather than let this go on!" At this, I turned and said, "Senator Dodd, if you feel so strongly, why don't you volunteer to go liberate Eastern Europe yourself?"

There was a stunned silence. The hostess, a perfect diplomat's wife, immediately stood up and cordially invited everyone to move into an adjacent salon. I was left alone with Henry Pleasants, a distinguished music critic and head of the CIA in Bonn, who said he found my remark interesting and he even tended to agree. We conversed for a while, just the two of us.

That evening, Herb appeared not to know who I might be.

He was not always quite that prudent. For one thing, he learned fluent German, which was already regarded as a bit suspect to the inspectors who occasionally came through. What is the point of learning German when you can get all the information you need, translated, from the American embassy? Still worse, Herb used his linguistic skill to have long conversational lunches with Social Democratic members of the Bundestag. Acquiring so much first-hand knowledge of German politics was beyond the call of duty. We once even invited a visiting Russian journalist to come for a drink and heard him lament that no one else would condescend to talk with him. There was no effort to convert us to communism, only distress at the exclusion.

Such eccentricities moved me to urge Herb to be very, very careful with his expense account. He was a superb agency reporter, faster and more thorough than anyone, flawlessly accurate, so they couldn't get him on professional grounds. But the expense account can provide a pretext. Watch out, I said.

My daughter Elizabeth was born in Bad Godesberg in February of 1959. That brought inevitable changes in my relationship with Herb. Early motherhood was easy, since we hired a lovely Italian au pair, but still, I no longer went along with Herb on all his various trips and could not supervise his expense account… or other matters.

The blow fell heavily in late 1960. I have something to tell you, Herb said. No, it wasn't about his expense account. He had been fired from the Associated Press because they had records that he had shared a hotel room with his secretary on one of his trips.

I was less surprised than shocked. I was disappointed regarding Herb, but my indignation was saved for the Associated Press, whose inspectors had obviously spied on one of their very best journalists in order to throw him out and give his job to some mediocre conformist. I publicly supported Herb as best I could, but the axe fell nevertheless. The high life in Bonn was over.

All this drama did not destroy our friendship, but it destroyed our marriage.

When I think about it, almost all the married couples we frequented in those days ended up in divorce. For one reason or another.

One strike against our marriage was his family. I met them during a visit to his home town in York, Pennsylvania, where his father owned a general store. They were Jewish, which meant nothing to me other than that we must do all we can for Jews because they were persecuted. Coming from such a Judeophilic background, I found it a bit ironic that in their milieu, marriage to a non-Jew was a bit of a disgrace. When I was taken with them to a bar mitzvah, I was obliged to pretend to be Jewish, which I thought rather fun. I did my best, so well that a man there confided to me that he "only felt comfortable" in the company of

Jews. That happened to me more than once. Herb himself seemed totally alienated from all that, but I think it contributed to a certain instability.

The emotional situation got so bad that on New Year's Eve, I packed my things and my daughter into my yellow Opel (separate from Herb's Citroen DS) and drove off toward Italy. In the Alps, the car spun around once on an icy road, but we got to Rome safely. We were welcomed by Ben and Liana in their third-floor apartment in the Via Giulia, which was sparsely furnished but large, as apartments in Rome tend to be. I had left my car parked just below and kept looking down uneasily as it was visibly packed full. After a pause I looked again and yes, both doors and the trunk were wide open and everything was gone. Everything, including a trunk full of all the things I had been writing over the years as I waited for Herb in *Konditoreien,* drinking coffee and eating German cakes. At the police station, I was obliged to tell them everything about myself, my mother's maiden name and date of birth, but they showed little interest in descriptions of what had been stolen, sure as they were that it would never be recovered.

With my little daughter, I spent about eight months in Rome. She had a great time, just learning to talk, with Italian as her first articulated language. She was very good humored and adaptable, and when we went to a restaurant, waiters would exclaim *"Che bella bambina!"* and take her into the kitchen to be spoiled. No need to look for a baby-sitter in Italy, they were everywhere.

Liana made half-hearted attempts to set me up with a promising young American writer, who published in *The New Yorker,* but I was not in the mood for a rebound.

I had come to Rome to be a writer, with absolutely nothing to show for it. Thanks to Ben and Liana, we were constantly in the company of writers, some of them famous, such as Swiss playwright Max Frisch, his companion the German poet Ingeborg Bachmann, American black novelist Ralph Ellison, a scattering of Irish poets and a wide selection of Italian writers, some of them famous and some not, but all working tremendously hard, writing novels, working for Cinecittà, giving university courses, all in the most impressive disorder. Other regular companions were our upstairs neighbors in the Via Giulia, Annette Fischer, whose Jewish family, owners of the Fischer Verlag (publishing house) in Frankfurt had fled the Nazis across Siberia to the United States, and her British companion Maurice, who had literary ambitions. I infiltrated this wonderful world in the guise of "a young writer," as Liana introduced me, but one day, Max Frisch pointedly asked me who was my publisher, and I realized the jig was up. I had felt I was a writer, but I was nobody. There were a few Americans who made ends meet by teaching English, but I was not particularly qualified and besides, observing the extraordinary culture, energy and talent of all these Italians, functioning in an environment of semi-chaos, I realized that I simply was not prepared to swim in this sea. Rome was heaven, but I was not ready for it.

I needed more culture, more discipline. And so it was that, with a boost from my father, I abandoned my temporary role as gay divorcee and returned to the University of Minnesota to work hard, as if in penance. It had been too easy and now it needed to be hard.

At the university, I could have entered graduate school in history, but was told that "the history department doesn't give teaching positions to women." Inasmuch as I didn't want to live off alimony, a teaching assistant position was necessary. This I found right away in the French department, consoling myself that French literature was close to history, while contributing to my literary culture. The party was over. Marriage was over, but it had been a learning experience.

PART II

The Right Thing To Do

4.

Vietnam Everywhere

When I was sixteen, all I wanted was to go to China with my father. But I was considered too young. I was told that once I finished high school, I could go to the University of Shanghai. A very large revolution got in the way. I didn't get to see China but I got to hear about it.

From Water Buffalo to B-52 Bombers

My father was sent to China in 1948 by the US government to dispense economic aid as a last-ditch effort to shore up the failing regime of Chiang Kai-Shek as the Communists moved inexorably toward victory. He managed to skirt around official corruption by importing water buffalo from Hainan Island to impoverished peasants of Guangxi province. But nothing could combat the futility of last-ditch efforts to stop the liberation of East Asia.[1]

The lesson learned from this experience was that a century of foreign exploitation, pillage and war had left China so destitute that the only resource for development was human energy—and this is what the Communists knew how to mobilize. For this reason, their victory was inevitable.

It seems that virtually all the American experts who lived through the final stages of the Chinese revolution came back with the same lesson. But they were prevented from sharing their understanding with the American people. Through a network of influential individuals whose fortunes were linked to the Kuomintang, known as the "China lobby," a media-political campaign sought to blame the Truman government for having "lost China." The notion that China—the oldest and most populous civilization on earth—was "ours" to lose or not to lose was repeated endlessly and would be applied subsequently to the rest of the world. The "loss" of China was used to brainwash the American public with the arrogant illusion that American "ideals" and American military power had the right and even the duty to "save" the world from

---

1 Paul H. Johnstone's experience in China is recounted in *From MAD to Madness* (Clarity Press, 2016).

itself. This attitude has long served as a barricade between the American people and the reality of the world.

As the United States plunged deeper into involvement in Vietnam in the 1960s, I was concentrating on my literary studies at the University of Minnesota and not paying much attention to world events. It was enough to see the photos of Vietnamese officers uncomfortably garbed in U.S. uniforms to realize that something was basically wrong. I rather distractedly saw the war in Indochina as a misguided effort that was bound to fail, sooner or later. Hadn't the Korean War sufficiently proven the folly of military engagement in Asia? I was fully occupied with studies, teaching and raising my small daughter. Had there not been committed pacifists and leftists providing organized opportunities to protest, I do not see how my own revulsion at the war could have found expression.

A Timid Militant

My clearest memory of joining the anti-war movement is of being scared. My first timid step was joining a scraggly "peace march" through the streets of the Twin Cities, from Minneapolis to Saint Paul. Although the logical purpose of a demonstration is to be seen by others, I was rather happy that nobody was paying much attention. Walking down the middle of the street carrying signs was not customary behavior in Minnesota in 1966, and I felt silly making a spectacle of myself in public. I didn't know the several dozen pacifists and leftists who had organized the march, except for the one university colleague who had persuaded me to come along. They looked pretty normal to me, contrary to the public image of demonstrators as crazies and weirdoes. I had joined the demonstration with the vague and foolish notion that if more respectable people got involved, the movement would have more impact—considering myself a respectable person. Actually, I was nothing but a graduate teaching assistant in the French department of the University of Minnesota, but I was not lacking in self-esteem.

The second step was much worse. It was an anti-war demonstration in downtown Minneapolis in the summer of 1966. A ladder was set up for speakers at the corner of 7th Street and Hennepin Avenue, and I was supposed to climb it and speak out loud to whoever would listen. Since I was used to teaching classes, the organizers may have assumed that I could speak in public. As the moment of my first political speech approached, I was terrified. I climbed the ladder as if to the gallows, speechless with dread.

Rescue came in an unexpected way. Suddenly, a squad of policemen descended on the gathering to break it up. An officer grabbed me by the arm to drag me toward a police van. I was already very nervous and I didn't like being grabbed. I told him to ask me politely what he wanted me to do instead of grabbing me. The officer paid no attention. Since the policeman kept his grip on my left arm, I used my right to sock him in the jaw. The expression is an exaggeration—although I am very tall, I am not at all athletic, and at most I only gently grazed his cheek. However, suddenly realizing that I had "assaulted an officer," I took the quickest way out by falling to the ground, as though it were he who had hit me.

A cry went up, "Let her go! Let her go!" The police at that time were no more used to this sort of thing than I was and turned their attention to the pacifists who were asking to be arrested. Thanks to the chorus of "let her go!" I slipped away. That evening I got to know the Trotskyists of the Socialist Workers Party (SWP) who had organized the aborted demonstration and covered my retreat with their timely chanting. I was relieved and exhilarated at having escaped—first from speaking on a street corner and then from going to jail. I had to thank them for that, and they praised my "revolutionary" response to police repression.

In truth, I was neither revolutionary nor even rebellious. But it was amusing to watch the scene on television, complete with a totally inaccurate commentary which identified me, by another name, as a Communist Party organizer. At that time I had never even met anyone who admitted belonging to the Communist Party, USA. In those days, almost all American Communists had "gone underground," in order to avoid being treated as agents of the enemy during the Cold War. Some of them had turned into fairly timid liberal Democrats. The fact that Communists were treated as pariahs aroused my sympathetic curiosity. Since there were none of them in sight, my curiosity had to make do with the Trotskyists of the SWP. That little party was a prominent feature of the local left. Minneapolis was in fact a center of SWP mythology, pilgrimages and training, thanks to a Teamsters strike in which they played a leading role back in 1934. The SWP held classes on the exotic theories of Marx, Lenin and Trotsky—while taking every opportunity to fiercely condemn "Stalinists," as well as various other even more obscure Trotskyist groups guilty of deviating from the correct Fourth International Line.

That incident on a Minneapolis street corner was amusing, but it was not at all typical of my subsequent involvement in the anti-war movement, much less of my views on what political action should be. I was always resolutely in favor of non-violent action, for various excellent reasons. I had nothing against policemen in general, or even the one I swung at in particular. My reaction was in reality not political at all, but the unthinking reaction of a woman grabbed by a strange man.

I did not join the antiwar movement out of any political convictions. I simply saw that the war was wrong on every count, and the pretexts given were false. I did not come from the Left, and it was not the Left that turned me against the war, but my opposition to the Vietnam War brought me into contact with the Left, so much so that I have been identified forever after as "on the left." My attitude toward leftist groups and their ideas always remained both friendly and deeply skeptical. The militants were devoted to an idealistic cause which deserved respect. My attitude toward the far left was similar to my attitude toward the nicest forms of Christianity—it was all too good to be true. I evaded all efforts to enlist me in the cause. However, without the existence of militant leftist groups, my opposition would probably never have found expression, much less become a central part of my active life for several years. Whatever their illusions about how to make a revolution, the Trotskyists knew how to organize a protest march, when nobody else did.

Vietnam in France

Shortly after my aborted debut as street speaker, I left for France. From September 1966 to September 1968 I was in Paris, working on my doctoral dissertation on "André Malraux and the Ethical Novel." My study of this particular writer was highly compatible with my effort to deepen my understanding of the Vietnam War by studying the history of French colonialism in Indochina. In 1923 Malraux, not yet 22 years old but already a self-taught expert on Asian art, left France with his wife, Clara, to rescue some ancient statues from the Cambodian jungle, as a novel way of getting rich. When he was imprisoned by the French colonial authorities for theft, a campaign on his behalf by French writers secured his return to France. In 1925 he went back to Saigon to co-found and edit a newspaper called *Indochine* which quickly aroused the wrath of the colonial authorities it criticized. Shut down after less than two months by official pressures, the paper reappeared for another short period as *Indochine enchaînée* (Indochina in chains).

In Paris libraries I was able to find copies of this ephemeral journal and read Malraux's articles, which were doubly fascinating to me at the time for what they told me both about Malraux's basically liberal reformist ideas and about the nature of French colonial rule in Indochina. As Malraux had found in Saigon, France brought principles of liberal democracy to Indochina and then, by the practice of colonialism, violated them. Those reformers who tried to appeal to those liberal democratic principles on behalf of the indigenous people were ignored or repressed. Like other East Asians at the time, the patriot scholar Ho Chi Minh studied Western principles for the secret of their strength. In searching for a modern path to liberating his people, he discovered Communism. While the Versailles Conference refused to consider his appeal for self-determination for colonized peoples, the Soviet Union took up their cause. Communism was above all the formula for mobilizing the mass of the population in a political struggle to win independence. It combined the preservation of national culture with the promise of social justice.

I arrived in France at a time when anti-war activity was expanding rapidly. On November 30, 1966, I attended a program of "Six Hours for Vietnam," held at the Mutualité Hall in the Latin Quarter. The meeting was a huge success, drawing constant crowds to the film-showings, displays and speeches by prominent intellectuals including Jean-Paul Sartre. As I recall, it was at such programs that I began to become acquainted with French experts on Southeast Asia. Paris was an excellent place to gain awareness of the historical context of the American war. The fact that Indochina had been part of the French empire naturally had created numerous academic and journalistic specialists in the region. They were politically diverse, but virtually all of them condemned the United States intervention.

U.S. policy saw culturally diverse Asian countries as so many "dominos" and communism as a diabolical world plot. After losing the battle of Dien Bien Phu in 1954, the French had realized that they could not restore the colonial control they had already lost when the Japanese conquered Vietnam during World War II. Ho Chi Minh had led the resistance to the Japanese and went on to declare national independence, appealing to the United States for support. Instead, the United States largely financed the hopeless French effort at reconquest, and when that failed, took over the war themselves. The United States policy-makers who set up a Catholic puppet government in Saigon fancied that they were engaged in "nation building," but the nation was two millennia old and was already rebuilding itself in its own way. In reality, the U.S. war was a violent attempt at nation-breaking, against a people with a strong sense of national identity who turned to communism precisely because it seemed to be the key to unity.

It was in Paris that I became really active against the war, in the context of three different organized elements: American, French and Vietnamese.

The Americans in Paris

In Paris, I quite naturally drifted into a newly-formed organization called the Paris-American Committee to Stop War (PACS), which had grown rapidly to several hundred members who met regularly at the Quaker Center on the Rue de Vaugirard, near Montparnasse. It was a very diverse organization, bringing together ancient pacifists, refugees from anti-Communist witch-hunts in the film industry, a sprinkling of relatively adventurous established expatriates and a wide range of radicalizing or simply curious students and young scholars. While not authorized to mount street actions of its own, PACS took part in broader French-organized anti-war demonstrations, notably against the visit of Vice President Hubert Humphrey to Paris on April 7, 1967.

There was an Austrian who frequented PACS who insisted on burning an American flag, an action that I personally did not care for. Flag burning and flag waving seem to me two sides of a similar fetish. Anyway, in the midst of a gathering at the Place d'Iéna, Tommy set fire to the U.S.flag, which served as signal for the French police to move in and arrest about a hundred people.

I was one of them. Indeed, I was filmed as I was led into the paddy wagon, and this time I went peacefully, even incongruously holding my umbrella. The footage of my arrest turned up in two films, "Loin du Vietnam" and "Le Fond du ciel est rouge" by Chris Marker.

At the police station I explained that I had to leave in order to fetch my young daughter when she emerged from kindergarten. The French police officer was quite courteous, and asked me whether I thought that demonstrating like that would accomplish anything. "I don't know," I replied, "but it is the right thing to do." He didn't dispute this, and let me free without delay.

Some months later, when I was elected to the board of PACS, I had to go to the police as part of the organization's legal registration. There again I was treated most politely, and gathered the impression that the French police were not at all hostile to our organization. After all, this was at a time when President Charles de Gaulle himself was openly critical of the U.S. war in Indochina. France allowed anti-war activities and even turned a blind eye to deserters from the U.S. armed forces.

PACS was far from being a radical organization. The president was a very rich American named Ira Morris. Its emblematic figure was Maria (pronounced Ma-rah-ya) Jolas, an imposing white-haired survivor of the great days of American literary expatriates in Paris. Born in Louisville, Kentucky, in 1893, Maria McDonald had gone to Berlin in her youth to study voice, but had settled in Paris to marry Eugene Jolas, who was remembered mainly for first having published James Joyce in his literary magazine *transition.* PACS board meetings were sometimes held in Maria's kitchen, whose cupboards were filled (she explained) with still unpublished manuscripts of James Joyce. Maria retained something of her southern lady manners, which contrasted, and frequently clashed, with the forceful personality of Rosette Coryell, the work horse of the organization. Born in Turkey into a Jewish family, Rosette was educated in French schools before becoming a Communist militant. For this reason, she was banned from the United States despite her marriage to an American citizen, Scofield Coryell. The Coryell couple were thus obliged to take refuge in Paris, where the mild-manned Sco always seemed a bit lost. Rosette, on the other hand, was capable and determined enough for two. Not surprisingly, the Great Lady from the South and the Communist militant from Istanbul did not get along. But there was a division of labor, with Maria in the limelight and Rosette in the background doing the thankless paper work.

PACS meetings occasionally benefited from the surprisingly vigorous and theatrical oratory emanating from a frail wisp of a man, Harvey Goldberg, professor of history at the University of Wisconsin. Harvey was both gay and an eloquent prophet of French revolutions, and as such, inspired a trail of students, male and female, who came to Paris in search of the revolutionary spirit that nobody in France could evoke as passionately as he.

My graduate school colleague, David Thorstad was also in town. A native of the large Norwegian-American community in northern Minnesota, David was raised as an Evangelical Christian, fearing the Rapture might sweep away his parents and leave him to Satan. He soon left that behind for language study and politics. During the Vietnam War, David joined the Trotskyist Socialist Workers Party and moved to New York as a journalist for the SWP newspaper, *The Militant.* Later he became an ardent gay rights militant, drastically overestimating the public's ability to make the distinction between pederasty and pedophilia. But in 1967 he was in Paris to work for "the Russell Tribunal," an international unofficial war crimes tribunal sponsored by philosophers Bertrand Russell and Jean-Paul Sartre to denounce U.S. crimes against the people of Vietnam. The sessions in Stockholm helped raise European awareness of U.S. violations of international law in Vietnam, but were largely ignored by U.S. media, of course.

In those days, George Whitman's now legendary bookshop in the rue de la Bûcherie opposite Notre Dame Cathedral was an even more frequent gathering place for anti-war Americans than PACS. It was open every day until late in the evening. George often invited me and my little daughter to stay for a modest meal on the premises. Maria Jolas was scandalized when Whitman changed the name of his bookshop from "Mistral" to "Shakespeare and Company," a name Maria maintained must be forever associated solely with the bookstore maintained by Sylvia Beach on the rue de l'Odéon in the 1920s. Whitman's generosity in providing a free lending library and even occasional free lodging for traveling writers aroused suspicious rumors (he was said to inform on his guests to the French police) but was rarely turned down. An energetic young literary scholar, Bruce Franklin, organized a Marxist study group in an upstairs room of the bookshop. Bruce Franklin had all the enthusiasm of the recent convert. I remember him exclaiming ecstatically, concerning his discovery of Marx, "the world makes sense!"

Accompanied by our children, his wife Jane Franklin and I leafleted the American Cathedral in Paris with a flyer "welcoming American visitors" and telling them that the French people liked Americans but did not approve of their war. Later, back in California, Bruce led a Maoist group called the Revolutionary Union, and although a tenured professor, was fired from Stanford University in 1972 for "inciting student disruptions" during antiwar protests.

If the somewhat reclusive Whitman was unlikely to be spying on such activities, others were. There can be no doubt that in those days, some of the people who showed up at anti-war meetings were there as informers or even as provocateurs, whether professional or amateur. I recall certain persons who betrayed themselves by trying to act the way they thought radicals must act. And there was the occasional outsider who tried to get PACS into trouble with the French authorities by advocating violence. At one meeting of PACS, I vigorously objected to the suggestion of a red-headed man, who appeared for the first (and last) time, that we organize a commando to attack the US Embassy. The suggestion was rejected, but as we left the Quaker hall, the redhead handed me a photo: of myself, carrying a banner in a peace march. The message: we are watching you. I kept the photo.

While concentrating on Vietnam, the antiwar movement had no objections to the aggressive little war launched by Israel on June 4. It lasted only six days, and, so far as I could tell, was applauded by just about everybody. It was understood that little Israel was fighting off—pre-emptively—a bunch of autocratic Arab countries that were ganging up on the only democracy in the Middle East. Personally, I was simply not interested in the Middle East. I don't even remember my own reaction to the event, but I remember how Paris reacted, with car horns honking in enthusiastic approval. At the time, I was friends with a young Israeli poet and classical scholar, Aaron Shabtai, and his wife, who were living in an apartment in the rue des Gravilliers, just down the street from my apartment on the fifth floor without elevator at 32 rue Pastourelle, on the edge of the Marais district. In the house where the Shabtais were living, the toilets were on the stair landing, for this was before the Marais became the gentrified, hugely fashionable center of gay life. I had met Aaron through our mutual opposition to the Vietnam War. Although antiwar on principle, Aaron accepted the idea that Israel's blitzkrieg was justified on grounds of self-preservation. For me, like many people at that time, my Jewish friends came first and I was ready to consider that what Israel did was their business.

I am inclined to believe that in June 1967, none of us grasped the significance of the punchy little Israeli war, and of the tragedy and devastation that was to follow for decades. The horrible truth is that Israel's rapid grab of territory from Egypt, Jordan and Syria, accompanied by the conquest and illegal occupation of the whole of Palestine, was accepted as "defensive" and inspired general admiration throughout the West.

Later Aaron became a recognized poet and extremely critical of Israeli conduct. Indeed, forty years later, in 2007, I met Aaron Shabtai again in Paris. He was separated from his wife and ten children and was leaving Israel forever on his way to New York with Tanya Reinhart, a prominent Chomskyan linguist known for her sharp criticism of Israeli policy. They had come to speak at the pro-Palestinian bookstore, Résistances, in the 17th arrondissement of Paris. While we were renewing old acquaintance, Jewish Defense League militants attacked the bookstore with tear gas and tried to break down the door and smash windows. Shortly after their arrival in New York, Tanya died suddenly, leaving Aaron devastated.

In 1967, opposition to the Vietnam War was increasing exponentially. One function of PACS was to provide American speakers for French anti-war meetings, where it was considered correct to include a Vietnamese and an anti-war American. I spoke in Strasbourg, in Montpellier, in Carcassonne. Indeed, my role as token American even took me to other countries. I spoke at rallies in Copenhagen, Milan and West Berlin. Copenhagen seemed just like Minneapolis, rather low key and pedestrian. Milan, on the other hand, was enormous, exciting, rapturous. The entire population seemed to be present, all united in passionate love for the Vietnamese. And to heighten the emotional tension, I heard that someone had been shot on the edges of the huge demonstration by police or fascists, I'm not sure which. The Italian Left was at its peak in those days. Vietnam was a unifying cause, before the fatal fragmentation of the 1970s totally changed the political mood of Italy.

Berlin was something else. The march through the streets was determined and angry, the protest by a conscious minority that felt itself in hostile country, quite unlike the Italian exuberance. After the march and the rally, I was taken along for a meeting by the organizers who meticulously analyzed the event, detail by detail. It had seemed to me that the demonstration was a huge success, and so I was particularly struck by the dissatisfaction of the German organizers. Indeed I was favorably impressed by their self-criticism, rare in such organizations, but more useful, I thought, than self-congratulatory triumphalism.

In France, the organized opposition to the war in Vietnam seemed to arise from very mixed motives. Unlike every other Western European country except Sweden, the French government in the person of de Gaulle was critical of the U.S. war in Indochina. The experience of Dien Bien Phu had convinced most of France that trying to restore Western colonial rule to Vietnam was a hopeless exercise. As a result of this particular circumstance, the French active opposition to the war in Vietnam was directed less at their own government than at other segments of the French Left.

The issue of the Vietnam War was uniquely ambiguous and complex in France. President Charles de Gaulle had recently taken France out of the NATO command and, in a resounding speech in Phnom Penh, clearly marked his distance from the American war. After defying the far right assassination attempts in order to make peace in Algeria, de Gaulle granted at least nominal independence to most of the rest of

France's colonial possessions in Africa and embarked on a policy of friendly relations with the Third World. The Gaullist government was both relatively tolerant of the antiwar movement and anxious to avoid any excesses that would wreck De Gaulle's bid to have Paris host eventual peace talks.

In contrast, various Trotskyist, Maoist and maverick socialist groups saw the cause of Vietnam as a way to outflank the French Communist Party (PCF), whose position was more anti-war than revolutionary. A few years later, in 1971 or 1972, I was invited to speak as token American at the annual convention of the *"Anciens Combattants du Métro,"* the Communist-led organization of Paris Métro employees who had served in the army or in the Resistance. Party spokesmen, a Vietnamese, an East German and I spoke to an attentive public that filled the room. To my surprise, when it was over, the back wall opened up, and we were suddenly in a vast hall with dining tables seating hundreds and hundreds of *anciens combattants* and their families in a festive mood. The organizers and speakers were seated at a special table, where people came up to give us flowers and collect autographs, as if we were celebrities of some sort in a Soviet bloc country. Enjoying the food and drink but somewhat embarrassed, I asked the organizer next to me why we were displayed to the crowd but not asked to speak to them. He confidently replied—citing as evidence some of the songs the crowd sang as the wine flowed—that the workers still had something of a colonial racist outlook and were not ready for our message of international solidarity with the Vietnamese. I wondered how, with such leadership, they ever would be ready.

Into the breach rushed the far leftist groups. The major ideological conflict between the Trotskyists and the "Stalinists," as they continued to call all the orthodox communist parties long after Stalin was gone, had always stemmed from the conflict between Trotsky's call for world revolution and Stalin's more conservative fallback position of "socialism in one country." Although the Western capitalist leaders appeared not to notice this fact, Stalin had realistically given up on spreading communism around the world. Indeed, his leadership of the Communist International, until it was disbanded, aimed more at defending the "socialist motherland" than at promoting revolution elsewhere. The Trotskyists excoriated him for this betrayal of the revolution, but their more radical stance was rarely regarded as more dangerous to capitalist leaders than the more conservative "Stalinists." In France, a whole generation of intellectuals passed through Trotskyism on their way into the political and journalistic elite.

In 1966, Alain Krivine, who had been expelled from the Communist youth organization at the Sorbonne, founded his own "Revolutionary Communist Youth" (JCR). The JCR went on to create Vietnam Committees which mobilized the intelligentsia to develop solidarity with the Vietnamese liberation. These committees were my initiation into public speaking at political meetings. On at least one such occasion, my daughter Elizabeth stayed with Alain Krivine and his wife while I was away for the cause. In short, my relations with the Krivine Trotskyists were always friendly, but basically distant because confined to the single issue of the Vietnam War. I was never interested in the doctrinal disputes which opposed one Trotskyist group to another, nor was I motivated, as were a number of militants in France and Italy, by belief that the Vietnamese national liberation struggle was the vanguard of world revolution. Many saw the revolt of the colonized, or "third" world, as a major historic stage in the world socialist revolution that was coming.

An important center of this revolutionary spirit of the times was François Maspéro's bookship, *La Joie de Lire,* in the rue Saint Sévérin just off the Boulevard Saint Michel in the Latin Quarter of Paris. It was essentially a stand-up bookshop, where readers stood reading books they only occasionally bought, mostly on the Third World and its struggles. (But they did not steal books, as became common after May '68.) Looking back on that period, it is easy to say that the spirit of the times was filled with illusions, but it was also a time of great curiosity about the world, and effort to learn. Oddly, as the world has "grown smaller" technologically, satisfaction with superficial impressions has tended to replace the effort to learn and understand.

While the Trotskyists tried, with some success, to shame the Communists for their inaction on Vietnam, they soon were confronted with another brand of communist rivals, the Maoists, who tried to shame *them* for being elitist. Like the Trotskyists, the Maoists were divided into rival sectarian groups, some of them claiming sponsorship by Beijing, others not. While they all condemned the Soviet Union for betraying the world revolution, some of them considered Stalin a hero and Trotsky a traitor. In general, they followed the Maoist revolutionary line of "the countryside surrounding the city," which led them to disdain urban intellectuals (which is what they were) and look hopefully to various provincial identity movements, such as the Bretons and Occitans in France as the key to future uprisings. While the Trotskyists appealed to students and intellectuals primarily, the Maoists pretended to be "just folks" and tried to appeal to "the people." I say "pretended," because their leaders came from the most elite *Grandes Ecoles,* notably the *Ecole Normale Supérieure,* and yet would not flinch from intimidating challengers as "too intellectual." This populist posturing had an irritatingly menacing character. The Maoists were the only ones who ever demanded to see the text of my speech in advance—a demand I rejected on principle, but I was allowed to speak anyway. There was a relatively large Maoist presence in the Marais section of Paris where I was living at the time, and while I was put off by both their ideology and their hypocritical leadership style, I found their activist style interesting. The Maoists organized "Base Committees" in neighborhoods and tried to reach a broader public by their presence in Sunday morning markets with visual displays and distribution of leaflets on Vietnam.

There were also other French groups who were active in opposing the Vietnam War. A center of such non-communist activity was the small Unified Socialist Party (PSU), which included a number of Christian activists, both Catholic and Protestant. For the Americans of PACS, the most impressive figure was that of Claude Bourdet, a celebrated independent journalist and French Resistance veteran who spoke perfect English and whose approach to political questions was much closer to Anglo-American pragmatism than that of the revolutionary groups. Free from any party line, Bourdet was more radical—that is, closer to reality—than they were. For many of us, he was our best guide to the unfamiliar scene of French politics.

The Vietnamese Diaspora

By far the most valuable aspect of my occasional stints as token American was the opportunity it gave me to encounter token Vietnamese. One of each of us was required at meetings, as evidence of true internationalism. For this, the French organizers were able to draw on the large, well-organized Vietnamese community in Paris. The community organized important events of its own, notably the annual Têt festivities, which included Vietnamese theater, music and food. Like others of my compatriots in Paris at the time, I was able to make friends with some of the leaders of that community, which was a revelation for Americans who had been told to fear the Viet Cong as savage cut-throats. In particular, I had frequent contact with Nguyen Ngoc Giao, of the Union of Vietnamese Students in France. Giao was a handsome man, highly cultivated and a dedicated patriot, with a good sense of humor and a calm, intelligent assessment of the situation.

It did not take long to realize that the Vietnamese were more civilized than we were.

This was evident first of all from their absolute absence of personal hostility or even the mildest reproach in the presence of Americans. They were serenely aware that the war was a mistake for which individual Americans were not to blame. They were glad to see us oppose the war, but no more surprised than at any other manifestation of human capacity to be reasonable.

It was politically significant that this Vietnamese community, and its leaders, could largely be considered "middle class"—small business people, students, professionals. Most of them, and notably the community leaders I befriended, were surely not communists. But whatever their long term political views, they were firmly united in support of the unification of Vietnam, which was what the US war of aggression was determined to prevent. Most Americans did not know that at the time, and many don't know it now or simply never cared.

While befriending Vietnamese, I also came to befriend scholars, both American and French, as well as Vietnamese, experts in Asian history, whose contribution to the anti-war movement was essential. Scholarship and honest journalism were necessary to combat the propaganda and the delusions spread by the United States in its foolish attempt to reverse history in Asia.

The essential facts were that in order to rob the Vietnamese of their victory over the French, the United States undertook to violate the unification agreement reached in Geneva in 1954, which called for nationwide elections in 1956. The United States blocked those elections for the simple reason that Vietnam's historic leader, Ho Chi Minh, was certain to win them, and he was a Communist. Instead, an ardent Catholic was found and put in place in Saigon to rule a Buddhist country, or half a country, severing permanently the southern half from the northern half. This led to creation of the Vietnamese Liberation Front in the south which the United States saw simply as "communists," "Viet Cong," and not as the patriots they were. Millions of Vietnamese were to be killed in this vain attempt to maintain a Western colony in East Asia.

My approach to the anti-war movement was to inform people about the truth in the expectation that popular opposition would force leaders to put an end to this flagrant injustice. This was grounded in a deep unquestioned faith in democratic process. If the anti-war movement also helped bring about world revolution, then so be it. If people wanted revolution, they should have it. But I doubted that they did.

May '68 seemed, for a moment, to show that I was wrong.

The Illusory Revolution

1968 began with the Têt offensive, when the Vietnamese national liberation struggle showed its strength as a military force. In the United States, Martin Luther King, whose open call for an end of the war clearly linked the anti-war cause to the battle for civil rights, was assassinated on April 4.

In France, reactions to the US war in Vietnam were viscerally linked to the war in Algeria, which was fresh in people's memories. For those who had supported Algerian independence, achieved only six years earlier, the Vietnamese people's struggle for independence was a natural continuation. On the other side were a smaller number of diehard colonialists who hated Charles de Gaulle for giving away Algeria and dismantling the French Empire. The youth group "Occident," rooted mainly in the law faculty in the rue d'Assas, organized commando groups to defend ill-defined "Western values" which they considered to be under threat. One evening, to my great surprise, I turned out to be one of those "threats." As I arrived late to take part in an anti-war panel in Saint Germain en Laye, near Paris, I smiled at a small group of men standing at the entrance who proceeded to knock me flat and bleeding, leaving a few of my teeth loose. That was my informal introduction to "Occident." This sort of encounter heightened tensions, and leftist groups strengthened their *services d'ordre* in self-protection.

Such minor incidents concerning Vietnam helped set the mood for the street fights that inflamed the Latin Quarter in the early days of May 1968.

The revolt broke out on May 3 after police entered the sanctuary of the Sorbonne and arrested student leaders protesting the shutdown of the university at suburban Nanterre. I don't think that at the time many people cared about the problem at Nanterre. But the sight of police occupying the Sorbonne aroused protests, and in the streets, police charged protesters. Some ran for cover, but many fought back with surprising determination. After several days of violent skirmishes between growing groups of students and baton-wielding security police (CRS, met with the slogan "CRS SS!"), within a week the entire Latin Quarter was in a state of siege. May 10 was the "night of the barricades." I happened to be there, in the streets near the Pantheon, and was struck by what seemed to me a certain mimesis. All night, students around the Pantheon calmly built barricades, passing the paving stones from hand to hand with the same gestures they had seen in the 16-millimeter films of Vietnamese peasant women rebuilding bombed dikes.

The next day, the streets were cluttered with debris from the police charge. The Latin Quarter was occupied by rows of armed CRS, and students who had been apolitical a few days before wandered in a new landscape, transformed into an oppressed people with an occupation army to overthrow. Was there some latent desire to be like the Vietnamese, who at the time were the object of widespread sympathy and admiration—even adoration?

In between my library research and my part-time work for a movie dubbing studio, I followed those events unroll as closely as I could. I was present at many of the key happenings, the major skirmishes in the Latin Quarter, the orations at the Odéon theatre, the night of the barricades, the big marches, the speech at the Sorbonne by Daniel Cohn-Bendit on his triumphant return after being expelled to Germany. I rushed to buy every edition of the daily *Action.* Yes, I was there.

But did I understand what it all meant? Hardly. Do I understand now? A little better, I think. But the French May '68 was too ambiguous and contradictory to be easily understood. I would even venture to say that nobody did, or could, fully understand its meaning because there were so many actors performing out of different motivations, often obscure even to themselves.

I recall overhearing a chic young woman in Saint Germain des Près remark that she had to rush to finish her shopping in order to "get back to making the revolution."

Paris was nearly the last student population in the world to get into the spirit of the times. But such was the mystique of Paris, capital of revolution, that it was only when students in Milan or Berlin heard of the Paris events that they thought something truly momentous was happening. Many set out on a pilgrimage to Paris heedless of transport strikes and gasoline shortages, to join the revolution in the Sorbonne.

However it may be interpreted, the massive French revolt of May 1968 quickly became the symbol of an era. The "events," as they were called at the time, featuring an ephemeral revolution at the Sorbonne and the biggest general strike in French history, momentarily created the illusion of Paris as center of a worldwide revolution.

The extreme ambiguity of the Paris revolt was expressed in the graffiti that appeared on walls around the city as if by magic. The walls seemed to talk—and indeed that was one of the slogans: *"Les murs ont la parole."* Indeed it seemed that the walls themselves were announcing a new dispensation: "It is forbidden to forbid," and in allusion to the paving stones being hurled at police, *"Sous les pavés la plage"* (under the paving stones the beach). Enjoyment without limits was the dominant message, down with authority of all kinds, down with work, *"L'imagination prend le pouvoir"* (imagination takes power), "Be realistic, demand the impossible!"

The myth of the spontaneous talking walls overlooked the fact that the most striking slogans were directly inspired by a group of radical libertarian theorists calling themselves the Situationists. Their best known exponents were Guy Debord, author of *La Société du Spectacle,* and Raoul Vaneigem, author of a *"Traité de savoir vivre à l'usage des jeunes générations"* which exhorted the young to total revolt against existing society.

Like other radicals of the period, Situationists considered genuine, non-existent socialism (as opposed to the Soviet variety of "real existing" but false socialism) to be the ultimate goal of social revolution. But their immediate target was "consumer society" and what Debord called "the spectacle society."

In May '68, they had the situation of their dreams. Their triumph was fleeting and deeply ironic. The liberation from all traditional authority that ensued paved the way to a far greater alienation in terms of consumerism and commercial spectacle than ever. "Anything goes" is a slogan that capitalism can live by.

The hedonistic spirit of "it is forbidden to forbid" was represented by the student rebel who came to personify May '68, Daniel Cohn-Bendit. A news photograph showing him staring impertinently into the face of a helmeted police officer at short range was a perfect image of cheeky defiance of skittish authority. For the media, it was love at first sight, and a love that lasted.

Cohn-Bendit was nicknamed by the media "Dany the Red." While it may have applied to his hair color, it did not fit his politics, insofar as "red" denoted communist or socialist. While loosely attached to the Anarchist Federation, Cohn-Bendit was much less concerned with liberating the working class from the chains of labor than with freeing the individual from social restraints on personal liberty. Born in France of German Jewish refugee parents, Daniel chose to retain German citizenship in order to avoid military conscription. Studying sociology at the University of Nanterre, he delighted his fellow students with his colossal nerve. Dany had attitude. He excelled at defying authority. This talent had been fostered in the ultra-progressive Oldenwald boarding school he had attended in Heppenheim, Germany, whose slogan was "Become What You Are." Its anti-authoritarian pedagogy had taken on a fresh luster in the 1960s as German authoritarianism came to be blamed for the rise of Hitler, notably by the Frankfurt School philosophers. In parallel to the political agitation going on against the United States war in Vietnam, Daniel Cohn-Bendit introduced an agitation against the authority of the university itself in regard to personal matters, challenging the ban on allowing male students to visit the rooms of girls in student dormitories. It was this incongruous mix of issues that exploded on May 3, 1968.

Alain Krivine's *Jeunesse Communiste Révolutionnaire* (JCR) was the most conspicuous leftist organization, which played a key role by providing the *service d'ordre* that protected the student demonstrators from right-wing provocateurs while preventing clashes with police from going too far. The chief of Paris Police at the time, Maurice Grimaud, later credited himself and Alain Krivine for keeping the war dance within certain bounds.

The leftists wanted to rouse the workers to make the Revolution. But when the workers massively joined the movement by going on strike in the greatest general strike in French history, the Communist-led CGT (General Confederation of Labor) succeeded in channeling the strike toward negotiations and wage increases.

For the ultra-lefts, that amounted to a cowardly betrayal by the union leadership. For several years, the most ardent militants, especially the Maoists, tried to relight the flame of revolt by courageously entering factories as ordinary workers.

While scorning the student revolt as *petit bourgeois,* the Maoists quickly adapted to the mood of revolt, shifting the focus of their *Comités de base* from Vietnam to French society. During the May events, they applied the Maoist theory of creating liberated territories in the periphery, making the revolution in cultural workplaces like schools and libraries. Employees everywhere were going on strike, reorganizing their own work, which often needed it.

Whatever its ideological significance, this tendency of over-managed people to take control of their work lives struck me at the time as the most positive aspect of the May events. A similar aspect was a seemingly spontaneous movement by artists to "serve the people" anonymously. In the Ecole des Beaux Arts, students produced the posters that symbolized May '68 even more than the Situationist graffiti. My close friend Yves Loyer, who before and after the revolutionary mood of the period strove to make a name for himself as an artist, was overwhelmed and for a while converted by the movement to produce art anonymously, for the benefit of the people, without thought of gain or glory.

While the Maoists pursued their cultural revolution and the Trotskyists tried to channel the street battles, political commentators and sociologists flocked to the scene to explain to the rebels what they were rebelling about. It was perhaps all the easier for French students to act out revolution in that they could situate themselves in a long national tradition running from the great revolution of 1789 through 1830 and 1848 to the Paris Commune of 1871. "The Student Commune" was the title of philosopher Edgar Morin's glowing essay opening *La Brèche,* the most widely noted of the shelf-load of books that appeared in shops more quickly than the streets could be repaved.

While the CGT worked to get the workers back on the job before they could be further contaminated, the massive strikes rekindled young intellectuals' interest in their own working class as a potential "revolutionary subject." Prior to May, seen from the vantage point of François Maspéro's crowded bookstore, La Joie de Lire, in the rue Saint Sévérin, it was clear that the contemporary front lines of the world revolution were in the imperialist periphery, in Vietnam or Latin America, and certainly not in France.

But even as it attracted the attention of the world, the May movement looked inward, turning its back on the Third World in its effort to unfold revolution according to national patterns. This was the start of the loss of interest in the Third World that soon ruined Maspéro (targeted for "revolutionary" anarchist shop-lifting to punish the publisher for "exploiting" the subjects he published books about, unlike all those other publishers only interested in making money). It is significant that La Joie de Lire was sold to Nouvelles Frontières, a budget travel agency. The sixties trips to Algeria, Cuba, China and even California in search of revolutionary models gave way to vacations in warm climates, period.

Edgar Morin described May '68 as an "osmosis" occurring between the "existential libertarian exigency" of some and the "planetary politicization" of the others.

The world seemed to be coming together politically when it was in fact falling apart.

The *gauchistes* were momentarily united by hostility to the French Communist Party. The leadership of the PCF was clearly convinced that revolution in France was a dangerous fantasy in a NATO member state and discretely worked with de Gaulle's prime minister, Georges Pompidou, to restore normal order.

The hatred of French intellectuals for the French Communist Party has been an obsession overflowing political categories. Hatred for the PCF came from right, left, and center. A specialist in the matter, Cornelius Castoriadis, writing under the name of Jean-Marc Coudray in *La Breche,* explained why: the PCF is *"neither* reformist *nor* revolutionary."

In 1968, both Maoist revolutionaries and budding technocrats saw the youth revolt as a blessed historic opportunity to snatch the working class from the clutches of the PCF. The PCF needed to be destroyed in order "to make the revolution"—or conversely to modernize French capitalism.

"Whatever comes next," declared Castoriadis, "May 68 has opened a new period in universal history."

This extravagant appraisal of the significance of May 68 was by no means unusual. The exaltation of May's spontaneity by established intellectuals was a way of celebrating the relegation of the PCF and its bureaucracy to the ashcan of history. Castoriadis perceived an explosion of creativity, "brilliant, effective and poetic slogans surged from the anonymous crowd," teachers were astonished to discover that they knew nothing and their students knew everything. "In a few days, twenty-year olds achieved political understanding and wisdom honest revolutionaries haven't yet reached after thirty years of militant activity." Did this stupefying miracle really take place? It was hailed in any case: for, if innocent youth could rise from its tabula rasa and make the revolution, there was obviously no need for a structured organization like the Communist Party.

There was immense joy among intellectuals at discovering a new revolutionary subject close to themselves. Castoriadis announced that in modern societies, youth is a *category* more important than the working class, which had become a dead weight on revolution.

But could spontaneous youth actually make the revolution? Even as he was extolling the glorious "explosion," Castoriadis pointed to its limits. "If the revolution is nothing *but* an explosion of a few days or weeks, the established order (know it or not, like it or not) can accommodate itself very well. Even more, contrary to its belief, it has a profound need for it. Historically it is the revolution that permits the world of reaction to survive by transforming itself, by adapting," he observed. The outcome could be "new forms of oppression better adapted to today's conditions."

Indeed, transformation and adaptation ensured that the real economic powers running the world were not seriously disturbed by all this turmoil.

All of this, I readily admit, went right past me at the time. The May events did seem to suggest that sudden, unforeseen changes were possible. That in itself was exhilarating. I watched in some wonderment as the French seemingly decided to make "the revolution." It was in their tradition, not in mine.

At the same time, I was not happy with May '68 because the Vietnamese and their struggle were forgotten. Ironically, one reason the French government clamped down so quickly on student activists may have been to prove Paris' fitness as a neutral and orderly capital for the talks that were opening there between the Americans and the Vietnamese. The rest of the world largely ignored those talks, and in Paris itself, they were overshadowed by the illusion of an imminent revolution at home.

Politically, the May '68 revolution was rapidly defeated at the polls. The majority of the population turned against the disorder, as is usual in similar cases, especially when no one could see where it was heading. In a snap election in June 1968, the Gaullists won an increased majority, and the French Communist Party won 20% of the vote compared to the 3.9% of votes that went to the only party openly representing the May movement, the PSU (*Parti Socialiste Unifié*).

Nevertheless, both De Gaulle and the Communists were badly wounded. Whatever else it didn't do, the May '68 student generation succeeded in discrediting and undermining existing authority, notably the political authority of De Gaulle and the PCF, and indeed authority itself. The illusion was widespread that spontaneity would undermine the ruling class and overcome consumerism and the "spectacle society." On the contrary, the result has been the triumph of the "spectacle society," the reign of images and financial power—the opposite of what May '68 claimed to promise at the time.

The "sexual liberation" aspect of May '68 has been exaggerated, as the French were not a puritan people to start with, just discreet. But it helped accelerate an evolution away from the legal imposition of Catholic mores, leading to legalization of abortion in 1975.

Many prominent '68 revolutionaries went on to highly successful careers, especially in communications, evolving into ardent defenders of the liberal Establishment. For one reason or another, fifty years later many young people in France regard May '68 as the mistaken illusions of their parents and grandparents.

Was this the first of the "color revolutions"? Since both De Gaulle and the French Communist Party were seen as enemies by the United States, a *cui bono* suspicion exists that May '68 must have been the result of CIA manipulation. Certainly, the CIA was active against both those forces of resistance to American hegemony and would no doubt have loved to engineer May '68. It may have tried to nudge things a bit here and there. But nobody could have foreseen, or engineered, the course taken by these events, not even the most ambitious intelligence agency.

5.

May in Minnesota

I returned to Minnesota in the autumn of 1968 with my daughter. In Vietnam, the war was as terrible as ever; in the United States there was a presidential election with two Minnesota candidates running. One was the poetic peace candidate, Senator Eugene McCarthy, who had been narrowly squeezed out of winning the Democratic primaries by JFK's younger brother, Bobby. Bobby Kennedy was assassinated at his victory party in California on June 5, ensuring the nomination of Vice President Hubert Humphrey, the loquacious pillar of the Minnesota Democratic Farmer-Labor Party, whose liberal anti-communism had succeeded in purging the DFL of its leftist FL elements. I felt no urge to get involved in that election campaign, since in Minnesota, Humphrey was certain to beat Republican Richard Nixon, for whatever that was worth—not much, as it turned out.

Family Values

Anyway, I had more personal concerns. I had to resume teaching and complete my thesis. But first of all I had to find a place to live. I thought this problem was quickly solved when I rented a spacious second floor (first floor European) apartment in a detached house on a tree-lined street in southwest Minneapolis, complete with lawn and shrubbery. The faulty plumbing in the house made itself known by occasional shrieks of agony, but nothing is perfect, and I set about fixing and painting, looking forward to restful moments in the sunny alcove with a bay window looking out onto the colorful Minnesota autumn.

What I had failed to reckon with were the neighbors. These turned out to be unmarried men in their twenties, no doubt employed somewhere in the lower reaches of the white color work force, who spent their nights (and part of their days) in revelry. They shared the house next door, which they used mainly, it seemed, as a center for emptying whiskey bottles and beer cans and strewing them across the lawn, the sidewalk and the street. That might have been, perhaps, just barely tolerable, but the noise that accompanied these folk customs was not. Shouts, booming music and the screeching of drunkenly driven vehicles at all hours persuaded me to abandon my newly painted nest in search of something more tranquil.

Luckily, I found just what I wanted in south Minneapolis, only a couple of blocks from Lake of the Isles on Humboldt Avenue. I was thrilled to learn from my Aunt Florence that some cousins of the Howard family had lived in that very same apartment in the first part of the twentieth century. This gave me a momentary false sensation of belonging here. It was a lovely spacious apartment, on the second floor (first, European) over the apartment of the owner, and I hastened to splurge on thick red carpeting and appropriate furniture. Here we were at last in a nice family neighborhood, ideal, I thought, for my daughter.

I was soon to encounter "family values," American style. To start with, although I was an employee of the University, I could not enroll my daughter in the University kindergarten because it was used by the psychology department to study child behavior, and a monoparental child would skew the sample.

At the local school, the very "nice" (the ultimate Minnesota adjective) doctor spread the word that my daughter was to be shunned because she carried tuberculosis. Parents duly ordered their children to ostracize my daughter. It took me some time to find out about this and to discover the cause. In Paris, my daughter had been inoculated against tuberculosis, as were all French children there at that time. This caused her to show "positive" on tests, while she was safer than the rest of the kids.

Now, had I been a thoroughgoing American, I'd have sued that doctor. But I had other things to do, including, within a few months, searching for another apartment. Practically on the eve of my oral exams, my landlady announced that I had to leave at the end of the month because she had decided to rent my apartment to a friend of hers.

This was another point for Paris. There, the tenant signs a lease and cannot be thrown out just like that. But this was the land of the free.

So again, in the midst of a critical period of my studies, and with a full teaching load, I had to start house hunting yet again. The magic of unknown relatives having lived in the Humboldt Avenue house did not work. And this time around, I felt the full brunt of reluctance of owners to rent to a "single mother." This despite the ease with which they could evict. Family values had other expressions. The local school refused to serve lunch, or even allow children to bring a bag lunch, primarily, it seems, because the housewives objected. They wanted nothing to distract from their own value as indispensable providers, and actively opposed moves to provide lunch possibilities for working mothers. Sisterhood was powerfully absent.

Finally, I did find a kindly landlord who rented me a whole big house with attic and cellar, garage, front and back yards and even an untuned piano in another nice south Minneapolis neighborhood near Lake Harriet. But there too, "family values" were at work, and although she kept it to herself for a long time, my daughter suffered from being excluded from playing with neighborhood children because she was living alone with a divorced mother. Nice Americans are easily frightened of all sorts of imaginary contagions, it seems.

Journalistic Values

The May '68 events were legendary across American campuses. The focus on Paris street battles between students and police tended to equate effective protest with street clashes rather than with the definition of coherent aims. I kept trying to explain the role of the anti-war movement in setting off the May protests, as well as the larger political context. This was my intention in accepting to be interviewed by the University newspaper, the *Minnesota Daily,* shortly after my return. The result, to my horror, was two large photos of myself featuring lots of leg (miniskirts were fashionable then) and a short, insipid and grossly inaccurate text which began:

> A Paris afternoon, May 13.
>
> Police were attacking people in the streets. Even tourists in cafes were teargassed. When asked if she was walking in the streets at the time, Diana Johnstone, a tall, dark-haired French woman, replied, "No, I was running."

The next day, on October 22, I wrote a letter to the editors of the *Daily,* as follows;

> When your reporter interviewed me on the subject of the May-June events in France, I attempted to give her the basis for a serious article clarifying an important situation little understood in this country, although, frankly, knowing the workings of the press, I didn't really expect a serious, clarifying article to

emerge. Neither did I expect quite such a classic example of what is wrong with American journalism.

The totally fabricated "human interest" lead and the waste of a quarter of a page on trivial photographs of myself at the expense of a clearly more valuable text are striking examples of the focus on unimportant "personalities" rather than on substantive matter that is typical of American journalism and a pillar of its unwavering mediocrity. In the few paragraphs left to the subject, my attempt at coherent analysis is reduced to a few disconnected comments which pose no threat to the public ignorance.

Your headline is an interesting example of journalistic deception through banality. Clichés are assumed to be true, and can be safely stuck on the top of any story. "Student discontent main cause of French riots, teacher says"—that sound like what anyone would say, doesn't it? "Teacher says" is a conventional lie to label the story an interview. A lie, because I never said that. I *did* say, most emphatically, that I objected to the American use of the word "riots" to cover what in France are termed "the events," because the events included a vast general strike, an enormous number of extremely constructive meetings and discussions throughout the most vital areas of French society, the discovery by a significant fraction of the young (and the not-so-young and middle-aged as well) of a sense of community and concern for the values implied in a society—and a few pitched battles between police and students, but never any riots, the word "riot" conveying an aimlessness and destructiveness which, as I took pains to point out, were notably absent. As to causes, "student discontent" is too vague to be informative (discontent about what?).

I regard the glaring factual errors in the story (I am not a "French woman" but a native of Minnesota; the police were not attacking anybody May 13, which happened to be the day of the giant protest march through the Latin Quarter) as mere peccadilloes in comparison to the fundamental distortion of reducing

> everything to incoherent trivia. I do not mean to single out your reporter for blame. Her story was probably edited, and she apparently did what was expected of her as well as anyone else. It is what is expected that I object to.
>
> I trust that the rules of the game provide at least one compensation to the unhappy interviewee—that of having her protest letter printed in full.

This trust was misplaced, as not a word of my protest was published or acknowledged in any way.

Black Values

In the spring of 1969, universities all over the country were the scene of black power demonstrations. Black students formed committees and took action centering on demands for incorporation of Black Studies into the university curriculum. The black power revolt was the major political event at the University of Minnesota in the spring of 1969. A small number of black students tried to occupy administrative offices and were charged with disorderly conduct. It was a marginal revolt compared to similar revolts on other campuses, and I was only very marginally involved as one of the junior faculty members who joined a support committee that met with representatives of the black students to discuss possible actions in defense of the arrested students.

The evolution of the civil rights movement into black power was no doubt inevitable, especially as the movement gained momentum in the majority of states where there was no legal segregation to combat, but racist discrimination still took many more or less subtle forms. Black power liberated the movement from the open influence of the churches and the less visible but crucial influence of the Communist Party, at least temporarily. It was an early harbinger of the shift from the broad old-left movement based on economic class to "identity politics."

White supporters of the black students were invited to attend a sensitivity session in the Student Union. This event turned out to be organized and led by a couple of young psychology graduates who ordered all the white students and faculty members to meditate on the connotations of the words "black" and "white." When you think of "black," what does it conjure up? Do negative connotations of the word "black" indicate a deep unconscious racism? Struck with guilt, students began to enumerate the awful things the word "white" suggested: pale, sick, hospitals, dead bones, a waterless desert, ghosts, toilets, gravestones... This exorcism of "white" took a remarkably long time, leading to the conclusion that Black is Beautiful.

As a literary scholar, I objected that what I'd relate to white or black could depend on what I had been reading, that this was a matter of individual culture that had nothing to do with racism, and that we would make better use of our time by discussing what strategy to use on behalf of the black students. But I was already a voice from the past speaking to a new age.

Guilt was always easier to feel, or to simulate, than thought. The guilty white activists of the solidarity committee carried their guilt into meetings with the representative of the black students, a formidable young woman named Anna Stanley. It became clear to me that Anna's strategy was to exploit white guilt to lure white students into a confrontation with police where young whites would get beaten by the police. This, she calculated, would arouse the white elite against the police. Whether or not it would work, it was at least a strategy. I was opposed, on the grounds that I could not in conscience lead young students into a situation where they might be injured. I called for a strategy that would broaden and popularize the movement and its aims, by intensified contacts with the general population of the Twin Cities. My white colleagues hesitated, until, in one memorable moment, Anna picked up a big stick and started swinging it at us all. The guilty whites ducked under the table, and so did I. But afterwards, I complained of this tactic.

The next day, Anna called me up and growled threateningly that I had spoken against her behind her back. That's true, I replied. I objected to using force instead of reasonable arguments. Her tone changed suddenly. "I can certainly use reasonable arguments when I want to," she said. I believed her.

About a year later, I found out how true that was, and why she had resorted to the big stick.

But already it was clear that this particular movement was poisoned by absence of mutual respect. Anna sensed correctly that she could bully the white radicals because they didn't expect her to act "reasonable," and this remnant of racist superiority enforced their feelings of guilt and their temporary submission. But in the long run, this could not last.

In any case, the black student movement suffered from its own contradictions, between symbolic advancement of a new intelligentsia and the welfare of the black population as a whole. The demand for "black studies" provided career opportunities for this new elite but did very little to bring up the educational level of the mass of the black community, which in subsequent years fell further behind the black bourgeoisie. This class distinction among blacks was welcomed as forging positive images of identity—the new expression was "role models"—which may have contributed to broadening the black upper middle class.

Non-violent Values

On October 15, 1969, the largest anti-war demonstration ever converged on the Pentagon. At a meeting in the Minneapolis auditorium two days earlier, a score of young men discarded their draft cards. Among them was Bill Tilson, vice president of the Minnesota Student Association, who was to play a leading role in the extraordinary events that occurred the following spring.

On April 18, 1970, it was still icily cold in Minneapolis. After some haggling with authorities, a peace march wound through downtown to Loring Park. There I gave a rather long speech which was my own personal political manifesto about how opposition to the war should be pursued. I referred to the peace talks going on in Paris which were widely ignored. I quoted at length Madame Nguyen Thi Binh, chief of delegation of the Provisional Revolutionary Government of the Republic of South Vietnam, who had been telling the American delegation for some time that the war could be ended simply by recognizing that "Vietnam belongs to the Vietnamese." The United States must accept this principle. Then concrete issues could be discussed, such as guarantees of safe troop withdrawal, and creation of favorable conditions for friendly relations between the South Vietnamese people and the American people.

The Nixon administration claimed to want to end the war. If it really wanted to end the war, I said, "It could send you or me or any one of us to Paris to talk to Madame Binh as one human being to another. The Government says, 'Those war protesters have no positive proposals.' Well, here's a positive proposal: let the Government prove its willingness to end the war by sending any one of us or ten of us or a thousand of us who want truly to end the war to Paris to work out the details with Madame Binh."

Only a short time later, events were to give me the opportunity to try to put this idea into practice.

At the time of that Loring Park peace demonstration, the war was already shaking up Cambodia. On March 18, while Prince Sihanouk was abroad, the United States had him overthrown and installed a prominent officer, General Lon Nol, as "provisional head of state." Sihanouk, whose popularity was a permanent fixture of Cambodia even in his absence, retaliated by allying with the Indochinese communist revolutionaries, including the indigenous Maoists he had himself labeled the "Khmer rouge." The Lon Nol regime sought nationalist legitimacy by a bloody persecution of Cambodia's 400,000 ethnic Vietnamese. Hundreds of Vietnamese residents of Cambodia were murdered and thrown into the Mekong, to float downstream into South Vietnam.

The United States had long been bombing Vietnamese liberation army supply lines across the border in Cambodia, but on April 30, President Richard Nixon announced that U.S. ground troops were about to be sent into Cambodia to capture the headquarters of the entire communist military operation in South Vietnam. This was to be a joint operation with the army of the U.S.-backed Republic of South Vietnam, then headed by General Nguyen Van Thieu as president and the flamboyant General Nguyen Cao Ky as prime minister. As usual, the President claimed the new military operation would "save American lives."

On May 1, 1970, American forces were launched into Cambodia for what was to be a wild goose chase, as Vietnamese forces melted into the forests to evade combat and Cambodian villagers bore the brunt of the ground attacks, in addition to U.S. bombing.

Across the United States, hastily called student demonstrations protested against this new escalation.

On May 4, I joined a spontaneous meeting of student leaders in the Student Union on the Minneapolis campus of the University of Minnesota. Nobody was quite sure what should be done, but all felt we had to do something. Word came that Ohio National Guardsmen had opened fire on an anti-war protest at Kent State University, killing four students. Without even being summoned, students began to gather in front of the Student Union, hundreds and then thousands. A movement was forming without leadership but looking for direction.

Across the country the word spread: students strike to end the war! Classrooms emptied and protests became constant, condemning the war and the murder of the Kent State students.

I have only blurred memories of those days. I hardly slept and rushed from one meeting to another. I remember the orderly determination of students I did not know who, with no political experience, quickly became leaders. I remember the solidarity of the professors in certain departments that endorsed the anti-war strike: my own department of French and Italian, the math department, the biology department. And I remember the look of obsequious panic in the eyes of a certain mainstream professor of political science at what he saw as practically a reign of terror.

What I remember best is an incident where I drew on what I had observed of Maoist activism in Paris.

I had just finished being interviewed by the University radio station and was heading across the Mall when I saw a crowd of students gathered in front of the Administration building. My heart sank. I understood immediately that the crowd was proposing to occupy the President's office and take the University president, Malcolm Moos, hostage. On the other side of the building, out of sight of the students, police forces were waiting. If students stormed the building, the police would intervene, and the rapidly spreading student strike in Minnesota would go the way of the student strikes in most other universities across the country. The police would shut down the campus, and the strike would be dead.

Alarmed, I pushed through the crowd and up the steps in front of the building where student leader Bill Tilson was holding a microphone. I took it and boldly harangued the crowd. The gist of what I said was this: "Grow up! The president is just a father figure. You have more important things to do than revolt against father! What we need is the support of the community. We must get out and explain the war to the people of Minneapolis and Saint Paul. Forget about the president, he is not important, let's organize to take the anti-war movement to the population of the Twin Cities!"

Bill Tilson had the presence of mind to call for a vote. Should we storm the president's office or go organize to take the movement to the community? The show of hands chose the community. The strike was saved. It went on for weeks, terminated only by the end of the spring quarter.

That evening, in the Student Union, a large meeting organized the Community Contact Program, as I had suggested. The Twin Cities were divided into sections, assigned to various teams of students. In connection with this program, it was decided to hold classes on the war, turning the campus into an anti-war university. Those of us who were a bit better informed than others led the classes, and a real expert was invited from the University of Wisconsin at Madison.

After launching the idea, I let it go. I had only to watch in admiration as students took it up, refined it and organized it with extraordinary competence and good sense. The university on strike was every bit as busy as the university in normal times, and perhaps more so.

There was no violence, no bloody clashes between students and police. And so, for national media, nothing happened in Minnesota. We had the best, most serious, longest-lasting student strike in the country, but it was not news. If some idiot threw a rock somewhere, it would make the television news. A serious, organized strike that transformed a whole university for two months was a non-event.

A few days later I happened to see a reporter for the local newspaper who had reported on the Administration building turn-around. I asked him why he had written that "President Moos calmed the crowd." You saw it happen, I said to him, you know that I was the one who calmed the crowd, along with Bill Tilson. He shrugged sheepishly. Perhaps it was his editor who wrote that; journalism works that way.

Still, Malcolm Moos deserves some credit for not panicking. Neither he nor the Governor called in the National Guard to shoot at students. Moos, a native of Minnesota, was the ghost writer of Eisenhower's famous 1961 farewell address warning against the "military-industrial complex." He was not responsible for the war. He was very probably against it. However, rebellion tends to turn on those who are within reach, triggering repression while those really responsible are far out of reach. We saved our movement and let it grow by rejecting violence.

Minnesota was so liberal then that local media actually published honest reporting. During the strike I was interviewed by a young woman reporter for the *Minneapolis Tribune,* a Texas blonde as tall as I was, wearing a bright red maxi coat. This was Molly Ivins, who would go on to take on the establishment in an exceptional career in Texas as an outspoken political commentator. She interviewed me on the Community Contact program and the workshops held to prepare students to talk to people at the cities. Her report began:

> Hundreds of University of Minnesota students have been leaving the school in small convoys early every evening to ring doorbells. "Hello," they say, "we're students at the University of Minnesota and we'd like to talk to you about why we're striking and about the war in southeast Asia."

As I told Molly, the students "feel they can't go into the community until they've informed themselves on the war, so they're studying like mad, attending teach-ins and workshops. If nothing else, this strike is going to produce a crop of Asia experts."

The May 9, 1970 issue of the *Minneapolis Tribune* published the report on the Community Contact program by Molly and her colleague Jack Miller. Visiting an introductory workshop, they quoted my French department colleague, Professor Peter Lock:

> "It's best to go in pairs of a student and a faculty member," said Lock. "People have all kinds of preconceptions about student irresponsibility and will put students on the defensive. But if there's a faculty member along to explain why he supports the strike, they tend to at least listen.
>
> "If you can't find a professor or a teaching assistant, go in boy-girl pairs—some women are afraid to open their doors to men. And we try to stop before it gets really dark. We also try to go in longhair-shorthair pairs—two longhairs together might really scare some people."

Harry Myers of the Speech department gave further advice.

> Be persuasive … And if you get a hostile one, listen to him. You may learn something and he may recognize some of the weaknesses in his own arguments as he speaks. You don't have to continually interrupt or contradict. If they're really nasty, just be as polite as you can and leave as soon as you can," Myers advised.

The students encountered varied reactions, sometimes hostile, sometimes indifferent, more often ignorant, but in general friendly and attentive. Often they were invited in for coffee to meet the children and have a chat.

No doubt different people experienced the Student Strike in contrasting ways. For me, and certainly for a number of others, it represented "higher learning" in the best sense of the term. While on strike we were studying, learning and teaching even more intensely than usual, using scholarly sources and methods, and immediately applying our learning to a socially useful cause. By "teaching" the community, we were teaching ourselves about that community, about its attitudes, its weaknesses and its potential.

As weeks passed, for striking faculty members the question became urgent concerning what to do about our regular courses. Specifically, what about exams and grades at the end of the trimester? Faculty members handled this individually, without collective consultation or decision-making. A few, at least, considered grades unimportant, and decided to give all their students good grades, without holding exams.

I did not feel that way. My view was that teachers owed it to students to give them grades as a form of feedback, to let them know how they were doing. So I arranged, somehow, to teach my courses enough to prepare the students for exams, which I gave and corrected. As instructor, I was teaching a very heavy load, as I recall, with courses in French history and culture, seventeenth century literature and my specialty, *explication de texte,* a course I used essentially to train students to read what was on the page rather than what was in their heads. I did not follow any school of literary criticism. The course was very much appreciated by students, or so I was told.

Meanwhile, the Trotskyists of the Young Socialist Alliance and the Socialist Workers Party did what they were good at and organized an "end the war!" march that may have been the biggest in Minnesota history. It was a far cry from the timid little trickle of people I had joined four years earlier. Masses of people filled the streets and spaces in front of the State House in Saint Paul. The student strike had succeeded in going beyond the campus and becoming a force in the community as a whole.

Having seen both May 1968 in Paris and May 1970 in Minnesota close up, I could not help feeling that, all things considered, especially the difference in the size of the population, the Minnesota May could be compared very favorably with the other one. It was proportionately just as big, but incomparably more focused and more peaceful.

Perhaps for those reasons, it went virtually unnoticed in the rest of the world, or even in the rest of the country.

6.

People's Diplomacy

The success of the Community Contact program inspired me to go a step further in putting into practice the ideas in my Loring Park speech.

For two years, United States and Vietnamese delegations had been meeting in Paris, supposedly to negotiate a peaceful end to the war. The talks were completely stalled, while the war raged on.

My idea was simple: since official diplomacy was getting nowhere, let's try people's diplomacy instead.

Underneath the apparent naïveté of this idea was a realistic reasoning. The war was increasingly unpopular. Since the Tet offensive, the U.S. government had largely abandoned the goal of actually winning the war and claimed to want to end it. For public opinion, the Nixon-Kissinger administration claimed that a peaceful settlement was not possible because of enemy intransigence. They claimed that if the United States simply pulled out, the Viet Cong, as the South Vietnamese National Liberation Front was called, would carry out a "bloodbath" against the freedom-loving people of South Vietnam.

But the United States was pursuing its own genuine "bloodbath" in South Vietnam, called the "Phoenix program." Citizens suspected of supporting the "Viet Cong" were summarily murdered. The idea was to wipe out the political base of the South Vietnamese resistance. This was supposed to strengthen the pro-US regime of Generals Thieu and Ky, for the day when the United States would withdraw. In reality, the Phoenix program could only strengthen the communist regime in North Vietnam relative to the broadly representative movement in the South, once Vietnam was unified, as it was sure to be.

American media largely echoed the official U.S. position.

This would be a good moment for ordinary responsible American citizens to go talk with the Vietnamese and determine for themselves whether or not a peaceful solution could be worked out. If the American people could come to terms with "the enemy," then the war should cease.

When I raised the suggestion with the main animators of the Community Contact program, they were enthusiastic. The contact program could serve as a sort of "talent scout" operation to find and select the members of a People's Delegation that would go to Paris, meet with the "enemy" Vietnamese delegations and report back to the American people on the chances of a peaceful settlement.

It is remarkable that most of us in the Community Contact Program scarcely knew each other, and yet the short time of our joint efforts had created an absolute trust.

We decided to move rapidly and confidentially. True, an elected delegation would have more legitimacy than a co-opted one. But the process of election would provide opportunities for all kinds of sabotage and infiltration. We decided on a procedure of selection that took only a few days. Members of the contact program suggested "typical Americans" from all walks of life. I would meet them and make the final selection, based solely on my intuitive judgment of their honesty and character. No questions were asked about political beliefs, but we did not want to include active members of political groups that might try to steer the operation in the direction of their sectarian goals, something which could cause unnecessary conflict within the group. Willingness to meet and talk with the "other side" was sufficient evidence of open mindedness.

When I met the people proposed by the student contacts, I was concerned with two main factors of character: common sense and the courage to withstand any pressures they might come under to back out of the project or turn against it. As I recall, only one of the nominees seemed to me a bit emotionally unstable and was dropped. The rest turned out to be extraordinary "ordinary" people.

The aim was to put together a group that was a representative cross-section of the population, by profession and social position. Among our first recruits were the following:

- Hubert Anderson, a high school teacher from Hopkins, Minnesota.
- George Bailey, a mechanic who worked for Minnesota Mining.
- Scott Berry, an architect.
- John Brooks, a stockbroker from Wayzata, Minnesota.
- Prudence Brooks, a Minnesota businesswoman.
- John Carney, a retired engineer.
- Dr. Charles Fisher, a dentist.
- Marianne Hamilton, a Catholic laywoman and mother of eight.
- Austin Hendrickson, electrician.

- Brian Mooney, a Vietnam veteran living in Saint Paul.
- Robert Nienkerk, a private investigator in Minneapolis.
- Dr. David Rosenbaum, a medical practitioner in Minneapolis.
- Margaret Thomson, a retired vocational high school assistant principal. At 70, she was the oldest in a group whose average age must have been around 40.

To provide some expert tutoring to the group, we invited Adam Schesch, the scholar who had come from the University of Wisconsin to help brief the community contact program in Southeast Asian history, to come along.

Otherwise, we did not want to load the group with academics. Out of thirty final members, only two belonged to the faculty of the University of Minnesota, myself and Roger Jones, a professor of physics who was eager to take part. The students in the community contact program disqualified themselves. To be sure of having a good student, I simply turned to my own best student, Mary Hoidal, age 19. I don't think she had any experience of political activity whatsoever, and I didn't know what she thought about Vietnam. In fact, I didn't know her outside the classroom. But I knew from her work that she was intelligent and serious. That was enough.

To meet the representatives of a rural population, we had to include farmers. The resourceful students of the community contact group came up with the names of two farmers who might be interested. First a couple of us drove into the country about fifty miles north of Minneapolis to meet George Panayotoff, a truck gardener in Big Lake, Minnesota. His farm was a lively business enterprise, growing a wide range of vegetables and preparing them for market. He showed us around, and after posing a series of questions, agreed to go with us to Paris.

The other farmer suggested by the contact group raised cattle a couple of hundred miles to the west, near the tiny village of Odessa five miles from the border with South Dakota. One of the contact students owned his own Piper Cub, and so the two of us took off and flew out to the farm near Odessa. For me, this was the high point of the experience in more ways than one. Western Minnesota was an unfamiliar landscape to me but seeking out the farmers was symbolically like seeking out my own forebears, who had been farmers in Minnesota and Iowa after pioneering westward from upstate New York and Pennsylvania. The family of Howard Hovde, like many other Minnesotans, had come from Norway. He was inordinately proud of the productivity of American farming, and

I thought that it was a bit incongruous to compare a spread the size of his with the family farms in the old countries of Europe and Asia. We had coffee in the Hovde kitchen and discussed the war in Vietnam. He must have been about forty years old, but like Panayotoff, he retained the forthright independent political spirit that in earlier generations helped build the Minnesota Farmer-Labor Party in opposition to the East Coast banks and foreign wars. Our history classes never taught us that at the turn of the twentieth century the state's independent farmers helped elect a Socialist governor and supported an anti-imperialist movement against Teddy Roosevelt's war in the Philippines. Minnesota's radical past had been largely forgotten, but something of its spirit still lingered on in 1970.

Howard Hovde was interested, but he was cautious and said he had to think it over.

The next day I received a phone call. "We've got a lot of work on the farm just now, it's hard for me to get away. But I talked it over with my wife, and she agreed—it's the right thing to do."

That was the farmer's response.

Labor was something else.

The Farmer-Labor Party had long since been absorbed by the Democrats and renamed the Democratic Farmer-Labor Party. For our project, labor turned out to be far more difficult to recruit than farmers. We did easily recruit an industrial worker, George Bailey, a mechanic who worked for Minnesota Mining, but our efforts to persuade union representatives to support our effort ran into a solid barrier: fear.

One evening a leader of the local United Electrical Workers (UEW) came to my home to discuss the project. He was totally opposed to the war, and thoroughly approved of the idea of a citizens' delegation to meet the Vietnamese and discuss peace. But he did not dare so much as show his approval publicly, much less participate. The UEW had once been one of the most combative and successful trade unions in the United States. Following World War II, the UEW had been subjected to a drastic anti-Communist purge led by Democrats, and since then nobody dared take a position that could appear to be on the wrong side of the Cold War.

Minnesota had its share of high-tech firms, such as 3M and Honeywell. About this time a charismatic independent radical named Marv Davidov was forming the Honeywell Project to protest against the company's manufacture of fragmentation bombs, used to spray deadly pellets into Vietnamese flesh. The project had great success in the Twin Cities and managed eventually to persuade an executive engineer to resign in protest. Stockholder meetings were disrupted in protest. But lower ranking workers and union officials never dared show even the slightest interest in the issue.

This was just one small indication of why the contemporary industrial working class was not the agent of revolution that Karl Marx and his followers had hoped—at least not in the United States. To put it simply, when the workers had next to nothing, they fought together to get something more, and once they got something more, they were afraid of losing it. In the United States, the very notion of solidarity had been defeated by an ideology of fear—fear of communism, fear of being called a communist, fear of losing a job, fear of the unknown. And there was a lot of unknown. Most American schools taught no geography and almost no history, so that for those who did not pursue higher education—the case of the lower ranks of the industrial working class—the world outside America was strange and perhaps threatening. My daughter's fifth grade text book introduced pupils to South America for the first time by telling them that people there were poor, and therefore jealous of the United States, and the Communists exploited this jealousy to make them hate the United States. My daughter herself showed this to me, out of indignation. She had started school in France and knew better.

Among many American workers, the only solidarity was against that threatening world out there.

In sharp contrast, farmers were sufficiently independent to have the courage of their convictions. They did not have to be afraid of being fired. They were not afraid of what their neighbors might think or say (their nearest neighbors were, in any case, miles away). Moreover, although they worked hard for long hours depending on the season, farmers had periods of relative leisure in the winter when they were snowed in and read a lot. Their very isolation tended to make them curious about the world. Perhaps that has changed, but it was true enough in 1970.

Despite the difficulties, we persisted in wanting to include a trade unionist. A colleague of mine knew someone in Cleveland, Ohio, and through that connection we recruited our union official, Leo Fenster of the United Auto Workers. He was a scrappy little guy and came the closest to cracking the extraordinary harmony that reigned in our group, but I suppose no union official less unmanageable would ever have joined us in the first place.

Of course we needed to have blacks in our group. At a time when the mood in the Black Power movement tended toward separatism, this might have seemed a greater challenge than attracting farmers or even trade unionists. On the contrary, our group had the good fortune to count five blacks out of a final total of thirty people. They were:

- Horace Huntley, student, University of Minnesota.
- Chester Oden, educator, St. Paul, Minnesota.
- Anna Stanley, student, University of Minnesota.
- Barbara Westberry, secretary and mother of five, Minneapolis.
- Milt Williams, black community leader, Minneapolis.

This strong representation was possible thanks to my brief clash with Anna Stanley during the black student revolt in 1969. That altercation was the basis for a mutual respect that allowed us to get to know each other. Anna was an intelligent and passionate woman who was aware that she had been used by male black students to bully whites while they took it easy. She complained of this but considered it her duty to the cause. I remember visiting her and listening to recordings of speeches by Martin Luther King, which brought her to tears. She was convinced of the connection between the black struggle for equality and opposition to the war. She helped locate and persuade the four other African-Americans to join the group. The fatal shooting of two black students and wounding of twelve others at the state college in Jackson, Mississippi, on May 14, was fresh in people's minds. Jackson State joined Kent State as symbol of repression and resistance.

I very much wanted to include Native Americans in the delegation. Minneapolis was the home of the American Indian Movement (AIM), so finding Indian leaders was easy, and they readily identified with the Vietnamese. But their participation ran up against an unexpected obstacle: their refusal to ask for passports from the government of the United States, which they considered had usurped their country. This intransigence was, in my view, symptomatic of a certain political confusion that has made AIM notorious at times but not particularly effective in the long run. AIM was built by city Indians, whose community was in reality deeply demoralized and subject to alcoholism and illness. Their original culture had been almost entirely wiped out, and they were struggling against heavy odds to rediscover it in a form that could be meaningful in contemporary society. Their situation contrasted sadly with the vitality and creativity of the black community. It seemed to me that slavery had been less destructive of its victims' spirit than the total conquest by an alien culture which had no use for the people it dispossessed.

At that time there were too few Minnesotans of Asian origin to speak of an Asian community. However, we did recruit an Asian-American to our group in the person of Bill Doi, a commercial artist of Japanese origin who had been interned as a child in the concentration camps where the U.S. government imprisoned Nisei during World War II.

We were rather astounded at our success. In a few days, we had discovered wide support for our project and recruited an impressive set of citizens willing to set off with people they had just met to meet the Vietnamese "enemy" in Paris. "Middle America" turned out to be full of people anxious to talk peace with the "Viet Cong." We began to think that this idea was too good to be limited to Minnesota. A national delegation would have more resonance.

In contrast to the world of the Internet, or to France in 1968, the United States in 1970 was a vast country where communication between different regions was minimal. Opposition to the war was taking active forms all over the country, but we had very little idea of what people were doing outside our own cities or States. For the national and international media, things happened only on the East or West coasts, preferably in New York or California. A place like Kent, Ohio, could make the news only if somebody was killed. Peaceful Minnesota was off the screen. And we were not able to measure the magnitude of what was happening elsewhere.

It was decided informally to send me to New York and Atlanta, where antiwar leaders were meeting, in order to offer them our project, to be extended to the national scale. My travels were paid for by colleagues from the biology department, who were heavily involved in the movement. In New York I met student strike leaders whose universities had been shut down almost as soon as the antiwar strike began. They had no base of activity, as we did on the Minneapolis campus of the University of Minnesota. As for going into the community door to door, my suggestion was met with incredulity. "In New York? Door to door? Here nobody would say 'it's the right thing to do'. At best, they'd say, 'What's in it for me?' Or slam the door in your face, or worse."

I can't judge whether this assessment was accurate. But in New York, Minnesota loomed as a sort of pristine paradise of civic virtue and innocence, a holdover from a vanishing world.

Atlanta was no better. I located the meeting of antiwar leaders and introduced myself discreetly into their midst to offer them the gift of our project. They were well-known at the time, but I scarcely remember their names, and what little I remember I prefer not to mention, out of politeness. They struck me as tired, unimaginative, and self-satisfied. No good idea could conceivably come from any source but themselves, and surely not from such a place as… what was that? Minnesota? Perhaps the problem was my inadequacy as a salesperson, but their lack of receptiveness was nevertheless striking for supposed leaders of a "movement." They were in slow motion, if not stagnation.

This was disappointing, but through telephone contacts we did broaden our delegation to the two States which, along with Minnesota, had the strongest anti-war movements: Massachusetts and California. We were joined in Paris by Jodie Jenkins, a school teacher from Weston, Massachusetts, and Pearl Levin, a mental health worker from Brookline, Massachusetts.

Peter Stark also joined us from Danville, California. At the time he was a banker but went on to be a Democratic member of Congress.

Our meetings in Paris were scheduled for late June. As the time grew near, the problem of money reared its ugly head. About a third of us were able to pay all our expenses ourselves. Most of the rest could pay about half, but a few simply couldn't afford it at all. We agreed that it would be totally contrary to our principle of representativity to exclude, for instance, the black mother of five children who could barely make ends meet as it was. We must stick together, all or nothing. But how?

My solution was simple: "We need a priest. Priests know how to raise money."

This was so true. Our member Marianne Hamilton, active in Catholic organizations, came up with an excellent young priest. Father Harry Bury was the cherry on our cake, as the French say. Aside from being an enthusiastic militant for peace, he indeed had plenty of ideas as to how to raise money. He got right to work, organizing fund-raising meetings (my colleague Suzanne Cowan contributed memorable cheesecakes to help the cash flow). Minneapolis was a generous city. As the hour of departure grew near, however, we were still short. Harry Bury arranged for a loan, to be repaid by a benefit concert on our return, given by the local—but nationally famous—singer, John Denver. The concert was a big success and covered all our expenses.

Through Paris contacts who helped prepare our visit, it was agreed with the Vietnamese of the South Vietnamese Provisional Revolutionary Government (PRG) to call our group the "People's Commission of Inquiry into the Solution to the War in Vietnam."

That defined our purpose quite clearly. By this time, everyone, even the Nixon administration, admitted that the war was a stalemate and claimed to want to end it. So why did it drag on? On June 25, the day we flew to Paris, Secretary of State William Rogers claimed that the Vietnamese demand that "we should get out—and then they will talk to us about a peaceful settlement." This was a slight but critical distortion. The Vietnamese demanded a promise to get out within six months, not withdrawal before negotiations.

Our mission was to sort this out. Did the Vietnamese really refuse to negotiate before a U.S. withdrawal? What were the Vietnamese conditions for ending the fighting? We knew that by now, the American people, and not least American draftees in Vietnam itself, wanted to end the war. If this could be done rapidly and with relative ease, this would be good news to bring back home.

To prepare our meetings, we met for informal discussions with several authors of books on Vietnam, including Jean Chesneaux, professor of Oriental history at the University of Paris, prominent historian Philippe Devillers, Australian journalist Wilfred Burchett and Peggy Duff, editor of the London-based *Vietnam International Newsletter*. They helped us grasp how little we knew and how much we had to learn.

And yet, we didn't need to learn all that much for our mission. We were not here to learn Vietnamese history, we were here to find arguments for ending the war. We knew very well that we risked being accused of "aiding the enemy," or at least of being naively fooled by the wily Viet Cong. But how were we to be fooled? All we were asking was their official position on how to end the war.

Anyway, the distrust generated by the Cold War was a two-way street. They were official diplomats, and we were anonymous citizens of the country that was devastating their homeland. Why should *they* trust *us?* And I do believe that they regarded us with some suspicion. After all, history shows that it is the wily Americans who have repeatedly violated agreements, usually on the pretext of their own moral superiority. Their entire intervention was a violation of the international accords reached in Geneva in 1954, providing for free elections and Vietnamese reunification. The United States persistently violates past agreements because their present leaders think it over and decide they know better.

On Saturday, June 27, our group of thirty spent the day in the pleasant villa in the Parisian suburb of Verrières-le-Buisson which housed the official delegation to the Paris conference of the Provisional Revolutionary Government of South Vietnam (PRG). The PRG was the political arm of the National Liberation Front, the clandestine coalition resisting American-sponsored repression aimed at preventing

Vietnamese unification. The peace negotiations were stalled because for the United States, the PRG was "the Viet Cong," not to be recognized, and the negotiations had to be between the Thieu-Ky military puppet regime held in place by the U.S. in Saigon and the Hanoi government, implying continued division of the country. So the key to a break-though could be recognition of the PRG, which is what we were doing.

There is no doubt that the PRG hoped we would succeed at least in that limited aim. We were very warmly welcomed by the acting head of the delegation, Mme Nguyen Thi Chon (replacing Mme Binh, who was absent), Mr. Ly Van Sau and Madam Nguyen Ngoc Dung (pronounced Zung), a remarkable woman whose warm intelligence won her a wide circle of friends and admirers in Paris. Everyone called her by her given name, "Madame Dung"—there are so many Vietnamese named Nguyen…

Obviously we were not there to negotiate but to play the role of intermediary, to listen and report, as media should but often fail to do.

Our talks were serious and factual. Our hosts provided us with their analysis of the situation and their proposal for its solution. The analysis was, unfortunately, all too accurate.

These patriotic Vietnamese were convinced—as indeed were American leaders at the time—that the United States had lost the ground war, as the entire armed "pacification" program aimed at gaining control of the villages had been defeated in all its forms. What was left was an air war directed, not against the guerilla forces, but against the population which provides food, shelter and recruits for those forces. In other words, it was an air war of terror to drive huge sections of the population out of the rural areas, to concentrate them where they could be controlled by the Saigon troops reinforced with new equipment and supported by the U.S. Air Force.

The Nixon Administration had stressed its readiness to withdraw combat forces, but the entire Air Force was categorized as "non-combat"—although, as one PRG delegate put it, "they do not drop flowers on us, but chemical defoliants and bombs." Nixon's "Vietnamization" policy was the attempt to abandon the unwinnable ground war, where casualties are sustained, to the Saigon armed forces, while continuing and intensifying the destruction of the Vietnamese countryside and rural society from the air.

It was the prospect of this continuing and intensifying aerial destruction that lent urgency to the PRG's demand for total U.S. withdrawal. They had laid out a complete and concrete timetable for the withdrawal of U.S. forces to extend over a period of six months. They understood the six-months timetable to consist of an orderly, staged withdrawal, not a mad scramble for the boats. They pointed out to the Commission that the U.S. command in Saigon had estimated a total withdrawal could be accomplished in only four months. They let it be understood that if the U.S. said seven or eight months, they would sit down and talk about it.

Years later it can be said that this solution would have been best for everyone. It would certainly have been better for the Americans and their closest Vietnamese collaborators than the ignominious flight from Saigon on April 30, 1975. But even when they know they cannot win a war, leaders of the U.S. empire are primarily interested in not *appearing* to lose it. They must build up a local puppet army to lose the war for them. Or they must use an assassination program—in Vietnam, the notorious "Phoenix Program"—to get rid of many of the potentially best people on the other side, weakening the human and political quality of the adversary. Or they must pretend that their purely destructive air raids are needed to "bomb the enemy to the negotiating table." All such evasions and pretensions keep wars going on and on, wiping out more and more lives.

After long detailed talks with the PRG in Verrières-le-Buisson, our meeting the next day with the Hanoi delegation to the peace talks was polite but largely limited to detailed condemnation of U.S. intervention. For political reasons, the North Vietnamese refrained from making proposals, insisting that the war was between adversaries in the South, and it was there that peace must be made. This of course went contrary to the U.S. position which claimed that the war in the south was due to a Northern invasion—which at the last minute, years later, it was forced to be, in the absence of the sort of orderly solution proposed by the South Vietnamese liberation front.

Probably nothing made what we had heard from Madame Dung and her colleagues more credible than meeting with members of the Union of Vietnamese residing in Paris at a reception organized in the Quaker Center. The unanimous support of these clearly middle class, Westernized Vietnamese for the war of national liberation against the United States strongly supported the PRG insistence that they were able to unite all segments of South Vietnamese society in a coalition government once the United States withdrew. It was all too obvious that communist organizing capacities were in the service of a deeply patriotic national liberation movement.

With the help of French friends, our group held a press conference in Paris on June 29, to explain our peace mission. Quite a number of reporters actually attended. But to my knowledge, not a single report was published. Questioned, a journalist for the Paris-based *International Herald Tribune* came up with this remarkable explanation for ignoring our meeting with the Vietnamese: "We are an international newspaper, and you are just a local story."

So there was nothing "international" about thirty totally independent American citizens crossing the Atlantic at their own expense to hold talks with the "enemy" Vietnamese.

Since my early education as wife of a foreign correspondent, I have no illusions about the media. Of course, when you think about it, the staff of the IHT had all been briefed by the information officers in the U.S. and British Embassies that no attention was to be given to the "Viet Cong" delegation. That is the way it works. But still I was disappointed. Much worse, and more painful, the Vietnamese were disappointed. I think they expected more to come of this.

It can rightly be objected that the media helped arouse popular opposition to the war in Vietnam. A relatively small number of journalists and photographers did indeed break the taboos to report on the horrors of the war. This happened relatively late in the game, at a time when the U.S. power elite had already decided the war was unwinnable. What even the best of the mainstream journalists did not do, however, was to provide real understanding of "the other side."

The media also, in my opinion, gravely distorted the anti-war movement. Television and print media ignored the serious political arguments of anti-war activists but rushed to pay attention to the most spectacular, least thoughtful aspects of opposition to the war. And this preference on the part of the media inevitably encouraged the movement itself to become more spectacular and less thoughtful.

The Home Front

As with the community contact program, once the People's Commission was formed I stepped back and let it carry me along. We agreed to rotate spokespersons at press conferences, and that is what we did. Three different members of the group spoke and answered questions at each press conference. I don't recall how the selection was made, but it was made with ease and without anybody shoving to get into the limelight. We insisted that we were a group of equals with no leader, and this was true. My own main contribution came at the end, in writing up the results of our mission for an unsigned pamphlet called "The Peaceful Solution" published by People's Press in Minneapolis in January 1971.

In contrast to the *International Herald Tribune,* Minnesota newspapers, far from the influence of U.S. government information officers, gave quite good coverage to our trip and its content. We agreed unanimously on a simple statement endorsing U.S. withdrawal from Vietnam, and many members of the group successfully spread the message wherever they could. Marianne Hamilton and Harry Bury organized a special "Catholic Commission of Inquiry" which went back to Paris to meet the PRG delegation and a Vietnamese priest in Paris, to obtain convincing confirmation that Vietnamese Catholics would not be victims of reprisals as a result of U.S. withdrawal (I accompanied this group).

While some members of the group were more inspired to spread the word than others, everybody agreed on the conclusions and nobody backed away. The vegetable farmer George Panayotoff was especially active in speaking to every meeting he could find, often together with Robert Nienkerk, a private detective. Nienkerk was truly amazing. He could speak to the most conservative groups, such as the Veterans of Foreign Wars, and with his Mr. America necktie, short haircut and straightforward manner, win them over with a speech like this:

> I'm a private detective. It's my job to tell whether people are telling the truth. Well, I can tell you, the Vietnamese we met were telling the truth. Now, I asked them about our American service men who are being held prisoner, and how to get them back. And they told me, those prisoners are war criminals. We won't harm them, but they are war criminals, and we will free them when the United States stops its aggression.
>
> Well now, I wondered about that and I did some research. And you know what? According to international law, yes, those American prisoners are war criminals. So what we need to do to get them back is to end the aggression and make peace.

What the anti-war movement needed was a lot more Robert Nienkerks. Of course, he did not interest the media, which focused on picturesque Hippies and Yippies, who mistakenly assumed that all that attention was helping the cause, when in reality such publicity helped marginalize the antiwar movement and contributed to increasing irrationality as an opposition stance.

In Minnesota, opposition to the war became so "normal" that the Minnesota legislature eventually passed a bill opposing the war. I believe the only other state that did this was Massachusetts.

Members of the People's Commission went to Washington, D.C., in September 1970, to discuss our views with whatever members of the Administration and the Congress would receive us. We found there an arrogant disregard for the views of the people of either the United States or Vietnam that surpassed our expectations. The manipulative attitude toward the Vietnamese was strikingly illustrated by a phrase used by the State Department spokesman we talked with when he said that the admitted difficulties of the Saigon regime in establishing its power were due to the fact that Vietnam has a "deficient sociology." This sort of jargon expressed the certitude of top American officials that they had every right to rearrange the "sociology" ("society" is what he must have meant) of a centuries-old civilization to make it less "deficient" from an American point of view—the means of correcting these "deficiencies" being massive bombing and dislocation of almost the entire rural population.

Members of the Congress who understood and shared our views reported their utter inability to influence the Administration. The top policy makers regarded American public opinion as something that comes and goes, while they go on forever.

We were told repeatedly in Washington that the war in Vietnam was "no longer an issue." Withdrawal of U.S. combat troops was supposed to cause the American people to forget about the war, so that the Pentagon could continue its work of destruction of a distant people, unimpeded by the indignation of decent Americans.

The sole exception was the Senator from South Dakota, George McGovern. As Democratic Party candidate for President in 1972, this decent man of peace lost to "Tricky" Dick Nixon in the greatest landslide in U.S. history. McGovern won only Massachusetts and the District of Columbia—not even his home state or neighboring Minnesota. Nixon had convinced the public that he was ending the war…

The Lessons of History

We did what we could, but it was not the antiwar movement that ended the war. It was the Vietnamese themselves who won their war of national liberation. Still, my hope was that the antiwar movement would be a significant learning experience for the American people, teaching them to pay critical attention to U.S. foreign policy in order to prevent such catastrophes in the future. Tragically, this did not occur. In the United States, the "lessons of Vietnam" have mainly been drawn by the same political and military institutions that got us into the mess and aim not at preventing another war but rather at preventing another antiwar movement.

The Vietnamese won their war, insofar as such a war can be won. They survived as an independent nation, heavily weighted down, however, by the sequels of the war, and still prisoner of a world economic order largely directed by the United States. The United States withdrew, refusing to help "heal the wounds of war," as the Vietnamese politely termed their request for reparations that never came, and continuing a sly combat by enforcing an embargo against humanitarian aid and secretly supporting Chinese and Khmer Rouge aggressions against Vietnam. The Americans orchestrated a shameful campaign demanding that the Vietnamese devote their scanty resources to a search for the bodies of American "MIAs" (missing in action, usually referring to aviators shot down while carpet-bombing civilians), a thousand times less numerous than Vietnamese still unaccounted for in their own land. Americans are masters of show business, and all this was part of a show to persuade the American people that they themselves, rather than the Vietnamese, were the real victims of a war fought in somebody else's country on the other side of the planet. Hollywood did its part. With a very few honorable exceptions (Stanley Kubrick's 1987 "Full Metal Jacket"), American movies portrayed the Vietnam War as a terrible ordeal for… the Americans. The Vietnamese were often reduced to the role of crafty Orientals who had lured innocent, well-meaning Yankees into a trap.

As for the American antiwar movement, half a century later, it has vanished almost without a trace as an influential political force. There are perhaps more intelligent critics of war than ever before, but they are largely confined to the virtual world of the web, without significant impact on a political system which is totally integrated into a military industrial complex that relies on endless conflicts to justify its perpetual renewal.

The public image of the anti-war movement has been largely reduced to certain aspects of its decadence—a commercialized "counter-culture" on the one hand and a mimetic revolutionary sectarianism on the other, elements that should be seen as two polarities that are both fatal to the development of a political consciousness capable of influencing the course of history. Starting in 1999, the United States has managed to wage at least three major wars of aggression without encountering any domestic opposition remotely comparable to the movement against the Vietnam War. The anti-war coalitions that exist are divided and distracted by their obsession with other causes, especially with the vague assertions of Identity Politics. Uncertain of their aims, they are without serious influence either on the population or on those in power.

A mass movement is always a conglomerate of misunderstandings. Unanimity of large numbers of strangers is always illusory. People came to the movement against the U.S. war in Vietnam for a variety of reasons and left for another range of reasons.

Did the movement make a significant contribution to bringing the war to an end? Not very, I would say, since the war dragged on for years even after most of the ruling establishment had come to the conclusion that it could not be won. But I still think that the experience I recount here suggests forms that opposition to war should take. It should stick to the point. It should educate. It should not be concerned with its own image but with reality. It should be open to everybody, eliminating preconceived ideas of what this or that category may think, and instead be based on the supposition that all people are able to learn, to change their minds, to gain in empathy with others.

The American anti-war movement could not end the war, but it could educate those who passed through it about their world. Some traces surely remain, and one day must be revived.

7.

Time to Go

After a spring and summer of intense antiwar activity, autumn brought the necessity of dealing with the practicalities of daily life. While I was obtaining my Ph.D. and teaching full time as well as opposing the war in Vietnam, my academic career was suffering from neglect. This was essentially my own fault. I had never really thought in terms of an academic career. I had considered teaching to be the line of work most compatible with motherhood, because of the summer holidays and hours at home. I chose a subject for my dissertation that really interested me, on an important author with whom I felt an affinity, André Malraux. A lot had already been written about Malraux, but I was sure I'd find a new idea, and I did. The thesis was in fact quite a readable essay, titled "Malraux and the Ethical Novel," which was very well received by my professors, but I never made the slightest move to have it published. Nor did I ever make any serious effort to find another university position after completing my doctorate. My sentimental attachment to Minnesota, based on the fact that I was born there and still had close relatives to see from time to time, was greatly increased by the solidarity built around opposing the war in Vietnam. I was ready to spend the rest of my life in Minnesota.

I enjoyed teaching—more than that, I *believed in it.* I felt strongly that teaching literature was an excellent method of sharpening critical intelligence. I did not subscribe to any school of criticism. I found that the first step was to entice students to read what was actually on the page. There is a natural tendency for people to read into a text their own ideas, or their own ideas of what a text should be saying, and this tendency was actually encouraged in some English literature classes I had attended. The classroom became a contest in individual sensibility. My approach was rather to ask two basic questions: what is the author trying to say, and to what extent does he/she succeed? Intention was an important factor and looking for intention is useful in every aspect of verbal life, notably in politics, where "What is he up to?" should be a constant interrogation. My class in *explication de texte* was extremely popular and inspired a few unfortunate students to decide to major in

French—unfortunate, because of the direction in which French literature departments were heading.

My common sense approach was much too simple to satisfy contemporary ambitions.

At the university, teaching was subordinated to the imperative "Publish or Perish"—and never mind that almost nobody reads what you publish, your list of publications will advance your career whereas good teaching will not. In our department, the most career-conscious professor was irritable and dismissive with students but was constantly publishing articles that said nothing of interest. I always thought that there is so much to read in modern society that publications should be kept to a minimum, so that the wheat isn't lost in the chaff. It also disturbed me that so many professors of literature did not really believe in the usefulness of what they were doing. Many even *said* they didn't see any point in teaching literature. They had been good in school and stayed there for the rest of their lives. They had no intellectual enthusiasm. Their conversation centered on their vacations.

I saw teaching literature as a way to train students in attentive reading, thus in thinking clearly and critically, the basis for intelligent politics. In addition, literary education created a common frame of reference that enriched social communication.[2] In addition, a foreign literature sharpens critical perception of one's own native culture. I wrote an article about this at the time for some leftist journal in Chicago. My simple point was that the social role of intellectuals was to raise the level of knowledge and critical thinking of the population as a whole, as the basis of democracy, or socialism, or whatever you want to call an advanced society.

As it happened, Professor Renaud, the head of my Department of French and Italian, shared this outlook and appreciated my enthusiasm. Only years later, meeting him and his wife in Paris, I learned that he had wanted to keep me on as assistant head of the department, but that this project had been vetoed by the male majority of the staff. In fact, French studies was on the verge of a transformation that would have put me at loggerheads with the vanguard of the profession. But I did not realize that at the time.

---

2 This role as frame of reference has been undermined by the Identity Political reduction of classical authors (except the female ones) to "dead white men."

Still, it was already clear that language teaching was under threat. When I first became a teaching assistant in 1963, I was supposed to teach language classes. But at that time, the expert advice of a strange couple had been imposed on the department from somewhere above. They were there to introduce a new "modern method." This consisted of eliminating all cultural content from language teaching and reducing it to exercises such as this one (it stuck in my mind):

Je voudrais une voiture aussi luxueuse que celle-ci.

Tu voudrais une voiture aussi luxueuse que celle-ci.

Tout le monde voudrait une voiture aussi luxueuse que celle-ci.[3]

And so on.

I said no, I absolutely would not teach French in such a fashion. I tried to get my colleagues to join my revolt, which some did, half-heartedly. Professor Renaud solved the problem by taking me out of language teaching and assigning me to teach the tragedies of Racine.

Later I was sent to a conference in Denver, Colorado, on "modern methods," which offered prizes for designing appropriate language programs. There it all became clear. This was sponsored by computer companies, and the idea was to replace teachers with computer programs. The whole revelation of another culture inherent in language study was flattened out to make way for commercially useful phrases such as "Everyone would like a car as luxurious as this one." I denounced this at the time, but to no avail.

French departments, and other language departments as well, were under a double pressure to be "useful." The language requirements for doctorates were fading as English became the dominant language of international scholarship. Language courses were to be a boon to computer companies. As for literature, well, what's the use of that? Since there is no clear and easy answer, French departments, in the coming years, were largely transformed into centers of post-modern theorizing, which was obscure enough to appear profound or at least "original" (the ways of being original are infinite) and to allow ex-rebels to feel revolutionary without having the slightest effect on the existing capitalist order or war economy.

In that summer of 1970, as the student strike against the war gave way to holidays, I was being eased out of my position in the French department by being pressured to accept a post as Assistant Professor

---

3 "I would like a car as luxurious as this one. You would like a car as luxurious as this one. Everyone would like a car as luxurious as this one."

in a newly created Experimental College within the liberal arts faculty of the University of Minnesota. This was the easy way to stay in my comfortable house near Lake Harriet, less than a block away from an elementary school and just across the street from a library—perfect for my daughter, I fancied. I could continue to visit my dear Uncle Bruce and Aunt Florence in Excelsior and see my youngest cousin, David, from time to time.

The Experimental College was a trap. I suspected as much at the time, but since it enabled me to stay put, I hoped I could make use of it to sustain the movement that had begun with the strike against the war. Indeed, this odd invention was precisely the reaction of Minnesota's very liberal rulers to the student strike. Minnesota was "nice." The untenured faculty and teaching assistants who had played prominent roles in the revolt were never reprimanded, much less fired. Mostly, they were told that, regrettably, their posts had been suppressed for economic reasons, but not to worry: "With your ability, you'll surely find an even better position somewhere else." This was the end of the academic road for some. For a few others, there was the possibility of setting off to sea in a leaky boat—the Experimental College. It was destined to sink, but meanwhile, it kept troublemakers busy—mostly disputing with each other.

I was the second ranking faculty member in this odd outfit. The top position went to Roger Jones, the physicist who had gone with our group to Paris. But Roger was no usual physicist. As it turned out, he was also an astrologer, and even a sort of New Age mystic.

Under Roger's direction, the Experimental College convened for the first time under a tree, on a sunny Indian summer day. Roger set the tone. "Now," he said, "the first thing we must do is to clear our heads of all the bad learning, before we set out on good learning. We must wipe away all our wrong habits of thought, before opening our minds to spiritual light." And how were we to do this? By plunging into deep silence for quite a long time.

As the others supposedly cleansed their minds in this mental purification ritual, I cheated by thinking. What I thought was that others had to be cheating too, because what Roger was asking us to do was simply not possible. Nor was it desirable. In my view, the only justification for an experimental college should be a reasoned critique of what already existed, as a basis for seeking improvements and alternatives. Throughout the rest of that absurd academic year, the Experimental College was the scene of endless quarrels between me and Roger, prefigured by the initial clash under a tree between an aspiration toward "innocent spirituality" and a demand for constructive reasoning.

The university authorities who put us in this leaking boat must have been very shrewd. Or could it have been by mere chance that the "experiment" served primarily to illustrate the fatal split in the intellectual dissidence of the time? Those who had momentarily come together in opposition to the war in Vietnam were destined to go very separate and indeed opposing ways.

Without realizing it at the time, I represented an "old guard" devoted to the rational search for factual truth and reasoned solutions to problems. The notion that nothing is exactly true, that there are multiple "truths," each one as true or not true as the others, was perhaps a phase of intellectual democracy that could not be avoided. My field of French literature was soon to be transformed into the headquarters of a critical movement to relativize everything, incidentally destroying the delight of reading good literature by promoting turgid "deconstructions" of "discourse" and "narratives," while rejecting the classics as "elitist." In reality, this would create an isolated academic elite of critics, claiming and very likely believing themselves to be leftist and even revolutionary, while abandoning teaching as I cherished it—the vocation of stimulating "elite" understanding in each and every person. The trend was to replace literature by esoteric postmodern studies at the top and empty "communications" at the bottom—each in its own way appropriate for "governance."

The students who had chosen to come aboard our leaky boat were torn between me and Roger. Since most were looking for an easy year of credits, most sided with Roger, whose demands for "spirituality" were easily met. This gave him a majority on most issues—everything was "democratic," of course. And virtually any activity could be considered part of the experimental learning process enjoying Roger's benediction. The educational activity I remember best was one young woman's "double marriage" with two men at the same time. She was very eager to talk about this to anyone who would listen. I also remember a woman student who insisted that having to read was discriminatory, since she personally did not like to read. However, my memory has kindly suppressed most of the details of that farcical experience.

I attracted a small but hard-working and loyal group of students who really wanted to do something to continue the activities of the anti-war strike. We formed a Vietnam Study Group and began a self-managed but quite serious study of Vietnam. We published a newsletter and organized a big anti-war meeting with Noam Chomsky as main speaker.

Outside our leaky boat, the powers that be were taking things in hand. If national media showed no interest in the extraordinary Minnesota anti-war movement, government agents of one sort or another were more curious. Some of their activities were revealed in documents obtained later by friends in Minnesota who requested their files through the Freedom of Information Act. I never bothered to ask for mine. But we could observe certain phenomena. Completely unknown individuals appeared on campus to cause trouble.

It was odd, to say the least, that the campus newspaper, the *Minnesota Daily* had on its staff an editorialist out of nowhere who announced our anti-war meeting in this elegant manner: "Chomp, chomp, Chomsky, here we go again…"

Nevertheless, the auditorium was packed to listen to the famous linguist, who at the time was an undisputed independent moral leader of the anti-war movement. It was the first time I met him—I would meet him and correspond with him many times in the future—and I was very favorably impressed by his unassuming, modest manner, and his willingness to spend time with my students who had worked hard to organize the meeting.

One of my precautions during this period was to avoid drugs, including marijuana, which was a fashionable social habit, but which could be used to "bust" political activists. Such abstention on my part was all the easier in that I was never attracted to the "substances" that were said to create mind-changing hallucinations. I simply didn't feel the need.

I was always adamant about staying within the law, for practical reasons. In the summer of 1970, some individuals set off 24 sticks of dynamite in the old Federal Building in Minneapolis, causing a large explosion that fortunately did not injure anybody. But the damage to the movement was psychological. Over and over, I heard students who had thrown themselves eagerly into the antiwar movement now react with revulsion, saying they never intended to get involved in *that sort of thing.*

One evening in the spring of 1971, when my father was staying with me as I recovered from an operation, we held a meeting of our anti-Vietnam war group in my home. They had just come from a meeting where the speaker was someone named Daniel Ellsberg. This was months before the Pentagon Papers were published by *The New York*

Times, and nobody had heard of Daniel Ellsberg. My father said, "Oh, I know Dan, we worked together on a study for McNamara."[4]

At that point I began to pay more attention to a stranger that my students had brought along with them. They seemed to have adopted him at the meeting for his zeal and his underdog status. He had just got out of prison, evidence no doubt that he was a victim of the system and a rebel against it. As we sat around the dining room table, when the discussion turned to what we should do next to stop the war, the stranger spoke up. He wanted "action," and exclaimed, "Let's get rid of the creeps!"

Since antiwar people never use such language, I instantly smelled, well, a rat. At our next gathering, I referred to the stranger who wanted to "get rid of the creeps," and told my students I didn't want them ever to bring someone like that into my home, because he might claim we were plotting something illegal and use the description of my furniture to prove he was there as a witness. (This sort of thing happened, notably to a local Catholic antiwar group.) My students were initially shocked at the suggestion that this poor victim of society could be an agent. "After all, he's been in prison. We must trust our brother!"

My father, who had been present at the first meeting, was present at this one too. My students turned to him, "You don't think he was an agent, do you?" My father replied with a shrug, "Of course he was an agent."

The newcomer vanished from Minneapolis thereafter. It was revealed later that Minnesota was awash with such transitory "newcomers."

I think that the Counter Intelligence people and I agreed on something: violence would destroy the mass movement. "Let's stop talking and *do something!"* was the line that always aroused my suspicion. I wanted to keep talking, to analyze the situation and plan strategy. But "doing something" without a precise purpose was either useless or, if the "something" was violent, harmful. Indeed, it was obvious to most people that when you are combating the system precisely because it is violent, a system that monopolizes violence and enjoys an overwhelming superiority in terms of violence, it is suicidal to challenge it on its own grounds, violence, where it is bound to win.

There are a few rare moments in history when people's turn to violence is justified and may even succeed. For example, when masses of people are desperate and exasperated with a power that reacts with repression to their just and feasible demands, successfully inciting parts

---

4 It was that study that came to be called the Pentagon Papers.

of the security forces—police or soldiers—to take the side of the people. In rare instances, this can be enough to reverse the relationship of forces. Every successful revolution splits security forces and wins some of them to its side. Premature violence simply solidifies the forces in power.

Conscript American soldiers in Vietnam could and did use violence effectively by turning on their officers. That caused the powers-that-be to reflect. On the home front, antiwar violence was counterproductive because the antiwar movement was based on rejection of violence.

This was so much the case that segments of the antiwar movement began to have doubts when U.S. propaganda developed the theme of violence on the part of the Indochinese who were defending themselves.

A start of this process can be seen in the uses of the "bloodbath" theme.

This theme developed under the Nixon administration, when the U.S. war was clearly lost, but U.S. forces were continuing to wreak as much damage as possible before their inevitable withdrawal. "If we leave," the argument went, "there will be a bloodbath." The idea was that the Vietnamese communists would take vengeance against the U.S. puppets, and therefore, the U.S. Air Force must keep killing Vietnamese, supposedly to prevent them from killing each other.

Years later, after the Americans and their closest Vietnamese collaborators fled Saigon in a panic, there was no such bloodbath in Vietnam. There were sessions in "re-education camps," without bloodshed. However, events in Cambodia provided the United States with the desired source of hypocritical indignation to justify its lost war and to be used to later to transform Washington into the world champion of Human Rights.

My reward for the academic year 1970-71 was working with the students in my Vietnam Study Group. They were exuberant and skilled. I was impressed that one of them, in that age of typewriters, had mastered cybernetic devices to print our bulletins and manage other practical tasks. We studied Vietnamese history, colonialism and the origins of the Cold War.

Otherwise, things were not going so well.

My daughter Elizabeth had demonstrated a strong character since she was two and this was bound to cause trouble. The elementary school just up the street had seemed perfect. It wasn't.

There is a tendency in American grade schools for the kids to gang up against whichever unfortunate schoolmate has been selected by class bullies for tormenting. In Elizabeth's class the victim (although not French) was named Pierre, and it may well have been the unusual name that singled him out for rejection, like the Roscoe Reeves Jr. of my own childhood. Elizabeth watched, powerless, feeling the unfairness as her classmates ganged up on Pierre at every recess. One day, the class teacher, Miss Hansen, announced that there was a problem with Pierre and the class should discuss it. And so, indeed, one child after another expressed what was "wrong with" Pierre, as Miss Hansen listened, apparently looking for a synthesis. When this was over, Pierre left, obviously devastated, as the others went home apparently satisfied. Elizabeth stayed and went up to the teacher and stated firmly, "Miss Hansen, you shouldn't have done that."

This was a declaration of war that made the rest of the school year unbearable.

I don't know how it is in other countries, and from my observation it is not like this in France, but in the United States the cult of popularity is so uncontrolled among schoolchildren that occasionally even teachers cater to it and join the pack in order to be popular.

At this time, a new sort of women's movement, to a large extent inspired by black power, was developing and detaching a certain number of women from other issues. At one women's meeting, I was informed that the Vietnam War was a man's affair, women had nothing to do with it and shouldn't be bothered opposing it. Women should concentrate on their own empowerment. Moreover, I was reproached by someone for being "a male identifier." I didn't object, because although I never doubted for an instant that I was a woman, I think it is good to identify even with people who are different. It's called empathy.

A meeting of the Experimental College was held at the end of the school year to decide what next. To get to the gist of the matter, students were complaining that they wanted more glamor, more excitement, more fun. I was dismayed by the superficiality and triviality of the whole enterprise. I suddenly said, "In any case, don't count on me. I'm leaving for France."

Just like that. It was a spur of the moment decision, but, on reflection, solidly based on many factors. My great interest was to pursue study of Vietnam and its history, and in France I knew experts and could consult libraries. And not least, my daughter was not happy in the nice school in the nice neighborhood in super-nice Minneapolis. She had started school in Paris, and it had left its mark; it represented something better. Going back to Paris meant that Elizabeth would go to a French school.

I held a house sale and sold just about everything—even books I later wished I had kept. My little back-engine Simca, which could beat bigger cars down Minnesota's snow-covered roads, got a good price. Always frugal, I had enough savings to last a while. Even so, I compared myself to a trapeze artist leaping from one swing to another without a net.

Before Elizabeth and I left for Paris, my father came to visit, regretting my decision. Although working for the Pentagon, he was as opposed to the war as I was. But, he said, to be effective in the sort of thing I was doing, I would have had to be rich and well-connected. I was neither. I had done too much, he said.

"If you had done more, I could have done less," I replied, without acrimony. It seemed to me at the time to be true. In retrospect, I was completely wrong. Each in our own way did all we could. And we failed. The relationship of forces was too much against us.

PART III

Lost Causes

8.

Decade of Uncertainty

When I brought my twelve-year-old daughter to France in September 1971, the prevailing mood in the circles I frequented was one of impending revolution. By that I don't mean "violent" revolution, but rather a sense of revolutionary evolution, hard to describe. The circles I frequented most were Asia scholars and "Science for the People" scholars from France, the United States and Italy. Such people did not see themselves "making the revolution" but serving a revolution which seemed to be underway, by "serving the people."

That sense of being part of a great revolutionary movement had a strong positive effect on human relations. The belief that we were all in this together inspired people to be extremely helpful to one another. Certainly, for over a decade I was a great beneficiary of this revolutionary helpfulness, which felt natural at the time. My feeling of "leaping from one trapeze to another without a net" was a genuine feeling, but in reality nets were there. During my previous stay in Paris I had been approached by a Frenchman who was writing a book on Black Power and wanted to consult me (although I was scarcely an expert). Yves Loyer had been a "suitcase carrier" during the Algerian war, that is, one who carried money and other useful things, I suppose, across national borders on behalf of the Algerian National Liberation Front. It followed that he was an ardent supporter of Vietnamese independence and other Third World national liberation movements. Yves came from a highly cultivated family and divided his time between his abstract painting and work in his father's patent attorney firm in the rue Mogador, next to the Galleries Lafayette in a main shopping district of Paris just behind the Opera. The classic Haussmann style building belonged to the Loyer firm, and it happened that a fifth floor apartment (with elevator), usually reserved for visiting business colleagues, was empty. That was where my daughter Elizabeth and I were installed. She was easily registered in a school in the 9th arrondissement. It was a strange neighborhood to live in, not normally residential, in between huge department stores, shops, snackbars, offices and, on the street corners, up-market prostitutes dressed like neat secretaries waited for customers.

Vietnam Solidarity

It was shared devotion to the Vietnamese cause that inspired Yves to arrange to allow me and my daughter to stay there for a year, paying only a small symbolic rent.

My project was to pursue my research on Vietnam, especially on the historic background of the Vietnamese war for independence from France—and subsequently, from the United States. I wanted to give my emotional attachment to the Vietnamese cause an intellectual expression that could be educational. Even some Americans who supported the Vietnamese thought of them as a primitive people, not realizing that this was a nation with a millennial history and long experience in defensive war.

To finance my research, I had applied for a grant from the Rabinowitz Foundation and for a while had the illusion that I would receive it. I did not. I went ahead anyway, spending my days in the Bibliothèque nationale, or getting advice and information from Paris university scholars, or visiting Mme Dung (Zung) at the PRG villa, or consulting the archives at the Overseas Ministry in the rue Oudinot. It was from informer reports in those archives that I learned how intensely French police had spied on Vietnamese patriots during colonial times. Yet despite all that, the Vietnamese had gotten their act together.

On my visits to Verrières-le-Buisson, Mme Dung might ask me to translate some PRG press release into English. I willingly complied, although I was highly skeptical of the usefulness of such texts. But I hoped in that way to learn more about Vietnam. As time went by, I did get the impression that the murderous Phoenix program, systematically eliminating South Vietnamese intellectuals and prominent individuals "suspected" of being "Viet Cong," was weakening the broad democratic nature of the South Vietnamese resistance. Decimation of the natural leaders of South Vietnamese society could only strengthen the influence of the more doctrinaire party in Hanoi. Finally, instead of the orderly withdrawal proposed by the South Vietnamese PRG, it was the North Vietnamese army that captured Saigon on April 30, 1975, sending the Americans and their closest Vietnamese collaborators stumbling into helicopters on the roof of the U.S. embassy in Saigon to flee in panic.

The victorious Vietnamese in France and Italy organized large gatherings to thank all those who had supported them in one way or another. Along with my friend Marianne Schaub, I attended such a large victory celebration in Rome. I took my daughter along, and that evening, after dark, we danced through the empty via Giulia, singing "We're off to see the Wizard." At the Rome conference, it all became clear. The North Vietnamese were in charge, and once the war was over, they thanked those of us who had independently supported them, but their priority was to strengthen relations with European Communist Parties. They needed them for reconstruction (since the U.S. blockaded reconstruction aid from the West) and, shortly, for international support in their brewing conflict with China. It seemed likely that the Vietnamese representatives never really trusted me, as an unlabeled independent. I could understand that. After all, what could they make of an American woman who seems to be a friend but might, after all, be an agent? They needed everyone when their country was being laid waste by U.S. bombing, but they were right to be suspicious, though wrong in their assessment. They were enthusiastic about Jane Fonda, because she was famous and went to Hanoi. When she passed through Paris on her way back to the United States, Madame Jolas got me to translate the star's documents from French into English, which she did not bother to do. There was an inevitable hierarchy of support: Communists, celebrities, and anonymous activists at the bottom. It could not be otherwise. I never visited Vietnam because I couldn't afford it, and I told myself that there were too many Americans there already.

But meanwhile, back in the summer of 1972, I had almost finished my book and was looking for a publisher when Back Bay published a book which largely accomplished what I had set out to do with mine by pointing to the cultural and political origins of the Vietnamese national liberation movement, ignored by Americans. The book was *Fire in the Lake: The Vietnamese and the Americans in Vietnam,* by Frances FitzGerald. As a matter of fact, I had learned that the book was being written, and had corresponded with Frances FitzGerald who reassured me that our books were surely different. Yes, but not different enough. *Fire in the Lake* was serialized in *The New Yorker* and won the Pulitzer Prize and the National Book Award. It was a good book, of course not exactly the book I was writing, but a good book and it largely filled the gap in knowledge I had wanted to fill, necessarily with different interpretations and emphasis.

Frances FitzGerald was the daughter of Marietta née Peabody, who divorced FitzGerald, and later became the lover and companion of two-time Democratic Party presidential nominee Adlai Stevenson, governor of Illinois and later U.S. Ambassador to the United Nations, with whom she corresponded regularly. Her father had been a deputy director of the CIA. She graduated magna cum laude from Radcliffe (the university I had wanted to attend, if not Shanghai, but nobody was willing to pay for it). She was a sincere and talented writer and in every way deserved her success. Perhaps being one of the best-connected women in the country had nothing to do with it, but it didn't hurt.

Anyway, my father had been right; I was doing more than I was in a position to do.

My manuscript was read by a few Asian scholars I knew, who found nothing wrong with it, and my friend Nina Adams, who had published a book on Laos and who had been researching in Paris at the same time I was, later used it in a course on Vietnam she taught at the University of Illinois in Springfield. She got the job teaching Vietnamese history—her specialty—only because she was hired primarily to teach women's studies. That is where academia preferred to place women. Indeed, leading American experts on Vietnam found themselves jobless as the war ended. Just when historic lessons should have been being drawn, America's institutions of higher learning had no place for those who knew most and, as a result, had been committed opponents of the U.S. war.

Much later, in May 1982, I once again met Ngo Vinh Long, who had been a pillar of the Concerned Asian Scholars in opposition to the American destruction of Vietnam. Although very young, Ngo was the top expert on Vietnam in the United States. He was staying for a while in Paris with his wife and their two awesomely bright small children. The descendant of generations of scholars, but living on modest means, Ngo Vinh Long had taught himself English by reading novels with the help of a small dictionary. Opposed to French colonial rule and more than slightly wary of communists, Ngo had first sympathized with American "aid" to South Vietnam, until he observed peasants starving from the U.S. policy of destroying crops around "Viet Cong" villages. After hectic years combining study with political protest, Ngo Vinh Long was accepted by Harvard in 1964 as their first Vietnamese student. At Harvard, he became the leading authoritative critic of the U.S. war in Vietnam, always informed, factual and balanced. His bulletin was a main source of information for serious critics of the American war. Fellow scholars predicted that Ngo should be in line to succeed the chair of the distinguished dean of Harvard Asian studies, John K. Fairbank. However, when the Vietnam War ended, Ngo lost the position to a Canadian woman; Harvard suddenly became interested in "parity" just in time to get rid of the country's best Vietnam scholar. For a time, Ngo was obliged to work as a janitor to support his family, with help from his wife.

Harvard's sudden awakening to the need to hire a woman was the perfect defense against accusations of political purge.

At the end of the war, many Vietnamese brought to the United States had been more or less involved in the U.S. military occupation. Ngo was not only isolated; in 1981, after speaking on a panel discussion at Harvard, he narrowly missed assassination. It wasn't until 1985 that Ngo Vinh Long obtained a secure academic post at the University of Maine.

Other concerned Asian scholars actively opposing the Vietnam War found jobs in Australia or by changing fields.

Americans' subsequent view of the Vietnam War was not to be formed by honest scholars but by Hollywood.

Years later, in 1979, lacking space in my tiny ground floor apartment near Père Lachaise cemetery, I stored the manuscript and notes in a trunk in the cellar, and when, getting ready to move to a larger apartment in a romantic old house in Belleville six years later, I opened the trunk, I discovered that the manuscript and the notes were all being eaten by small worms.

The end of the Vietnam War was the end of a chapter in my life, and in many other lives. Opposition to the massive U.S. destruction of a harmless Asian country had united millions of people all over the world who had little else in common and whose unity soon disintegrated. The standard explanation for the strength of the antiwar movement in the United States was that young men, especially students, did not want to be sent to Vietnam to be killed. On the basis of that analysis, the United States and various NATO governments abolished conscription and built up professional (or mercenary) armies, more appropriate for foreign wars that have nothing to do with "defense." But there are reasons to question the centrality of the draft. The movement was indeed strongest among students, but many students were able to avoid the draft, or at least to get relatively safe assignments. Most conscripted GIs were from the working class, and that was not where opposition was strongest.

There were more general emotional and aesthetic factors that stimulated the movement. The visible disproportion between Vietnamese peasants and the monstrous American military machine was simply horrifying. The Vietnamese, by prevailing standards, are a delicate people, the men small and slim, the women and children pretty—up against U.S. military men each carrying a veritable warehouse of arms and equipment.

The images were emotionally powerful, and the lesson was duly drawn by U.S. communications experts: no such wealth of heart-rending images was to be shown to the public in future military interventions.

The war salesmen and women in Washington had the institutional structure to "learn the lessons of Vietnam" and prepare means to prevent another such antiwar movement in the future. They had spies infiltrating the movement to study its mechanisms, they had permanently employed propaganda specialists, they had increasing symbiosis with mass media, they had think tanks, they had Hollywood.

The veterans of the antiwar movement were dispersed, without institutional coherence, and had lives to get back to. Whatever drew them into the movement, they came out of it with differing lessons and convictions. In Paris, where the revolutionary past breeds expectations of a revolutionary future, sects proliferated devoted to the overthrow of the system, usually called capitalism, but fiercely disagreeing with each other on how to go about it, and farther and farther from any social reality. For me, the priority was not to "overthrow capitalism" which might be a very good idea if anyone knew how to do it, but rather to demilitarize the United States and put an end to the American crusade to remake the world in its own image.

Even without any definable prospect, the mood of "revolutionary solidarity" did not fade overnight and continued to provide safety nets. After not selling my book, and with my savings running low, I had to find a job. I had left the Loyer apartment after a year, and Elizabeth and I shared a tiny apartment in the rue de l'Agent Bailly in the 9th arrondissment, where the main feature was the violent quarrels of a drunken couple across the courtyard. For heating, I had to drag large gas canisters up the hill from time to time. Luckily, a black American from the old Paris Americans Against War was working at the Agence France Presse and informed me of the scheduling of a recruitment test for the English desk. Had he not gone to the trouble of informing me, I would never have known such an opportunity existed. This was an example of the sort of solidarity that emerged from shared opposition to the war in Vietnam, a solidarity that is worth much more than personal ambition. So I took the test and for the next seven years worked on the English desk of the French news agency.

Watching the Tide Change

It was a good spot for watching the tide change.

The big story of 1973 was Watergate, which totally enthralled most of the Anglo-American press corps, who saw in it the heroic saga of the free press defeating the ogre of power. I didn't see it quite that way at the time, and even much less so as years went by. *Washington Post* reporters were celebrated for revealing the perfidy of Nixon. However, the *Washington Post* owned *Newsweek,* and I was aware from my experience in Bonn that *Newsweek* was particularly close to the CIA—and so was the *Washington Post.* Is it really a model of journalism for a reporter, on assignment from the most politically influential newspaper in the country, to take notes for his story from an anonymous informer in secret meetings in a garage? The informer was revealed much later to be Mark Felt, assistant director of the FBI, disgruntled at not being chosen to succeed J. Edgar Hoover. In short, Watergate was the first big eruption of the Deep State into open politics, as the alliance between secret services and leading media brought down a President of the United States. As with Russiagate, the story dragged on and on, hogging the news pages with ad hominem gossip.

My misgivings about Watergate centered, however, on its role in manipulating the mood of the United States as it was emerging from a war it had failed to win and that had aroused much of the world against America, severely jeopardizing its role as model for the world. Suddenly the United States, and its Western satellites, were invited to forget Vietnam and join in hating the villain: Richard Nixon. Nixon was not being condemned for prolonging the (already lost) Vietnam War by bombing the North, defoliating the south with massive spreads of poisonous Agent Orange, and targeted assassinations of civic leaders. No, Nixon was not condemned for genuine war crimes, but for an obscure, bungled burglary of the Democratic National Committee (which should, theoretically, have nothing much to hide) and for his own rude remarks which he had taped "for history."

Nixon was a scapegoat. Never mind that he was unlovable: it takes someone unlovable to be an effective scapegoat. Getting rid of Nixon was a brilliant coup that united generations, torn asunder by opposing attitudes toward the war, who could now agree that Nixon was bad. Watergate washed away the national sins. It prepared America to be "born again" first as the innocent Gerald Ford and then as the good Christian Jimmy Carter, champion of human rights.

The shenanigans around Watergate were a distraction from the most significant acts of the Nixon administration, in particular the shakeup of the world economy by the August 1971 decision to suspend (meaning to end) the convertibility of the dollar into gold. This was a direct result of the huge U.S. debt resulting from the cost of the Vietnam War. Since the rest of the world was holding dollars, they had to be worth something, and in fact the gold standard was replaced by the oil standard, as the dollar maintained its worth as a required currency to pay for petroleum products. The worldwide dollar surplus was drastically reduced by the October 1973 decision of the Organization of Petroleum Exporting Countries (OPEC) to triple their prices—ostensibly on political grounds, to punish consumers for supporting Israel. Some time later, I shared a first class compartment on a long train trip from Nice to Paris with an executive of Shell Oil, who passed the time explaining to me that the U.S. government was in cahoots with the Arab oil producers. The Americans made up for the higher cost of oil by transforming the Arab world into a lucrative market for U.S. weaponry. I never wrote about this, because I had no proof, but it sounded plausible enough. Be that as it may, the oil shocks of the 1970s were disastrous for a number of countries, including Yugoslavia, creating an indebtedness which eventually had dramatic political consequences.

The last gasp of the revolutionary Left in Europe took place in Portugal, when romantic revolutionaries in the armed forces overthrew the clerical dictatorship in Portugal, just about the last remnant of Europe's fascist past, in a bloodless coup on April 25, 1974. The overthrow of the Lisbon government was intimately linked to Third World liberation struggles, as it was in large part inspired by the disaffection of soldiers sent to combat independence movements in Portugal's African colonies. In both Lisbon and Paris, I met and conversed lengthily with the hero and leader of what was called "the Carnation Revolution," Lieutenant Colonel Otelo Saraiva de Carvalho, who impressed me as an honest idealist eager to serve the freedom and well-being of the people of Portugal and of Africa. I also observed how Otelo's progressive popular revolution was little by little stolen from him. There was a strong orthodox Communist Party in Portugal whose leader, Alvaro Cunhal, had been in exile in Moscow and remained pro-Soviet. That was enough to mobilize NATO, and the Portuguese revolution took on the semblance of an East-West contest, which the West was sure to win, considering the geography. Otelo dreamed of a non-bureaucratic people's revolution in Portugal as in the African colonies, with peasants taking control of the land and workers improving their lot. Having no base outside his military comrades, Otelo had to look around for other leftist support, which inevitably brought him into contact with a dubious far leftist group calling itself the Popular Forces 25 April (FP-25), which allowed the forces grouped against him to accuse him of association with terrorists.

The CIA and NATO forces would surely have intervened directly had Alvaro Cunhal been close to taking power, but this was out of the question. U.S. Ambassador Frank Carlucci studied the situation and opted for "soft power" to calm the revolutionary fervor. Carlucci perceived that among the potential leftist leaders in post-revolutionary Portugal, the one that was in reality the least leftist was the Socialist foreign minister, Mario Soares. With the approval of Carlucci, the German Social Democratic Party (SPD) took things in hand, providing political and material support to Soares, whose Socialist Party came in first in July 1976 parliamentary elections, with the communists coming in second. In that period, on my visits to Lisbon, I kept running into friendly Germans, who were clearly establishing a dominant influence in Portugal. The tamed Portuguese Left became a satellite of the Friedrich Ebert Stiftung, the foreign policy foundation of the SPD, which exercised an overwhelming influence in the Socialist International.

On April 17, 1975, the Cambodian Communist Party, called Khmer Rouge by the world, captured Phnom Penh from the U.S. puppet government. The predictions of a "communist bloodbath" if the Viet Cong came to power had not come true, but the violent repression exercised by the radical revolutionaries in Kampuchea, as they insisted on having foreigners call the country, gave the anti-communists more than enough grist for their mill.

Pol Pot and other Khmer Rouge leaders had been converted to communism in France, and at various public meetings I had the opportunity to hear their representatives speak. I was struck by how different they sounded from Vietnamese spokespersons. Whereas the Vietnamese were always diplomatic, welcoming support and encouraging open discussion, the Khmer Rouge I heard were dogmatic and openly unfriendly. I well recall hearing one of them say aggressively, to a large supportive crowd, "We don't want or need support from anyone, we shall do it ourselves." Thus I was not entirely surprised to learn that things had turned very nasty in Cambodia.

Cambodia was a small rural country whose traditional culture had been drastically disrupted by outside influences: in previous centuries, expansionism of the more vigorous Thais to the West and Vietnamese to the East, followed by French colonial rule, and finally, a brutal bombing campaign by the United States intended to weaken Vietnamese supply routes (the "Ho Chi Minh trail") but which in reality devastated the countryside and incited the rural population to justified rage against the aggressors—and against those of their own people who collaborated with them.

The Khmer Rouge acted as fanatic ideologues act: they explained the disaster in terms of their doctrine, which did not grow out of their national experience but had been learned as abstractions. Thus, in echo of the Chinese Cultural Revolution which was raging at the time, the Khmer Rouge blamed their national disaster not so much on the Americans—who were far out of reach—as on their own bourgeoisie, meaning the hapless city dwellers.

The catastrophe that struck this small country was undeniably caused by the secret war waged against it by the United States. The historic paradox is that pro-U.S. propaganda used the "killing fields" of Cambodia to retroactively justify their own years of killing.

Within public opinion, many who had joined in protests against the war could now emotionally "come home" to America, since the communists had turned out to be so awful and Richard Nixon was gone.

My work on my lost book on Vietnam had brought me into contact with most leading French scholars on Indochina. Outstanding among them was Serge Thion, an opponent of Western imperialism, whose book *Des Courtisans aux Partisans* gave a uniquely balanced understanding of turbulent Cambodian politics. Serge introduced me to the leading Cambodian poet, linguist and philosopher, Keng Vannsak, who at the time was living with his French wife in a Paris suburb. Keng had designed the first Khmer typewriter in 1952 and had studied together in France with Pol Pot and other future Khmer Rouge leaders, but was far too moderate to follow their violent course. He was very eager to have his original ideas on the background of the Cambodian disaster recounted in English, and after listening to him expound, I would much have liked to do the job for him. But I had to earn my living, and nobody I knew of in the United States was interested in a scholarly analysis that departed from the prevailing Manichean view of Cambodian "self-genocide." The Khmer Rouge slaughters rapidly came to symbolize "what communism leads to" and there was no great desire to learn about local historical factors that made the Khmer Rouge quite unique, having nothing in common with most other communist movements in the world.

It should be recalled that after the Vietnamese reacted to persistent border violations from the Cambodian side by overthrowing Pol Pot in 1979, the United States continued to recognize the "genocidal" regime and secretly armed and supplied the remnants of the Khmer Rouge in their refuge along the Thai border.

At an international news agency such as the AFP, news from all over the world is coming in over the wires. I was much more fascinated by dispatches from Africa (about which I had previously known next to nothing) and Latin America than by the usual semi-official press releases that make up most of local agency coverage. Thus my request was accepted to work at the English desk on the overnight shift, from 11 p.m. to 7 a.m. This had the advantage of having every other week off, to do as I chose. It also provided a larger paycheck. It was a topsy turvy life, going from dinner to work and getting off work just as cafés are opening for breakfast, but I made the most of it.

During the work week, my interest centered especially on Latin America, as part of my job was to rewrite dispatches from Spanish into English. During the free weeks, I often went to Italy, staying with friends there and following political developments. My old friend Liana was no longer in Rome. She had broken up with Ben years ago, then been involved with one of Rome's ubiquitous but quite unreliable Irish poets, giving birth to his son, before meeting the highly successful novelist Anthony Burgess (best known for *A Clockwork Orange*), who was recently widowed. The very British Burgess was completely enthralled by the lively and fanciful Italian beauty. He married her and pretended to be the father of her son from an earlier secret relationship. That was totally false, but from my time spent with the couple, I realized that a good writer of fiction may have a very loose contact with factual truth. His imagination was everywhere. He presented Liana as a countess, which may be true, since there are a lot of countesses in Italy, but I had never heard of that before.

They had a flat in London and a house in Malta, but in those years seemed to live mainly in airports, as Anthony flew from one book signing to the next university conference, and they could describe in detail the topography of scores of airports.

I had new friends in Italy, from my days in the Department of French and Italian, especially Gordon and Renata Poole in Naples, and Tita Viviani in Florence. In the late 1960s, Tita had accompanied her husband Paolo Viviani to the University of Minnesota where he was doing graduate work in psychology, and having nothing else to do, actually drove a taxi in the Twin Cities without really knowing her way around. This was the source of anecdotes that her friends must have found more amusing than did her dismayed clients. In the 1970s, she lived back and forth between her family home in Florence and the couple's apartment in Paris as her marriage fell apart. Paolo, son of a celebrated Neapolitan playwright, Raffaele Viviani, prided himself on being a communist, but was cynical enough to accept a Stanford contract to develop military uses of psychology. He was politically prescient enough to predict confidently that Nixon and Kissinger would seek reconciliation with China in order to isolate Russia.

Tita was a woman whose lack of confidence prevented her from pursuing the intellectual career of which she was capable. We were coming home together from seeing an Ariane Mnouchkine play at the very politically engaged Cartoucherie theatre in the Bois de Vincennes when I suddenly had my brainstorm: I would write my own newsletter and call it "The Owl." Tita was incredulous, but that is exactly what I did.

It was a spur of the moment idea, like going back to France, but such ideas can in fact mark the conscious emergence of a mature project. I had asked for a grant to write a book on Vietnam, had not gotten the grant, had written the book, and that was that. I would never ask for another grant. I would just do what I thought I could do, and see what happened.

This was before computers, before internet, before blogs. The Owl had to be typed, pasted together and photocopied, stuck into addressed envelopes and mailed. For this dull work I was helped by a generous and committed young Japanese-American, Lillian Ginoza, at the very beginning of her career in journalism.

The newsletter was sold by subscription, and my very first subscribers were Professors Edward S. Herman and Noam Chomsky. This was more than a decade before they published their classic critique of mass media, *Manufacturing Consent.* My own criticism of mass media came from inside, or from the edges, as during my marriage to Herb Altschull. In fact, four years before the Herman/Chomsky book came out, Herb published his own critique of news media: *Agents of Power: The Role of the News Media in Human Affairs* (by J. Herbert Altschull, Longman, 1986), in which he thanked me for "steering (him) in the right direction many years ago."

The main point of Herb's book was that mass media, whether State-controlled (as in the Soviet bloc) or privately owned, select and interpret the news to serve their interests; and in the case of the United States, those private interests coincide quite closely with those of the U.S. government, since the same economic powers are behind both. This has become much clearer since the 1980s, as the influence of the Military Industrial Complex and certain lobbies has increased drastically.

In fact, media were more open then than they later became. Within a short time, my Owl was getting around, and led to invitations to write for various publications. The high point was the invitation by Claude Julien to write an article on Jimmy Carter for the highly respected monthly, *Le Monde diplomatique.* My article appeared on the front page of the November 1976 issue, with the title "Une stratégie 'Trilaterale'." From then on, I was kept busy at the AFP at night and during the day writing for numerous publications in various countries. At the new Chicago weekly, *In These Times* (ITT), co-editor John Judis saw my work and asked me to write for ITT, using "the same style." I took up the invitation. With all this, I often had the image of myself struggling to keep my head above water in the middle of an ocean.

The 1970s were a messy decade politically. In France especially, the Left was split between its traditional currents, notably the French Communist Party with its working-class base and its patriotic legitimacy stemming from the Resistance, and on the other hand, an array of contentious grouplets, tendencies and individuals each striving to claim the heritage of May '68. Finally, the winning tendency was the one that coincided with the post-Vietnam strategy of the United States.

The unsatisfactory results of U.S. intervention in North Korea and in Vietnam inspired U.S. policy-makers to shift strategy from direct military assault from the outside to undermining unfriendly governments from the inside. That had already been done in Iran and Guatemala. But the new strategy put more emphasis on the ideological offensive, broader than anticommunism, based on occupying the high moral ground of "human rights." Mainstream media were fully enlisted in this offensive.

Sympathy for Third World liberation struggles was eroded by denunciations of the failure to respect human rights on the part of new independent governments.

In Europe, the rise of Human Rights as a dominant ideology resulted from a lengthy diplomatic process. It began in response to Moscow's wish to solidify the Soviet Union's Eastern European buffer zone but finally contributed to its collapse.

Hosted by Finland, the Conference on Security and Cooperation in Europe opened in Helsinki in July 1973, initiating what was called the "Helsinki process" of negotiations among both Eastern and Western governments which culminated with the Helsinki Final Act which was signed on August 1, 1975 establishing the Organization of Security and Cooperation in Europe (OSCE). Hardline "roll back" Cold Warriors in Washington denounced this process as being soft on communism, since it accepted existing borders. However, the Final Act balanced the affirmation of "territorial integrity" and "non-intervention in internal affairs" (sought by Moscow) with affirmation of "respect for human rights and fundamental freedoms, including the freedom of thought, conscience, religion or belief." This became the key instrument of political intervention.

The required monitoring of "respect for human rights" offered the opportunity for those who did not share the "religion or belief" of the country they lived in to organize opposition, on the expectation that they would receive political support from abroad—which was the case.

In 1973, New York publisher Robert Bernstein founded the "Fund for Free Expression," the parent of Helsinki Watch established in 1978, which ten years later changed its name to Human Rights Watch. The idea of Helsinki Watch was to monitor the "human rights" provisions of the Final Act, supposedly everywhere but in practice supporting dissident groups in the Soviet Union and Eastern Europe. This required close cooperation with Western media, which could be relied on to highlight whatever "abuses" were denounced by Helsinki Watch.

What I witnessed at the AFP was the choice of news that gets to the public. The news that came onto the main desk appeared to be reasonably comprehensive, but the reports that actually got published in newspapers were highly selected. An example that struck me at the time was the contrast between treatment of two stories, one from Czechoslovakia, and the other from Argentina. In Buenos Aires, a left-wing lawyer was dragged from his apartment in the middle of the night, with traces of blood in the elevator as the only clue to his fate. In Prague, dissidents returning to their cars from a meeting expressed outrage because someone had let the air out of their tires. The second report got more attention than the first.

But the most effective "human rights" campaign was carried out in support of Jewish citizens of the Soviet Union who wanted to emigrate to Israel. The refusal of Soviet authorities to allow them to leave without reimbursing the cost of their free higher education was widely denounced as a violation of "freedom of religion," namely Judaism.

On May 12, 1976, a Moscow Helsinki Group held a press conference held at the apartment of Andrei Sakharov and his wife Yelena Bonner. My boss at AFP called me to assign me to write the English version of Sakharov's statement, stressing its exceptional importance. I never saw such concern for any other story.

For all my efforts to keep up with everything going on the world, I don't think I at all understood the long-term political significance of the Russian human rights movement.

Soviet leader Leonid Brezhnev was making every effort to promote "détente," meaning a relaxation of tensions, with the West, with a view to promoting trade, disarmament and good relations. Refusal to allow Russian Jews to go to Israel, presented as anti-Semitic persecution, turned out to be a main obstacle to détente. It was ironic indeed to portray the desire to keep educated Jews *in* Russia as "anti-Semitic," a term which historically suggested a desire to get rid of them. Brezhnev's 1972 "diploma tax" was intended to stop the brain drain but could have been overcome by paying the tax. However, the refusal to allow Jews to emigrate—the "Refuseniks"—was blown up as a major human rights issue, more important than pursuing peaceful East-West relations. Nobody remembered that not so very long ago, the United States had banned communists, or suspected communists, from either entering or leaving the country—as it did, for example, to the great black singer, Paul Robeson. And in the American case, the motives were more unequivocally political.

The issue marked the start of heavy Israeli influence on the U.S. Congress, notably in the office of Democratic Senator Henry "Scoop" Jackson of the State of Washington. Known as the Senator from Boeing for his big appetite for Pentagon contracts, Jackson was advised by Richard Perle, the original pro-Israel neo-con. Influenced by the Refusenik movement, Jackson co-sponsored, with Representative Charles Vanik of Ohio, an amendment to the 1974 Trade Act which conditioned trade relations on respect for the right to emigrate. This was a milestone in the rise of the Jewish/Israel lobby.

In Paris, the mood was not all that different. On June 21, 1977, as Brezhnev arrived to sign a trade agreement with President Valéry Giscard d'Estaing, big name intellectuals protested by organizing an evening reception for Russian dissidents at the Theatre Récamier in the chic sixth arrondissement. I was the anonymous mouse among the big names, a Cinderella at the party because I had to leave in time to get back to the night desk at the AFP and the party seemed scheduled to last past midnight. The most famous dissident of all, who had been elevated by the "New Philosophers" to the status of Saint, Alexander Solzhenitsyn, refused to come, ostensibly because of his objection to sharing the event with Jean-Paul Sartre.

A pitiful ghost of Sartre arrived rather late, flanked by Simone de Beauvoir who appeared somewhat out of place. Sartre had not aged well, to put it mildly. In reality, the relations between the two famous writers were strained, as Sartre in his last years came increasingly under the influence of a certain Benny Lévy, aka Pierre Victor. As a student of philosophers Louis Althusser and Jacques Derrida at the elite Ecole Normale Supérieure, Benny was a Maoist during May '68, and taking the name of Pierre Victor, became the leader of a radical revolutionary group, *la Gauche prolétarianne,* the only one of the May '68 offshoots to flirt with "armed struggle," before backing off. As a revolutionary, Victor impressed Sartre, who took him on as his personal secretary in 1974. The mentor in the pair was not the famous philosopher, but Victor, who reverted to his original name of Benny Lévy and undertook to initiate Sartre into Judaism, with some success. Simone de Beauvoir couldn't stand him but was helpless to break his hold on the celebrated writer.

That evening, Sartre was brought onto the stage, a pathetic figure too weak to speak. This was the heyday of the "new philosophers," in reality a clique of highly educated young writers promoted by the weekly *Nouvel Observateur* in an obvious campaign to turn public opinion to a more pro-American position in the Cold War. The main theme was to denounce the Soviet Union by identifying it almost exclusively with "the Gulag," although by the time they went into action, conditions had improved considerably in the Soviet Union since Stalinist times. Moving rapidly from doctrinaire Maoism to doctrinaire anti-Sovietism, André Glucksmann was the leading *passionario* hurling rhetoric at the Kremlin oppressors. His latest book, *Les Maitres penseurs,* accused enlightenment figures including Karl Marx of responsibility for the Gulag and Auschwitz, for structures and ideologies that oppress what he and Michel Foucault called "the plebe." That vague concept is explicitly anti-Marxist, since it avoids naming the working class as the defensive party in the class struggle.

Glucksmann used Foucault's books and concepts as his main ideological source, and Foucault returned the compliment by lavishing praise on Glucksmann, thus contributing to Glucksmann's stature as a new "philosopher," rather than simply a polemicist.

Glucksmann's admirers were particularly taken with his good looks, exclaiming that "at last, we have a handsome philosopher"—an obvious mean allusion to Sartre, who was nothing to look at even in his prime.

I dared suggest to Glucksmann that there were other dissidents in the world, notably in Latin America and even in the United States, and it would be more balanced to defend them as well. This was clearly out of the question.

I had come with the intention of interviewing one of the more political dissidents, in particular the mathematician, Leonid Plyushch. I addressed this request to the master of the proceedings, the philosopher Michel Foucault. Turning on me with a singularly hostile smile, Foucault advised me to interview Dr. Stern instead. Dr. Mikhail Stern was a Ukrainian Jewish sexologist who had been sentenced to seven years in prison for swindling and bribery in 1974, but who had just been released and allowed to go into exile. Of course, in the West nobody doubted that the charges were trumped up and that Dr. Stern was a victim of persecution. This case dealt with events in the Soviet Union which I could not verify, and Dr. Stern, living in the Netherlands, had no need of defenders, who were numerous and influential. I, however, was interested in more general political issues than sexology in the USSR. I never got past Foucault, certainly one of the most unpleasant people I have ever met, and finally had to leave without an interview and return to my job at the AFP.

I met him again several years later, as recounted further on.

An American Dissident?

I had had other worries during the 1970s. On arrival in France in September 1971, I had applied for a resident's card (*carte de séjour*). In January 1972, I was granted a normal one-year card, but a year later, in January 1973, instead of renewal, I has told by the Prefecture de Police that henceforth I could only receive a three-month card, for political reasons that were not explained. Confident that I had never done anything the slightest bit illegal, I requested to go to the Ministry of Interior in order to clarify the matter, as I was ready to answer all questions about my activities. I was told that "the Ministry of Interior does not receive." The trouble with a three-month card was that it did not authorize a work permit, which became an acute problem when I was hired by the AFP. My good friend Yves Loyer got in contact with a prominent Socialist, Jean-Pierre Cot, who wrote to the Interior Ministry, which replied that there were orders "from the highest level of the ministry" to oblige me to re-apply every three months for permission to stay in France. Monsieur Cot managed in 1974 to take my case to "the mediator," a special trouble-shooting office, which enabled me to get a work permit, but still blocked me from getting a proper residence permit. Everything in France (and elsewhere perhaps) depends on *relations,* on contacts. Fortunately I had a few. One day at the apartment of Madame Jolas—a veritable center of *relations*—I met the wife of author and publisher Jean Lacouture, who advised me to write to her husband, which I did, in detail. Lacouture replied that he had "greatly appreciated my articles on the Trilateral Commission in *Le Monde diplomatique"* and would take my case to the highest level.

Thus, on August 26, 1977, Jean-François Poncet, Secretary General at the Elysée Palace, and thus President Giscard d'Estaing's closest aide, wrote back to *"Cher ami"* Jean Lacouture, replying that: "Upon verification, the facts that you bring to my attention are correct: the conditions of renewal of Mme Johnstone's *carte de séjour* were directly linked to events which today belong to history."

That seemed to be that. Upon instructions from the Elysée, I was finally granted a resident permit. And yet, there was one last episode indicating that my status was never altogether secure. On November 7, 1979, I went to the press service of the Foreign Ministry to obtain my accreditation as correspondent of *In These Times*—my new job. After inspecting that very bland social democratic weekly and asking about the content of one of my articles, the head of the press office, Monsieur Garidou, treated me to a little speech making it clear that freedom of the press exists in France, but that if I forgot that I was a foreigner in France, I could nevertheless lose my resident permit. When I asked whether he made the same speech to the correspondent of *The New York Times,* he said no, but confirmed that he said the same thing "to certain Arabs."

As correspondent of *In These Times,* I became a member and at one point even an officer of the Foreign Press Association. It is noteworthy that my compatriots were elsewhere, in the Anglo-American Press Club, which kept clear of all the contaminating influences in the FPA.

In fact, I was very happy to steer clear of *them.* I knew from Bonn the power of Anglo-American group conformity, and the difficulty of being honest when it goes against the prevailing doctrine of one's milieu.

Much of my attention in those days was centered on Italy. Opposition to the war in Vietnam had situated me "on the left," since that was where most of the opposition was, but in Italy I discovered two—or even more—lefts increasingly at war with each other.

In These Times persuaded me to abandon the AFP and The Owl to become their full time European correspondent. I took a 50% pay cut in order to enjoy the greater freedom, but was rewarded by the huge increase in the exchange value of the Reagan dollar, which eventually (in 1985) enabled me to undertake purchase of my first property, a third floor (fourth American) apartment between two courtyards with trees in a romantic 1830 house with statues in niches on the façade.

I was hired not only because they liked my writing style, but especially because the weekly's founder and editor, James Weinstein, was fascinated by Eurocommunism. A gentle and rather whimsical man, Jimmy Weinstein had inherited money from his capitalist father and the politics of his communist mother and tried to combine them as best he could. Aside from writing histories of the American Left, stressing the importance of socialism in the United States prior to the First World War, in 1976 he founded *In These Times* to provide a voice for the reformist Left. Although a New Yorker who had lived in California, Jimmy set up his new shop in Chicago, in the middle of the country, more "American" than the coasts. The weekly focused on labor news and domestic political issues, so that taking me on was an anomaly, not, I think, always appreciated by the Chicago staff.

McCarthyism was long gone and the civil rights and antiwar movements had raised hopes for the development of a genuine democratic socialist movement that could actually influence policy in the United States. That was Weinstein's ambition, and he saw in the new concept of Eurocommunism a possible model for the future of the American Left. The death of Spanish dictator General Francisco Franco had allowed the Spanish Left to emerge from underground, which aroused special enthusiasm among the old veterans of the Abraham Lincoln Brigade that had fought on the republican side in the Spanish Civil War. These veterans, many of whom had become quite successful businessmen while hiding their political convictions, were the main supporters of ITT in its infancy. I visited some of them in California, including one who was living in the Spanish style villa that had belonged to Marilyn Monroe. In turn, they took me on a nostalgic visit to sites they remembered from their heroic days in Madrid.

In 1977, the three main European communist party leaders, Santiago Carrillo of Spain, Georges Marchais of France and Italian Enrico Berlinguer, meeting in Madrid, agreed on the concept of Eurocommunism, meaning a socialism clearly integrated into Western European democracy, rejecting the Soviet Union as model. I was largely free to choose my subjects and to write what I wanted, but Jimmy had a definite preference for events concerning Eurocommunism.

9.

Italy's Hot Cold War

That brought me back to Italy. I had spent enough time in that country to have acquired a certain feel for the political mood. I had friends I could stay with in major cities, who told me a lot about what was going on. One thing was perfectly clear: the Italian Communist Party brought together many of the "best people" in Italy, from workers in Bologna to aristocrats in Naples, the most honest, the most rational, the most generous, the most competent people in the population. This was demonstrated in the local governments which they controlled. If Italy had been free, truly free, I have no doubt that the Italian Communist Party would have been providing leadership in a social democratic system, still capitalist and not communist, but better than the corrupt and disorderly state of affairs in Italy governed by the Christian Democrats.

But Italy was not entirely a free country. When a great power "frees" a country and then stays there, the country is occupied. The American occupation of Italy was politically more subtle than the Soviet occupation of Czechoslovakia—except in the eyes of a number of Italian communists, especially the more radical youth. The United States had colluded with the Vatican to ensure a seemingly permanent domination of the political scene by *Democrazia Cristiana* (DC), the Christian Democratic Party. Through the Marshall Plan, the U.S. gained economic domination over its beneficiaries. The CIA established close links with Italian secret services, where fascist sympathies remained active. To aid in its invasion of Sicily, the United States had revived the Sicilian mafia to combat the communist resistance. In countries where the culture is not thoroughly Americanized—and Italy was such a country—and where the *best people* are likely to resist American domination, for reasons of patriotism and dignity, U.S. officials tend to favor the *worst people*—the most sly, the most corrupt, the criminal, the disloyal and the just plain stupid—because those are the ones most eager to enjoy protection of a foreign power.

In its own half of divided post-war Europe, on the basis of the fantasy that the Soviet Union would break the tacit Yalta agreement and invade the West, the United States established secret armed groups whose task was to stay behind in case of communist invasion, in order to be able to attack the occupier by "unconventional warfare." In Italy the secret "stay behind" group, called *Gladio* (sword) was formed by the CIA with close links to NATO and to fascistic leftovers in the Italian secret services, especially the sinister *Servizio Informazioni Difesa* (SID), welcoming the chance to be able to crack down on communists with impunity. Precisely because of the strength of the Italian Communist Party, Gladio was far more extensive and active than such groups in other countries and tended to confound its mission of opposition to a foreign invader with battling against its own domestic adversaries. The existence of Gladio was not confirmed until long after its units had been involved in mysterious acts of violence.

In the immediate post-war years, Italian Communist Party (PCI) leader Palmiro Togliatti, no doubt in complete accord with Moscow, led his followers away from the revolutionary aspirations of the anti-fascist resistance toward acceptance of electoral politics. This took a dramatic turn when a right-wing student wounded Togliatti in an attempted assassination in July 1948. Armed workers seized power in factories throughout Italy. At a giant rally in Rome, on his return from medical care in Moscow, Togliatti himself called on workers to lay down their arms, go back to work, and vote.

This clear rejection by PCI leaders of a Bolshevik style revolution in favor of bourgeois democracy did nothing to dissuade Washington from pursuing its anticommunist crusade in Italy, by whatever means necessary.

The realism of the PCI leaders was largely accepted until a strong labor movement met with violent repression in the late 1960s. A new generation revived the revolutionary enthusiasm of their predecessors. Unlike the "68" of Paris, in which worker radicalism was eventually upstaged by student libertarianism, the Italian "68" was totally centered on the struggles of the industrial working class. The massive strikes revived the notion of revolution, whereas the PCI intended to obtain gains for workers through elections and legislation.

The industrial working class in Italy differed from that of other major European industrial nations in that period by its social composition. The demand for labor in Germany and France was met by "guest workers" from Turkey or North Africans from France's former colonies. In Italy, the demand for labor in the northern factories was met by a huge influx from the south of the country, still largely feudal in its culture. These factory workers, filling the least skilled jobs, were both Italian and at the same time, in the north, aliens. They came by necessity, but their material conditions were harsh and they were deprived of the social integration they had left behind. They were not used to the discipline of the northern factories and their rebellious tendencies were fed by long traditions of anarchism and peasant uprisings. In southern Italy, well before the Communist International gave the term a modern meaning, peasants rebelling against wealthy landlords' appropriation of communal lands were called *comunisti.*

The leaders of the Italian Communist Party had a much more pragmatic attitude.

Finding themselves in the sphere of the Western great power, the United States, Italian communist leaders decided that they had to live with that reality and attempted to adapt to it. Vague "fear of communism" should not apply to *them.* They wanted to show the Western world just how democratic and respectable they really were. That led the PCI to make more and more concessions, which in turn led elements of the radicalized post-68 Left to condemn the PCI for selling out the working class. The reformist Left was caught between doctrinaire anticommunism on the right and ultra-revolutionary disruptions on its left.

The story of the Italian Left in the 70s was unique, and yet it illustrated more sharply than any other the crisis and defeat of the Marxist concept of the working class as the "revolutionary subject" destined to bring about communism in advanced industrial societies.

In the 1960s, a number of radical academics, of whom Toni Negri was the most influential and the most extreme, turned their attention away from Third World struggles to concentrate on the need to bring down capitalism by workers' struggles. They saw factory worker struggles for higher wages as the crucial attack on surplus value and thus the most revolutionary demand. And indeed, worker struggles in Italy in the late 1960s were massive and intense.

Potere Operaio (worker power) was formed in September 1969 as a highly disciplined neo-Leninist vanguard party aimed at leading factory workers' wage battles into "movements of mass collision able to corrode the reality of the state," in the words of Negri. This approach disdained political efforts to improve workers' conditions through legislative reforms and collective bargaining, as pursued by the Italian Communist Party. At its peak around 1971-72, *Potere Operaio* had some 4,000 registered members, about a thousand of them full time militants, spread through 150 sections and cells in key factories.

Potere Operaio was a victim of its own success. In the March 1973 "Red Week," workers occupied and shut down the gigantic FIAT automobile plant in Turin. This led to deadlock. What next? Most workers, especially the most experienced, were not ready to smash their source of income for a revolution that was nowhere in sight. Finally, the industrial workers movement turned to the trade unions and the PCI for leadership.

The reaction of Toni Negri was what the French call a *fuite en avant*—just keep going in the wrong direction. Three months later, he called for spreading the rebellious worker behavior which had failed in the big factories—non-collaboration, endemic conflict, absenteeism, refusal to work, sabotage of profit-making—throughout the whole economy.

This was the radical response to a phenomenon which was recognized not only by Negri, but also by his opponents. It was clear that advanced capitalism was moving production of surplus value out of the range of potentially rebellious concentrations of productive workers, primarily by automation, but also by limiting labor's share of income by setting the moment of maximum profit-taking either before industrial production, as with increased oil prices, or after it, in the services sector. This was a step in strengthening financial capital at the expense of industrial production.

But Negri's reaction was unique. Since production was diffused through society, the "revolutionary subject" must also be diffused through society—if a 'revolutionary subject' indeed exists. Negri had no doubt of it. He picked up the pieces of this shattered, reshuffled, dispersed and divided working class—including unemployed, lumpen, students—and united them in the figure of the "diffused" or "societal worker," not marginalized, but rather the new producer of surplus value whose rebellion against it, whose refusal to work for capital, whose struggle of "self-valorization" and expression of "needs" can sabotage capitalism's latest (last?) strategy and create communism.

To this purpose, Negri led the creation of a new movement, *Autonomia Operaia* (worker autonomy), which quickly gained followers among radicalized students.

The so-called "Autonomy area" was a loose web of collectives and militant groups often at odds with each other but all fiercely hostile to labor unions and political parties—especially the PCI. Unlike the obsolescent "mass worker," the "societal worker" was dispersed in precarious part-time jobs throughout society and was urged to express their "needs" (the key term in the radicalism of the seventies) by direct action.

By advocating autonomy from everything organized, *Autonomia Operaia* entered into direct conflict with political parties and trade unions seeking socialist reforms. Negri wanted a total revolution, which he claimed would come from an uncompromising confrontation between capitalism in its highest stage and the "societal worker" whose violence expressed the "need for communism." Negri's Marxism interpreted working class struggle in an almost mystical way, that is, by final causes, by the vague utopian "communism" that the "revolutionary subject" is historically destined to bring about.

Negri's *Autonomia* could be considered the student branch of the violent working class revolution which other Italian groups—notably the Red Brigades—were undertaking.

Suspicious persons could find it strange that such a dogmatically unorganized movement produced handsomely designed slick magazines such as *Metropoli* to expose the tortuous ideas of *Autonomia* theorists. There was clearly a lot of money coming from somewhere.

I toured the FIAT plant in Turin in those days and saw clearly what rapid progress was being made to render the "mass worker" obsolete.

Negri's most eloquent adversary was Bruno Trentin, a brilliant and highly influential leader of the Italian Metal Workers before becoming second in command of the huge PCI-linked General Confederation of Italian Labor (CGIL). Trentin was born in France, the son of a liberal professor who had gone into exile for refusing to sign allegiance to Fascism. As an adolescent, Bruno disobeyed his family to return to Italy to join his father in the resistance and briefly got captured by the retreating fascists. Finally, moved by the tremendous popular enthusiasm of the postwar years for socialism, Bruno Trentin decided to serve the working class movement instead of pursuing an academic career. During the wave of labor militancy in the late 1960s, as *Potere Operaio* was trying to use that militancy to destroy capitalism, Trentin's leadership succeeded in achieving practical gains for workers in the work place, through factory councils, shared management, increased knowledge, and in society, by building political support for the working class.

The opposition between the two visions could hardly be greater.

I met Trentin several times in those years, for interviews in his office or just for conversations in some trattoria near his apartment in Trastevere. From a certain reasoned elation in the late sixties, his mood grew more pessimistic as time went on. I remember him telling me of his youth, when he left school to go join the resistance in Italy, where he was arrested but got away, as part of a mass popular fight against fascism. "Things were so much clearer in those days," he reflected.

Apparently, things were also much clearer to his adversaries on the extreme Left, who imagined themselves to be still fighting the revolution, as the armed branch of the working class. The radical groups that took up arms had no doubts about what they were doing. They were completing, they imagined, the communist revolution which should have emerged from the fight against fascism, but which was interrupted by the United States, subjugating Italy to the imperialism of the multinationals. There was some truth in this, but the response proved tragic.

The revolutionary mood in Italy in the 1970s was incomprehensible to most of the world then, and must be even harder to grasp decades later. In his prison notebooks, the Italian Communist Antonio Gramsci, contemplating the causes of the triumph of Mussolini's fascism (which kept him in jail for most of his life), developed the view that the revolutionary struggle for the means of production (communism) must be preceded by a struggle to gain "hegemony" in the war of ideas.

The mood of Italy in the 1970s was such that many young radicals could believe that the hegemony had been achieved, and that the revolutionary moment had come. They simply ignored the large sectors of the population who had no interest in such adventures.

The Hegemony of Revolutionary Romanticism

In that period, much of the Italian far left was bracing itself for a military coup on the Greek model. Between 1969 and 1974 there were a series of fascist terror bombings and coup plots. On December 17, 1969, an explosion in Piazza Fontana in Milan killed seventeen people and wounded 88. This was apparently a "false flag," initially attributed to anarchists, carried out by members of the fascist organization, *Ordine Nuovo* (New Order) who, while finally identified, were never adequately punished. On December 8, 1970, in considerable confusion, followers of World War II fascist hero Prince Julio Borghese actually attempted to take over the government of Rome in a botched coup d'état which received help from the Sicilian mafia and was expected to eventually receive aid from the CIA and NATO forces. These and other acts of neo-fascist violence were understood as the counter-revolution, heralding the revolution itself.

In 1970, the Red Brigades were founded by Trento University student Renato Curcio, his companion Mara Cagol and Alberto

Franceschini, as an urban guerrilla to serve as the "military arm" of worker struggles, mainly by intimidating bosses and foremen. In 1974 it turned its attention outside the factory, kidnapping and then releasing a Genoa judge after he "repented," but also killing two neo-fascists in Padua.

In the late 1970s, the Red Army Fraction was also engaged in violent urban guerrilla warfare in Federal Republic of Germany (West Germany). Although their actions appeared similar, the context was totally different. Also known as the Baader-Meinhof Band after leaders Andreas Baader and Ulrike Meinhof, the RAF committed kidnappings and assassinations out of a sense of desperate isolation, inflicting moral punishment on a capitalist society they considered guilty of past Nazi crimes and current wars against the Palestinians and other Third World peoples. Except for a network of intellectuals who offered them shelter when they were fleeing police, the RAF knew they were acting alone in Germany, without popular support, but felt themselves to be a fraction of a worldwide communist movement, especially in the Third World, with some clandestine support from the German Democratic Republic (East Germany). In Germany, the communists were in the East and the anti-communists were in the West, and nothing could change that.

The urban guerrilla groups in Italy were operating in a totally different context, riding what they felt to be a massive wave of revolutionary fervor in their own country. This euphoria attracted romantic revolutionaries, such as Ariana Faranda, from a rich family and known as the most beautiful girl in her Sicilian village, who as a student joined the Red Brigades. The strong remnants of feudal society in Italy were reflected in the social composition of the group, bringing together glamorous intellectuals with an aristocratic sense of duty fighting ostensibly on behalf of the least qualified levels of the working class against the selfish bourgeoisie. The Red Brigades enlisted old-line Stalinist factory workers and dockers in Turin and Genoa, to the unspeakable horror of the PCI. That small hardline faction of the Italian working class had always felt betrayed by PCI leaders who told the Partisan anti-fascist resistance to lay down their arms at the end of World War II and agreed to play by the rules of bourgeois democracy. This faction, ignoring Stalin's respect for the Yalta spheres of influence, preserved Stalin as its symbol of uncompromising communist revolution, against "revisionist" PCI leaders.

This key factor of reality was clearly understood in the PCI and ignored by both the United States and the ultra-left: Stalin accepted the Yalta dividing line. There are always wild cards in secret services, but

Soviet leaders in the 1970s had absolutely no desire to promote communist revolution in Western Europe, which could have led to a major war which Moscow was steadfastly determined to avoid. Only the ultra-left and Washington saw such a possibility, and indirectly strengthened each other.

Ultra-right violence, ultra-left violence, plus constant streams of false reports and wild rumors created an atmosphere of confusion in the late seventies, when it was unclear who was doing what. Were the young radicals whose revolutionary actions ranged from disruption to armed violence merely carried away with their own illusions, or was CIA-backed infiltration a factor in the chaos? There were constant rumors of plots, which could never be proved or disproved, especially with a judicial system more focused on oral testimonies than on material evidence. Italy has a long tradition of conspiracy theories as well as of conspiracies, and hardly anyone believed that things were just as they seemed.

In the late seventies, the PCI's austere secretary general, Enrico Berlinguer, seemed to be succeeding in making the party eligible to take part in a coalition government, by a rapprochement with the left wing of the Christian Democrats, who had been in power for over thirty years. This policy was called the Historic Compromise. According to normal Western democratic standards, that would have been a totally natural development. In the June 1976 parliamentary elections, the PCI won 34.4% of the vote, barely trailing the Christian Democrats' 38.7%. And the PCI had gained 7% since the previous elections and showed every sign of gaining more in the future. Aldo Moro, one of the leading Christian Democrats who alternated with Giulio Andreotti and lesser members of Democrazia Cristiana (DC) in the role of Prime Minister, saw advantages in such a coalition.

But the Historic Compromise was an abomination for a wide range of political forces: the revolutionary Left, which considered it a sell-out; and just as fiercely, the extreme fascist right hidden in security agencies; some Catholic conservatives who still worried about atheistic communism, and various branches of the Italian mafia, which had no desire to see progress toward honest government; not to mention certain foreign powers and last but surely not least, the United States…

The Declaration of War

In February 1978, a Resolution by the Strategic Leadership of the Red Brigades amounted to a declaration of war against the Italian State. By this time, Mara Cagol had been killed in a gunfight with police and both Curcio and Franceschini were in jail. The new Red Brigades had been taken over by Mario Moretti, who further expanded and militarized the organization.

The Resolution was 27,000 words of rigid pseudo-Leninist analysis. The various levels of the Italian working class and their relative readiness to install the dictatorship of the proletariat were categorized like Lego pieces in a construction: *Operaio massa* (mass worker, on the factory assembly line, "the most revolutionary"); the professional worker (a step above, the worker aristocracy, a bit too high); and the non-industrial working class divided into six categories, of which manual service workers and the "extralegal proletariat" (criminals) were considered to have revolutionary potential, whereas the "sub-proletariat" was rejected in the terms of Marx and Engels as "the passive rot of the lowest levels of the population susceptible to be led by the reaction…" (Ironically, it was that bottom level that was being idealized by Toni Negri's revolutionary friends in France, Félix Guattari and Michel Foucault.)

The RB saw Italy as a "weak link in the imperialist chain" whose combat must contribute to a world proletarian revolution which they saw as getting underway. Civil war waged by imaginary European Communist Combat Organizations could deter the main enemy, the *Stato Imperialista delle Multinationali* (SIM), from its tendency to initiate World War against "Social Imperialism" (their name for the Soviet Union and the Warsaw Pact countries). The group's ambitions had grown from supporting factory workers to designing world history.

The Sacrifice of Aldo Moro

On March 16, 1978, a major step toward the Historic Compromise was scheduled to take place in the Italian parliament. That is, the DC would continue to form the government, but with the necessary support of the PCI. However, the process ended that very day when it was announced that former prime minister Aldo Moro, Chairman of the Christian Democratic Party and the main sponsor of collaboration with the communists, had been kidnapped by the Red Brigades.

The kidnapping operation was strikingly brutal and professional. As Moro was being driven to work that morning, his car and an escorting police car were blocked in the via Mario Fani by three other cars, whereupon gunmen posted on either side massacred Moro's two bodyguards, including his driver, and three (unarmed) policemen in the escort vehicle behind him. Moro was immediately seized and whisked away in another car.

Two days later, the Red Brigades began to issue communiques explaining their action and making their demands.

There were three stated reasons for the abduction, and a fourth, hypothetical, but widely accepted as decisive.

The first and main reason was to strike at the heart of the "Imperialist State of the Multinationals," to show its weakness and display the force of the Red Brigades—the central purpose of guerrilla action spelled out in the Strategic Resolution a month earlier. In this, the operation was a huge success.

The second reason was to put their prisoner "on trial" and interrogate him in expectation of uncovering the assumed crimes of his party for which he shared guilt. This was not a great success, since Moro's most damaging statements against *Democrazia Cristiana* concerned the party's betrayal of himself, rather than revelations of its alleged crimes against the people. It is quite probable that Moro himself knew nothing about whatever crimes were committed by secret services and Gladio, linked to the CIA.

Thirdly, the capture of Moro could have been the basis for a prisoner exchange, releasing Moro in return for the release of imprisoned members of the Red Brigades. This was a habitual demand in such cases. It was particularly timely, because at that time a tumultuous trial of Renato Curcio and a dozen other *brigatisti* was underway in a Turin courtroom.

But the fourth reason, unconfirmed but widely accepted as crucial, was to block the realization of the Historic Compromise between the DC and the PCI.

The weakness of the Italian state had already been illustrated by the abduction exercise. Aware that he was under threat due to his key political position, Moro had apparently requested a bullet-proof vehicle but had not got one. More amazing, none of his five-man escort were armed. From then on, Italian security forces displayed almost unimaginable incompetence in their fumbling gestures of searching for the place where Moro was sequestered.

The tragic irony was now that the Italian State had proved its weakness, the ruling Christian Democrats were determined to prove the strength of the State by refusing all negotiations with the kidnappers who had murdered five security personnel in cold blood.

That was not the opinion of Moro himself, who, well-treated physically if not psychologically in his secret hideout, was allowed to write many long letters addressed to his wife, Noretta, and to his Democratic Christian colleagues. There were only two possible ways to save Moro. One would be a police rescue, a possibility that appeared increasingly remote, as the investigators ignored hot trails and followed cold ones. The other would be to negotiate with the captors. This was rejected out of hand by the DC-led government. Enrico Berlinguer supported the hard line, both because the PCI advocated a stronger state and because it was necessary to dissociate the legalistic "communists" from "communists" trying to overthrow the state.

A week after Moro was kidnapped, the Red Brigades assassinated a former mayor of Turin. Two weeks later, in Genoa, they fired shots crippling Felice Schiavetti, president of the Italian association of industrialists. Other attacks continued to remind everybody that the Red Brigades were a force to be reckoned with.

To back up their refusal, a number of politicians and media commentators dismissed Moro's pleas on the grounds that as a prisoner, he must be under pressure from his captors. The term "Stockholm syndrome" is one of the gems of popular psychology that manage to reduce complex mental and emotional reactions to an automatism denying human conscience. In his narrow political prison, questioned interminably by Mario Moretti in terms of Marxist-Leninist jargon, Aldo Moro, steeped in Catholic doctrine, language and ethics, must have understood rapidly that he was confronted by a different logic from his own. Since he was intelligent, he had to try to understand. But it must have been clear that it was hopeless to argue with the Red Brigades, and that his life depended more on arguing with his fellow Christian Democrats, who subscribed to his own philosophy.

During his long career, when much younger, Aldo Moro had been *Ministro di Grazia et Giustizia*—Minister of Grace and Justice, a post prosaically titled "Attorney General" in the United States, a nation run by lawyers. The Italian title was more poetic and above all more Christian, giving "grace," forgiveness, priority. There are profound differences between Italian and American culture, and this is one of them.

The political fortunes of Christian Democracy, however hypocritical, rested on a vague confidence in Christian charity.

Ironically, while Minister of Grace and Justice in the 1950s, Aldo Moro had made a point of making long visits to prisons to see to the welfare of prisoners. At the moment he was kidnapped, his wife Eleonora was teaching a catechism class. Aldo Moro was as profoundly Christian as his captors were Marxist-Leninist. But they too were Italians, and not indifferent to Christian culture.

Subsequent testimony by *brigatisti* indicates that Moretti wanted to extract from the government a political reason to free Moro. He had to satisfy his constituency, that is, his secret army that would be dismayed that such an operation had been carried out for nothing. The interrogation had produced nothing worthwhile. Finally Moretti informed Moro's wife by telephone that the only way her husband could be saved from the death sentence would be for the government to recognize that this was a civil war, that the Red Brigades were an enemy army rather than a criminal group, opening the way for an exchange of prisoners.

In his many long letters to his political colleagues, Moro indirectly alluded to their supposed underlying Christian values, recalling that he himself, in a totally different context, had advocated accepting prisoner exchanges in order to save lives. A DC colleague, Paolo Emilio Taviani, claimed this was not true in an attempt to suggest that the prisoner was no longer thinking clearly. Moro responded with indignation. Taviani, he recalled, had served as minister of both Defense and Interior, and had long collaborated with Admiral Eugenio Henke, chief of the SID, closely linked to the CIA and NATO. "In the two delicate posts he occupied, [Taviani] had direct confidential contacts with the American world. Does the fact that he so strongly held out against me suggest some American and German indication?" And it was true that Taviani had always been a leader of the pro-American "Atlanticist" branch of the party, whereas Moro sought more independence, political and cultural.

On April 23, over a month after Moro was seized, Pope Paul VI wrote a note in his own handwriting pleading with the Red Brigades to release Moro, who was a close personal friend since student days. "I am writing to you, men of the Red Brigades … you, unknown and implacable adversaries of this deserving and innocent man, I pray to you on my knees, liberate Aldo Moro simply and without any conditions."

The "without any conditions" meant more to Moretti than the prayers. None of his conditions would be met. There are rumors that the

Pope offered to pay a huge ransom, but the point was to prove that they were a revolutionary army, not common criminals.

On May 9, 1978, Aldo Moro's bullet-riddled body was found in the trunk of a Renault parked in the historic center of Rome, in the Via Caetani, near the headquarters of the PCI and only a bit farther from the headquarters of the Democrazia Cristiana.

The Italian government had saved face by not giving in.

The Red Brigades had saved face by not giving in.

Pope Paul VI, reportedly heartbroken, died three months later, on August 6, 1978.

Italy After the Moro Tragedy

Everyone was suspected of everything. By all indications, the Italian secret services, noted for fascist holdovers, had infiltrated radical groups, and radical groups had apparently infiltrated the secret services. The radical groups were suspected of having been infiltrated by the CIA, the KGB, the Mossad, the German BND and MI16—or more precisely, by Italians working for one or several of those agencies. Suspicions were voiced that Moretti, the BR chief who "executed" Moro, was himself an infiltrated agent of someone or other. I find that hard to believe. But it was strange that the building where the RB had set up a headquarters at 96 via Gradoli, a building with its own tennis courts in a very exclusive suburb of Rome, a few steps away from the American Overseas School of Rome, was itself heavily inhabited by Italian secret service agents—as was the entire neighborhood. A tip-off to the police that the Red Brigades were "in Gradoli" led police to go looking in a town of that name a hundred miles north of Rome, claiming they didn't realize that there was a via Gradoli right there in Rome.

Moro's widow bitterly accused the government of doing nothing to save her husband. He could easily have been found "if things had been done with the common sense of a housewife," she told a Rome court. Eleonora Moro was convinced that international forces wanted to get rid of her husband. He had told her that "Kissinger warned him ominously: either stop courting the communists or you will pay dearly for it."

Eventually, a number of the perpetrators were captured, tried and convicted, spent time in prison and were eventually released. Others escaped, and Red Brigade actions continued for about a decade.

On December 17, 1981, it was reported that the Red Brigades had kidnapped an American officer, General James Lee Dozier, from his apartment in Verona, where he was deputy chief of staff at NATO's Southern European headquarters. He was rescued on January 28, 1982.

Perhaps this comes from spending so much time in Italy, but from the start I believed this kidnapping was staged. There were too many details that didn't ring true. Already it was very odd for four men posing as plumbers to steal a ranking officer from his apartment in a town that was the center of NATO operations in northern Italy, in the part of Italy most infested with fascistic networks. Then, in a press statement, the captors stated that they had kidnapped Dozier because he was an American soldier invited to work in Italy and paid tribute to the German Red Army Faction. Such a mild reproach was not at all in the style of the Red Brigades, which would have denounced him as a mercenary of Multinational Imperialism, at the very least. After his release, much was made of the torture to which Dozier was subjected. But as the Italian writer, Leonardo Sciascia, pointed out, even though they might kill their prisoners in the end, while in captivity they treated them very well (soft bed, good meals) in order to emphasize their difference from the imperialist state prisons which were very much a target of leftist criticism under the influence of Michel Foucault. Finally, Dozier was rescued by a special post-Moro anti-terrorist unit of the Italian police, without firing a shot, letting loose a storm of praise for the efficiency of Italian anti-terrorist operations and pledges of eternal U.S.-Italian brotherhood in arms, including warm congratulations from President Reagan. It was just all too good to be entirely true.

Meanwhile, my friend Tita Viviani had returned to Florence. Her mother had died and she went home to comfort her father, or rather her stepfather, whom she found disconsolate. She was disappointed not to be able to cheer him up, but when she told me her story, I began to understand.

As a young actress in Milan, Tita's mother Silvia was engaged to be married to a banker who in some unclarified incident was shot dead in Buenos Aires. The young woman found herself pregnant, without a husband, in Catholic Italy. A rich mattress factory owner from Pavia, a textile center near Florence, was smitten with the beautiful actress and undertook to rescue her from dishonor by marrying her in time to give the newborn baby a father and a name. Silvia settled with Berto in a spacious bourgeois apartment in Florence, which seemed to have been built for formal receptions, with a vast marble entrance and formally furnished salons. But nobody came. The romantic actress continued to dream of her lost banker and shared her bed with her baby daughter Tita more than with her husband. As for Berto, a staunch Catholic, he forbade his wife to work as an actress or in any other capacity, although he finally allowed her to open a flower shop. Berto was a somber type, saying little, but consuming elegant liqueurs at the end of his meals no doubt contributing to his cirrhosis. The bed had been shared just long enough to produce a second daughter, Barbara, whose overriding interest was clothes. At dinner, Tita would try to liven things up, like a great bird flapping its wings, telling charming anecdotes. But the gloom persisted.

Her renewed contact with a lover she had had before her marriage turned out very badly.

In 1979, Berto died, and Tita discovered that she had been completely disinherited.

The personal rejection hurt her deeply.

She found a secretarial job in another textile firm in Pavia, and began to commute by car, while looking for a small apartment in Florence. A short time later, she was killed instantly when her car drove off a cliff. No one knows how this happened.

In the late seventies, *In These Times* arranged for me to go to California for speaking engagements, on the subject of the European Left. I was hosted by veterans of the Abraham Lincoln Brigades in the Bay Area and in Beverley Hills. The University of California at Santa Cruz struck me as a little paradise on earth, with its majestic redwood trees, its nearby port and beaches. This natural luxury was the setting for utopian ideas of socialist revolution to flourish. Students and faculty committed to radical change were eager to hear of advances toward socialism in Europe. From Santa Cruz I went to Los Angeles, where I was introduced to the veteran American Communist, Dorothy Healey, and her aged mother, who had been among founding members of the Communist Party USA. After World War II, when the CPUSA had "gone underground"—in other words, disappeared almost entirely—Dorothy Healey courageously stayed visible and audible, with her own regular radio broadcast on political issues. She underwent less harassment than certain others whose refusal to acknowledge their beliefs was exploited to imply dire intentions, which never existed.

I also spoke at a community college in the Los Angeles area, where the reception was much cooler than in idyllic Santa Cruz. After my talk, in the questions and answer period, I was somewhat taken aback when a student demanded crudely, "Why are you doing this? What's in it for you?" In prosperous Santa Cruz, it had been taken for granted, as I took it for granted, that I was doing this because it was "the right thing to do," as when we opposed the war in Vietnam. A bit lower down on the social scale, the ethical outlook was somewhat more cynical and individualistic. Finally, I couldn't say exactly why I was doing what I was doing, it always just came naturally.

On one of these trips to the United States, I visited old friends from the University of Minnesota—Fran Shor and his wife (at that time) Peggy, Jim and Suzanne Cowan—whose devotion to socialism and the working class had taken them to Detroit, where they gave night school courses to factory workers. Even then, Detroit looked like a throwaway city, where people and their homes were used and discarded. In the residential neighborhoods where every other house seemed to be boarded up or falling apart, the "business district" street was devoted mainly to saloons and store-front churches. Drink and pray, the two consolations. I was also surprised to find a town with the daunting name of Hamtramck stuck inside Detroit, which was very visibly a Polish town, full of Poles, Polish signs, Polish restaurants, and leftover signs of New Deal days, such as a portrait of Franklin D. Roosevelt on a café wall. By now, the ethnic composition has changed completely, and I read that it is mainly inhabited by Bangladeshis.

Certainly this was a working class center. My idealistic friends set out to educate the working class, but they soon found that their students were not there to advance the working class, but to get the hell out of it, one by one. Looking around Detroit, that was understandable. But for my friends it was a disappointment that soon sent them elsewhere—the Cowans, to Santa Cruz, the Shors, to Venice.

Back in Italy, the working class movement was experiencing significant setbacks. The most significant political outcome of the Moro assassination was to eliminate the option of the Historic Compromise and to introduce a period of infinite mutual distrust. Extreme left and extreme rightwing violence continued to perturb political life. The horror peaked on August 2, 1980, when a powerful explosion tore apart the central railroad station in Bologna, killing 85 people and wounding some two hundred. This was attributed to a neo-fascist group, as an element in what was called the "strategy of tension," an extreme right effort to cause panic and, if not a right-wing coup, a public desire for order. But it was also an implicit warning to the Left, including to the peaceful Left around the PCI, that repressive force was always waiting in the wings to crush any real move to socialism.

In 1980 the Italian labor movement suffered an historic defeat when a long strike at the FIAT plant protesting against layoffs split the working class. The issue was very complicated, as I described in two articles in *In These Times* (12 and 19 November 1980). After five weeks of strike, on October 14, up to forty thousand FIAT employees marched on the factories demanding that the pickets get out of the way and let them go back to work. To a large extent, the split was categorial: the forty thousand included mostly foremen, white collar workers and women employees. This breach of solidarity was a road mark in the disempowering of the "mass worker." Automation and outsourcing would do the rest.

Everywhere, the working class was being put on the defensive. Elected in 1980, U.S. President Ronald Reagan went on to break the air controllers strike in 1981. Three years later began the epic struggle in which the government of Margaret Thatcher defeated the National Union of Mineworkers led by Arthur Scargill. Thatcher would take the lead in a deindustrialization policy that crippled the British labor movement and dedicated the UK to finance and a service economy. In reaction to these shocks, and to accompanying ideological campaigns linked to "human rights," the European left increasingly turned away from the working class in search of other crusades.

Nobody could know it at the time, but decades later, Italy's little hot cold war has been largely forgotten, or remembered only as an incomprehensible episode of senseless terrorism. In a sense, everybody lost. Not only the Red Brigades, but in the long run, all the players in this passionate political drama. For over two thousand years, history washes over Italy like a series of tidal waves on a rocky shore, but as everything changes, everything remains the same—almost.

10.

Land Where My Father Died

In August 1978 I received a letter from my father that meant a lot to me.

> You seem to be reaching the peak of your powers and living life to the full. You've done it all on your own, against great odds, and what you have done is good. The last because the prominent deeds of so many achievers are most definitely not good. Anyway, not only do I love you as a father should, I am enormously proud of you. You are doing much that I wish I had done, but somehow did not do. I tell myself that I would have if only I had been more gutsy, had not lost confidence in myself just about the time I should have been starting to accomplish the most, but I may be just telling myself that to console myself.

The next year, over the objections of his wife, Polly, who claimed he was too weak, my father visited me and Elizabeth in Paris. A kindly Breton gentleman who kept a pied-à-terre in my building lent it to me to give him a comfortable place to stay during his visit. The three of us visited rose gardens—in the Bois de Boulogne, in the Jardin des Plantes, at l'Hay les Roses and finally at the Chateau de Malmaison where the ex-Empress Josephine retired with her roses. It was a very happy time.

The greatest single influence on my life was certainly my father. As influences go, I could certainly have done much worse. It has become fashionable to speak of "role models," a concept that does not mean much to me. Considering we as simians are always aping each other, from teachers, to characters in books or movies, or simply each other, for better or for worse, I suppose we are all exposed to a kaleidoscope of "role models" which come and go. Rather than in terms of "role," I would say that my father's influence was above all an ethical model. I was susceptible to this influence no doubt because of some innate similarities in temperament—for instance a tendency to worry, to be serious, to be cautious.

This was very different from my mother, Dorothy Bonnell, whose optimism caused her to have several serious accidents (for instance, breaking most of the bones in the right side of her body by riding a rented motorcycle downhill into a wall in the Bahamas. She recovered of course, thanks to that same optimism). She was a living encyclopedia: she could name every type of everything, from dairy cows to ships rigging. I admired my mother, and always got along with her; in fact, I can't recall ever having a quarrel with her. (It was not a quarrelsome environment.) But I did not have the same empathy with her as with my father; I could say that I did not know her as well. However, when she was in her eighties I took her on a tour of Southwestern France where she was thrilled at having "seen Carcassonne," as it was a literary reference.[5]

From my father I assimilated opinions and especially attitudes. He was a rationalist, a realist, a self-declared Voltairian, one who believed in clarity and simplicity of expression. There were also traces of a Victorian and even Puritan heritage in his behavior. I never in my childhood heard a "four-letter word," as they used to be called before they took over colloquial speech. There was great precision of language in my family, which implied truthfulness, something that seemed so fundamental that I was amazed as I discovered that people lied. Nobody ever tried to make me pretend I believed in Santa Claus. Politeness to others was taken for granted. In contrast to the Manicheism so prevalent in America, I appreciated my father's suspension of judgment, his generosity in seeking the best rather than the worst in others, even though I was rather less generous than he was. Finally, most important of all was the combination of intellectual curiosity and modesty, expressed by an image that he often repeated, of the expanding circumference of knowledge: "As our circle of knowledge expands, so does the circumference of darkness surrounding it." (He couldn't recall the source.)

The more we know, the more we know how little we know. But we keep trying.

5 Poem by Gustave Nadaud.

The Last Days

The following are notes mostly taken at the time, for letters to my daughter, and thus some of it is written in the present tense.

10 October 1981, 1:30 a.m. The Call.

The telephone must have been ringing for quite a while before I woke up to answer it. Immediately the sound of the Atlantic waves announced the news I had been dreading. "Your father is dying. They're afraid he won't last through the night."

The voice was that of my friend Joyce. Nobody in my family had bothered to inform me.

It was just past midnight in Paris. No way to leave before tomorrow morning.

And tomorrow morning I was supposed to leave for Bonn to report on the huge October 10 demonstration against nuclear weapons. An event that my father himself would have judged of prime importance for me to attend, especially if he were to die before I got to him.

I took the first plane for Washington at 11:30 a.m. In the plane I wept a lot, thinking of how disappointed he must be to be dying. At 78 I'm sure he wanted to live longer. He wasn't counting on dying just yet.

Only when I got to the hospital and was taken to him did the tears stop. Weeping is a way of rebelling, a refusal. Faced with reality, the emotional rejection has to dry up.

He is very thin, already nearly cadaverous. His eyes are closed by an immense fatigue, and his head rises and falls, rises and falls, as all his effort goes into breathing, with the intensity of an anemone at the bottom of the ocean whose regular opening and closing is the sole and eternal gesture of life.

And yet his high forehead is smooth and he is still handsome, perfectly recognizable even in that solitary concentration on the sole task of breathing, just as he was solely concentrating on tending his rose garden before he was struck down by a stroke.

His wife Polly, sitting on the porch nearby, failed to notice for quite some time.

The rose man is dying.

I am uneasy about describing a seriously ill person as "battling" his illness. Obviously, it is impossible to defeat death, but some can fight better than others, just as it is impossible to defeat gravity but it's always possible to jump higher than others. The omnipresent spirit of competition. Occasionally someone is celebrated for a successful fight against death, like having managed to climb a mountain, or achieve some such physical exploit, before eventually dying anyway.

He doesn't seem to be struggling... no pain, no physical suffering, only weakness.

My father is an emotional man, visibly so. Since childhood I have always been very sensitive to his feelings, his joy, his anger, his sadness. I always hated to see him be disappointed. And dying must be the biggest disappointment of all. Even at age 78. But both the fight and the disappointment blurred and were disarmed by fatigue.

There he is breathing, exhausted, on that adjustable hospital bed, not in a room but an alcove, one of a dozen alcoves arranged in an oval around a command and control center, just like in Houston where they send astronauts into space. Lit screens on which can be read the cardiac rhythm, the vital signs of all the exhausted old men lying in their alcoves attached to electronic apparatuses and dextrose tubes. Will he be sent into space or is it a false alert? In the neighboring room their wives and other close relatives wait.

Outside, the trees are as colorful as the roses. Here, October is the most beautiful month of the year. There are still magnificent roses in my father's garden. But for me, Northern Virginia is hardly a real place. You must find your way along the motorway by counting the shopping centers with their parking lots vast as Boeing runways. Geographic curiosity is missing here and besides, everything changes too often to bother to make a map. One is vaguely aware that at Langley (but where exactly is Langley?) the CIA hides behind lots of trees. The Pentagon, where my father worked, is clearly visible. With Reagan, especially with Reagan, Northern Virginia has one of the richest populations in the United States. For while in the District of Columbia government employees are being fired by the truckload, as a result of cutting the budgets of social programs, the affluence of businessmen and lobbyists is greater than ever in the vicinity of the Pentagon, so many runners running in the great arms race. They rest from racing in four-bedroom houses with two-car garages surrounded by trees and lawns.

The climate is favorable to roses. My father's devotion to these flowering plants led to his becoming President of the Colonial Rose-Growing Society, writing in their bulletin, offering advice to amateurs and creating a rose garden for the nearby Episcopal Church. The roses are his attachment to a land where he does not really feel at home. In recent letters he complained of the smothering heat. He certainly would have been happier in the Minnesota of his youth, near his younger brother Bruce, a botanist as handsome as the male stars of mid-century Hollywood. On our last visit to a large family reunion at Bruce's place, my father showed me the lake where, as boys, they had gone fishing through the ice. Little Bruce had fallen through the ice into Lake Anoka and my father succeeded in pulling him out. Bruce still spent weeks each summer in the Northern Minnesota forests fishing and watching the clouds move rapidly across the blue sky reflected in the lakes. They would have liked to keep going camping together forever.

But we are in Northern Virginia, which is as far as his second wife Agnes, called Polly from her maiden name Pollock, wants to be from her family in New Bern, North Carolina. This attachment was not at all diminished by the resentment Polly harbors toward her elder sister, named Emily but called "Sister," whom Polly accuses of unfairly making off with part of her inheritance. This obsession with inheritance is one aspect of the "interesting sociology" which may have contributed to my father's rapid decision to marry a Southern woman, at full speed after my mother left for another man. Minnesotans do not worry much about inheritance, because they expect to go their own way and prosper. In New Bern, in North Carolina's old South tidewater area, there are not such expectations. Fortunes were made before the Civil War and are clung to. The town lives in its past, with plaques on houses where some forgotten general once stayed. They live around the country club and their ignorance of the rest of the world is stunning. Polly's niece thought that skiing was only done on water. A street bears the name of Polly's family, and she grew up in a town where it was "not done" to greet a black person in the street, even if it was the Mammy who had always cared for her and who knew her better than anyone. Her first husband had left her quickly for her best friend, a subject of which she never spoke (but certain friends knew and told). Beneath her falsely flirtatious ways, Polly suffered from a terrible, angry insecurity.

Polly says now that for a certain time, Paul has been calling for his "loved ones." "An awesome dependence," she calls it. And I am certainly the one he most wanted to see. She hadn't called me, however.

And there is my unknown brother, Paul Jr. He is, above all, Polly's son. He was born when I was sixteen, and I haven't permanently lived with them since he was an infant. On my visits, Polly has always arranged to keep him out of the range of my inevitably bad influence. I don't know him and he doesn't know me, but he has ideas and watches me suspiciously.

11 October 1981. The Lazarus effect.

Once he feels surrounded by his loved ones, he tries to be there, to stay there… Today we experience the Lazarus effect.

There are three candidates for the attribution of this miracle: the daughter who came from Paris, the medical treatment, and God, who is very much respected in these parts.

For my part, I think that what brought him back to life was above all his hope that I will be able to get his memoirs published. He spoke of it as soon as he awakened. His eyes brightened. The manuscript, Diana must take the manuscript. It was his final hope.

We are obliged to keep our visits to the patient short. That leaves me a lot of time left to think about this country where I do not feel at home. I go to the cafeteria for coffee. The nurses who stop by are often obese—yet professionally they know that obesity is bad for their health. Eating is a form of happiness when others are missing.

The only reading matter in the waiting room is a book in the style of "Dick and Jane learn to read." It is *Bible Story I,* that is, the Old Testament, a collection of barbaric tales in which God is constantly perpetrating massacres and genocides that "they had coming to them." How is it that the second volume is missing, the one where gentle Jesus preaches turning the other cheek? I suspect American ecumenism of having reduced the Christian Bible to what it shared with the Jews. American Protestantism depends heavily on the Old Testament. And one can see the United States become more and more Israeli, apocalyptic, paranoiac: "The others don't appreciate how wonderful we are, but we are God's favorites," that adorable jealous, vengeful God. Qualities to emulate.

Three clergypersons from the Fairfax, Virginia, Episcopal Church of the Good Pastor succeed each other on shifts at the patient's bedside. He is a bit special because he provided the church with its rose garden, where his ashes are to be spread. He doesn't want a tomb or other "barbaric customs." As he awakens, his preferences clearly go to the attractive woman minister, very soothing in her manner, who shows no interest in sin or anything else unpleasant. This is the Episcopal Church, after all. Probably a tacit compromise between Polly's aggressive Calvinism and my father's politely concealed agnosticism. The youngest of the three comes to pray, a bit clumsy in his mastery of ideas.

It's Sunday, and so early in the morning I went to the services with my unknown brother. The gist of the sermon: "God loves you, so don't worry about that," and (literally): "The stubs of your checkbook show how you're spending your money and how you're spending your life." Moral of the story: contribute to noble causes by writing a check made out to the Church of the Good Pastor.

I told my father that I went to church out of filial rather than any other kind of piety. I wonder whether he remembers that incident over thirty years ago when my father suggested that my devotion to Jesus might waver. Neither of us ever mentioned it.

This afternoon, he can speak, he even spent a few minutes sitting in a chair… We can agree that it would be more appropriate in church to speak of astronomy, of black holes, which fascinate both of us.

He is still there, he is holding on, and to the general astonishment he has refused to be sucked into the black hole, at least for now. I think it's especially because he wants to finish his memoirs.

He has always needed a project. That and to get along with people, with everybody, to like others and to be liked. That "awesome dependence." Americans are particularly eager to be liked, to be popular. At least compared to the French, I find Americans particularly characterized by an insecure need to be liked. What distinguishes my father is that he has succeeded in being liked by a great number of people (as is clear today) very different from each other. He is at the center, because his personality is richer, with multiple facets. The rest of us are simpler, each in his or her own way, and he is the synthesis.

I am not "his reflection" (as someone said) but rather the reflection of one of those facets. The trying-to-understand-everything side, which alone does not make one particularly liked in these parts. The curiosity and skepticism, the Pascalian sense of being a fleck of dust in the universe, which in his case is balanced by more down to earth things: sports, gardening, helping his neighbors fix things, conformity to the social norms, respectable career, competence and much work according to what organized society demands… And he so excelled in all these acceptable activities that even the heretic facet was seen in him as an extra charm, a whiff of "originality" that needn't be examined in detail.

In any case, in the case of his son, that side is visibly absent. Paul Jr. is his mother's son. He has her southern drawl, her attitudes about things, and she has consistently "sheltered" him from his father, almost as much as from me. Among all these "normal" people who gather, how many recognize the paradox that the strange "daughter from Paris" is the very opposite of a rebel? She is doing what her father would have liked to do.

To cover up the scandal of having tried to pursue wisps of truth (rather than "happiness," whatever that is), I can pass as "a career woman" in journalism—an excuse for the suspicious fact of living in Paris. Conversation is difficult with all the friends and neighbors. Nobody asks me about Europe. Well, almost nobody.

"Do they have ham in France?" It is the unknown brother who poses this question. He is visibly disappointed by the affirmative. He would obviously prefer to have scored a point. I try to build bridges by assuring him that McDonald's are doing quite well in France. "They must hate that," he responds grimly. "The Americans are coming." I reassure him that the French don't hate Americans, and that it seems more to me that Americans are not crazy about the French. He doesn't appear to want their affection.

The night before, the first question he asked to try to maneuver on "my" territory: "What do the French think about the American hostages?" (Referring to the Americans held in the U.S. embassy in Teheran between November 4, 1979 and January 21, 1981.) Sensing a trap, I replied, "the same as Americans, but naturally a bit less." He persevered, suspecting that I was hiding something. "I wonder what would have happened if a country took Russians hostage." Translation: we Americans are too nice, everybody takes advantage of us. My efforts at historic contextualization get nowhere. "The Iranians are criminals, they should be punished."

Paul Jr. tells me that he has some very daring ideas. Contrary to majority opinion, he prefers a conscription army to a professional army. Seeking some common ground, I say that like most French people, I share that preference. He is not interested. He is not looking for complicity.

The old patriarch studied the whole world with curiosity and affection, and thoughtful tolerance. For him, the world was his friend. But the son feels obscurely rejected by the world outside his own day to day experience.

October 13, 1981

Vaguely surprised, transformed from a semi-corpse into a weak old man, the fugitive from death was today transferred from the technological control room to a room with a window.

Polly is collapsing. Amid the Hosannahs and Halleluyahs to a merciful God, she sees herself faced with a period of full-time nursing which can end only in a repetition of the drama we've just been through.

Her dismay could explain why she exploded against me yesterday afternoon. Papa told me that he would really like some ice cream, chocolate if possible. I went to the cafeteria, got the ice cream, brought it back and helped him eat it. Everyone else had left and Polly was still in the waiting room, ready to go. We are not supposed to stay too long and tire the patient. I said goodbye. Papa shook his head, he wanted me to stay a little longer. I hesitated.

Suddenly Polly burst into the room, furious, grabbing me and exclaiming, *"I'm* his wife and don't you forget it!"

I was stunned. I tried to make myself invisible, only answering in a semi-whisper. When we got home, I tried to say that I understood her sacrifice, that she was doing all she could all the time.

But how can I fail to notice that among the many family photos on the recreation room wall, someone is missing?

And despite all that, she knows that there is something between me and my father that is special. And why not? It doesn't hurt anybody. Is this the effect of patriarchal society? Female jealousies of all sorts. The truth is, I was always aware that the bonds between my father and Polly were tenuous, based on very little in common, especially since he married her rapidly on the rebound. I always tried to stay out of the way. I don't think she could recognize that.

Europe and America are two worlds that are moving away from each other much more rapidly than either recognizes. I feel that all that ties me still to America is my frail father, such a slender thread…

October 16, 1981

The hospital called us out of bed shortly after midnight. This was it.

Oddly, Polly chose to wait outside as Paul Jr. and I entered the small room where my father was laid out to die.

A few last looks in each other's eyes, a few words, even a smile.

And then he plunged, almost resolutely, into the black hole…

I was at his side, holding his emaciated shoulder, looking into his half-open eyes. His blood pressure went down, down… The terrible lines on the cardiographic screen zig zagged frantically up and down, then flattened out into a straight line, toward infinity.

The unknown brother was sobbing uncontrollably. I had cried before and now I was silent, in a trance. I understood that his terrible grief was sharpened by regret, regret for what had not been realized between father and son, regret for what should have been.

I had nothing to be sorry for.

The Heritage

According to his wishes, he was cremated and his ashes spread on the church rose garden. I stayed away and later went alone for my own private ritual at the rose garden, where I recited into the air words that seemed appropriate:

> I returned, and saw under the sun, that the race is not to the swift, nor the battle to the strong, neither yet bread to the wise, nor yet riches to men of understanding, nor yet favour to men of skill; but time and chance happeneth to them all.

Then it all turned into a social event. My Uncle Bruce and Aunt Florence had come from Minnesota and their presence was quiet and comforting. Once it was all over, Polly was jolly, back to her Southern belle manner, enjoying the attention. I went out in the woods to shed a few tears.

Now I was totally obsessed with my father's memoirs. They were handwritten on lined yellow paper, quite legible. There were some personal, rather poetic writings. But the bulk of his memoirs was his recollection of his twenty years spent working at the Pentagon. In his few last days of life, the future of his memoirs had been his sustaining preoccupation. Would I take them, would I get them published? Certainly, I vowed. It mattered so much because he could not die without doing something about the distress, perhaps a certain sense of guilt for what he had not been able to do, an anxiety that he suffered from those years in the nuclear war planning machine. He couldn't stop it, but at least, or at best, he could tell about it.

But Polly was already in full Southern concern with who gets the inheritance. I heard hints that there was so little in the will that it was not worth probating. Her anxiety that I might take something else was palpable. It was so overpowering that she would not allow me to take the manuscript unless I left her a copy. It was my mother who helped me find a shop in Washington to copy all those pages.

I flew back to Paris with a mission: to publish my father's memoirs of Pentagon nuclear war planning.

I received one letter from Polly after that, and then silence. I never again heard from either her or Paul Jr, although I wrote to him.

After a month or so, I received roundabout news that Polly had rapidly sold the house and moved to New Bern, North Carolina. She took everything, including certain things my father had brought from China and meant to give me. The will was never probated. In North Carolina, where she was extremely well connected, there was no chance that a court would rule against her in favor of a daughter whose reputation was automatically under a moral cloud by the suspicious fact of living in Paris. I let the matter drop.

My energy was devoted to finding a publisher for my father's memoirs. I contacted the few publishers I knew at the time, to no avail. One of them, Verso, did not want to publish the paternal memoirs but instead asked me to write a book on the subject I was covering at the time. This led to my first book, *The Politics of Euromissiles* (1983).

Thirty-five years later, Paul H. Johnstone's memoirs were published by Clarity Press as *From Mad to Madness: Inside Pentagon War Planning*. The promise was kept.

It must have been around this time, or later, that some news came to me from Minnesota, from some members of our group that went to Paris to meet the Vietnamese. Our cattle farmer, who understood what was the right thing to do, Howard Hovde, had hanged himself. And a bit later, our vegetable farmer, George Panayotoff, also took his own life. They had been enticed into borrowing money in order to further modernize their already productive and prosperous enterprises. They had been caught in the debt trap. They had bravely defended Vietnamese farming people, living in indescribably poorer conditions, but were unable to defend themselves.

This debt trap for farmers was the subject of a 1984 film, "Country," starring Jessica Lange, born in a northern Minnesota village on the edge of the Red Lake Indian Reservation. What to think of a rich country that drives its best farmers to suicide?

PART IV

The Plots Thicken

11.

From Afghanistan to Iran

While the 1970s were wracked by conflicting passions unleashed by the revolutionary fervor of the late 1960s, the following decade marked its definitive defeat, for at least a generation.

There are signs of the times that are trivial but telling. One that struck me was the transformation of Jane Fonda from antiwar militant "Hanoi Jane," a role that brought her under sharp criticism, into a fitness advocate, one which won unanimous approbation. The new emphasis was on neither the mind nor the heart, but on the body. I was reminded of the old classic movie, "The Women," where bourgeois ladies spent their time in beauty parlors and exercise gyms as they concentrated on keeping or exchanging their husbands. Hippies were out of style. Jogging was in.

The French daily *Libération* was a mirror of these changes, especially as it evolved from base demagogy (an early crusade of that broadsheet was to accuse a notary of child murder, essentially on grounds that French notaries have high social status and thus feel free to kill proletarian children) into apologies for hedonism. The liberation it advocated was no longer socio-economic but strictly sexual. This was the new spirit of the times. Sex was liberated from reproduction, of course, and was increasingly a commodity or a sport—even a competitive one. Instead of "making love," one henceforth "had sex."

These changes perfectly reflected the rise of Margaret Thatcher in the UK and Ronald Reagan in the United States. The period of collective passions was giving way to the age of self-love. "My Way" was the hymn of the period.

Journalistic attention was turning toward the Middle East, an area definitely outside my limited experience or knowledge. In the seventies, there was media interest in Palestinian terrorists, such as Ilich Ramirez Sanchez, dubbed by the press "Carlos the Jackal," who led the 1975 attack on the OPEC meeting in Vienna. I was simply never interested in such adventures, and so when, on a visit to the *Playboy* office in New York, I was offered a generous remuneration in exchange for "an interview with a terrorist," I was silently offended. The editors seemed to think that because I was "on the left," I must have an affinity with terrorists. In fact, I always hated violence and wanted nothing to do with it.

As a funny anecdote, on that trip to New York, where a friendly agent was trying to improve my career, I was told by a leading editor that I would do better if my name were "Johnstein." I suppose that sort of joke is common in New York, but I never really liked New York nor wanted to spend much time there.

Afghanistan: Introducing Islamic Jihad

The fairly dormant Cold War suddenly took on a new strategic dimension when the Soviet Union intervened militarily in Afghanistan in late December 1979. The chorus of Western Cold Warriors rejoiced at condemning what was called an invasion, a term they had never used for the U.S. intervention in Vietnam. The floods of crocodile tears left me unimpressed as I read about it, mostly in French publications which were less biased than they have become since. As my focus was on Eurocommunism, I was attentive to the contrasting reactions of the Italian and French Communist Parties. Georges Marchais created a scandal by going to Moscow and approving the Soviet action, whereas Berlinguer's party used the occasion to attempt to increase its respectability by condemning the invasion. But ironically, it was Marchais' party that got into the French government two years later, whereas the PCI was out forever.

Western strategists sagely interpreted the Soviet invasion as a geostrategic move to penetrate southward to the "warm seas" of the Indian Ocean. In reality, Pakistan was very much in the way, and the Russian move was motivated by the desire to keep civil war between two rival communist groups from getting further out of hand. Moscow intervened on behalf of the moderates, with no intention of staying very long. But this was not completely clear at the time.

The Afghan crisis stemmed from failed attempts by Westernized urban elites to modernize the huge, ethnically divided Muslim country. In many Third World countries, "Westernized" meant Marxism-Leninism, seen as the most advanced Western doctrine offering a base for modernizing traditional societies. This choice of allegiance was all the more natural for the educated elite in Kabul since the USSR was a neighbor and the main partner in whatever limited exchanges took place. In the 1960s, the modernizers founded the People's Democratic Party (PDP) which, although small, divided into two opposing tendencies: one (Parcham) which ascribed to the "stages" theory, advocating a slow democratic transition, and the other (Khalq) calling for immediate passage to "communism." On April 27, 1979, the PDP came to power with Mohamed Taraki as head of state.

Radical PDP leader and prime minister Hafizullah Amin took it upon himself to go beyond the "democratic national" stage and try to launch "socialist construction" by drastic reforms in the countryside which the feudal populations rejected. Khalq schoolteachers rushed enthusiastically into the countryside to spread modern education. In the villages, men, women and children were summoned to learn to read and write. Rather than expose their women to such dishonor, the villagers assassinated the schoolteachers. This was leading toward a regional conflict as Pakistani dictator General Zia and anti-Soviet Maoist groups supported by China prepared to exploit the turmoil.

As I reported to *In These Times*:

> Babrak Karmal, brought to power by the Dec. 27 Soviet invasion/coup that overthrew and killed Amin, explained in an interview with the weekly *Afrique-Asie* that Amin's 'massive repression was the conscious application of a plan worked out by the CIA. We know Amin was a CIA agent. His role was to destroy the party from the inside, by physically eliminating all its cadre and leaders, to discredit socialism and the Soviet Union in the people's eyes.'
>
> Babrak Karmal claimed that by attacking 'our Islamic values,' by disrupting the state apparatus and the economy, Amin was creating the best possible conditions for 'an invasion of our country by imperialism according to a concerted plan of the U.S., China and regional reactionary circles'.

In my report, I treated this as a mixture of communist paranoia and vain apologetics.

But it wasn't that simple.

In reality, at the time, President Carter's National Security Advisor, Zbigniev Brzezinski, of Polish nationalist background, was working with Washington's Pakistani vassal and anti-Soviet Maoists to use conflict in Afghanistan to weaken the Soviet Union through its "soft underbelly" of Islamic peoples. Soviet leader Leonid Brezhnev was extremely reluctant to intervene but was misinformed by his security people that the intervention could stabilize the situation rapidly and allow for quick withdrawal. In reality, the USSR found itself bogged down in what the Western strategists triumphantly called "Russia's Vietnam."

Brzezinski himself revealed this in the course of a January 1998 interview with the center-left French weekly *Le Nouvel Observateur:*[6]

> **Q:** The former director of the CIA, Robert Gates, stated in his memoirs [*From the Shadows*], that American intelligence services began to aid the Mujahadeen in Afghanistan six months before the Soviet intervention. In that period you were President Carter's National Security Advisor. You therefore played a role in this affair. Is that correct?
>
> **Brzezinski:** Yes. According to the official version of history, CIA aid to the Mujahadeen began during the course of 1980, that is to say, after the Soviet army invaded Afghanistan, on December 24, 1979. But the reality, kept secret until now, is quite different: in fact, it was on July 3, 1979 that President Carter signed the first directive for undercover aid to the adversaries of the pro-Soviet regime in Kabul. And on that very day, I wrote a note to the president in which I explained to him that in my opinion this aid was going to bring about a Soviet military intervention.
>
> **Q:** Despite this risk, you were an advocate of this covert action. Could it be that you yourself hoped for this Soviet entry into war and sought to provoke it?
>
> **Brzezinski:** It isn't quite that. We didn't push the Russians to intervene, but we deliberately increased the probability that they would.
>
> **Q:** When the Soviets justified their intervention by claiming that they intended to combat secret United States meddling in Afghanistan, nobody believed them. However, there was an element of truth. You don't regret anything today?
>
> **Brzezinski:** Regret what? That secret operation was an excellent idea. It had the effect of drawing the Russians into the Afghan trap and you want me to

6 The translation by David Gibbs and Bill Blum was published by *In These Times* on January 15, 1998. This is my translation, with no significant differences.

regret it? The day that the Soviets officially crossed the border, I wrote to President Carter: We now have the opportunity of giving the USSR its Vietnam war. Indeed, for almost 10 years, Moscow had to carry on an unbearable war, a conflict that demoralized and finally broke apart the Soviet empire.

Q: Nor do you regret having favored Islamic extremism, giving arms and advice to future terrorists?

Brzezinski: What is most important to the history of the world? The Taliban or the collapse of the Soviet empire? A few overwrought Moslems or the liberation of Central Europe and the end of the Cold War?

Q: A few overwrought Moslems? But people keep saying that Islamic fundamentalism now represents a global menace.

Brzezinski: Nonsense! It is said that the West should have a global policy toward Islamism. That is stupid. There's no such thing as global Islam. We should look at Islam in a rational manner and without demagogy or emotion. It is the leading religion of the world with 1.5 billion followers. But what do fundamentalist Saudi Arabia, moderate Morocco, militarist Pakistan, pro–West Egypt or secularized central Asia have in common? Nothing more than what unites Christian countries.

What this totally unprincipled statement really implies is that the United States can make use of Islamic extremist groups whenever this is handy, even if they are trying to subvert more secular Muslim states and hate the West—meaning us. And thanks to Brzezinski, the United State began to ride the tiger of fundamentalist Islam in Afghanistan, by arming the most fanatic Mujahadeen against the modernizers, because the modernizers were backed by the Russians. This was the beginning of the clandestine alliance between the CIA and Osama bin Laden, which is still very far from being fully revealed.

Brzezinski thus opened a new chapter in the saga of "the Great Game" pursued by the British Empire against the Russian Empire in Southern Asia in the nineteenth century. Such distant adventures always give rise to a wealth of pretensions, tall tales, intrigues and deceptions which can only be unraveled by historians, if ever.

The U.S.-backed Jihad against Russia in Afghanistan provided fake philosopher Bernard-Henri Lévy (called BHL) with the opportunity for his first major international grandstanding. Having won media notoriety as a *"nouveau philosophe"* in the mid-seventies, the egocentric pamphleteer used this status to present himself as heroic champion of Afghan freedom fighters. In June 1981, Bernard-Henri Lévy flew to the mountains west of Peshawar, ostensibly to deliver material to enable Afghan Mujahadeen to create a "resistance radio." With his entourage, he spent ten days in the mountains of Pakistan, unable to enter Afghanistan, but taking the time to be photographed in the costume of Afghan fighters. Years later, BHL claimed a twenty-year friendship with anti-Soviet Afghan military commander Ahmad Shah Massoud, whom he had met only once in 1998.[7] A small deception among so many big ones, but a hint as to the publicity methods of BHL.

Iran for the Iranians

While the United States was drawing the Soviet Union into Afghanistan to be attacked by Islamists, it was being kicked out of neighboring Iran. The Shah, Reza Pahlavi, notoriously installed by a CIA coup in 1953, was unable to put down a powerful social revolution fueled by Muslim revival, which looked to exiled Ayatollah Ruhollah Khomeini as its spiritual leader. Needless to say, Washington's sympathy for Islamic Jihad in Afghanistan did not extend to the Muslim uprising in Iran. When Khomeini was forced to leave his Iraqi exile in October 1978, he was allowed to take refuge in France, for geopolitical reasons that remain unclear. In Paris, French experts on Iran were on close terms with an exiled Iranian scholar, Abolhassan Banisadr, whose Ayatollah father was a friend of Khomeini. The secular Banisadr aspired to a modernized, democratic Islam in Iran. This connection may have encouraged optimism as to forthcoming changes in Teheran.

The Ayatollah Khomeini was installed by his supporters in the town of Neauphle-le-Chateau west of Paris, where he defined the aims of the revolution and received visitors and journalists. In November 1978 I went to Neauphle-le-Chateau to interview the Ayatollah. I came wearing

---

7 "Massoud, cet ami récent," L'Express, October 1, 2005, https://www.lexpress.fr/culture/livre/massoud-cet-ami-recent_487406.html.

a headscarf, which didn't bother me as I believe "When in Rome, do as the Romans," and this compound was provisional Iranian territory. Forty years later, it may be hard to grasp how much the Iranian Islamic Revolution was welcomed by the Left, which saw it above all as an end to the brutal rule of the SAVAK secret police, closely linked to the CIA and, less openly, to Mossad.

There was no scoop to be had from such an official interview, which by the way was not my usual way of proceeding. But Khomeini was a phenomenon not to be overlooked. His words were reassuring, both for the West and, more crucially, for his own people. Khomeini promised that the revolution he called for would introduce parliamentary democracy, which was true, but not for very long. The dynamic of a genuine revolution is almost impossible to channel into peaceful electoral politics, and this was soon illustrated.

In December 1978, as a result of truly massive popular protests and violent repression in Teheran, soldiers mutinied and attacked SAVAK agents, causing the Shah to flee. This illustrated an ineluctable rule of revolutions: to succeed, part of a regime's security forces must desert the ruling power and side with the people. Faced with military repression, winning over soldiers is a key element in a successful uprising.

Khomeini returned triumphantly to Teheran in February 1979. On January 25, 1980, after having served in a transitional revolutionary government as minister of economics and foreign affairs, Abolhassan Banisadr was elected Iran's first President, with 79% of the vote. This looked very promising, but the post-revolutionary troubles were already making peaceful transition impossible. The main trouble was the U.S. embassy hostage crisis. Radical revolutionaries demanded that the United States allow them to extradite the Shah and put him on trial. The Carter administration naturally refused to turn over their own client, all the more in that the Shah was ill with cancer. On November 4, 1979, Revolutionary Guards stormed the U.S. embassy, taking the 52 employees hostage to exchange for the Shah. The anti-Americanism of the action aroused enthusiasm among crowds who cared little about the repercussions. Banisadr's presidency was burdened from the start by this crisis, which he deplored but was powerless to resolve. Then on September 22, 1980, Saddam Hussein's Iraq invaded Iran, triggering a long and bloody war, supported by the United States and applauded by Israeli leaders happy to see the two Middle East rivals kill each other. Banisadr narrowly escaped death as he commanded forces near the front lines.

The hostage crisis can be said to have brought down two Presidents. Carter's defeat in 1980 is attributed in part to the inability of his administration to free the hostages. The hostages were released while Banisadr was still president, a day after the election of Reagan, according to a secret deal. But the propaganda success of the hostage taking had strengthened Banisadr's enemies. He lost his power struggle with radical clerics and was impeached by the Majlis in June 1981. The radical revolutionary group, People's Mujahedin-e-Khalq (MEK), led by Massoud Rajavi, helped him escape back to France, but this time the refuge was permanent.

In October 1982, Rajavi married Banisadr's daughter Firouzeh, but the couple were divorced in 1984. A year later Rajavi married the ex-wife of one of his associates, Maryam Qajar, and moved the MEK to Iraq, where it became an ally to Saddam Hussein in the war against Iran. After the United States invaded Iraq in 2003, Rajavi "disappeared" and Maryam took over as leader of the MEK, which is considered to be carrying out subversive actions within Iran in collaboration with Israel and NATO secret services.

So long as he was linked to the MEK, Banisadr and his aides were holed up in the village of Auvers-sur-Oise, known for its appeal to celebrated painters, notably Van Gogh. The atmosphere there was somewhat tense. After his break with Rajavi in 1984, the former first President of democratic Iran was settled permanently into a highly guarded estate in Versailles, where he has remained ever since.

Over the years, I interviewed him many times. He always received me in the most friendly and courteous way. Whatever the purpose of what he told me, I was too obscure to be a useful channel of communication. I welcomed whatever glimpses of the Iranian mystery he offered, but I never flattered myself that I could begin to understand the affairs of a nation I had never visited and whose culture and politics were so remote from my own experience, especially since out of sight, underneath the Iranian drama, the "deep states" of several nations were playing their own covert war games.

12.

Heresy Defines Religion

Around the turn of the decade 70s-80s, a major ideological offensive was underway to erase all traces of the anti-Americanism and Third World sympathy that had characterized the left during the Vietnam War.

In that period, Maria Jolas continued in her role as the American *Grande Dame* in Paris. Her modest apartment on the rue de Rennes still served as a meeting point between American and French intellectuals, such as Arno Mayer and Pierre Vidal-Naquet, who had opposed the U.S. war in Vietnam. Noam Chomsky might stop by when he came to Paris for meetings on linguistics. His contacts with Paris were mostly by air-mail letters in those days when computers were still rare. Chomsky was a prolific letter-writer, and even I got a share.

One of Chomsky's Paris contacts was a mutual friend, Serge Thion, who had drawn on his expert knowledge of Cambodia to defend Chomsky from malicious insinuations that he was "soft on Pol Pot" simply because, in a joint article, he and Ed Herman had pointed to contradictions in reports of death counts under the Khmer Rouge reign of terror. Chomsky was immensely annoyed by those attacks, whose bad faith seemed evident.

I had a clear idea of what was up.

The launch of the "New Philosophers" in the mid-seventies by the weekly *Nouvel Observateur* was implicitly designed to render obsolete "old philosophers," notably Jean-Paul Sartre, who had rejected Cold War anticommunism and sympathized with revolutionary movements. The new, improved brand of philosophers, who had earned their revolutionary credentials by passing through the elite *Ecole Normale Superieur,* May '68 and certain Maoist groups, claimed to have awakened to the horrors of communism when they dramatically "discovered" the Gulag (a very belated discovery, since the Soviet prison system was no longer what it used to be in the 1930s). This epiphany was their way of combating the prospect of the French Communist Party joining in a coalition government with the Socialists. It involved discovering that in terms of human rights, they were on the American side of the Cold

War. The American antiwar movement, which previously had stood as a model, now had to be dismissed as naïve.

Chomsky was the most famous figure in the American antiwar movement, and it was clear to me that an attack on him was an attack on us all.

Chomsky had a fairly low opinion of the most visible aspects of Parisian intellectual life, the faddishness and superficiality of its "star system." He respected Thion for his independence, serious scholarship and free-thinking libertarianism. Chomsky had a record of defending academic freedom, even in the case of such a fierce political adversary as Walt Rostow, whom he considered "a war criminal." Thus when Chomsky was asked by Thion in the fall of 1979 to sign a petition calling on the University and the Government to protect the right to free expression of a nonconformist professor who was being "subjected to a vicious campaign of harassment, intimidation, slander and physical violence in an attempt to silence him," Chomsky readily complied.

The professor was Robert Faurisson of the University of Lyon. On December 29, 1978, *Le Monde* had published a letter from Professor Faurisson on "the problem of gas chambers." The letter began by recalling that early reports of homicidal gas chambers in Nazi concentration camps at Oranienburg, Buchenwald, Bergen-Belsen, Ravensbrück and Mauthausen had all turned out to be unfounded, which showed that rumors could be mistaken. Faurisson, a half-Scottish professor of literature whose specialty was solving the mysteries of obscure texts by French poets, had visited Auschwitz-Birkenau, and found no evidence of gas chambers used to kill people. Whereas every other aspect of the installations was well documented, Faurisson said he found "no order of construction, no study, no orders, no blueprint, no bills and no photos" of gas chambers used for extermination purposes. He concluded, "The nonexistence of 'gas chambers' is good news for poor humanity. A good news that it would be wrong to keep hidden any longer."

I was a regular reader of *Le Monde,* but I missed that letter and would never have heard of it had it not raised a storm of denunciation, demanding that all available retribution be visited on the errant professor. That was what led to the December 31, 1979 petition that Chomsky signed, along with over 500 others, defending Faurisson's right to free expression.

I first got wind of this from the uproar it caused in the Maria Jolas circle when Pierre Vidal-Naquet wrote an article in the September 1980 edition of the intellectual magazine *Esprit* denouncing the petition as a "scandal" because it "never asks whether what Faurisson said was true or false."

That, for Chomsky, was the whole point: when it comes to defending the principle of free speech, you don't ask whether the statement concerned is true or false. And if you disagree with it, then defending the right to express it is that much more imperative.

This led to a lengthy exchange of letters, published and unpublished, between Chomsky and outraged French intellectuals. This quarrel was carried on with rising animosity.

Chomsky fumed that French intellectuals today, despite the tradition of Voltaire, totally failed to understand the principle of free speech. As a didactic exercise, Chomsky wrote an essay entitled "Some elementary comments on the Rights of Freedom of Expression" and gave it to Thion, telling him to publish it as he saw fit. Chomsky's irritation with his critics was not concealed, as he alluded to their "Stalinist" past, to the "communist" nature of their attitude and to the "lack of respect for facts or reason" of certain sectors of the French intelligentsia.

Thion, meanwhile, had befriended Faurisson, who was writing a book defending himself against court suits being brought against him. Thion arranged to have the Chomsky text published as preface to the 1980 Faurisson book, *Mémoire en défense.* Chomsky apparently did not anticipate that this would cause quite such an uproar. As Chomsky was far better known than Faurisson, he became the main target of endless vituperation in Parisian intellectual circles and their related media, virtually equating him with Faurisson's "negationism" even though Chomsky never for a second endorsed Faurisson's findings.

The irrational tone of the attacks led Chomsky to be more angry and dismissive. To show the low caliber of his critics' attacks, he cited as an example a piece published in *Le Nouvel Observateur* by Jean-Paul Enthoven, a close friend of Bernard-Henri Lévy, which claimed that Chomsky's theory of language, generative grammar, "does not allow the means to think of the unimaginable, that is, the Holocaust." The Holocaust was being moved out of the realm of reason.

I had a lot of respect for Thion's intellectual integrity, so I read books he gave me and listened to his lengthy arguments in defense of Faurisson's theories. But I listened with deaf ears. In my precarious social and economic position, I was certainly not going to venture into that particular lions' den. Besides, the issue of gas chambers simply didn't strike me as all that significant; Jews were persecuted and killed, did it matter so much how? In fact, witnessing the effect this was having in the circles I knew, I was ever so slightly annoyed with Noam for turning the Paris intelligentsia against him, because he was indeed the very symbol of the American antiwar movement and any opprobrium that fell on him fell on all of us. Mine was a selfish rather than a principled position, but it was not unfounded. Those who were looking for an excuse to dismiss antiwar Americans as naïve supporters of totalitarianism had found their pretext. There may be no connection, but although I lived in France, my articles were never again published here, although they might appear in Spain, Italy, Germany or elsewhere.

Since no court had ruled that Faurisson was deliberately falsifying history, this episode led to the adoption of the so-called "Gayssot law" in July 1990. Based on an idea of former Socialist Prime Minister Laurent Fabius, and responding to a campaign by the highly influential *Ligue International contre le racisme et l'antisémitisme* (LICRA; originally LICA) the bill was introduced by Communist deputy Jean-Claude Gayssot as an amendment to previous laws on freedom of the press. The novelty was its article 9, which defined as a crime any challenge to existence of crimes against humanity as defined in Article 6 (c) of the Statute of the Nuremberg International Military Tribunal:

> *Crimes against humanity:* namely, murder, extermination, enslavement, deportation, and other inhumane acts committed against any civilian population, before or during the war, or persecutions on political, racial or religious grounds in execution of or in connection with any crime within the jurisdiction of the Tribunal, whether or not in violation of the domestic law of the country where perpetrated.

That is a long list, but what is remarkable about that law is that it has been very selectively applied to alleged denial of gas chambers in Auschwitz, although there is no mention of gas chambers in the law. Even more selectively, "human rights" organizations like LICRA are authorized to sue and collect damages from individuals whose ambiguous remarks fall far short of "denying the Holocaust."

In 2005, Bruno Gollnisch, professor of Japanese language and civilization at the University of Lyon, when plied with questions by an interviewer, said that such questions should be left to competent historians. As a result, he was sued by LICRA and suspended from his university at half salary, until his conviction was overturned by the highest court five years later. It is not far-fetched to suggest that this was due to his important position in the leadership of the National Front.

The strenuous objections by many French jurists and historians to setting a precedent of defining historic truth by legislation have been ignored.

The application of this law is less significant than its ideological function. It legally establishes the Holocaust as a sacred event above ordinary human history—not so much the event as a whole (as nobody questions the persecution and murder of Jews by the Nazis) but specifically the use of homicidal gas chambers. Instead of Holocaust, the French have adopted the term Shoah, with even more religious connotations. In all of history, this is the only version of events which is protected by law from revision or even questioning. This amounts to a religious dogma. It distinguishes the massacre of Jews during World War II as belonging to a category apart from other genocides, which is perfectly appropriate for the Jewish religion, but which clashes drastically with French *"laïcité,"* meaning the absence of government support for any religion. The Shoah is celebrated officially and unofficially, not only in the annual Shoah commemoration but almost constantly in school rooms, trips to Auschwitz, radio and television programs, books and films. It has *de facto* replaced Christianity, which indeed had succumbed to *laïcité* over a century ago, as the State religion. It has its martyrs and saints, its holy scripture, its rituals, its pilgrimages, everything that Christianity had except redemption.

The proof that a doctrine is a religion is when any questioning of it is regarded as heresy. Any challenge to the Shoah faith is blasphemy and can be punished.

Under the religion of the Shoah, France is in eternal repentance for having allowed, while under German military occupation, Jewish children to be deported with their parents by the Nazis. Even the French railroads are sued for complicity. The Shoah religion has cast a veil of shame over France which has undefinable effects. A major contributor to this national shame has been the ineffable Bernard-Henri, whose early writings declared "fascism" to be the very essence of France.

The sense of national shame surely had its origins in the sudden 1940 military defeat and occupation by the German Wehrmacht, despite de Gaulle's extraordinary efforts to restore pride by managing to situate France among the victorious Allies. But in recent decades shame has shifted from the 1940 humiliating military defeat to complicity in the Shoah.

French intellectuals have lamented that "after Auschwitz" it is impossible to write, or even to think. The gas chambers are portrayed as having cast guilt on rationality itself, based on an all-encompassing chain of causality that the Enlightenment led to industrial society and from there to the gas chambers. Suspicion of technology might not be a bad thing if it led people to condemn the military industrial complex, nuclear arms manufacture and war—a more plausible response. The result, however, has been quite the opposite. The Holocaust religion has created an attitude in which war is justified in order to prevent massive slaughter of innocents, the very tragedies that in fact are perpetrated during wars—notably the Holocaust, which took place during World War II.

It is quite thinkable that the mood created by the Shoah religion has contributed to the explosion of irrational, subjective "philosophy" in France. Does "post-modern" mean post-reason, or post-Auschwitz, or both? French intellectual life has become characterized by proclamations of "truth" based on subjectivity uncontrolled by factual analysis.

Who profits from this religion? The first—but not the only—answer is obvious: Israel.

Israeli leaders and the pro-Israel organizations have shamelessly draped themselves in the martyrdom of the Holocaust as the absolute defense of the Jewish State, whatever that State does in persecuting the dispossessed Palestinians or in fomenting endless wars in the Middle East to strengthen Israel's regional position. In France it is widely considered taboo to refer to Israel's vigorous defenders as a "lobby," although in the United States that reality has become too blatant to ignore.

The power of the Holocaust religion owes much to its adoption by the United States, as symbolized by its central shrine, the Holocaust museum in Washington (and similar temples all over the country). By sacralizing the defense of Israel, the Holocaust religion provides yet another pretext for more and more arms manufacture, the solid center of the U.S. economy.

It was not clear at the time, but the main importance of the Faurisson scandal is that his contentions were the first to be officially denounced as heresy, thereby establishing the sacred nature of the Shoah. This sacralization of the Shoah grew just as Israel was becoming more aggressive and more in need of ideological protection.

13.

Deep State Power Struggles

On May 4, 1978, Henri Curiel was murdered in the elevator of his home just off the Place de la Contrescarpe in Paris. The news was a shock, especially as the assassins got away without a trace other than a message sent to the AFP signed "Delta" and announcing: "Today at 2 p.m. the KGB agent Henri Curiel, militant of the Arab cause and traitor to France who adopted him, definitively ceased his activities. He was executed in memory of all our dead."

I never met Henri Curiel. But around 1980, I met a couple who knew him well, and who became my dear friends.

The American George Pumphrey and his wife Doris were living and working in Paris, where they had been granted asylum by the liberal government of President Valéry Giscard d'Estaing. George was a black American from a Maryland suburb of Washington D.C., where his mother was a schoolteacher. George was handsome and smart and studied theater in hope of becoming an actor but was drafted into the Army during the Vietnam War and posted to Germany.

In Germany, George undertook anti-war educational work among fellow soldiers. This led him to meet Doris, the idealistic young daughter of an anti-Nazi Protestant Pastor. Opposition to the US war in Vietnam was her way of carrying on the fight against fascism and war. This activism led George to be dishonorably discharged from the Army in 1970. The young couple married and after considerable difficulties moved to Rockville, Maryland, where they devoted themselves to black community aid projects. At the height of the FBI crackdown on the Black Panthers, George had a sharply conflictual encounter with an armed policeman, which, given the atmosphere of repression, had led them to flee to Canada and from there to France.

In France they were taken under the wing of a highly discreet network called *Aide et Amitié* (Help and Friendship) run by Henri Curiel and his wife Rosette, which worked with Christian organizations to provide shelter and jobs for political refugees, mostly from Latin America and Africa. They helped Doris find a job in the Christian humanitarian organization CIMADE and a job for George as a woodworker in a furniture factory. But their debt to Curiel was much more spiritual and political than material.

As George explained to me, the Pumphreys arrived in France in 1973 with the impatient radical attitudes of young leftists of the period. Curiel calmed them down, teaching by discussion and example the need for revolutionaries to be practical, clear-sighted, non-violent and kind to others. For Curiel the vocation of a revolutionary was close to the vocation of a saint. Curiel himself had been through a lot. He was born in Cairo in September 1914 to a rich and intellectually accomplished Sephardic-Italian Jewish family.[8] Aspiring to a genuine national independence that could lift the Egyptian masses out of dire poverty, he founded the Democratic Movement for National Liberation, one of three or more communist-oriented groups at a time when Marxism was widely considered the key to Third World liberation and development. He was later jailed and then expelled from Egypt by Nasser for his defense of Israel's right to exist.

George and Doris were determined to devote their lives to the revolution, although the shape of that theoretical revolution changed with the times. Kindness was a part of working to improve the world. I moved several times in the following years, and they were always there to do the heavy lifting and furniture arrangements.

They were understandably shattered by the murder of Curiel. So were many others whom he had inspired or helped. Who hated him so much to have him killed? The clues are naturally to be found in his activities leading up to his assassination.

Curiel was deeply involved in efforts to foster reconciliation between Palestinian Arabs and Israelis. He had made practical arrangements for talks in Paris between a Palestine Liberation Organization (PLO) delegation and leaders of the Israeli Council for Israeli-Palestinian Peace, including Matti Peled, Uri Avnery and Jacob Arnon van Amerongen, in the presence of former French prime minister Pierre Mendes-France.

As reported by *Le Monde,* Curiel was in trouble over two kinds of activity: not only helping arrange meetings between Israelis and Palestinians with a view to settling the Middle East conflict, but also due to South African objections to Curiel's aid to anti-apartheid militants who took refuge in France.

---

8 The journalist Alain Gresh, a former editor of *Le Monde diplomatique* and an author of books on Middle East affairs, is his son.

Reproached by interior ministry officials for his "constant secret intervention…in the margins of the Middle East conflict," Curiel replied in a 1977 letter:

> The chance to intervene is something I have acquired at considerable personal cost. I have spent nearly two years in a concentration camp in the Egyptian desert for having defended Israel's right to national existence alongside a Palestinian Arab state. But I have also spent nearly two years in prison in France for having defended Algeria's right to national existence. Although I am a Jew defending Israel's right to exist, Arabs, Egyptians and Palestinians have confidence in me. Although I am a communist defending Palestinians' right to their own state, Jews, Israeli Zionists have confidence in me. That is why I can intervene.
>
> But the second question is even more important… What is the goal of my efforts?
>
> I have not only been a determined defender for 30 years of the right of both peoples to national existence, but also have worked tirelessly to bring them together. As for solving the present crisis, everyone knows my efforts at rapprochement are based on Israeli evacuation of territories occupied in 1967 and the establishment on those territories of a sovereign Palestinian state. Now, those are precisely the positions of French diplomacy…

Yes and no. And here lies the crux of the problem.

President Charles de Gaulle set out a clear policy in favor of decolonization, starting with recognition of Algerian independence, despite violent resistance from colonial diehards who even resorted to assassination attempts. He believed that the era of European empires was past, and that the role of France should be to set the example of an independent nation fostering good relations with independent nations around the world, notably in Latin America and Africa. The policy described by Curiel was indeed the position of French diplomacy—under de Gaulle. But since de Gaulle resigned as President of France in 1969, concerted efforts were being made to reverse that policy. These efforts were mostly out of sight and were intense within Western intelligence agencies.

The Curiel assassination was one of the first events that brought to my attention the deadly conflicts going on in and between Western intelligence agencies. Glimpses of these conflicts, and clues to their meaning, could be drawn from statements by their unofficial spokespersons: that is, by journalists who wrote articles on the basis of "unidentified intelligence sources."

The battleground within intelligence agencies is not simply between agencies of separate countries. Indeed, especially as they grow more complex, more compartmentalized, each intelligence agency is a battleground for its own control, for its own policy line. And according to policy lines, alliances can form between different intelligence agencies, or sectors of them, against opposing sectors in their own agencies.

Every nation needs an intelligence agency with serious analysts to keep its government informed—that is why such agencies are called "intelligence" in English (but more accurately, *renseignements,* information, in French). But much of the work of an agency such as the CIA in actuality is not devoted merely to gathering and analysis of information, but to "Operations"—secret operations which can go from assassination to the spread of false information and creation of "false flag" events. These activities can be designed not only to harm an enemy, or deceive the public, but also—most critically—to influence the leaders of their own governments.

French newspapers linked the Curiel assassination to obscure battles within and between France's two main intelligence agencies, the DST, mandated to protect domestic security, and the SDECE, the secret service supposed to operate only outside the country, comparable to the CIA. During World War II, Curiel and his wife had helped the Free French mission in Egypt, and thus had a special relationship with the Gaullist officers in the DST. Thus, although a stateless political refugee since his expulsion from Egypt and kept under close surveillance, Curiel's activities had been allowed in France, since they corresponded to de Gaulle's conceptions of France's long-term interests in the Third World. De Gaulle saw that by riding with the historic tide of anti-imperialist revolt and capitalizing on France's prestige as *patrie* of revolution, and offering refuge to political fugitives who might be their countries' future rulers, France could best hope to maintain good relations with countries in Asia, Africa and Latin America.

But this policy was always detested by elements within the SDECE, especially those close to the United States CIA. And even more fiercely within the Israeli MOSSAD.

After de Gaulle died in 1970, President George Pompidou named a new director to the SDECE, Alexandre de Marenches who, according to *The Tribune de Genève* on March 5, 1979, "broadened its field of activity, bringing it closer to that of the American and British services, with a new tendency to exercise a 'right of pursuit' onto French territory, through a new division of research on 'subversion and terrorism'."

A crucial aspect of such "research" was to feed undocumented stories of "terrorism" to chosen journalists. The reported source would be "intelligence sources" or "informed sources" or "reliable sources"—never identified by name.

The Watergate scandal did immense harm to journalistic ethics by glorifying "Deep Throat," the anonymous source of major revelations. Deep Throat was in fact Deep State—an unidentified spook. The glory enjoyed by the Watergate journalists accredited in advance a long torrent of such "reliable intelligence reports" of which the most notorious are the "weapons of mass destruction" cited to justify the catastrophic invasion of Iraq in March 2003.

Personally, I was never tempted to cite "unidentified intelligence sources" since they never picked me out for their leaks. You have to be a well-paid reporter on a major newspaper to have such a privilege. I would not have done so anyway. As an obscure correspondent for an obscure weekly, I relied on open sources and thoughtful analysis of known facts. This method turned out to be more accurate than spook revelations.

As an example of the other method, on June 21, 1976, the French weekly *Le Point* published a front-page article by its editor, Georges Suffert, which insinuated that Curiel's organization was cover for a network of "terrorist" organizations, starting with the African National Congress (ANC) and mostly made up of Communist Parties in various countries. The article was addressed to Christians, warning them against being "manipulated" by the KGB on behalf of terrorists. Sued for libel by Rosette Curiel, Suffert acknowledged that Curiel was no terrorist but in his defense produced a letter from a famous Belgian-American journalist testifying that Curiel's membership in the KGB was common knowledge in the Western intelligence community. The letter was from Arnaud de Borchgrave, a mysterious figure who seemed to live in that "community," indeed in several branches of it. I had briefly met him at a reception in Bonn twenty years earlier and was put off by his "I know everything but can't tell you more than this" manner.

Suffert's article, based on de Borchgrave's gossip, was widely seen later as having marked Curiel for elimination, even though Suffert probably had no idea of such consequences. An article that suggests that an individual may be a KGB agent running a terrorist network makes his subsequent assassination seem almost normal.

At this point, Curiel was taken into house arrest in the south of France, officially because of his political activities, although it is more likely that the DST took him out of Paris precisely to protect him from assassination. On his return to Paris, he was finally granted full legal residence. He was assassinated shortly thereafter.

So who did it? Who was "Delta"?

It was generally assumed that this professional killing was the work of some foreign secret agency, possibly with French complicity enabling the assassins to escape. Suspicion fell heavily on the South African Bureau of State Security (BOSS), which was the main source of accusations of "terrorism" lodged against Curiel for his aid to ANC political refugees, particularly his clandestine aid in providing false papers to allow national liberation militants to go back to their countries. (This hypothesis was strengthened by the similar assassination on March 29, 1988, of ANC Paris representative Dulcie September as she was entering her office.)

The Curiel case helped bring to light the symbiosis between certain journalists and elements of Western, Israeli and South Africa intelligence agencies keen on identifying Third World liberation movements as part of a worldwide KGB plot to destabilize the West through terrorism. The purpose of this campaign was to pressure Moscow to cut ties with such movements, to promote the use of the term "terrorist" to stigmatize opponents, and above all, to back a rightist power play within intelligence agencies, especially the CIA.

A milestone in this operation was a 1981 potboiler entitled *The Terror Network* by Rome-based New York journalist Claire Sterling. As I wrote at the time:[9]

> At the start of her chapter on Palestinian Ahmed Jibril, she remarks with false modesty that she

---

9 "The 'fright story' of Clair Sterling's tales of terrorism," *In These Times*, May 20–26, 1981.

> "cannot in his case provide all the usual documented footnotes. A good deal of my information about him came from intelligence sources in Israel and Western Europe." The joke is that almost all the "information"—or accusations—in the book came from the same sources—if not directly in interviews with unnamed intelligence specialists, then indirectly from published reports leaked by those same sources. [...]
>
> [Sterling] has carefully selected only those intelligence sources that uphold her theory that the terrorism of the past decade was all part of a deliberate KGB plan to "destabilize and thus defeat the West."
>
> Thus this book is definitely not a simple product of the CIA. It is, rather, part of a political offensive by a particular faction within the Western intelligence community that seems to be aimed at obtaining operational space within, if not over, the various agencies.

The political offensive operated as a circuit between a handful of journalists, intelligence agency sources, think tanks—especially the Georgetown Center for Strategic and International studies (CSIS)—and politicians. On the basis of her totally unprofessional book, Claire Sterling was called to appear as the opening "expert" witness before the new Subcommittee on Security and Terrorism chaired by Alabama Senator Jeremiah Denton, clearly eager to hear stories that would justify the existence of his subcommittee—as well as providing incentives to heat up the arms race. Other witnesses were Michael Ledeen and Arnaud de Borchgrave.

Exhibit A of Sterling's "terror network" was a "Tucuman Plan" allegedly drawn up in Argentina's Tucuman province in May 1975 by Trotskyist guerrillas of the ERP (People's Revolutionary Army) "under KGB supervision" calling for creation of a "Latin American Europe Brigade" of "1,500 qualified Latin American terrorists" to go off to Europe for "an orchestrated assault on the continent."

Anyone who knows anything about Latin America at that time can recognize this as a total absurdity. But of course provincial U.S. politicians like Senator Denton don't know anything about anything in the greater world out there. The Argentinian police, whom Sterling claimed "discovered" this plan in an ERP safehouse, were part of the repressive forces of the Argentine military dictatorship which at that time were vigorously assassinating, torturing and "disappearing" all resistance. Such beleaguered South American revolutionaries' only interest in Europe was in hope of finding a bit of sympathy and support. How did Sterling come by this preposterous "secret" information? The contents of the Argentinian police report "were told to me by one of the best-informed intelligence analysts in Europe." This source appeared to be Robert Moss, editor of the *Economist Foreign Report* in London, a confidential platform serving up Western intelligence leaks to subscribers. A favorite Robert Moss source was the BOSS. He was co-author, with Arnaud de Borchgrave, of *The Spike,* a fiction characterizing all opinion circulating in the Western world that differed from those of the authors as Soviet disinformation.

Clearly needing to pad out her "terror network" with whatever she could lay hands on, Sterling devoted a chapter to Henri Curiel, insinuating that he was involved with the German Baader-Meinhof band, a connection that no one else had ever even suggested. Eleven footnotes to the chapter on Curiel referred to the already discredited Suffert article in *Le Point,* whose source was gossip repeated by Arnaud de Borchgrave. One referred to the CIA, five to confidential police sources and eight to Robert Moss' *Economist Foreign Report.*

In concluding her smear of Curiel, Sterling used a familiar trick of deniability: "If he did work for the Russians, he was of no use to them once his cover was blown, and what he knew could hurt them."

So, she implied, the Russians both used him and assassinated him.

But the idea of assassinations did not always shock her.

> One of my more memorable conversations in France was with a personage of vast charm and qualified experience who assured me that he would brand me a compulsive liar if I quoted him. If, now and then, I should notice a small news item about a body washed up on a beach, he said, it might well be that of some trained and unregenerate professional terrorist, sent on 'a long, long voyage—very long, madame', in the interests of preserving public order.

This sounds like the late Alexandre de Marenches. She found his subtle boast of assassinating "terrorists" part of his charm.

Sterling's book was promoted by Michael Ledeen, perhaps the most openly unprincipled of the neocons who were beginning their successful infiltration of centers of U.S. power. The Sterling-Ledeen collaboration had its glory days before it.

14.

The Bulgarian Disconnection from Reality

On May 13, 1981, a 23-year-old Turk named Mehmet Ali Agca shot and wounded Pope John Paul II in Saint Peter's Square in Rome. This criminal act initially seemed unrelated to the Italian affairs I was usually following.

The would-be assassin of the Pope was a notorious militant in the neo-Nazi Grey Wolves and a convicted assassin. On February 1, 1979, Agca and an accomplice had murdered the respected editor of the liberal daily *Milliyet,* Abdi Ipecki, an advocate of improved relations with Greece, of separation between religion and State, of defense of minorities—everything the Turkish fascists detested. That summer Agca was arrested, confessed and put in prison, but not for long. On November 24, he "escaped," that is, he was smuggled out of prison, with evident complicity of guards. In hiding Agca told an interviewer: "The secret services are protecting me. I am not worried—no one can hurt me."

John Paul II was then planning to visit Turkey, which enraged Turkish nationalists as a Western intrusion on Islamic soil. Once free, Agca wrote a letter to *Milliyet* warning that if the "crusade commander John Paul" goes ahead with his visit, "I shall certainly shoot the Pope." The visit went ahead, but Agca did not shoot the Pope—until nearly two years later, in Rome.

Then, easily captured in Saint Peter's Square, rapidly tried and convicted, Agca either refused to talk or changed his story constantly. At various moments after his rapid condemnation he claimed to have been ordered to kill the Pope by the Turkish mafia, or by the Popular Front for the Liberation of Palestine, or even by Cardinal Agostino Casaroli, the Secretary of State of the Vatican. Nobody took any of that seriously.

But almost a year and a half later, in his Italian cell, he came up with a new story, which unlike all the others was widely welcomed as a "confession" of the truth: he had shot the Pope on instructions from Bulgarian agents, acting on orders from the Kremlin. The Russians did it!

That was the infamous "Bulgarian Connection" story. After a period of rumors, the story hit Western media with Claire Sterling's article "The Plot to Kill the Pope" in the September 1982 *Reader's Digest.* For Sterling, this was a new chapter in her "terror network," linking Warsaw Pact member Bulgaria, the KGB and Agca's intermittent claim to have once been trained in a Syrian PLO camp in Lebanon—by the way, just as Israel was invading Lebanon in order to destroy the PLO leadership there.

An Italian Story, After All

Since events were happening in Italy, involving Italians in key roles and amply covered by Italian media, I saw this largely as an Italian story. Using open sources, I tried to analyze available facts according to a simple criterion: what makes sense and what doesn't. The "Bulgarian Connection" was presented by its promoters as primarily a Polish story, linked to the Solidarnosc labor uprising. According to this theory, the assassination attempt was a KGB plot to prevent the Polish Pope from going to Poland to stop a Soviet invasion. But despite the Pope being hospitalized, there was no Soviet invasion. In reality, both the Vatican and the Kremlin were fundamentally conservative organizations, with more serious ways of dealing with each other than bungled assassination attempts.

In January 1983, I observed that accusing the Kremlin did not square with "the delicate 'historic compromise' between the Church and Communist authorities in Poland where Catholicism has thrived under Communist 'totalitarian' tyranny as it rarely thrives anywhere else in the modern 'free world'. … In recent months, the mediating role of the Catholic Church may be all that has saved Poland from civil war and enabled General Jaruzelski to keep the lid on without major bloodshed."

But the most suspicious part of the story was Agca's belated confession itself.

> In an all-day parliamentary session devoted to the Bulgarian connection on December 20, Defense Minister Lelio Lagorio did his best to link Bulgarians to the Red Brigades and a drug and arms smuggling ring (whose more flagrant 'American connection' was quickly swept under the rug), but he failed to provide any solid evidence.

> But Lagorio said something else that was much more significant. He explained that Ali Agca had been persuaded to disclose the Bulgarian connection by Italian intelligence agents who visited him in Ascoli Piceno prison in late December 1981 and throughout 1982. He added that Italian and Turkish secret services had cooperated on the case and had attended a high-level meeting in Ankara in April. …
>
> Lagorio also disclosed that the Italian intelligence agency SISMI had put together a photo album of all Bulgarians residing in Rome, especially those working either for the embassy or for commercial or tourist agencies. What convinced investigating Judge Ilario Martella to take Ali Agca's accusations seriously and to issue warrants for the arrest of three Bulgarians working in Rome was the Turk's ability to identify his three alleged Bulgarian accomplices from photographs shown to him.
>
> But what if SISMI had already shown him the same photographs during one of their prison visits while he was being persuaded to 'tell the truth'? Everything Ali Agca has reportedly told Judge Martella incriminating the Bulgarians could have been learned from coaching by SISMI agents.

Later revelations confirmed my suspicions. As time went by, numerous witnesses confirmed that Agca's story was a result of SISMI coaching.

Agca was clearly someone ready to say absolutely anything. In fact, he ended up years later proclaiming himself to be Jesus Christ. But he had every reason to go along with the Bulgarian Connection story. He could be assured that it would guarantee comfortable prison conditions. It made him a media star. And shifting the blame to the communist Warsaw Pact enemy was a neat twist.

The accusation in Claire Sterling's article was taken up on a special September 1, 1982 NBC television report by Marvin Kalb, claiming that the Kremlin decided to eliminate the Pope after he wrote a personal letter to Brezhnev in August 1980 saying that if the Soviets invaded Poland, he would give up the papacy to return to Poland and lead the resistance.

Kalb did not get this shattering information either from the Vatican or from the Kremlin, which both denied the letter's existence. Kalb's sources were essentially his "consultants," Claire Sterling and the former CIA station chief in Turkey, Paul Henze.

The motivations of Claire Sterling, who was building a profitable career as a specialist in KGB-inspired international terrorism, and of CIA propaganda specialist Paul Henze, are not hard to guess. But the ones actively pursuing the case were Italians. What about them? That particularly interested me.

> Defense Minister Lagorio is a Socialist, and the Italian Socialist Party (PSI) has been leading the charge against the Bulgarians. The domestic political reasons for their zeal are not hard to spot. One is the usual desire to put strains on the Italian Communist Party, whose pro-Soviet minority and Eurocommunist majority may be driven into sharper conflict by attacks on the Eastern bloc. The clamor to break off commercial relations with Bulgaria and other Eastern countries might also hurt the PCI financially, since part of that trade is in the hands of companies close to the PCI.
>
> But the most serious motive is the Socialists' desperate attempts to attract the favors of the Reagan administration. [...] How can the PSI, with its 'Socialist' label, gain the preference of the right-wing ideologues in the Reagan administration over a party that calls itself 'Christian' and is adopting Reagan's economic policies?
>
> The obvious answer is: take the lead in the anti-Soviet crusade.

Defense Minister Lagorio was then stressing his commitment to installation of U.S. cruise missiles in Sicily, and the "Bulgarian connection" provided a public relations pretext. This was the way that the much smaller Italian Socialist Party could win favor in Washington over the Christian Democrats, who had always been the American favorite but which recently had suffered from multiple scandals and whose leaders were wary of pro-Israel U.S. policy in the Middle East.

As I saw it then, and still see it today, the Bulgarian connection was an episode in the all-out drive by the "war party" in Washington to gain control of the CIA and the U.S. foreign policy establishment. And this was done with help from NATO allies who had internalized the need for U.S. protection, whether from Russia or from their own domestic left.

As I wrote in January 1983, "It should never be forgotten that the success of an imperialist power like the U.S. is due to the presence in every client nation of an elite that pleads for U.S. protection. And these elites may go to great lengths to exaggerate, distort or even invent threats likely to impress American leaders."

The trial of three Bulgarians and five Turks charged with conspiracy in the 1981 attempt on the life of Pope Jean Paul II opened in Rome on May 27, 1985. The trial ended on March 29, 1986 with a verdict of acquittal for all the defendants. Thus, although finally totally discredited for lack of evidence, the Bulgarian connection story colored public consciousness for years and probably still lingers on in many minds as a vague impression that the Bulgarians tried to kill the Pope. The whole story was meticulously recounted and debunked by Edward S. Herman and Frank Brodhead in their 1986 book, *The Rise and Fall of the Bulgarian Connection.* In the preface, they mention my reports to point up the failure of mainstream media:

> The failure of the western media to meet its own alleged professional standards is illustrated and dramatized by comparing its handling of the case to that of a single reporter, Diana Johnstone. It is our belief that between May 13, 1981, and August 1985, Johnstone, writing on the Bulgarian Connection and related issues for a small weekly newspaper, *In These Times* (circulation about 30,000), conveyed more relevant facts, used more pertinent documentary materials, and provided more intelligent analysis and insight on the Bulgarian Connection than the entire U.S. mass media taken together—radio, TV, newspapers, and weekly news magazines. While this is a testimonial to Johnstone's abilities, it is also indicative of structurally based blinders that hamper and constrain mass media investigative efforts and reporting.

Indeed, that is the final point of the Bulgarian Connection: it illustrated how easy it was to build a major international political scandal out of a "confession" methodically extracted by intelligence agents from a convicted pathological killer and sold to the public by mass media. It is all too easy to tell the American public wild tales about "the rest of the world," about which their school system has taught them little. Instead of serving to educate the public, mainstream media easily go along with a story that conforms to standard prejudices and power interests. This was a very bad lesson for the future. It is a lesson that has notoriously been learned and applied. The story was used and thrown away, but it was useful while it lasted.

Hints of the real story sometimes trickled into mainstream media. In January 1983, Henry Kamm of *The New York Times* noted the skepticism within Western intelligence agencies, which suspected that "rivalry within the Italian internal security agencies, doubtful evidence or outright 'disinformation' may have played a role" in the accusations against Bulgaria. But *New York Times* editors never assigned Kamm or anyone else to do a thorough and unbiased investigative series, exploring all the open sources which I used and which anyone else could have used as well or better. The difference was that *In These Times* didn't assign me to anything; I was free to pursue my search for reasonable explanations as far as I was able. Working for a major media has obvious advantages, especially economic, but it entails a loss of freedom.

A Cast of Shady Characters

The Bulgarian Connection was indeed an Italian story.

Efforts to piece together the intrigue beyond this hoax led to a labyrinth of intrigue revealing some of the sources of the systematic deception which did not end with the Cold War and has been pursued even more vigorously ever since. It took only a small number of people to create and promote a major hoax that thrived for years due to the passive complicity of mainstream media. It succeeded partly because it was "a good story" that fed on stereotypes but more significantly because it served the foreign policy objectives of those who wanted to use the newly elected Reagan administration to reinvigorate the Cold War.

The Bulgarian Connection seems to have originated in the imagination of one man: Paul Henze, described in his *Washington Post* obituary in 2011 as "a National Security Council specialist in psychological operations." His career went from Radio Free Europe in Munich in the 1950s to CIA chief of station in Ethiopia to CIA chief of station in Turkey (1974-1977) to CIA representative to the National Security Council in the Carter Administration, where he served as Brzezinski's chief of propaganda. He was also involved in creating the new policy of exploiting anti-Christian Muslim extremism in Central Asia as a weapon against Russia. For Henze, as for Brzezinski, Russia was the perpetual enemy.

The first public hint of the story came on a right-wing British broadcast over Thames Television, T.V. Eye on September 3, 1981. With Paul Henze as "consultant," Italian Undersecretary of Security Francesco Mazzola presented one hypothetical motive and one fact incriminating the KGB and the Warsaw Pact. The hypothetical motive was that the Kremlin wanted to get rid of the Pope to maintain control of Poland. The fact was that Agca, in his travels between his two crimes, had spent several days in crossing Bulgaria. There was nothing odd or incriminating about that, since millions of Turks constantly pass through Bulgaria for geographic reasons, as a glimpse at a map makes clear. Moreover, there are Turkish criminal gangs in Bulgaria that Agca might have found interesting.

It was Henze who got *Reader's Digest* to assign the story to Claire Sterling. Michael Ledeen joined the press campaign. Thus the whole connection story was ready and waiting for Agca's "confession" to confirm it.

As I reported in June 1985, "Paul Henze has been described by many Turkish writers as the man who has controlled counterterrorism, and with it a series of military coups, in Turkey for the last 25 years. A long investigation by Turkish journalist Mehmet Ali Birand, reported in the Italian weekly *Panorama* last May 26, attributed coups and repression in Turkey to the ultra-secret Counter Guerrilla Organization founded in 1959 and still controlled by Paul Henze, now age 60."

After concocting the story, Henze, Sterling and Ledeen were accepted as "expert witnesses" by major newspapers, widely viewed television programs, and Senator Denton's Subcommittee on Security and Terrorism. Challenging their testimony could raise suspicion of being an apologist for the Soviet Union.

By mid-1985 the Bulgarian Connection story was falling apart, as more information emerged concerning the agitation around Ali Agca's cell in the period when he was preparing his "confession." There were strange comings and goings of intelligence agents, corrupt officials and gangsters such as Agca's fellow inmate at Ascoli Piceno prison, Neopolitan Camorra boss Raffaele Cutolo. Other inmates later said that Cutolo had been warned that he might be killed by guards for "attempting to escape" if he failed to persuade Agca to accuse Bulgarians.

After Henze and Sterling, the third American architect of the Bulgarian Connection was Michael Ledeen, perhaps the most versatile of the so-called "neoconservatives" who have led U.S. policy astray for nearly half a century. Ledeen's relationships with U.S., Israeli and Italian secret services as well as with the media made him the perfect go-between. Originally a scholar of Italian fascism, at various times in his remarkable career Ledeen was Rome correspondent of *The New Republic,* in charge of State Department relations with the Socialist International, a co-founder of JINSA (Jewish Institute for National Security of America), a paid "consultant" of the Italian intelligence agency SISMI, an advisor on Italy to the Center for Strategic and International Studies (the first highly influential think tank advocating what was later called "neoconservative" foreign policy), National Security Council consultant on Iran in the Reagan administration at the time of the Iran-Contra scandal, and an American Enterprise Institute "freedom scholar." As advisor to Secretary of State Alexander Haig, Ledeen had responsibility for dealing with the Socialist International—a sensitive political position, as we shall see, both because Socialist Parties could be a useful tool against their Communist Party rivals in Italy and France and because of relations with Israel.

In Italy, he was widely criticized for trying to influence Italian policy by peddling his own fanciful report on "international terrorism," and for seeking to set up anti-communist "counter-guerrilla training camps." A July 31, 1984 article in the leading Italian daily, *La Repubblica,* declared: "Undesirable individual? The historian Ledeen should stay away from Italy."

Ledeen has been credited by his colleague, Jonah Goldberg, with this colorful definition of U.S. foreign policy: "Every ten years or so, the United States needs to pick up some small crappy little country and throw it against the wall, just to show the world we mean business." True or not, nothing Ledeen has ever said or done has gotten him into trouble or harmed his standing in Washington, D.C.

During the 1980 U.S. presidential election campaign, Ledeen joined with his Italian colleague, high-flying SISMI agent Francesco Pazienza, in a caper intended to contribute to the Reagan campaign against the incumbent, Jimmy Carter. Using Pazienza's connections in the Arab world, they lured Carter's not-too-bright hayseed brother, Billy, into escapades in the Rome Hilton and with Libyan contacts that they then used to accuse him of having made compromising contacts with Yasser Arafat, leader of the Palestine Liberation Organization (PLO).

Ledeen and Arnaud de Borchgrave wrote articles exposing the scandal which, however, never really took off. Carter lost for other reasons (not necessarily more noble). But this helped promote Ledeen onto the CSIS Reagan administration transition team as consultant on Italy, communism and terrorism.

Pazienza was a far more flamboyant international con man than the drab Ledeen. Unlike Ledeen, he got into trouble with Italian law for his role in every major scandal of the period, notably his close involvement with the sinister Propaganda 2 Masonic Lodge, the spider in the net of Italian intelligence agents. Charming and multilingual, Pazienza was a master manipulator but eventually got caught in the cross-fire between opposing sectors of the Italian deep state and fled to the United States for cover. In January 1986, jailed in Manhattan while the Italian government sought his extradition, Pazienza wrote a letter to his Paris lawyer accusing SISMI colleagues of setting him up to take the blame for the Bulgarian Connection hoax once the story was discredited. He said that both Michael Ledeen and Claire Sterling worked for SISMI. By that time, nobody in Italy doubted that they did.

Perhaps this story—and it doesn't stop there—was just too complicated for American mass media.

The classic critique of mainstream media by Edward S. Herman and Noam Chomsky, *Manufacturing Consent,* includes this comment:

> In June 1983, Diana Johnstone, the foreign editor of the newspaper *In These Times* submitted an Op-Ed column to the *New York Times* and the *Philadelphia Inquirer* that summarized the evidence and claims of intelligence-agency visits, the reported threats to Agca that his open and pleasant prison conditions might be terminated if he remained uncooperative, and [investigating magistrate] Martella's proposed deal with Agca. This Op-Ed offering was rejected, and no commentary or news along these lines was permitted to surface in the *Times* or the *Philadelphia Inquirer*—or elsewhere, to our knowledge.

I am pretty sure, although I can't remember exactly, that I wrote and submitted that Op-Ed at the urging of the authors of *Manufacturing Consent.* Perhaps it was meant as an experiment. The results were clear.

Perhaps editors just wanted to keep the story simple, so that readers would easily understand it. Even if simple means false. But it should be noted that "the Bulgarian connection" was useful to various parties. It was useful to Agca, keeping him amused and famous. It was useful to the Italian right in its relentless effort to destroy the Italian Communist Party. It was useful to the American war party, represented by Henze, Ledeen and CSIS, in gaining influence in the Reagan administration. It was useful to the Vatican, not only as anti-communist propaganda, but also as the occasion to enact a characteristically Christian morality play, in which the Pope pardons a repentant Agca in his cell. Nor could leaders of Turkey, a NATO ally, mind having blame shifted to Bulgarians.

The one who had no reward was the hapless Bulgarian travel agent, Sergei Antonov, who spent over three years in prison before being acquitted, a broken man.

15.

The Israeli Connections

It wasn't until around 1980 that I began to pay serious attention to Israel. By then it had become unavoidable, as the repercussions of Israel's "wars of self-defense" had become a major factor in European politics that was impossible to ignore.

As far as I can reconstruct the past, the first time I broached the subject of Israel was in an interview in Paris with exiled Lebanese Christian leader Raymond Edde. At that time, the Maronite Christian community had been taken over by the Gemayel family, which ran a fascist militia called the Phalange. The Edde family, prominent bankers, were rival leaders of the Christian community. Raymond's father, Emile Edde, was a founder of the Lebanese republic and one of its early presidents. Raymond Edde was forced into exile in 1977, and I went to see him at his Paris hotel in May 1980 to learn something about the conflicts between religious communities in Lebanon.

He was a courteous and affable man. He had a lot to say. His words were prophetic.

> We are faced with an American plan aiming at Lebanon's partition, which sooner or later will lead to the breakup of Syria. The objective is to create a number of religious states alongside Israel, small buffer states to contribute to the security of the Jewish state.

Edde explained that American agreement to Israel's plan to partition Lebanon was a result of Kissinger's "shuttle diplomacy" in the early 1970s.

The idea, said Edde, was to dissect Lebanon into geographically based political units corresponding to its major religious communities. This was deemed favorable to Israel because it would make religiously based states the rule rather than the exception and remove the dangers of Arab nationalism or of political movements transcending ethnic barriers. Of course, Israel would be the strongest of such religiously based states, or semi-states.

Throughout the 1970s, Israel helped arm and train the Phalange militia, whose drive to dominate the whole of multi-ethnic Lebanon produced endless civil war. The Israeli aim was not to help the Phalange achieve that domination, but to lead to creation of a separate Maronite state dominated by the Gemayel family, as the first step in dismembering this small but traditionally rich country. The second step would be to support the Druze as they created their own separate enclave, leaving the largely Shi'ite Muslim south unprotected, and vulnerable to invasion from Israel just across the border.

Edde pointed out that Israel did not mean to stop with Lebanon.

"Israel's idea," he told me in the 1980 interview, "is to divide up Syria between an Alouwite state, the minority President Assad belongs to, with 10 percent of the population, a Sunni Muslim state and a Druze state."

I began to get confirmation of Edde's analysis from other sources. At the time, I had met independent progressive Egyptian journalists in Paris, who gave me contacts to interview editors of *Al Ahram* in Cairo during a trip to Egypt.

(The oddest thing about that trip was a rather insistent proposal of marriage from the Imam of Al Azhar mosque, who invited me to tea with his daughter, gave me his photo and wrote to me in Paris to renew his offer.)

An important person in that phase of my education about Israel and Palestine was Livia Rokach, whom I must have met through Chomsky, because he wrote an introduction to her 1980 study of the personal diaries of Moshe Sharett, written between October 1953 to November 1957, when he served as Israel's first foreign minister and briefly as temporary replacement of Ben Gurion. The study, entitled *Israel's Sacred Terrorism,* never found a commercial publisher but was published by the Association of Arab-American University Graduates in Belmont, Massachusetts.

Livia lived in Rome, and for a few years I visited her regularly in her apartment near the Ministry of Grace and Justice ("Grace" was dropped from the name in 1999, as Catholic influence declined). Or we met for lunch in the Campo di Fiori. Livia was in the emotionally difficult position of being a "Palestinian Jew." Her family had lived in Palestine before the State of Israel took most of it. Her father, Israel Rokach, had been a mayor of Tel Aviv and a minister in several Israeli governments in the 1950s, notably Minister of the Interior in the government of Moshe Sharett. Livia was very much an insider and very much an outsider at the same time. She was increasingly embittered by the impossibility of her position and was never a happy person.

Sharett was for using diplomatic means to advance Israel whereas Ben Gurion favored the use of force. This basic difference underlay Sharett's copious diaries. He denounced the crimes in his private diaries but never in public. Livia wrote that Sharett's "intrinsic weakness consisted in his seemingly rational hope that the so-called liberal West would prevent the implementation of his opponents' designs. He relied on the West rather than on the awakening of a local, popular conscience which he had the power and the information to provoke but which as a Zionist he could not and dared not do."

The most striking information from Sharett's diaries concerned Israeli violent attacks on Palestinian villages, airplane hijacking (before Palestinian "terrorists" did the same), hostage taking, provocation, terrorism and "false flag" massacres. They also abundantly confirm the intentions of Israeli leaders in the 1950s to exploit internal difficulties in neighboring countries, both Lebanon and Syria, to break them apart. Everything I had heard from Raymond Edde was more than confirmed.

In a significant passage on the instinct of revenge, Sharett wrote on March 31, 1955 (p. 36): "...we have eliminated the mental and moral brakes on this instinct and made it possible to uphold revenge as a moral value. This notion is held by large parts of the public in general, the masses of youth in particular, but it has crystalized and reached the *value of a sacred principle* in [Sharon's] battalion..."

In July 1954, an action was carried out that says a great deal about the methods used by Israeli leaders toward their allies. The purpose of the action was to prevent or postpone a planned Anglo-Egyptian agreement. Israeli military intelligence issued these instructions:

> Our goal is to break the West's confidence in the existing Egyptian regime... The actions should cause arrests, demonstrations, and expressions of revenge. The Israeli origin should be totally covered while attention should be shifted to any other possible factor. The purpose is to prevent economic and military aid from the West to Egypt. The choice of the precise objectives to be sabotaged will be left to the men on the spot, who should evaluate the possible consequences of each action... in terms of creating commotion and public disorders.

These orders were carried out between July 2 and July 27, 1954, by a network of about ten Egyptian Jews under the command of Israeli agents. British and American cultural and information centers, British-owned cinemas, but also Egyptian public buildings were bombed in Cairo and Alexandria. Suspicion was shifted to the Muslim Brotherhood. The Israeli ring was discovered and broken up on July 27, when one of its members was caught after a bomb exploded in his pocket in Alexandria. This Israeli false flag operation came to be called "the Lavon Affair," after the Israeli defense minister at the time, Pinhas Lavon.

Israel invaded Lebanon on June 6, 1982, primarily to destroy Palestinian refugee camps and drive the PLO leadership out of Lebanon, which it achieved. In September, ostensibly in "revenge" for the assassination of Bachir Gemayel, whose perpetrator was unknown, Phalange militia, urged on by the Israeli Defense Forces, massacred hundreds, perhaps thousands of Palestinians and Shi'ite Muslims in the refugee camps of Sabra and Shatila. The widespread indignation did not harm Western support of Israel in the slightest.

The invasion of Lebanon also corresponded fully with Raymond Edde's analysis. Israeli forces enabled the Phalange to maintain control of Beirut. Then Israel began shifting its praises and military support to the Druze as exceptional fighters. In October 1983, I wrote to *In These Times:*

> What is the U.S.—along with its French, Italian and British allies—doing in Lebanon?
>
> There is a simple, obvious answer: propping up Amin Gemayel's control of his Beirut enclave during the difficult period when it is being abandoned by its Israeli protectors…
>
> Thus the U.S. is doing exactly the opposite of what it says it is doing in Lebanon. It says it is there to support the country's legitimate president Amin Gemayel who represents the last hope of uniting and saving Lebanon. In fact, by saving the Gemayel enclave, the U.S. is making sure that the partition of Lebanon proceeds apace.

Livia Rokach was persuaded by some prominent Arabs to go to Lebanon during the war with the intention of doing public information work for the PLO. She came back disillusioned and depressed. She complained that the "Arabs believe too much in social hierarchy to try to touch public opinion. They prefer oil magnates." It was a "take me to your leader" mentality which Livia felt was totally inappropriate under the circumstances.

Mutual friends told me that Livia grew increasingly bitter and distrustful, and I found that to be true the last time I saw her in Rome. I am not sure exactly what happened, but I learned much later that she faced eviction from her apartment. This could have been too much for someone who suffered from not belonging anywhere. On March 31, 1984, on the day of her eviction, she was found dead in her bathtub, almost certainly a suicide. Finally, her body was repatriated to Tel Aviv.

False Flags and Aliyah

The conflict between Israelis and Palestinians includes a demographic competition. To maintain a Jewish state, Jews must outnumber Palestinians. Indeed, the birthrate among Israelis is very high, but it is also high among Palestinian Arabs.

In addition to the Jews who already lived in Palestine when it was part of the Ottoman Empire and later a British protectorate, the Zionist Jews who settled in Palestine between the two World Wars, and the Jews who fled Europe as a result of unprecedented Nazi persecution, Israeli authorities have gone to great lengths to attract their coreligionists from Jewish communities that had lived peacefully for centuries in Iraq, Iran, Syria or Morocco. It is certain that for Zionists, this was a matter of life and death. Thus they were ready to go to extreme measures to incite Jews into leaving their ancestral homes and move to Israel.

There is some controversy as to how this was done. As I began to pay attention to the Middle East, to read and speak to fellow journalists from Arab countries, especially Egypt (at the time I was a member of the Foreign Press Association in Paris), I learned that it was taken for granted in that part of the world that Israel had used "false flag" violence in order to scare Iraqi Jews into fleeing to Israel.

As usual, there are conflicting accounts of such events. What is certain is that there was a series of bombings of Jewish targets in Baghdad in 1950 and 1951. In eight separate incidents, grenades were lobbed into Jewish targets in Baghdad. The attacks seemed to be essentially symbolic, since few people were killed (four altogether, as reported). Iraqi authorities attributed these bombings to Zionists' effort to accelerate "Aliyah" from Iraq. A score of Iraqi Zionists were tried and convicted by an Iraqi court for having carried out the bombings, and two were executed. Needless to say, Israel has always denied all responsibility. But what is significant is that Iraqi Jews themselves, whether those who stayed or those who left for Israel, believe that the attacks were carried out by Zionist agents as a part of "Operation Ezra and Neremiah" designed to transfer the Iraqi Jewish community to Israel.

False flag attacks, meaning acts of violence carried out by one side to be attributed to another, are a constant of history. They happen in war, and on a smaller scale they happen even in daily life, where they are called "framing." But wartime false flags are not taught in American schoolbooks. At least until fairly recently, it is my impression that most Americans considered it absolutely unthinkable that a belligerent would attack its own people or friends for any reason whatsoever. But it can be a most effective way of influencing public opinion, not only to induce condemnation of an adversary, but also as a means to incite a third party to join the fray.

Middle East conflicts no doubt count numerous false flags, but the most spectacular must be the failed false flag operation that took place during Israel's six-day war in 1967. That was the June 8 Israeli air and naval attack that attempted to, and almost succeeded in sinking the *USS Liberty*, a lightly armed US Navy electronic surveillance ship sent into nearby Eastern Mediterranean waters to monitor Israel's military advance into Egypt.

On June 8, waves of clearly identifiable Israeli planes targeted the US vessel with rockets, machinegun fire and napalm, setting the ship aflame and killing many of the officers and men. Israeli planes had jammed the ship's radio to block distress calls. Next, Israeli naval vessels launched two torpedoes into the flaming ship and strafed life rafts as they were lowered in an attempt to save survivors. The clear intention was to sink the ship with its entire crew. Despite 34 dead, 171 wounded and a big hole in the hull, the crew kept the ship afloat to return to port. Ironically, a Soviet destroyer was the first to offer help, but was turned down by the Americans, who can distinguish their friends from their enemies.

The U.S. government ordered the survivors to keep silent about the event. It was decades before news of the attack trickled out, and mainstream media have persisted in ignoring what happened, even as evidence accumulated that General Moshe Dayan personally ordered the attack.

Why? At first, insofar as it was mentioned at all, it was described as a "mistake" by both Israeli and U.S. officials. Just one of those things that happen in the fog of war. But the survivors saw very clearly that the attackers knew the ship was American and persisted in trying to sink it without a trace.

Again why? The favored theory that they wanted to prevent the Americans from learning about Israeli massacres of Egyptians makes no sense, especially since even sinking a U.S. naval vessel did nothing to shake U.S. support for Israel—on the contrary, arms deliveries only picked up after the six days war. There is only one possible logical explanation for the attack: it was a false flag that went wrong. Had the ship sunk, it was to be blamed on Egypt—or even on the nearby Russians. And this would have been used to strengthen U.S. support for Israel. But this turned out to be unnecessary.

I knew nothing about the USS Liberty until decades later. The presidency of Lyndon Johnson kept it secret, and succeeding administrations did the same. To such an extent that the U.S. government was complicit in the murder of its own service men. The game of chess includes a basic rule of war: you can sacrifice your own pawns.

In France, as I reported in the summer of 1982, the invasion of Lebanon had shaken the strong solidarity with Israel of the French people, even of French Jews, that had been fortified by the six days war in 1967. This was different. Making war against several Arab countries at the same time seemed heroic. Attacking Palestinian refugee camps in Lebanon was something else. This was the act of a bully. Also, there was a strong historic bond between France and Lebanon that did not apply to other countries in the region.

Around lunchtime on August 9, 1982, two well-dressed gunmen suddenly appeared at the end of the rue des Rosiers, the narrow main street of Paris' historic Jewish quarter in the Marais district, and began firing automatic weapons as they proceeded calmly up the street, stopping briefly at Goldenberg's famous Jewish restaurant to lob in grenades and spray customers and employees with submachinegun fire. They vanished as suddenly as they had appeared, leaving behind six dead, including two American tourists, and 22 wounded.

This was more than enough to revive ancestral fears in the Jewish community. Shocked local residents turned their fury against journalists, against President Mitterrand, as if they were responsible, shouting "Mitterrand assassin!"

Was this what the killers were after? Most French political commentators thought so, as I reported at the time:

> The reactions of the people in the Rue des Rosiers were, predictably and understandably, highly emotional. But the crime itself was committed with cold calculation. All witnesses were struck by the easy professionalism of the killers. They behaved like guns for hire.
>
> "So the question being asked all over France is, 'Who profits from the crime?'
>
> In Israel, Prime Minister Menachem Begin lost no time issuing a statement. "Again the cry 'death to the Jews' can be heard in the streets of Paris as it was during the time of the Dreyfus affair," he claimed. "I am proud to be the head of democratic Israel, but above all I am a Jew. If France does not prevent the appearance of neo-Nazi manifestations, of murder of Jews just because they are Jews, I will not hesitate as a Jew to call upon our young people living in France to actively defend the lives of Jews and their human dignity."
>
> In Paris, Begin's statement sounded like a threat to export the Middle Eastern Arab-Israeli war to France, unless France kept its nose out of Lebanon.

Of course there were no "neo-Nazi manifestations," nobody was shouting "death to the Jews" in the streets of Paris. But for decades to come, Israel has quite officially made every effort to present itself as the real homeland of all Jews everywhere, and above all to lure French Jews into making their "Aliyah." The highly educated, successful French Jewish population, the largest in Europe outside Russia, is a main target for Zionist recruitment. Every anti-Jewish act, large or small, is greeted in Tel Aviv as another advertising opportunity. U.S media eagerly echo the claim that "France is anti-Semitic."

The Rue des Rosiers massacre preceded by only a couple of weeks the vastly larger massacre of Palestinians in the Lebanese refugee camps of Sabra and Shatila. If the fascist Phalange did Israeli a favor by mass killing of Palestinians, who did Israel a favor by a shooting spree in a famously Jewish street in Paris? The crime was claimed by the Abu Nidal group of killers, which claimed to act on behalf of the Palestinians. The action could only be meant to distract from the massacres in Lebanon.

What I wrote was the objective truth, considering that what such an action provokes people into thinking is part of the objective truth. I could not be surprised when a Jewish political science professor wrote to *In These Times* complaining about this article, in much milder terms than those employed by Israel's defenders in later years. Professor Isaac stated that he had "discerned an anti-Israeli bias in her reporting, coupled with a troubling insensitivity to the problem of anti-Semitism." He accused me of failing to recognize Jewish critics of Israel. On the contrary, my principal source of information about Israel and Palestine in those days was French-born Israeli poet Maxim Ghilan, director of the International Jewish Peace Union, and editor of *Israel and Palestine Political Report.* He contacted me to ask for my collaboration, and we dined frequently together in the mid-1970s, in a reasonably priced restaurant with Art Nouveau décor near where I was living in the Impasse de l'Astrolabe near the Gare de Montparnasse in Paris.

My American critic wrote that my "Manichean account" had reversed a simple dichotomy of good Jews against wicked Arabs with an equally simple dichotomy of wicked Zionists against good Arabs. I replied in personal terms:

> I grew up at a time and in a family haunted by Nazi persecution of the Jews. Nothing so much marked my early imagination. It was many years before I thought critically about Israel. And I confess that, contrary to Isaac's assumptions, what got me to pay more attention to negative aspects of Israel (all learned from Israeli or Jewish sources) was not so much the Palestinians (whose approach to the political defense of their cause put me off) as alarm at Israel's increasingly dangerous role in the world. Ironically, Professor Isaac is right when he accuses me of not having the same sympathy for Jews as for Arabs, but he has it backward: my adult recognition of the plight of the Palestinians does not equal the sympathy I felt in my early years for the Jews.
>
> In that distant time the horrors of the death camps had not yet been taken out of the realm of

> immediate reality by the word 'Holocaust', with its otherworldly religious connotations [...]
>
> I would not presume to say what is 'the moral inheritance of the Holocaust' The word is strange to me. Over the past years it has seemed to swallow up the events that had such real meaning and transfer them into some closed temple. The Holocaust is being made as remote to non-Jews as the Crucifixion is to non-Christians. Those who do not belong to the religion are told to stay out and feel guilty about it. This does not work, any more than Jews feel guilty for 'killing Christ'. It is perhaps an inevitable part of the whole tragedy that the crime of Nazi genocide, of the 'final solution', has been increasingly turned into a theological concept. This denies its universality and sets up a separation between Jews and non-Jews that did not exist at the time, when opposition to Nazism brought Jews and non-Jews together."

The Palestinian Dilemma

Aside from contacts with Livia Rokach and Maxim Ghilan, both Israeli Jews, one factor that moved me toward sympathy with the Palestinians was the increasing insistence on "the Holocaust" as justification for Israeli cruelty toward the Palestinian inhabitants of the land they seized for themselves. Even in personal terms, I always declared myself immune to emotional blackmail, and this was turning into emotional blackmail on a world scale. Sympathy is one thing, exploitation of sympathy is another.

Ironically, the Israelis from their position of strength appealed to the world on the basis of their suffering (or rather, the past suffering of other Jews), whereas the Palestinians eschewed sentimentality in favor of appeal to their right to their land. Palestinian leaders tried to act tougher than they were. But spectacular acts such as hijackings and the attempt to kidnap Israeli athletes at the 1972 Munich Olympics did not advance their cause. The Palestine Liberation Organization had the disadvantage of being an umbrella organization including radically opposing strategies which had to act by consensus. This no doubt contributed to ambiguity, evasiveness and bluff. For a people who had lived under Ottoman rule and then the British, without strong State institutions of their own, it was difficult to establish leadership legitimacy. As leader of Fatah, Yasser Arafat gained leadership of the PLO, more like a feudal lord than a party chief. Thus he had difficulty in defining a clear strategy that could be accepted by various conflicting resistance forces, especially since the international relationship of forces was too unfavorable to point to any viable strategy. As a dispersed and conquered people, Palestinians were extremely vulnerable to infiltration and manipulation, not only by the Israeli Mossad but even more easily by the agencies of Arab States, all using them for their own purposes, when they were not themselves under Israeli influence.

To put it briefly, the PLO was torn between three potential strategies: armed struggle from bases in friendly neighboring Arab countries, in the context of Arab nationalism; spectacular actions such as hijackings, intended to call international attention to their plight; and negotiations. None of these approaches could be called promising.

Israel's military victories in 1967 and 1973 demonstrated a relationship of forces extremely unfavorable to the Palestinian cause. They illustrated the extreme improbability of a liberation of Palestine by "the Arab nation," which lacked the unity or the capacity. Guerrilla incursions from Jordan were brought to an end in "Black September" 1970 when King Hussein ordered his army to attack the PLO. The PLO base in Lebanon was wiped out by the Israeli invasion and obliged to take refuge in distant Tunisia. For a while, the impossibility of armed resistance encouraged maverick militant groups to carry out actions designed primarily as attention-getters, but Arafat called for a halt in 1974.

What was left? The brutal invasion of Lebanon had aroused unprecedented condemnation of Israel in the West, even among Jews. Perhaps, Western public opinion and Western leaders were ready to pay attention to the Palestinian cause and to sponsor a peace agreement between two States, Israel and Palestine, which was in fact the official position of the "international community." But this would require negotiations: willingness on both the Israeli sides and also with Great Powers as guarantors not to allow any agreement to be sabotaged. Despite strong opposition from militant groups considering any recognition of Israel to be treason, by the mid-seventies the PLO was ready to move toward peace negotiations, which necessitated recognition of Israel, but by this time Israeli leaders were much too sure of themselves to be interested.

PART V

The Fate of Peace-Seekers

16.

Dinner with Dr. Sartawi

The 1980s were marked above all by the aggressive adoption by both the British and United States governments of economic policies that favored capital over labor and deregulation over social services. While the Anglo-Americans were setting the agenda for the next decades, continental Europe seemed to be safely ensconced in its own variations of social democracy. The term "welfare state" is an exaggeration, but Western European countries enjoyed universal health insurance, decent unemployment and retirement benefits, labor protections and a range of essential public services.

As "neo-liberalism" was asserting itself under Reagan and Thatcher, social democracy was pretty much taken for granted on the continent. This was the heyday of the Socialist International, made up of parties which were either in government (in France, Italy, Austria, Sweden, Portugal) or influential leaders of the opposition, as in Germany. The drastic decline of the Italian and French Communist Parties contributed to this preeminence of the Socialist Parties. Social democracy was tacitly accepted as the inevitable wave of the future, and there is little doubt that such a prospect strongly influenced the reformist leaders of the Soviet Union around Mikhail Gorbachev. There, it gave rise to the illusion—very widespread in the European Left—that the only obstacle to universal democratic socialism was the negative image of Stalinism. Get rid of Stalinism and the whole world would become social democratic. And Gorbachev himself seemed convinced that a reformed Soviet Union could be part of "our common European house" along the lines of European social democracy.

In those years I attended various conferences of the Socialist International, with overly optimistic hopes of finding more principled leaders opposed to U.S. aggressive militarism, whether in Vietnam or directed against other Third World countries, such as Swedish Prime Minister Olof Palme and Austrian Chancellor Bruno Kreisky. However, there were not many like them. Palme, Kreisky and Charles De Gaulle were the only European leaders who dared publicly criticize the U.S. war in Indochina.

It was by interviewing him in his London office that I first met Bernt Carlsson, secretary general of the Socialist International from 1976 to 1983. Carlsson was a protégé of Olof Palme and shared his strong commitment to supporting Third World decolonization. They provided political and financial support to liberation movements in Southern Africa. At various Socialist International conferences and on his occasional visits to Paris, Carlsson and I would meet over coffee or dinner, when he would help educate me about Europe's Socialists. From him I learned that SPD troubleshooter Hans Jürgen Wischnewski had not only secretly supported the Algerian National Liberation Front during its war for independence from France, but had actually acted as its treasurer. French intelligence had a huge file on him which De Gaulle shrewdly used to alienate the French Socialists from the German SPD. Another hug in the Franco-German couple. Wischnewski had so many Arab friends that he was nicknamed Ben Wisch.

It was not to be concluded from this that the SPD was devoted to Third World liberation—rivalry with France might be more like it.

In December 1982, Bernt had just come from a Socialist International meeting in Paris, where the SPD had given in to "brazen" insistence by the Israeli Labor Party delegate on sitting in on a confidential discussion of Israeli conduct (notably in Lebanon) in order to derail criticism. Although Mario Soares had been chosen to be spokesman at the subsequent press conference, the Israeli delegate "brazenly" went and sat down next to Soares, who tried to lean away from him. The usually calm Carlsson was so angry at this "grotesque scene" that he walked out of the meeting.

I was interested in the 1980 Brandt Commission Report calling for massive transfer of wealth from the rich North to the impoverished South. Bernt told me that my articles were too kind to the SPD. Willy Brandt is not good on the Middle East, he said. The Brandt Commission assumes mild compromises can solve problems, but this is not possible, and the SPD did nothing constructive when it was in office.

Carlsson told me that he wanted to stay on in the Socialist International but was considering resigning for political reasons. He would say a lot and raise the question: is the Socialist International to be truly international or a mere instrument of the Germans? Was this a socialist international or a German international?

His main concern was Southern Africa. He was beginning to fear that the Third World was losing its struggle for independence. All around him he felt growing exasperation with Third World incompetence, which was accompanied by a new resurgence of admiration for America. He had to hire Canadian or Swiss secretaries because others didn't get the job done. He predicted that as a result of ongoing poverty in the South, the problem for the United States would be to keep out all the people who want to move there. Large scale migration might cause panic in the European middle classes, he predicted, pushing them far to the right.

Backed by Palme, Carlsson sought to use the Socialist International to advance a peace settlement between Israel and Palestine. The political incompetence he deplored was all too common among Palestinian representatives. They did not know whom to address nor how, finally delivering no clear message to anyone. But Bernt Carlsson had found the ideal Palestinian to speak clearly to the West: Dr. Issam Sartawi. He hoped to use the influence of Europe's Socialist Parties to oblige the Israeli Labor Party, which was then in power in Tel Aviv, to accept talks with Sartawi as the start of negotiations for a viable two-state solution.

I met Issam Sartawi in Albufeira, Portugal, in April 1983. He was an impressive man, ruggedly handsome, forthright and articulate. Thanks especially to Bernt Carlsson, I had read and even written about his friendly contacts with Uri Avnery and Matti Peled, prominent Israelis who had responded to PLO overtures for dialogue with progressive and democratic forces in Israel. These contacts were the most positive sign of a possible Middle East peace settlement since 1948.

Dr. Issam Sartawi had worked as a heart surgeon in the United States. After Israel occupied the rest of Palestine in 1967, Sartawi gave up his medical career and founded his own military unit dedicated to liberating Palestine by armed struggle, from bases in neighboring Jordan. After the "Black September" expulsion of Palestinian militants from Jordan, Sartawi became convinced that armed struggle was getting nowhere and that the way to save Palestinian national rights was through negotiations and reconciliation. This was the basis of his new friendship with Avnery and Peled, the search for a "peace of the brave" between former enemies. ("Peace of the brave"—a noble concept America's current leaders seem never to have heard of.)

Sartawi was perfectly suited to seek Western support for Palestinian peace efforts. From his time in the United States he had gained a perfect command of English and his straightforward style appealed to Westerners. After much insistence, he gained Arafat's cautious support for his peace initiatives. That was why he was in Portugal in April 1983, invited by Bernt Carlsson to the annual week-long conference of the

Socialist International. As an unofficial PLO representative, Sartawi hoped to win enough support from the world's Socialist parties to enable him to meet and talk with Israeli Labor Party leader Shimon Peres. That could be the informal start of peace talks.

In the Montechoro resort hotel where the Socialist International conference took place, Dr. Sartawi, accompanied by his assistant Anwar Abu Eisheh, was a brave but lonely figure as he attempted to engage in conversation with the delegates. Socialist Party leaders were intimidated by Shimon Peres' threats to walk out if the Socialist International recognized the PLO. I can recall the face of Peres, frozen in an expression of eternal suffering, as he walked past the smiling Sartawi, pretending not to see him at all.

In a tone of reluctant but righteous respect for order and decency, Peres refused any dialogue with "the representative of a terrorist organization."

I was flattered when Dr. Sartawi invited me to dinner. I had no illusions; if he invited me, it was because he was being shunned by more important people. But I was very happy to accept the invitation. Anwar Abu Eisheh drove us to the popular A Ruina seafood restaurant on the port. Cheerfully, Sartawi ordered "the biggest fish in the house," explaining that, "if we are to die, we might as well die of eating fish."

When we went to our table, although I always prefer to sit with my back to the wall, I quickly took the opposite seat, instinctively letting Sartawi sit where he could see who was entering.

As we enjoyed our fish and white wine, Sartawi spoke at length about his ambitions to make Palestine a paradise. We had spoken with locals in Albufeira who deplored the destruction of their way of life to make way for mass tourism. Sartawi dreamt of a prosperous Palestine without the huge "plastic" hotels booming here in the Algarve region of Portugal. He wanted development to be designed to benefit the people.

"I dragged the PLO kicking and screaming, like a little child, to the Socialist International," he told me. He was all too aware of opposition to peace endeavors on both sides among those who believed that their side could win by force. At the Algiers meeting of the Palestinian National Council the previous February, he was kept from speaking on procedural grounds by those who condemned any peace initiative. He resigned in protest. Arafat rejected his resignation, but his status remained ambiguous—just like his invitation to the Socialist International Congress "as an observer."

"I wanted to insist that the invitation be addressed to the PLO, not to me," he told me. "I pointed out that I might be killed, or thrown out of the PLO, or resign. And you see, I was right to foresee this problem."

Sartawi deplored the "dangerous rhetoric" with which many PLO leaders smooth over defeats, getting farther and farther from reality.

And then he told me an anecdote from his life as a resistance fighter, making incursions from Jordan into the West Bank—Israeli-occupied Palestine. He was leading a military unit at night across the border. There were lights somewhere indicating that the enemy knew they were coming, and that they were going into a trap. And yet it would be wrong to turn back… I can't remember how the story ended. I was too transfixed by its implications.

It was a lovely evening in Portugal.

Two mornings later, when I entered the lobby of the Montechoro hotel, Dr. Sartawi was lying on his back in a pool of blood. He had been shot four times pointblank in the head. He was 48 years old, with a wife and two children. The assassin got away without a trace.

My memories of the immediate aftermath are all the more blurred in that I was in such a state of shock that I lost my eyeglasses. Bernt Carlsson was devastated since he felt responsible for having invited Sartawi into the trap. We met in his hotel room to talk and he would not say a word until he had inspected everything, including my miniature tape recorder. He suddenly distrusted everything and everyone. And his distrust focused particularly on the German Social Democratic Party. The SPD was the leading power in the Socialist International. The SPD financed the Portuguese Socialist Party that hosted this conference. The SPD paid for everything and provided security. How then did an assassin penetrate the hotel, shoot Dr. Sartawi in the head point blank, and then escape down an unwooded hill without being stopped?

With restrained Swedish bitterness, Carlsson went before the delegates to read the letter that Sartawi had addressed to Socialist International Chairman Willy Brandt:

"It is indeed an historic occasion of particular importance and significance that the PLO was invited to the Socialist International Congress as an observer and that it has accepted," he wrote.

The historic significance was that the Middle East "peace process" had been killed before it was born.

Dr. Sartawi was unique because he was able to understand all sides. He could see through everything—including the trap he walked into. He kept hoping that even if killed, he was advancing the cause of the Palestinian people. But no, he died in vain. Without a negotiator of his insight and courage, the so-called "peace process" has been a game of dupes, as Israeli leaders use Palestinian mistakes as excuses to hold onto the whole of historic Palestine… forever.

Aftermath

The assassination was claimed by the Abu Nidal group, which specialized in killing moderate Palestinians on grounds that they were betraying the cause of recapturing the whole of Palestine—a cause which such groups obviously did not succeed in advancing. Once Sartawi was dead, Shimon Peres praised his courage, and publicly noticed for the first time that he personified "moderation." Crocodile tears mixed with the blood on the dull red tiling of the hotel Montechoro lobby.

On May 13, 1985, after two long and confused trials in Albufeira, before clearly baffled local jurors, an inadequate prosecution and a bewildered court-ordered defense, an obscure Mohammad Hussein Rachid was acquitted of having assassinated Dr. Sartawi. He had been identified, and then not identified, as the killer. Although there seemed little doubt that he had been involved, he might have been a decoy. Finally, he was convicted of using a false passport to enter Portugal and sentenced to three years in prison, but the three years had already run out and he went free. The prosecution commented: "Portuguese justice emerges from this affair without prestige and the crime remains unpunished."

Suspicions lingered on. How had a killer been able to enter a hotel where heads of government were gathered, commit a point-blank murder and then walk out and escape down a visible hill? Were Israeli secret agents involved in the murder? Had friends of Israel in the Socialist International simply let this happen? (Bruno Kreisky had warned of secret reports of a plot to kill Sartawi in Portugal, but no special precautions were taken to protect him). Or had the PLO secretly paid Abu Nidal to do the job? And what was the role of Sartawi's young assistant, who quickly recovered from a bullet fired into his leg, but who later retracted his identification of the killer? Such layers of distrust have a demotivating effort on those who might want to be helpful.

The simmering quarrel between Bernt Carlsson and Willy Brandt soon exploded. Resigning from the "German international," Bernt went back to Sweden where he became Palme's special emissary to the Middle East and Africa, entrusted with attempting to promote peace between Iraq and Iran.

17.

The Mysterious North

My memory of Olof Palme is of his sharp eyes as he took in everything around him at one of those annual meetings of the Socialist International. He had the air of someone who took it all in. Palme was unusual in combining a keen knowledge of world affairs with the courage to follow his convictions when they went contrary to the Western consensus made in Washington. In early 1986, he planned an early meeting with the new Soviet leader, Mikhail Gorbachev, to explore ways to respond to Gorbachev's offers of peace and disarmament.

On February 28, 1986, Olof Palme was assassinated in downtown Stockholm as he walked home from a movie with his wife.

A prominent national leader was murdered right in the middle of his capital and a year later, nobody knew who did it. I went to Sweden to learn how the investigation was going. My main discovery was political: After nearly half a century of Social Democratic government, Sweden's security police remained firmly in the grip of right-wingers whose notorious hostility to the late Prime Minister Olof Palme made them prime suspects, if not as perpetrators, then as accomplices of the friendly security forces of another country.

This was based on talks with knowledgeable Swedes in Stockholm and at Lund University. By all accounts, almost everybody in the Swedish Security Police (SäPo) "hated Palme's guts." They had detailed files on him that were by no means for his protection.

I spent a long time listening to Melker Bentler, a retired SäPo officer, in his neat apartment in Stockholm. He explained that right-wing indoctrination of Swedish security police went back to pro-German sympathies in the 1930s. When the Nazis overran Europe, Sweden was allowed to remain neutral perhaps for that very reason. At the end of World War II, the pro-German attitude changed to pro-Americanism. The constant factor was viewing Russian communism as the enemy.

Bentler, who retired in 1980 at age 65 after 27 years with SäPo, told me that the Swedish secret services depended heavily on the CIA, the West German BND and the Israeli Mossad. "What the CIA says is the word of God. They depend on it 200%."

Palme's sympathy for political refugees was not shared by the security services that were theoretically under his command. Bentler recalled that during the colonels' dictatorship in Greece, SäPo passed along information on Greek political exiles to the Greek junta's police via NATO secret services. Although the Swedish Social Democratic government gave aid to the Mozambique liberation movement, FRELIMO, that led the country to independence from Portuguese colonialism, SäPo regarded FRELIMO as terrorists.

Having heard his SäPo colleagues wish that Palme would be assassinated, Bentler's first thought was that the murder was committed by some rightist group with help from SäPo. But such a possibility was never officially investigated.

The investigation of this highly significant political crime was taken over by Stockholm Police Chief Hans Holmer, an administrator with no experience as an investigator, but who basked in media praise as a master sleuth as his inquiries got nowhere. For a year, police were mobilized in the attempt to find evidence that the assassination was committed by some unknown Kurd.

The idea that the Kurds did it came from SäPo, which had long files on political refugees from Turkey associated with the Marxist-Leninist Workers Party of Kurdestan (PKK), which SäPo considered terrorists. SäPo leaked information about "dangerous Kurds" to Swedish media, which eagerly took the bait. Now, whether or not the PKK exiles were terrorists in Turkey, there was no conceivable reason for them to be terrorists in Sweden, least of all at the expense of the Social Democratic leader to whom they owed their safe asylum. But as SäPo and mainstream media saw it, who but a terrorist from a Muslim country would do anything so rude as to gun down a Prime Minister? The invisible Kurd was the perfect decoy. Especially since SäPo had been trying for months to have the PKK refugees expelled. "We told you so!" was their line.

I went to Lund University to learn of the independent investigation by historian Wilhelm Agrell, a prominent expert on Swedish military doctrine and (from 1990) a member of the Royal Swedish Academy of War Sciences. Agrell had examined the case from the logical premise that one can seek a solution from two directions: from technical examination of material evidence and from intellectual analysis of motivation. In an article in a major Swedish newspaper, Agrell complained that there had been no systematic study of the "motive line" and then offered one of his own.

The assassination was clearly a liquidation, not an act of terrorism, he observed. In terms of motivation, a prime suspect was apartheid South Africa, due to Palme's strong political and financial support to the ANC.[10] Nevertheless, Agrell concluded that foreign governments such as that of apartheid South Africa were not ready to go so far as to eliminate a head of a foreign government. Finally, he settled on the "patriotic" motive: the explanation that Palme was eliminated by elements within Swedish security or armed forces that considered him a threat to the nation.

In the years of his leadership, Palme had endowed Sweden with an image as the vanguard of social welfare and peaceful international cooperation between East and West, North and South. Sweden was admired as the ultimate land of peace and progress. Out of sight of the rest of the world, Palme's independent foreign policy, often at odds with Washington, was loathed and detested by a large part of Sweden's upper classes (from which Palme himself originated), by its CIA-linked intelligence services and by Sweden's relatively small but ambitious military-industrial complex.

What made Palme personally most controversial, Agrell told me, was relations with the Soviet Union and the "submarine question": a peculiar hoax that greatly excited the frustrated cold warriors in Sweden's armed forces, who yearned for a good reason to drop the nation's historic neutrality in favor of joining NATO.

Melker Bentler called Russian submarines "Sweden's Loch Ness monster." It had become a national sport to "spot" the shadow or the periscope of an intrusive Russian spy sub among the gliding swans in Sweden's peaceful fjords. For true believers, the fact that none were actually found was proof of the Russians' advanced technology and sinister slyness. But the one time a Soviet sub did actually materialize, it indicated an absence of both. On November 29, 1981, a Russian copy of a 1945 U-Boat of a type called the Whiskey ran aground on the southern coast of Sweden. The crew said they got lost because their compass didn't work. Even British Admiral Ian McGeoch, a commander of NATO subs in the Eastern Atlantic and editor of *The Naval Review,*

---

10 On a September 8, 2010 TV program, Tommy Lindström, head of Swedish Police Authority at the time of the Palme assassination, stated flatly that South Africa was the number-one suspect. The motive would have been to stop secret payments by the Swedish government via Switzerland to the African National Congress. This was not followed up and was one of a dozen or so unproven theories put forward over the years.

said it was "unlikely in the extreme" that this obsolescent U-Boat was on a spying mission. Nevertheless, this clumsy incident, dubbed "Whiskey on the Rocks," gave rise to a Russian submarine spotting mania, which mobilized the Swedish Navy and media on a great Russian submarine hunt. Tabloids even headlined that a sinister underwater Slavic vessel had been cornered and that the trapped Russian crew must "give up or be blown up." But without ever being captured or photographed, the elusive ship vanished—or rather, never appeared. There was not the slightest proof it ever existed. The public alarm engendered by the imaginary Russian U-Boat invasion created a political climate enabling the Navy to demand and obtain increased appropriations from parliament.

Prize-winning documentary film-maker Maj Wechselmann claimed that the whole uproar was a farce staged by the Swedish Navy in order to get more money for equipment. She was sure that Palme didn't believe the submarine incursion stories. "He knew the Russians and the Swedish military too well," she told me in Stockholm. Palme had begun his career in military intelligence and was certainly harder to fool than many other political leaders.

The political risk of contradicting the official military version was daunting. Mass media were also committed to the story. Palme was planning to settle the troublesome submarine dispute in talks with Gorbachev during his planned state visit to Moscow in April. It was his firm intention to use this visit to promote a new era of peaceful relations with Russia and Western Europe. But he had already had to postpone this trip as ultra-conservatives accused him of planning to sell out his country. Top SäPo officials were quoted as describing Palme as a "security threat."

Not only the motivation factor but also material evidence suggested an inside job.[11] Who would have known exactly when Palme would be walking down a main street next to an uphill passageway ideal for a quick getaway? The only obvious answer is the security police who tapped Palme's phone when he spoke of his plans for the evening. It was easy to figure when the film would be over and the Palme couple would leave the theater. The killer had only to wait at the corner for a short few minutes. Several persons were seen in the vicinity of the crime

11 Late testimonies strongly implied Swedish security services, but the case remains officially unsolved. For further developments, see Al Burke, "With Licence to Kill and Cover Up," January 1, 2017, http://www.nnn.se/nordic/palme/licence-to-kill.pdf, and "Death of a Troublesome Socialist," February 28, 2011, http://www.nnn.se/nordic/palme/assassin.pdf.

with walkie-talkies, Agrell told me, and police vehicles were observed in places they should not have been but could have facilitated the killer's escape. But Police Chief Holmer was too busy with his publicized hunt for a guilty Kurdish terrorist to pursue such leads.

As Holmer's investigation collapsed a year after the assassination, and about the same time I visited Sweden to seek explanations for my small weekly, *The New York Times Magazine* sent one of its star reporters to Europe for a month-long inquiry involving more than 100 interviews in five countries. The difference between our investigations was that I gave the names of my sources but Richard Reeves, as is common in the mainstream press, cited well-placed officials who preferred to remain anonymous. And the conclusions were quite different. Reeves found an unwillingness in high places to solve the crime, and a vague theory that the assassination must have something to do with Palme's secret meddling in the Persian Gulf War. There had been secret Swedish arms shipments to Iran, and Iraqis were reportedly angry that Swedish hospitals had treated Iranian victims of Iraqi poison gas. This hypothesis shifted responsibility from the secret services and the military to the Foreign Ministry which, the sources said, had been too involved in Middle East affairs. This was a not too subtle way to condemn the peace efforts of Palme and his emissary, Bernt Carlsson. But for this theory there was not a shred of material evidence and no plausible motive either.

Reeves' article[12] stressed one element which was indisputable: feelings about Palme were very divided in Sweden, and many people in prominent positions were quite content to see him dead. We both also reported that the murder was almost certain not to be solved.

Palme was rapidly replaced as Prime Minister by a modest Social Democratic Party functionary, Ingvar Carlsson, with no interest in or knowledge of international affairs, and whose mediocrity seemed to reassure Sweden's famously conformist population that the excitement was over.

Unofficially but definitively, Palme's death marked the end of Sweden's role as the only Western European country with a foreign policy not dependent on the United States and NATO. While remaining formally on the edge of NATO, Sweden has become one of the most

---

12 Richard Reeves, "The Palme Obsession; The Murder Sweden Can't Forget—Or Solve," *The New York Times Magazine*, March 1, 1987, https://www.nytimes.com/1987/03/01/magazine/the-palme-obsession-the-murder-sweden-can-t-forget-or-solve.html.

ardent supporters of United States renewal of NATO buildup to counter the alleged "Russian threat."

In post-World War II Europe, only two Western countries deviated sharply from the line laid down in Washington. One was France under De Gaulle and the other was Sweden led by Olof Palme. In both cases, the independent policy depended on a single man, who was never fully understood by his people and whose disappearance led to a major reassertion of U.S. dominance in Europe.

Only one other nation west of the Iron Curtain deviated from the Washington line, and that was Yugoslavia. We shall see later what happened there.

After Palme's death, Bernt Carlsson was a political orphan. His experience in international affairs, especially concerning Third World liberation, led to his designation in July 1987 as United Nations Commissioner for Namibia during the Southwest African nation's decolonialization. Carlsson publicly sought U.N. action against foreign companies illegally exploiting Namibia's diamonds, uranium and other natural resources. Carlsson worked hard to overcome U.S. delays to Namibia's independence.

In late 1988, Namibia's independence was finally in sight. On his way to a crucial United Nations meeting in New York, on December 21, 1988, Bernt Carlsson was one of the 243 passengers aboard Pan Am flight 103 when it was blown up over the Scottish town of Lockerbie.

The most plausible explanation of the Lockerbie massacre has always been that it was an act of Iranian revenge for the U.S. Navy July 3, 1988 shooting down of an Iranian civilian airliner flying over the Persian Gulf six months earlier. On July 3, 1988, the *USS Vincennes* had fired a guided missile at the regularly scheduled flight to Dubai that was flying in Iranian air space, and killing all 290 people aboard, including 66 children. Far from apologizing, the United States decorated the military officers responsible.

Many years later, former British diplomat Patrick Haseldine came up with a new conspiracy theory to explain the Lockerbie massacre. Carlsson, the most prominent person aboard, was en route to New York to advance Namibian independence. The South African Apartheid regime probably feared Carlsson's public denunciation of illegal uranium mining in Namibia. According to Haseldine, an official delegation of

22 South African diplomats changed their flight reservations from Pan Am 103 at the last minute.

This proves nothing. It merely shows that the combination of secretive powers and unsolved mysteries are bound to cause people to seek explanations, however erroneous. When so many strange things are happening, it is normal that individuals try to figure them out, at risk of being labeled "conspiracy theorists."

PART VI

The Franco-German Couple

18.

Mitterrand Meets the Markets

Jimmy Weinstein had taken me on as European editor of *In These Times* primarily because of his hope that the European Left, especially in its new form of "Eurocommunism," would encourage the revival of socialism in the United States. I say "revival" because Jimmy was primarily a historian whose books recorded the long forgotten, or buried, history of socialism in America. It was this historical perspective that set him apart. Among his books, *The Decline of Socialism in America, 1912-1925* was a revelation to many who were unaware that there had ever been enough socialism in America for it to decline. The subject was not in the school curriculum, even in a State like my native Minnesota with a history of socialist candidates winning elections. It was this sort of electoral socialism that Weinstein wanted to revive. He spent his life promoting the cause of socialism in America. Despite his deep identification with the Socialist Party of Eugene Debs, Jimmy abandoned that model on grounds that in the United States there is no escaping the two-party system, coming around to the firm conviction that the only way to promote socialism in the United States was to go by way of the Democratic Party.

The multiparty parliamentary systems of continental Europe could not easily serve as models for a rigid two-party system. I am not sure exactly what practical or ideological transfer was anticipated. But if Jimmy Weinstein had been as skeptical as I was, I would never have had this most desirable job. In this way I became an assiduous observer of the socialist and communist parties of France, Italy and Germany, attending their conventions and interviewing their activists.

There was no Eurocommunism in the Federal Republic of Germany (FRG); after being banned in 1956, a small communist party was reborn in 1969 but totally marginalized. In Germany, the Left was totally dominated by the venerable Social Democratic Party (SPD), which had officially abandoned Marxism at its 1959 conference in Bad Godesberg. SPD leader Willy Brandt headed a coalition government as Chancellor from October 1969 to May 1974 when he was forced to resign as a result of an irrelevant spy scandal.

Aside from their contrasting ideas and programs, I felt important differences between them in terms of human relations and mood. The German SPD, in that period, was both friendly and business-like, with important members willing to talk at length about serious matters with a minor journalist such as myself. The French Communist Party (PCF) was rather more like a church, where doctrine was unquestioned but which generated fellowship and solidarity. Attending a PCF conference always entailed a hearty lunch with lots of red wine and good feelings. Everybody left with a warm glow. The French Socialist Party was quite the contrary: torn by rivalries between personal ambitions and conflicting policy lines, a real can of worms.

The only French Socialist I found at all interesting was Jean-Pierre Chevènement, whose study group, the *Centre d'Etudes, de Recherches et d'Education Socialistes* (CERES), had serious policy aims. Chevènement played a key role toward uniting the splintered left around a progressive program, negotiated notably with the PCF. At the time, the PCF was the leading opposition party. The Socialist Party could not form a governing coalition without the PCF.

In 1972, at a time when the afterglow of the May '68 revolutionary fervor suggested the possibility of an electoral victory for a unified Left, the PCF, the Socialists and some Radicals adopted a joint platform, *"Le Programme Commun de Gouvernement."*[13] However, the liberal Giscard d'Estaing won the 1974 presidential elections, and the Common Program had to wait seven years.

The Common Program proposed a long list of 101measures: an increased minimum wage; elimination of all wage discrimination based on age, sex or nationality; lowering the retirement age to 60 for men and 55 for women; numerous measures concerning job creation, public housing, transportation and education, and so on. Many of these measures were adopted without delay.

The crux of the matter, however, was the ambitious program to "democratize the economy, develop the public sector and plan economic progress." This involved considerable enlargement of the public sector, including public service enterprises, companies living off government subsidies, monopolies, mining, arms aeronautics and space, nuclear power and pharmaceuticals. This strong government intervention was intended to bring about French industrial recovery after the negative

---

13 http://www.m-pep.org/IMG/pdf/Texte_Programme_commun_gauche.pdf.

effects of the oil crises of the 1970s. This would have amounted to reviving the highly successful proactive industrial policy of President Charles De Gaulle, with additional social measures.

In foreign policy, the influence of the Left was seen in opposition to interference in the internal affairs of other States—expressed as support for peaceful coexistence, respect for territorial integrity and national sovereignty—as well as for efforts to advance universal nuclear disarmament. The program did not advocate leaving NATO but favored continuing de Gaulle's refusal to reintegrate its joint command while calling for "simultaneous dissolution of NATO and the Warsaw Pact."

The Common Program reflected an illusion that was widespread in the left: the belief that economic unification of Europe could "free it from the domination of Big Capital," democratize its institutions and above all, "preserve French freedom of action to carry out its political, economic and social program."

On May 10, 1981, Valéry Giscard d'Estaing lost his bid for a second term to veteran politician François Mitterrand, whose metamorphosis into leader of a renewed French Socialist Party won him a seven-year term as President, to be followed by a second seven-year term. This would have been impossible without support from the French Communist Party, then at the peak of its electoral strength, which was rewarded by four cabinet posts. In 1936 and 1937, Communists had already taken part in the anti-fascist Popular Front government before leaving in protest against the Munich agreement. The progressive program adopted by the *Conseil National de la Résistance* (CNR) for France's post-war government, gave the PCF a place in that government—until it was evinced in May 1947 as the wartime alliance with the USSR turned into the Cold War. But this time, the victory of the Common Program brought the PCF in out of the cold. U.S. commentators sounded alarmed, which seemed to signal the seriousness of the changes.

In May 1981, the Left was euphoric. This time, nothing stood in the way of strong steps toward democratic socialism. Jimmy Weinstein was enthusiastic.

Ironically, this great new path to socialism was led by François Mitterrand, a basically conservative politician of considerable manipulative skill. He had a great ability to command personal loyalty, even devotion, from his party colleagues. By various manoeuvers, and with sincere prodding from the CERES current, the "Florentine" (as he was called in allusion to Machiavelli) had managed to build a new Socialist Party out of the political debris from the May '68 explosion. With veteran Lille

Socialist Pierre Mauroy as prime minister, and a cabinet including both Communists and a record number of women, the new government of the left embodied more appearance of change than it would be able to carry out.

A year later, the single great accomplishment of the new government was abolition of the death penalty, a personal commitment of Mitterrand. Thus the Socialists began their identification with reforms that were less "social" than what came to be called "societal," more ethical than economic.

As for the economic changes that were at the heart of the Common Program, the world context could not have been worse. Thatcher in Britain and Reagan in the United States were pushing through strong monetarist economic policies that went in the opposite direction. Capital began to flee France as the country experienced repeated currency devaluations. The program of nationalizations was designed to preserve control of capital investment—the absolute key to development—but before taking State control, peaceful nationalizations required paying compensation to private investors.

A major weakness of the Common Program was that it was not propelled by strong popular movements demanding these radical changes. The self-styled "revolutionary" left that emerged from May '68 was largely obsessed with its distrust (even hatred) of the PCF. To go against the dominant current of the capitalist world, a country must be in a mood not of reform but of revolution—ready to accept sacrifices for the sake of a better future. French society was not in a mood for such drama.

The Turning Point

Moreover, the conservative backlash did not take long to materialize. Nationalizations were stalled by litigation and bureaucratic obstacles. Other measures ran into corporatist resistance. Prison guards demonstrated against measures to humanize prison conditions. Hospital directors struck against measures to abolish the private sector in hospitals and physicians struck against measures to equalize medical studies between Paris and the provinces. Truck drivers disrupted traffic to protest against the Left's desire to favor railways.

Meanwhile, both labor and progressive citizens waited passively for things to happen.

In foreign policy, Mitterrand totally ignored the Common Program's leanings toward détente and instead aligned with the Atlantic

Alliance and Reagan's revival of Cold War hostility toward "the Evil Empire" (USSR).

It didn't take long to reach "the turning point," that is, the abandon of the major economic policies. A new policy of budgetary "rigor" was adopted in March 1983.

Finance Minister Jacques Delors presented Mitterrand with a stark choice:

- Either a socially generous Keynesian type economic policy entailing further devaluations that would oblige France to withdraw from the European monetary system (the distant forerunner of the euro); or
- Reverse economic policy in order to remain in the European monetary system.

On March 21, 1983, Mitterrand went for the second option. This was called *le tournant de la rigueur,* an about-face toward adopting programs of austerity.

French workers felt betrayed, and it was the French Communist Party that paid the immediate political price, losing half its electorate in June 1984 European elections. The disillusion of the Left led to a conservative victory in 1986 parliamentary elections, obliging the President (secure in his seven-year term) to take on right-wing leader Jacques Chirac as his Prime Minister.

Meanwhile, Jean-Pierre Chevènement resigned from his position as Minister of Research and Technology (one of the few real successes of the early Mitterrand presidency), and soon the old Socialist, Pierre Mauroy, was replaced as Prime Minister by a slick young socialite, Laurent Fabius, introduced to the public by Mitterrand as the young man France needs. Fabius was prime minister, incidentally, when the Greenpeace ship *Rainbow Warrior* was sunk by French intelligence agencies in a New Zealand port on July 10, 1985, but blame was placed on the Defense Minister and Fabius escaped the scandal unscathed, still as Mitterrand's young heir apparent.

As Fabius took over the government, PCF leader Georges Marchais announced that his party would no longer participate in the government. By July 1984, the *Union de la Gauche* was dead.

The decline of the Communists may have been an intentional object of Mitterrand's strategy. At least, that is what he told the Americans, who feigned to be alarmed by the presence of four PCF cabinet ministers in the French government.

President Reagan, who seemed less than terrified, dispatched his vice president, George H.W. Bush, to Paris on June 24, 1981 to enquire into the communist threat. It is uncontested that Mitterrand explained to the Americans that his strategy was to weaken the PCF by way of alliance with the Socialists. "Having them (the communists) in the government," he explained, "makes them lose their originality, since they are associated with the socialists in all the decisions. Thus they should be less and less able to win independent votes."

The Italian Communist Party had been defeated by covert plots, violence and murder. Mitterrand crippled the French Communist Party by a warm embrace.

But to what extent was that his purpose? Saying things to reassure American masters that their control of Europe is not in jeopardy need not be the expression of the most profound conviction. "Leave us alone, we can handle this," is what Mitterrand was saying. But in fact, intentionally or not, his policy of bringing communists into a coalition and then reneging on the social promises did set the PCF on a path of decline. But that was not the only factor, and its inability to handle the legacy of the party's longstanding allegiance to the Soviet Union was another. The relationship of forces was shifting toward finance capital at the expense of traditional working-class organizations. The French abandonment of the Common Program was a milestone in the shift in the identity of "the Left" away from its connection with working class struggles throughout the West, as "the Left" began to take on new meanings.

The dream of *Liberté, Egalité, Fraternité* in the form of democratic socialism faded, as "Europe"—meaning the institutions of the European Union—became the new horizon of the Left.

Redefining "the Left"

To justify abandoning his social democratic program, Mitterrand needed two things: excuses and a new set of values.

The excuses were provided by all the experts, starting with Minister of Economy and Finance Jacques Delors, a devout Catholic with a social conscience, whose attachment to European unity brought him under the influence of much more orthodox champions of "the Markets."

In the period after Mitterrand and his government abandoned the principal measures of the Common Program, a change took place in the meaning of "the Left," which was increasingly identified with attitudes rather than with practical programs. The new left attitudes proved to be quite compatible with adaptation to neo-liberal policies designed to meet the demands of finance capital.

Reduced to good thoughts, the Left could aspire to fulfill the only available political role in neo-liberalism: that of friendly salesman who justifies the need for unwelcome economic policies on the grounds of expertise—or by assorting unwelcome economic measures with generous attitudes in other areas.

The Left and Expertise

François Mitterrand was a man of literary culture, skilled in persuasion. He had no culture in economic matters, and certainly came to the Presidency with a great capacity for secrecy and intrigue (throughout his time in office, he managed to prevent the public from knowing of his close relationship with his mistress and their daughter, even while going on holiday with them), a strong measure of intuition concerning people he dealt with, and a solid knowledge of his own country and its history. But he was plunged into a much larger world with problems and contradictions that neither he nor perhaps anyone else knew how to solve.

Socialist leaders are easily accused of "treason," when they may simply have no idea what to do. They were better at gaining public confidence than at changing material reality. Their facility in dealing with people does not extend to modern technology and a globalized economy.

It may have been a sign of how out of place he felt in the contemporary world that Mitterrand turned for advice to much younger men, more confident and brilliant, who seemed to know what needed to be done. One of these was Laurent Fabius, the prime minister of "the turning point." More significant was his extraordinarily close relationship with a very young man on his way to becoming an almost permanent power behind the throne, who indeed may have introduced Fabius to Mitterrand, Jacques Attali.

Attali is an extraordinary figure, a sort of Rasputin of the French Left. His advice may be good or bad, it is habitually delivered in prophetic tones and with an unshakable air of confidence and good humor. He became President Mitterrand's constant intellectual companion, they were photographed walking in the gardens of the Elysee Palace, with Attali pouring his wisdom into the presidential ear. Instead of youth seeking wisdom from old age, it was the other way around.

Jacques Attali is undeniably extremely clever. Born in French Algeria in 1943, he and his family moved to France in 1956, two years after the start of the Algerian war of independence, and proceeded to attend every elite school in France, often at the top of the class. He has written, or at least signed, an infinite number of books on every possible subject, whose accuracy has occasionally been severely questioned. He plays the piano well and has even directed a symphony concert.

It was in 1965, when he was a student at the ultra-elite Ecole Polytechnique, that he first met François Mitterrand in the central French district of Nièvre, which Mitterrand then represented in Parliament. They hit it off so well that in 1974, he directed Mitterrand's first presidential election campaign (which he lost). For ten years, from Mitterrand's election in 1981 until 1991, Attali was his "special advisor," his omniscient expert on everything.

Like many well-rooted politicians, Mitterrand's familiarity with the world outside his own country was limited. In contrast to De Gaulle, who spoke fluent German, or Chirac, who learned perfect English in the United States, Mitterrand spoke no foreign languages. The polyglot Attali came in handy as his "Sherpa," that is, as his guide to summits with other leaders.

Early on, Attali advised Mitterrand that the Common Program economic measures were unworkable and would have to be abandoned. He was certainly far from being the only one giving the President this advice, but he seems to have been the one the President trusted most. As advisor to private companies on economic strategy, corporate finance and venture capital, Attali was a credible guide into that unknown realm of finance capital. His talent for instant rationalization could come in handy to a politician who was reversing the policies that got him elected.

In December 2014 the daily *Libération* (not an unfriendly newspaper), opened its article on Attali with the rhetorical question, "And what if it turns out that Jacques Attali, 71, is the real President of France?"[14] This thought was inspired by the fact that at that very time, Attali was guiding his protégé, Emmanuel Macron, through his first big political job as Minister of Economy in the Socialist Government of François Hollande, designing laws to reduce worker rights. Attali had also sponsored the rise of Hollande himself and his ex-companion,

---

14 Grégoire Biseau, "Attali, l'homme qui murmure à l'oreilles des présidents."

Ségolène Royal, who unsuccessfully ran for President against Nicolas Sarkozy in 2007.

Through all this, Attali maintains his adherence to "the Left," which is itself a contribution to changing the meaning of the term. Above all, Attali claims sweeping good intentions, looking forward to the establishment of universal justice under Global Governance, with Jerusalem as an appropriate capital. Attali readily identifies with the Jewish prophetic tradition, always represented as concerned for the betterment of humanity, whose future he predicted in 1980 as that of "transhumanism," a bright future of people enhanced by spare parts.

Attali is simply the most dazzling example of semi-official intellectuals who have transformed "the Left" into an elite claiming to possess expertise in doing what is best for the people. The Left has evolved from a program to an attitude.

The Left as Minority Protection

Especially in the prosperous 1960s, formal agreements between Paris and various African governments allowed for large numbers of immigrant workers to come to France to meet the growing demand for factory labor and other jobs.

In the 1970s, the liberal government of President Giscard d'Estaing adopted family reunification measures, allowing immigrants (who initially had been vaguely expected to eventually return to their native lands) to bring in their close relatives. The result was a large influx of wives and children who, since they lived outside the work force, tended to stay among their own people rather than integrate into French society. This was the beginning of the concentration of unassimilated populations in suburban high-rise housing areas of major cities, notably Paris, Lyons, Marseilles. These neighborhoods were not initially built as "ghettos" but as vastly improved housing for working-class people. In the 1960s and 1970s, the French Communist Party was very much present in these developments and played an important role in social integration, providing unifying aspirations, cultural events and actions bringing together people of varied backgrounds.

In the early 1980s, immigration emerged as a political issue as it had not, up to then. In October 1983, following the murder of a young adolescent, residents of a largely Arab neighborhood in Marseilles, supported by local clergy, set out on a long anti-racist march, protesting against police brutality against young North Africans. A delegation was received by President Mitterrand, who promised improvements in residence and working papers, a law against racist crimes (measures which were adopted) and the right to vote for foreigners in local elections (a measure which has so far never been adopted except for citizens of European Union member states; it was blocked by conservative parties considering it a gimmick to enlarge the Socialist Party constituency).

Contrary to Britain, where the option of multiculturalism has led to the growth of completely separate, self-contained communities (notably Muslims practicing Sharia law among themselves, as in Bradford), France has always pursued a policy of assimilation. This is readily denounced in the English-speaking world as "racist," when the case could be made that it is precisely the opposite. What is racist about considering that any individual, regardless of origin, can become French? This worked very well with Italians, Spaniards, Portuguese.

However, the growing influx of immigrants proudly attached to their own customs and religion made traditional assimilation more problematic.

The Socialist Party managed to co-opt the budding political movement of second generation immigrants from North Africa by a propaganda campaign.

SOS Racisme was founded in 1984. The operation was initiated by Socialist Party apparatchik Julien Dray,[15] with the organizing help of the *Union des Etudiants Juifs de France* (UEJF) and both government and private subsidies. The UEJF saw to it that *SOS Racisme* never took an interest in Palestinians, a fear aroused by keffiyehs spotted in the 1983 demonstrations.

The organization made a big media splash by its yellow logo, an open hand with the slogan, *Touche pas à mon pote* (hands off my pal), written on it. A principal backer of *SOS Racisme* was Pierre Bergé, business manager and lover of the top designer, Yves St Laurent, and the very personification of French radical chic. Show business adopted the cause with enthusiasm, mobilizing everyone from the comedian Colluche to Bernard-Henri Lévy. The association chose as its president a nice-looking student leader of mixed French ancestry (father from Martinique, mother from Alsace) with the predestined name of Harlem Désir. After

15 In 2009 Dray would be charged with embezzling the organization, but got off with a timid reproach for having bought himself a 7,000-euro watch with an *SOS Racisme* check.

his stint as symbol of racial equality, Désir was provided with a very successful career in the Socialist Party.

This was a sign of the growing professionalism of politics, using established techniques of communication rather than relying on militant activism.

Twenty years later, socialist historian Max Gallo criticized the yellow hand logo for evoking the Star of David that Jews were obliged to wear under Nazism. "It was totally created from above, by ideologues who knew what they were doing and thereby giving the impression that recent citizens were in effect the Jews of today…From the yellow star to the little yellow hand of SOS Racism, they created the first of those historic confusions that were to poison French debates." That is, it was a step on the way to enforcing the anti-racist, pro-immigrant creed by arousing the guilt associated with Nazi extermination of the Jews.

The limit of the *"pote"* campaign was that it set out to correct bad attitudes rather than to provide practical remedies. It was essentially an advertising campaign, selling anti-racism as "defense of a pal," even, or especially, on the part of those who had no such "pal" to defend. It implied situations where white activists stepped in heroically to defend a minority "pal" from attacks by hypothetical racists. This triangle bad guy-victim-good guy is the moral pattern of American movies rather than a political program that brings people together around common goals and shared social aspirations.

The campaign marked the beginning of the primary identification of the Left with the single issue of anti-racism and support for immigrants. Defense of undocumented immigrants (*les sans-papiers*) was to become the primary identifying cause of the moral Left. Cinema naturally played a huge role over the next decades in exalting ethnic minorities, as the indigenous working class was ignored or belittled. In the 1930s, a charismatic actor like Jean Gabin portrayed working class men who were strong, acute and sensitive. From the 80s on, the French worker was a clod, probably racist. Instead of promoting a healthy blend of those already here and those arriving, anti-racism has tended to exercise a transfer, taking away respect for the traditional working class and giving it to immigrants instead.

The Timely Demon

Establishing the post–working class Socialist Party as the center of the Left owed a great deal to the emergence on the political scene of the perfect foil, Jean-Marie Le Pen. Le Pen, a nationalist veteran of the Foreign Legion, started his political career in the 1950s as a verbally gifted parliamentarian representing a rightwing party of shopkeepers engaged in tax revolt (*Poujadisme*). In 1973 he became leader of a coalition of varied remnants of far-right movements of the past: the National Front. It brought together traditionalist Catholics, Pétainists, royalists, and assorted reactionaries, including genuinely fascistic groups such as *Occident* (whose militants had greeted me with fists at a 1967 meeting against the Vietnam War). Le Pen held together these disparate malcontents by the force of his rhetoric and his charismatic presence as jovial tough guy.

In 1982 and 1983, the National Front suddenly became visible by winning up to 10% of the vote in municipal elections. Due to the proportional voting, Le Pen was elected to the European Parliament. As the Socialist Party turned to anti-racism as its central ideological identity, an opponent who could be identified with racism added a touch of urgency to the cause. The fact that Mitterrand agreed to allow national television authorities to grant Le Pen more speaking time could be considered only fair. But conveniently, Le Pen's increased media visibility took votes from the "respectable" right which did not dare consider allying with the pariah. This use of Le Pen to keep the right divided is generally attributed to Mitterrand as one of his most skillful political gambits.

It didn't work all the time and it backfired seriously in the presidential election of 2002, when Le Pen's notoriety was such that with 17% of the vote he made it to the second round, ahead of Socialist candidate Leonid Jospin, thus giving Chirac an unprecedented landslide victory of over 80%.

The focus on Le Pen led some alarmists to claim that there was a "rise of fascism" in France. There were real fascists in the National Front, but Le Pen's party never aspired to seize power by violence, as fascists did. Or even to take power at all—it was a conglomeration of lost causes, on their way out, not on their way in.

The anti-racist campaign also contributed to weakening the PCF, since its leader, Georges Marchais, clung to the traditional left working-class position of calling for limits to immigration (as did Chicano leader Cesar Chavez in the United States).

Le Pen's infamy rested on remarks for which he was taken to court by the LICRA (*League Internationale contre le racisme et l'antisémitisme*). The most notorious of these was his answer to a question in a September 13, 1987 interview: "I ask myself several questions. I'm not saying the gas chambers didn't exist. I haven't seen them myself. I haven't particularly studied the question. But I believe it's just a detail in the history of World War II." For this, he has been fined over a million French francs and has had his parliamentary immunity revoked to allow for additional prosecution. Both his Paris apartment and his party headquarters were firebombed in retaliation.

But was he ever a threat? I doubt he ever thought he was. Even his most scandalous remark, the above-mentioned about the gas chambers, was surely designed less to influence popular opinion than to amuse his followers, like an impertinent student showing the rest of the class that he dared contradict the teacher. Jean-Marie Le Pen was a talented public entertainer who used his unquestioned verbal gift to show that he didn't care what respectable people thought. He seemed to relish being denounced, which is not exactly the approach of a genuine demagogue with dictatorial ambitions. Jean-Marie was a bon vivant, who could recite classic French poetry and sing French popular songs, and who seemed to be having a hell of a good time as he aroused the indignation of all decent people.

19.

The Ideological Pendulum

It is not possible to observe French politics without paying attention to the ideas and influence of French intellectuals. Nowhere do public intellectuals, essayists, commentators, and especially those labeled philosophers (an expandable category), exert such extraordinary influence as in France—or at least in the Parisian circles where "public opinion" is manufactured. It is a small, exclusive world crisscrossed by rivalries and mutual admiration societies, where the chosen few promote each other for the benefit of their shared prestige. As another instance of bad timing, the Union of the Left came into office at a time when the Paris intellectual fashion had turned drastically against the sort of politics represented by the Common Program.

In the years following the end of World War II, intellectuals were understood to be on the Left, often communist sympathizers, even though the French Communist Party was always wary of independent intellectuals. But the Party was identified with the Resistance, a desirable identification. Marxist references were standard if superficial. The leading writer of the period, Jean-Paul Sartre, popularized his own philosophy of existentialism, which was not Marxist but did not preclude debate with Marxists. Sartre adopted a critical rather than hostile attitude toward the French Communist Party and stood up against the extreme anticommunism of the Cold War. In the 1950s and 1960s, Sartre was the undisputed dominant figure in French thought, not only because of his popular writings (essays, plays, novels) but also because, alongside Simone de Beauvoir, he was the epitome of the *intellectuel engagé,* actively committed to the leftwing causes of his time, especially Third World liberation struggles.

In his popular 1946 pamphlet, *L'Existentialisme est un humanisme,* Jean-Paul Sartre exalted the self-creating role of the individual and the importance of taking social responsibility. Subsequently, the French philosophical pendulum swung from one extreme to the other. The individual was no longer a subject but became the object of unconscious or external forces, swept along by inherent power drives or ideological structures that shift from one period to another.

The Death of the Human Agent

The strong point of Marxism, as emphasized by Engels, the point that gave Marxism ideological hegemony over the socialist movements of the 19th century, was the identification of the working class—in particular, the industrial working class—as the agent of revolutionary change. More perhaps than Marx's monumental analysis of capitalism, it was this apparent key to success that gained influence in revolutionary socialist and labor groups.

But that strong point became Marxism's chief weakness when, in the twentieth century, the working class failed to make the revolution in the industrialized West. Some leftists, notably disciples of Trotsky, blamed this failure on the "Stalinist" leadership of the Communist Party, whereas there were many other objective causes. But even though the chosen "agent" of revolution was not doing the job, many leftists retained their devotion to the goal of "revolution," even communist revolution, and looked around for alternative agents to make it happen. The choices ranged from the Third World, youth, blacks, women, gays to the elimination of the human agent altogether—the approach that dominated philosophy in France in the sixties.

The elimination of the human agent—that is, of the ability of the human being to act deliberately and rationally to bring about social change—owed a lot to cultural anthropology. The sharp differences between cultures fostered "nurture over nature" theories, seeing humans as totally conditioned by their cultural surroundings. Pushed to extremes, insistence on isolating cultural modes from each other led to the notion that even Western science is a cultural construct, denying the very possibility of a single concept of truth.

One of the last ostensibly Marxist French philosophers was Louis Althusser, whose great novelty was to "free" Marxism from the human being as agent of change. In a sense, Althusser was attempting to revive Marx by fitting him into the structural mode. Althusser attempted to save Marx from the disgrace of his youthful humanism by discovering an "epistemological break" (a sort of paradigm shift) in his work, which fit in with structural determinism. The revolution still remained an aspiration (whose is not clear).

Althusser's 1965 writings on Marx[16] were intended to stimulate a renewal of Marxist analysis on a scientific basis within the French

16 *Pour Marx* (*For Marx*) and *Lire le Capital* (*Reading Capital*), avec

Communist Party, of which Althusser remained a critical member. As he admitted, he was above all a very skillful writer, and I don't think that he himself was totally convinced by what he wrote, because he was intelligent enough to be aware of his limits.

I read his work as I read philosophers in general, as a tourist, who might enjoy the view but wouldn't want to live there. More than his ideas, I appreciated his views on international affairs, less marked by the rabid anticommunism of post-May '68. That must be what led to my spending a long evening, sometime in the late 1970s, conversing with him in his cramped quarters in the elite Ecole Normale Supérieur where he tutored many future intellectual stars, notably Bernard Henri Lévy. Although he was born in Algeria and had spent the World War II years in a German prisoner of war camp, Althusser gave the impression of a man forever in bedroom slippers cut off from the outside world by ceiling-high shelves of books he had read and forgotten. In contrast to the characteristic arrogance of Paris intellectuals, Althusser was kindly and excessively modest, telling me that Spinoza was the only philosopher he really understood. This modesty, I learned later, was surely linked to his deep depression, on the edge of insanity. On November 16, 1980, he strangled his wife Hélène Rytmann in a fit of dementia and was confined to mental hospitals.

Althusser was the last big name French philosopher attempting to come to terms with Marx. But already, his structural determinism marked a sharp break from Sartre's focus on individual freedom and social responsibility. It didn't have much to do with Marxism either.

Pendulum Philosophers

As Sartre's star faded, you could see the up and coming word masters jostling to take his place. The most assertive was Michel Foucault.

On January 21, 1982, Professor Jean Chesneaux, whom I knew from Vietnam War days, summoned me to meet with Michel Foucault. Both were enthusiastic supporters of the rebellious Gdansk dock workers movement called *Solidarnosc* (Solidarity)—less, I strongly suspect, because of their concern for the welfare of Polish dock workers than because it gave them a welcome opportunity to denounce the Soviet Union. They were eager to persuade me to spread the anti-Soviet message to the

---

Etienne Balibar.

Left in the United States. I should drop criticism of U.S. foreign policy and concentrate on denouncing the Soviet Union as pure power facing pure resistance in the form of *Solidarnosc.* My position then as always is that it is more appropriate to criticize the misdeeds of one's own side rather than to join the chorus denouncing "the other side." Even if not motivated by pure animosity (as is often the case), criticism of the other side will be so interpreted by it, leading to it having no positive effect.

Chesneaux had spent years as a member of the French Communist Party, whereas the exceedingly versatile Foucault had, as he proudly asserted, had his moments as PCF member, anarchist, leftist, ostentatious or disguised Marxist, nihilist, explicit or secret anti-Marxist, technocrat in the service of Gaullism, neoliberal, and so forth.[17] (So many French intellectuals had passed through the PCF that it was nicknamed "the Gare St Lazare.") Somewhere between Kuhn[18] and his own rapid change of phases, Foucault invented his concept of "episteme" to account for ideological periods, vaguely enough defined to keep scholars working to figure it out.

As Asia historian, Chesneaux had been well treated by the Party, whereas Foucault deeply resented the Marxist influence in French academia which remained indifferent or hostile to his theories. May '68 brought them together in common hatred of the French Communist Party, ostensibly because it was not sufficiently revolutionary. Chesneaux's reaction was to go from one "spontaneous" revolutionary movement to another before settling on anti-modernism as his doctrine.

Foucault passed his brief post-May '68 revolutionary moment close to the most important of those movements, *la Gauche prolétarienne* (GP), in which nary a genuine proletarian was to be found, and certainly not Foucault, who came from a well-to-do bourgeois family of cardiologists in Poitiers. True, inspired by the Great Proletarian Cultural Revolution in China, some GP members left their studies to work in factories hoping thereby to further the revolution. Thanks to the Soviet-Chinese split, a main attraction of Maoism at the time was that it defied both the USSR and the PCF for being insufficiently revolutionary. The leader of the GP was Benny Lévy (a former student of Althusser), then

---

17 "Polemics, Politics, and Problematizations: An Interview with Paul Rabinow," in *The Foucault Reader,* ed. Paul Rabinow (New York: Pantheon, 1984), 383–84.

18 Thomas S. Kuhn, *The Structure of Scientific Revolutions* (Chicago: University of Chicago Press, 1962).

using the *nom de guerre* Pierre Victor, and its members included Serge July, founder of the daily tabloid *Libération,* which was eventually to become the principal organ of postmodern hedonism. Pierre Victor turned to Jean-Paul Sartre for protection of GP's newspaper, *La Cause du Peuple,* and the two grew so close that Sartre ended his days fascinated by Judaism, to the consternation of Simone de Beauvoir and other old friends and associates. Fortunately for everybody, Victor/Lévy dissolved the *Gauche prolétarienne* to prevent it from turning to violence on the model of the armed Italian ultra-left groups.

In France, the "discovery" of the Gulag occurred decades after the Stalinist repression had ended, at a time of relaxed tensions both internationally and within the Soviet Union. Denouncing the Soviet Union was primarily a means of combating the French Communist Party through a sort of guilt by association.[19] Foucault was in the forefront of those who equated the USSR with the Gulag, concluding that mass imprisonment was the inevitable outcome of totalitarian communism. This campaign intensified as the PCF risked being elected to government positions in coalition with the Socialists.

The PCF's much deplored reluctance to perform "revolution" did not exempt it from being accused of all the crimes of Bolshevism at its worst. In reality, the PCF had been elected to run a number of French municipalities, which it governed correctly according to the law, with marked concern for social and cultural services, without ever instituting concentration camps.

The past hegemony of Marxist thought in the French intelligentsia lent a tone of bold non-conformism to the new "far left" anti-communism. It may not be surprising that Foucault, who was then becoming the high priest of resistance to authority, was himself extremely authoritarian. His thought boiled down to reducing every human action to a lust for "power" and he gave the impression that this emphatically applied to himself. And indeed he acquired an extraordinary ideological power, still exercised today. Confronting his imperative manner, the power I most immediately wanted to resist was that of Michel Foucault.

After Foucault's exhortations to focus primarily on the Polish *Solidarnosc* movement failed, I learned from my friend, University of Wisconsin Professor Harvey Goldberg, who spent much time in Paris, that Chesneaux had accused us both of "appeasement" of the Soviets

19 See Michael Christofferson, *French Intellectuals Against the Left: The Antitotalitarian Moment of the 1970s* (Oxford: Berghahn Books, 2004).

who "destroy the spirit." But the meaning of "the spirit" is hard to grasp in the context of French theory.

Harvey's passionate lectures in Madison on French Revolutionary history inspired many of his students to become politically active. That is, it inspired them to take on the big issues, in view of big changes.

Foucault was preaching a very different message. While in the USSR, power meant the Gulag, here at home it was everywhere. The ubiquitous nature of "power" virtually eliminated the focus on hierarchies of power, on the possibility of consciously organizing individuals to work together against the major political power centers. If power is everywhere, power is nowhere in particular. Resisting power can mean resisting your teacher, your parents, the law, even your doctor. Foucault's immense influence on American academia can be seen in today's resistance to every possible "micropower," taking the form of witch hunts against alleged instances of discrimination, racism, exclusion, professors, speakers or texts which use words that might hurt somebody's feelings. Meanwhile, opposition to the macropowers of finance capital, the military industrial complex, NATO and the pro-war leaders in the West is weak, marginalized and ineffective.

Philosophy for Neoliberalism

For those who situate Foucault "on the left," it is worth noting that his reduction of socialism to the Gulag went hand in hand with a certain positive interest in economic liberalism, or neoliberalism, as less oppressive. This corresponded to the mounting political power of "the markets" at the time. The clash of micropowers and the absence of human agency are quite compatible with the idea of "freeing the market" to take decisions mathematically, regardless of discredited human rationality.

Initially (in his 1961 thesis *L'Histoire de la Folie* and in *Surveiller et Punir*),[20] Foucault attacked social institutions stemming from the enlightenment for instituting a "great internment" of marginal individuals, not only in prisons but also in schools and hospitals. Historians have pointed to the gross inaccuracy of this attack, which

---

20 Michel Foucault, *Surveiller et Punir: Naissance de la prison,* (Paris: Gallimard, 1975); *Discipline and Punish: The Birth of the Prison* (New York: Pantheon Books, 1977).

used cherry picked and invented facts to prove its point. Foucault settled on the image of a 19th century prison layout, the "panopticon," as the symbol of the surveillance state. In that model, a single guard was in a position to survey all the prisoners at once, so all could feel watched even when they weren't—a variation on Orwell's Big Brother. (Foucault died precisely in 1984, and never lived to see the electronic realization of his fantasy as revealed by Edward Snowden.)

By 1976, Foucault had already shifted his criticism to a different method of control, coining the term "biopower" to indicate an historic shift from discipline of individuals to governance of populations. With Foucault, this does not apply, as it might seem, to contemporary manipulation of the masses by "communication," propagating lies to justify militarization and wars. For Foucault biopower acts on bodies more than on minds, enforcing normalization. There can be little doubt that Foucault's own personal sadomasochistic homosexuality, unacceptable to his father and to society in his youth, were central to his philosophical obsession with revolt against all forms of normalization.

When he was dying of AIDS in 1983, just as the Pasteur Institute was first to identify the HIV virus, Foucault singled out France's comprehensive universal health care system as target. He denounced French systems of social coverage for "imposing a specific life style," and as a result "whichever individuals or groups who, for one reason or another, don't want to share that life style find themselves marginalized by the play of institutions." By means of social security, he maintained, the State exploits anguish, uncertainty, insecurity so that people "accept everything, taxes, hierarchy, obedience, because the State protects and guarantees against insecurity."[21]

Since both the bourgeoisie and the proletariat willingly accepted such oppression, Foucault sought his own agent of rebellion in what Marxists called the *Lumpenproletariat,* the idle poor, which he vaguely identified as "the plebe," all those who refuse to accept such powers. He perceived a spark of mass rebellion in "those youth gangs in the suburbs and certain Paris neighborhoods, whose delinquency takes on political meaning."[22]

---

21 Jean-Loup Amselle, *Critiquer Foucault: Les années 1980 et la Tentation néolibérale, ouvrage collectif dirigé par Daniel Zamora,* (Editions Aden, 2014), 96–7.

22 Ibid, 62.

In 1971, the expectation of revolution, or of revolutionary movements, was prevalent in the Western left. This valorization of revolution was the one thing that seemed to bring together two leading intellectuals of the time, Noam Chomsky and Michel Foucault, but their divergences were pronounced in a debate that clearly marked a parting of the ways.[23]

Chomsky set out by advocating political combat to liberate positive aspects of human nature in a society offering people an opportunity to realize their capacity for creative work. As example, he cited his preferred organizational model, the Spanish anarcho-syndicalists.

The specific nature of the example gave Foucault a good opening to reject not only that model, but any model. Chomsky was thinking in terms of defining goals for political combat, Foucault was looking for opportunities to revolt, regardless of outcomes. "If you say human nature is repressed," said Foucault, "you risk having to define it in terms of our own society." Marxism claimed that human nature was alienated in bourgeois capitalist society, yet it accepted "bourgeois virtues" and such values were reproduced in the Soviet Union.

Chomsky conceded the point but insisted that it was important to have a purpose, to have a direction for action, to try to conceive of a just society.

Foucault retorted that justice means one thing for the working class and another for the bourgeoisie. For the working class, justice means making demands and for the bourgeoisie it means rejecting them. "In a classless society," he concluded, "I am not sure that in a classless society, we would still have any notion of justice."

This was the crux of the debate.

Chomsky firmly disagreed, maintaining that a sense of justice was not just a product of bourgeois society, it was a feature of human nature. He argued that it was too hasty to reject our current systems of justice as merely the expression of present class society.

Foucault rejected this, claiming that our "notions of human nature, of goodness, justice, of human essence and realization are concepts and notions created within our civilization, in our type of knowledge, in our form of philosophy. As a result, they are part of our class system and, however regrettably, we cannot advance those notions of justice in a combat which should overturn the very foundations of society."

---

23 "Chomsky & Foucault - Justice versus Power," Philosophy Overdose, YouTube, https://www.youtube.com/watch?v=J5wuB_p63YM.

Foucault adopted the notion of "class struggle" not out of concern for the class but for the struggle. He was not speaking of "justice" at all, but of the exercise of power, of a Nietzschean will to power. In his view, the search for justice is a search for what one wants, period. A group's search for justice is a demand for what the group wants, regardless of relations with other groups. This is an idea which has spread.

Foucault made it clear that he had no goals beyond destruction of existing society, resisting powers where we find them, without worrying whether those powers are good or bad since there is no good or bad. Rebellion for the sake of rebellion.

Structuralism started with anthropology, observing radical differences in cultures. There are also observable shifts in Zeitgeist from one period to another, which anyone who lives long enough has experienced. But this can be and has been pushed *ad absurdum.* Since Foucault's time, evolutionary psychology has been advancing evidence for "human nature," as we are all evolved mammals and as such all have certain psychological characteristics, which do not disappear from one period to another but take on a wide variety of forms. There are exceptions but there are also norms. The human norms, which allow society—any society—to function include such virtues as altruism, and the capacity to reason (however the factual suppositions at the basis of the reasoning may differ) which is essential to the sense of justice in its variations. These norms find widely diverse expression in different groups and societies, and some exceptional individuals may be devoid of any or all these impulses. Psychopaths, for instance, do exist. Such deviations cannot be the basis for any durable human society or civilization.

In practice, in this postmodern period influenced by Foucault, we have seen that structuralism leads to the notion of incommunicability between periods or cultures. This fosters the social fragmentation of identity politics, anti-rational subjectivity and social chaos. Did Foucault foresee this? Did he even, in some way, *want* it? Nothing is impossible to deniers of human nature.

20.

The New Germany

On February first, 1982, a European Meeting for Nuclear Disarmament was held at the Paris Mutualité hall (the habitual scene of large political gatherings). This was a French response to the growing movement against nuclear weapons in Germany. The main speakers were Claude Bourdet, author and veteran of the French Resistance, a true conscience of the independent left; 1966 Nobel Prize winning physicist Alfred Kastler; and celebrated biologist Théodore Monod. These were among the grand old men of French intellectual life, principled and outspoken critics of militarism and nuclear armament.

Also present was a representative of the upcoming May '68 generation, François Gèze, whose publishing house, La Découverte, had pretty much replaced François Maspéro as the independent left publisher. The outlook had changed. Interest in the Third World shifted to tourist trips to warm climates, or to lectures on their failure to respect human rights. While others spoke against the danger of nuclear war, Gèze focused on the Polish *Solidarnosc* movement, criticizing Germans whose fear of the risk of war kept them from showing sufficient enthusiasm for the Polish uprising. Gèze called for boycotts and economic pressure on the Eastern bloc.

At this point a spirited German woman with long red hair bravely stood up and defended the priority of promoting peaceful relations between East and West. Further acts of hostility toward the Soviet Union could only make matters worse for the Poles. Her name was Eva Quistorp—one of the first German Greens I befriended. Like a disproportionate number of German peace activists, Eva was the daughter of a Protestant pastor. She was among the founders of *Die Grünen,* Germany's Green Party, whose growth was linked to its role in the budding peace movement.

The clash between Quistorp and Gèze illustrated a sharp difference at that time between a new generation obsessed with atoning for Germany's crimes and the French May '68 generation whose hostility toward the Soviet Union was linked to negative feelings toward the French Communist Party. This difference also corresponded to the contrast between France's status as a nuclear power, with its own *force de frappe* (strike force) and defeated Germany where opposition to nuclear weapons could only be to those of other countries.

The military and moral defeat of the Third Reich had even turned German army officers into pacifists. Gert Bastian, a 57-year-old decorated veteran of World War II and a General in the Bundeswehr, the West German army created under U.S. auspices, believed that the first duty of the new German officer corps was to speak the truth rather than blindly obey orders. He was one of the very first to raise the issues that dominated German politics for much of the decade.

The Euromissile Threat

In the 1970s, while U.S.-Soviet proxy conflicts continued in the Third World, notably in Africa, the spirit of détente prevailed on the European front. On May 26, 1972, President Nixon and Soviet General Secretary Leonid Brezhnev signed the Anti-Ballistic Missile (ABM) Treaty as the first achievement of the ongoing Strategic Arms Limitation Talks (SALT) and the first step toward nuclear disarmament. These moves toward relaxation of East-West tensions were greeted with approval and relief by many Europeans, especially Germans who had no desire to be the battleground for yet another war of massive destruction.

U.S. acceptance of détente provided space for German Chancellor Willy Brandt to pursue an *Ostpolitik* (East policy) of reconciliation between the Federal Republic and the Soviet bloc. Ostpolitik acquired its visual symbol when Brandt fell to his knees before the Monument to the Heroes of the Warsaw Ghetto on December 7, 1970. As Brandt was known as a firm adversary of Nazism, his gesture was understood to be on behalf of his people. Brandt abandoned the policy of isolating the German Democratic Republic, recognized the Oder-Neisse line separating East Germany from Poland and in 1972 signed the Basic Treaty which established relations between the two German States, the FRG and the GDR, for the first time since their post-World War II separation. Brandt's key advisor, Egon Bahr, helped negotiate these bilateral treaties which he saw as the first step in a process to overcome the division of Germany. The second step was creation of the multilateral Organization for Security and Cooperation in Europe (OSCE) and the third step, according to Bahr, would be to "transfer détente to the military field." But that would take time.

Ironically, the measure that interrupted détente, reviving Cold War hostilities and leading to mass opposition, was taken by Jimmy

Carter and Brandt's successor as Chancellor, Helmut Schmidt—by no means the fiercest Cold Warriors. Supposedly as a countermeasure to the upgrading of missiles long stationed on Soviet territory—the SS-20—NATO decided in December 1979 to deploy a total of 464 ground-launch cruise missiles and 108 Pershing 2 systems in five NATO countries, starting in 1983. At the time, Carter and Schmidt were both facing elections under a barrage of attacks from the right for being too soft. Acting tough, Schmidt gave his approval, on condition that the U.S. missile deployment plan would serve to stimulate further disarmament negotiations between the two superpowers. But after Carter lost, the newly elected Reagan administration decided to go ahead with the deployment no matter what.

In February 1980, General Gert Bastian wrote a memo leaked to the *Frankfurter Rundschau* (close to the SPD) providing strategic arguments against deployment of the U.S. missiles. There was no reason, he said, to regard the modernization of the SS-20 as a threat, since the Soviet Union had had medium-range nuclear missiles pointed at Europe for some 20 years without any need for counter measures since "nobody doubted U.S. determination to counter the threat with its own nuclear forces and to retaliate to any destruction of Europe with similar damage to the USSR." In short, Europe had been protected by the danger of Mutual Assured Destruction (MAD), which the Pershing 2 and cruise missile deployment threatened to weaken. MAD depended on the "global balance" of terror and not on regional symmetry, he argued.

The deployment of U.S. nuclear weapons in Europe had two negative effects. It suggested that the United States was no longer willing to shelter Europe under its "nuclear umbrella" but instead considered responding to East-West hostilities by waging a limited nuclear war in Europe. It suggested to the Soviets that the Americans were seriously contemplating a "first strike" to knock out Soviet command and control centers, as recklessly advocated by certain neocons. Thus, if tensions rose dangerously, Soviet commanders might feel "flatly obliged to get rid of this new risk through a nuclear preventive strike."

It is part of the job of a strategist to sense dangers. Whatever the intention of the U.S. missiles, they would in fact increase the probability of a limited nuclear war that would destroy Germany. It is remarkable that the biggest antiwar movement in history was initiated by military men, officers who had fought in the Wehrmacht in World War II, who had tasted victory and defeat, and who felt their mission was to prevent this from happening again.

If any single individual could be considered the initiator of the German peace movement of the 1980s, it was General Gert Bastian. It was he who wrote the text which, adopted at a meeting in the small Rhineland city of Krefeld on November 16, 1980, became the manifesto of the movement to stop the scheduled missile deployment.

The Krefeld Appeal declared that:

> It is becoming increasingly obvious that the NATO resolution of December 12, 1979, to 'close the arms gap' was a fateful mistake. The expectation that agreements between the United States and the Soviet Union aimed at limiting strategic weapons systems in Europe could be reached before a new generation of American intermediate-range nuclear weapons is deployed in western Europe does not appear to have been fulfilled.
>
> A year has passed since Brussels and not even the commencement of such talks is in sight. On the contrary: the newly elected president of the United States has frankly declared that he does not want to accept even the already signed SALT II treaty to limit Soviet and American strategic nuclear weapons and therefore does not wish to pass it on to the Senate for ratification. […]
>
> The participants of the Krefeld talks on November 15-16, 1980, therefore appeal jointly to the federal government to retract its endorsement of deploying Pershing II and cruise missiles in central Europe and, in the future, to adopt a position within the alliance [i.e., NATO] that no longer exposes our country to suspicions that it is seeking to pave the way for a renewed arms race, which would endanger Europeans primarily. […]
>
> All citizens are therefore called upon to support this appeal, so that public opinion will create unremitting and growing pressure in order to force a security policy that:

- *rejects the arms buildup that would turn central Europe into a nuclear weapons platform for the United States;*
- *values disarmament over deterrence;*
- *directs the development of the army of the Federal Republic toward this aim.*

The success of this appeal was astounding. Initially signed by a few prominent individuals under the coordination of the German Peace Union (DFU)[24] in Cologne, signatures soon began to pour in, and by September 1981, three million had signed, and one year later the figure had risen to five million. The Krefeld meeting brought together for the first time General Bastian and 34-year-old Petra Kelly, co-chair of the newly founded Green Party. Aside from their conservative Catholic backgrounds, they had little in common but soon became inseparable.

The Last Great Popular Movement

The movement was by no means limited to Germany. Missiles were also scheduled to be deployed in Italy, Belgium, the Netherlands and the United Kingdom. But Germany mattered most, because it was in Germany that the consequences of this movement were truly historic.

Because of my father's death, I missed the first great meeting in Bonn on October 10, 1981, when some 300,000 people gathered to demand disarmament negotiations to rid Europe, both East and West, of nuclear weapons. At that occasion, former Berlin mayor, Lutheran pastor Heinrich Albertz, reportedly exclaimed, "Just look at these young people! When has there ever been such a thing in Germany?"

Seventy German soldiers in uniform marched to express their opposition to NATO plans to deploy nuclear weapons on German soil.

A new Germany, a peace-loving Germany, was displaying itself before the eyes of the world—not least before observers in the Soviet Union, where fear of German "revenge" was deeply rooted.

A few days later, record-breaking demonstrations were held in London, Rome and Brussels.

---

24 The DFU was headed by another World War II veteran, retired Colonel Josef Weber, who advocated joint nonalignment of East and West Germany.

In the early 1980s, I attended international European Nuclear Disarmament (END) conferences in the countries where NATO was scheduled to deploy the Pershing and cruise missiles. Considerable support came from peace activists in the United States. A high point was the wildly applauded appearance of Harry Belafonte, singing "We shall overcome."

The movement enjoyed considerable support from Christian Churches, which made it that much easier to reconnect with peace activists in Minnesota. Marianne Hamilton, who took part in the 1970 trip to meet the Vietnamese in Paris, together with Polly Mann and Mary Shepard, had founded an organization called Women Against Military Madness (WAMM), which had attracted quite a number of influential wives and professional women in the Twin Cities, including the wife of the police chief, who arrested her in the course of a demonstration against the fabrication of fragmentation bombs by Honeywell.

With a bit of scouting on my side, WAMM organized peace exchanges between New Ulm, Minnesota, and Neu Ulm, Bavaria, the site of a U.S. Army base earmarked for Pershing nuclear missiles.

The peak year of that campaign was 1983, since NATO governments were scheduled to say yes or no to the missiles at the end of the year. It was a year full of conferences, marches, petitions and mass demonstrations denouncing the threat of nuclear war.

On January 20, I was in the press gallery watching French President François Mitterrand address the Bundestag in Bonn. Since Christian Democrat Helmut Kohl had succeeded Helmut Schmidt as Chancellor, the SPD was now in opposition and many Social Democrats were active in the peace movement. Some hoped for support from France's Socialist President. I saw the stiff looks on their faces as Mitterrand defended the missile deployment with a phrase that became a battle cry for NATO: "The missiles are in the East, the pacifists in the West." Some Social Democrats felt that Mitterrand had stabbed them in the back.

The point was that the missiles were scheduled to be deployed in Germany, not in France. The French policy, initiated by De Gaulle, was to stay out of the NATO strategic command and count on France's *force de frappe* to keep France out of eventual East-West conflict.

Sitting next to me in the press gallery, Erich Weser, chief editor of the business magazine *Wirtschaftsbild* ("economic picture") was aglow with satisfaction. He was glad that the French Socialist President had seen the light. In his good mood he confided to me that "after all, the French have no sense of how to do business, unlike we Germans and you Americans." That is one of the common attitudes that contribute to making the "Franco-German couple" a loveless marriage.

At that time, I was also writing occasional articles for the British socialist weekly, *The New Statesman.* I was told by the editor of an SPD journal, with whom I occasionally had lunch in Bonn, that Mitterrand had dispatched the secretary general of the French Socialist Party, Jacques Huntzinger, to London to tell *The New Statesman* to stop running my articles. I can't know whether this rather surprising story was true, but in fact *The New Statesman* never again asked me to write for them.

Mitterrand's sage advice did not slow down the movement. In February, a citizens' "International Tribunal against First Strike and Mass Destruction Weapons" was staged in Nuremberg, with Petra Kelly, Barry Commoner and Daniel Ellsberg participating.

The movement grew in reaction to the bellicose turn taken by the Reagan Administration. The former Hollywood actor certainly had little experience of foreign affairs and allowed his government to be infested with neocons such as Richard Perle and Paul Wolfowitz, whose notions of limited nuclear war in Europe ("flexible response") threatened to undermine the MAD doctrine, which effectively ruled out the possibility of nuclear war due to the certainty of Mutual Assured Destruction if it ever began.

To further threaten—or incite—the Soviet Union to ruinous arms expenditures, Reagan in March 1983 popped up with the idea of the Strategic Defense Initiative (SDI), an anti-missile missile project, derisively dubbed Star Wars, which would clearly violate the ABM Treaty, and undermine MAD, by theoretically defending the West from Soviet retaliation should the United States carry out a first strike. The stationing of U.S. Pershing and cruise missiles, plus the "Star Wars" project, lent credibility to the possibility that such a first strike was really in the works.

German parliamentary elections were held on March 6. For the first time, the *Grünen* passed the 5% threshold and made it into the Bundestag with 5.6% of the vote.

Three days after the Greens were elected to the Bundestag, I rented a pied-à-terre with a neat little garden in Bonn, in order to be close to the action. I bought a bicycle to take advantage of the quiet city's bicycle paths and enjoy biking along the Rhine to the Bundestag, far from the perils of Parisian traffic. I even brought my remarkably tame Burmese cat Coco with me to explore the garden.

The leading figure of the early German Greens was Petra Kelly, an intense little blonde activist with dark circled eyes who was the most eloquent spokeswoman of the German peace movement. She could easily relate to the American anti-war movement, because that was where she was coming from. Petra Lehmann, born in U.S.-occupied Bavaria in 1947, abandoned by a father traumatized by his past as a prisoner in a U.S. POW camp, took the name of her stepfather, U.S. Army officer John E. Kelly, who moved the family to the United States when Petra was thirteen. She was educated in the United States and came of age in time to be deeply marked by the Vietnam War and the assassinations of Martin Luther King and Bobby Kennedy, whose presidential campaign she worked for. Back in Germany, impressed by Willy Brandt's gesture of humility in Warsaw, she joined the SPD but left when Brandt's successor, Chancellor Helmut Schmidt, accepted the stationing of a new generation of nuclear missiles on German soil.

Her gaunt beauty and rapid-fire articulate answers to all questions made her an outstanding figure, the superstar of the German peace movement. Invitations and demands for interviews flooded in from all over the world. I heard her, haggard and on the brink of exhaustion, complaining that she and her small staff were unable to cope with all the messages and requests pouring in.

Foreigners tended to overlook that fact that the German movement was run not by Kelly but by a Coordinating Committee which was far more representative of society than were American peace movements. Initiated by the church-supported Reconciliation Action Peace Service and a half dozen other groups in 1981, it kept expanding to include a wide range of citizens groups, both the Green and the Social Democratic parties (after Schmidt failed to win re-election) and even the German Trade Union Confederation (DGB).

The ability of these diverse groups to quarrel openly and finally reach agreement was impressive. Eva Quistorp attributed this to the absence of a "correct line." The prevailing political culture seemed heavily influenced by a Protestant tradition of "examination of conscience" which requires a self-critical effort to understand the other person's point of view. France was not like that.

Eva, as representative of Women for Peace on the Coordinating Committee, was disappointed by her visit to the United States in 1983. The highlight was her contact with Congressional Black Caucus leader Representative Walter Fauntroy, who spoke out publicly against the missile deployment. Otherwise, she found no interest in real dialogue in a country that is "so huge, with such powerful media." Born in 1945, "the year of Hiroshima," she was surprised to discover that in America, whose armed forces had devastated Indochina, she as a German was expected to bear a certain "burden of guilt" in contrast to the deep and pervasive sense of national self-satisfaction that prevailed in the United States, unburdened by the bad conscience expected of Germans.

In mid-May, a major European Nuclear Disarmament (END) event held in Berlin was an occasion for the Western peace movement to call for "a nuclear weapons-free Europe." East German party leader Erich Honecker reluctantly received Green leaders Petra Kelly, Gert Bastian, Otto Schily and Dirk Schneider. Petra Kelly's public demand to Honecker to respect the East German peace movement's rights of free expression made it clear that Mitterrand was wrong in claiming that "the pacifists are (only) in the West."

The Autumn Peace Action on October 22, 1983, was the largest demonstration in German history, with half a million people in Bonn, 150,000 in West Berlin, 300,000 in Stuttgart and Neu Ulm and 400,000 in Hamburg, a record number. A "human chain" was built linking people hand in hand from Eucom U.S. forces headquarters in Europe at Stuttgart to Wiley barracks (a Pershing site) in Neu Ulm, which required not only 170,000 participants but also highly efficient organization to spread them out at the right places at the right time. Among them were four women from Women Against Military Madness in Minnesota, while a "celebration NEIN" was being held in solidarity in New Ulm, Minnesota. Military men in uniform carried a banner saying "No!" to missiles. There was huge Christian participation: a group of more than 150 monks and nuns from various religious orders walked through the Rhineland calling for refusal of the missiles as a first step toward complete nuclear disarmament. A group of Lutherans pinned on church doors a continuation of Martin Luther's historic 95 theses up to 100, mixing Biblical passages with condemnation of nuclear weapons.

Speakers at the main rally in Bonn included retired U.S. Admiral Gene LaRoque, who acknowledged that the Pershing II and cruise were first-strike weapons; East German Protestant pastor Heino Falcke calling for "an end to the war that has long been waged against the Third World and the environment; an official of the DGB Trade Union Confederation; and a communist, Etty Gingold, speaking for survivors of the anti-fascist resistance.

The major political news of the October 22 event was the participation of Willy Brandt, and his clash with Petra Kelly. They addressed a huge crowd packed into Bonn's vast Hofgarten. Peace movement leaders were suspicious that Brandt would not directly contradict his party leader, Helmut Schmidt, and allowed him to speak only after he had promised that he would finally say "no" to the missiles. His way of complying was to say that Germany needed "not more means of mass annihilation, but fewer. Therefore, we say no to ever more new nuclear missiles." Echoing Schmidt's original argument, Brandt called for "serious negotiations instead of deployment" and came up with a long-term goal: a superpower agreement first to freeze and then to destroy nuclear weapons, and a transfer of money spent on arms to combat hunger and poverty. His statement was above all diplomatic, designed to reassure Washington and Moscow at the same time. He urged "friends and partners in East and West" not to fear Germany but to "make use of" Germans' desire for peace. He wanted blocs to be overcome, but "we belong to the Western Alliance," he concluded.

This did not satisfy Petra Kelly, who had arranged to speak right after Brandt on the speakers' platform. There should not be just fewer mass annihilation weapons, but none at all. Moreover, saying "no" to the missiles and "yes" to NATO, was absurd, she retorted.

Brandt appeared furious at these reproaches and accused Kelly and the Greens of partisan attacks.

Despite the clear message that German public opinion was overwhelmingly opposed to stationing the U.S. nuclear missiles on German soil, the German Bundestag voted on November 22 to go ahead with the deployment, and the missiles started arriving.

Not only in Germany.

Also in Italy, the Netherlands, Belgium, despite huge protests. In the United Kingdom, the missile deployment and police repression failed to put an end to the protests of Greenham Common women, which continued until the missiles were removed under the Intermediate-Range Nuclear Forces Treaty (INF) agreed to four years later by Ronald Reagan and Mikhail Gorbachev.

Was that the happy ending? Unfortunately, it was not.

Looking back on all this, one could say that the anti-missile movement of 1983 was an immediate failure, and a few years later a partial success, and in the still longer run, a failure. As I write, in 2019, the United States has decided to scrap the INF Treaty as it recklessly pursues an arms race more dangerous than that of the 1980s. So far, there is no hint of a protest movement that could begin to resemble that of thirty-seven years ago. Why is that? What follows suggests answers. But so far as Germany is concerned, the principal difference between now and then is Reunification.

We Are One People

When the Bundestag failed to reject the missiles, the movement did not immediately die but began to take divergent directions. The SPD undertook to try to define a new "security policy," while the Greens, increasingly fragmented and disoriented, began to split between those labeled by the media as realos (realists) and fundis (fundamentalists). Of course, for the media, the realos were the sensible ones, and the fundis must be a bit crazy. Josef "Joschka" Fischer, with a background in anarchistic house occupation and street fighting, who had never been either a pacifist or an environmentalist, quickly became the media's favorite "realo," due to snappy rhetoric in the Bundestag of no great political consequence. The difference between "realo" and "opportunist" was hard to discern and would even become much harder.

Within the inevitably demoralized peace movement, many Greens, notably Petra Kelly, decided to turn their attention to promoting partnership with independent peace groups in Eastern Europe, with the objective of attaining a non-aligned bloc-free Europe.

From early on, it was clear to an attentive observer that the peace movement was part of a tide turning toward rapprochement between the two Germanys. For even if the movement had failed to stop the missiles, it had spectacularly demonstrated the emergence of a "new Germany," after forty years of silence. Awareness of Germany's division was sharpened while at the same time it aroused profound feelings of German identity.

I saw this clearly at a regional conference on "German policy" held in Karlsruhe on March 10, 1984, organized by the Green Party of Baden-Wurttemberg, considered a conservative branch of the party. On that evening, a concert hall packed mostly with young people timidly joined in singing for the first time an imaginary national anthem for an imaginary reunified Germany. Political cabaret singer Wolf Biermann, thrown out of the GDR in 1976, introduced the "Children's Anthem," written by poet Bertolt Brecht for communist East Germany. In contrast to "Deutschland Über Alles," the gentle song calls for "a good Germany," "neither over nor under other peoples," and for a day when other nations do not "turn pale" at the sight of Germany but stretch out their hands in friendship as they do with other peoples.[25]

People sang with tears in their eyes.

The conference organizer, Thomas Rauberger, explained that the demand to get rid of ABC (atomic, biological, chemical) weapons runs up against belonging to a bloc. "We must get to the root of the problem: this is an occupied country. We must organize to demand a peace treaty. My utopia is a neutral federal republic, like Sweden and Austria."

Attending numerous meetings, held exclusively in German, and hearing the carefully guarded briefings of Egon Bahr, it became increasingly clear that the peace movement was not only about nuclear missiles. It was also—and perhaps primarily—about the division of Germany, and the prospect of reunification, which was clearly Egon Bahr's lifelong passion. Sensing that this peace movement was a step toward German reunification helped explain its unfriendly reception by Honecker—and Mitterrand.

Two clichés of the period summed up the latent Franco-German split over what then seemed a remote prospect of bringing together the capitalist Federal Republic and the communist Democratic Republic. Of the Germans, it was said "They think about it all the time but never mention it." And of the French it was said that "they love Germany so much that they want two of them." Leading French expert on Germany, Alfred Grosser, observed that "the Western Allies want reunification only so long as it is impossible."

Among other things, the Euromissiles were a way to make reunification impossible, in line with the undeclared purpose of NATO to "keep the Russians out, the Americans in, and the Germans down."

The nuclear missiles, even if the prospect of using them was dim, served to enforce the opposing military alliances, NATO in the West and the Warsaw Pact in the East, thus cementing the division of Germany into two States. There was, and still is, little recognition in the West of what the division of Germany was all about. The Cold War dogma is that the Soviet Union conquered Eastern Europe as part of a drive to impose communism on all of Europe. Therefore, Western Europe needed U.S. military defense to keep from being overrun by a red tide. There is no evidence for this belief. Stalin was intent on maintaining control of Eastern European countries occupied by the Red Army in its victorious

---

25 "Children's Hymn," Wikipedia, https://en.wikipedia.org/wiki/Children%27s_Hymn.

war against the Third Reich, not in order to spread communism, but to secure a buffer zone that would protect the USSR from sudden Western invasion. At first, the Soviets established coalition governments, "people's democracies," but faced with Western-backed opposition, found themselves obliged to install nominally communist puppet governments to maintain control.

Eastern Germany was always a special case. In contrast to heavily Catholic neighboring Poland and other post-war Soviet satellites, there were many ardent supporters of communism in the Eastern part of Germany. It is well-known that many Germans fled from the communist East to the capitalist West—notably from parts of Germany that were integrated into Poland, east of the Oder-Neisse line. Less known is the exodus of a much smaller number of Germans from West to East, out of political conviction and the feeling that the GDR was "the better Germany," farther removed from the Nazi past than the U.S.-occupied zone where "denazification" often resembled blackmail or plea bargaining.

West to East migrants included Angela Merkel's Protestant pastor father and author Berthold Brecht, who founded his own theater in East Berlin. This crisscrossing migration deepened the ideological gap, and yet helped underpin the nostalgia for a single German nation.

It was an open secret in Bonn that the first Chancellor of the U.S.-sponsored German Federal Republic, the Christian Democrat, Konrad Adenauer, who could count on votes from the Catholic Rhineland and Catholic Bavaria, was quietly content with the division that excluded traditional socialist strongholds in the Protestant east. As a Rhinelander, Adenauer felt at ease being anchored to the West. So there was a certain measure of satisfaction with the division of Germany by leaders on both sides. From the very start, the least satisfied were the social democrats, and it was in the SPD that the policy of reconciliation was developed by Willy Brandt and his key advisor, Egon Bahr—the *Ostpolitik*.

The Good Spies

Mutual espionage flourished in the period of separation between the two Germanys. Nothing was easier than to spy on than one part of your own country on behalf of another part. All this spying was probably mostly useless, sometimes harmful, but at times a factor for peace. In East Germany, the internal division of the notorious Stasi *(Ministerium für Staatssicherheit)* spied on virtually their whole population with

Germanic thoroughness, trying to root out dissidents and eventual plotters working for the West. The major effect of this effort was to create an atmosphere of suspicion that, far from protecting the State, was a major factor in its downfall, as it radically alienated people who had done nothing wrong, starting with the intelligentsia, who were the most concerned with ideological freedom.

The foreign intelligence division of the Stasi headed by Markus Wolf was another story. As Wolf recounts in his book, *Memoirs of a Spymaster,* he had great success in recruiting agents in the Bonn government. Indeed, his agency was a victim of its success, as the revelation of the presence in Chancellor Willy Brandt's office of one of his spies, Günter Guillaume, caused an uproar that led to Brandt's fall from office, which was not at all what was intended.

But there were also many individuals in West Germany, including among the German Greens, who possessed no State secrets but acted as regular informants on the mood in the West. One of these was Green Bundestag member Dirk Schneider, whom I saw a lot of in those days, because he was well-informed on strategy and disarmament issues (none of them secret) as well as serious in his analysis. I had no idea at the time of Dirk's extra-curricular activities. After reunification, he spent time in prison for his harmless activities. And he was far from the only one. Although every country tends to make heroes of its own intelligence agents, those of other countries are portrayed as diabolical. The outrageous behavior of the fictional James Bond made him hugely popular in the West, but the routine nonviolent intelligence work of the young Vladimir Putin, when he was a KGB agent in East Germany, is denounced as particularly sinister. This obscures the fact that genuine, non-fictional intelligence agents, when not engaged in the adventurous criminal activities of "operations," but merely gathering information, contribute to international understanding. At the end of the Cold War, the KGB felt that it was so well informed about the West that it propelled the Westernizing reforms of Gorbachev. But perhaps it was not quite as well informed as it thought, when it came to future intentions.

The ordinary work of informants can be highly positive if it helps to overcome dangerous illusions and fears. A famous example is that of Rainer Rupp, who spied for the GDR out of sincere political conviction. Promoted to a key position in the NATO bureaucracy, he was able to caution Moscow not to get too excited about Reagan's Star Wars, since U.S. experts told him it wouldn't work.

By 1983, the division of Germany had lasted for nearly forty years. The Federal Republic had given up denying the very existence of the Democratic Republic, which had an international presence of its own, especially in support of African liberation movements. The Western informants, whether in the Greens or in other political parties, believed that the division was enduring, but sought to bring about a rapprochement between the two States. After all, Germany had historically been divided, and the FRG was, after all, a federation of Länder enjoying considerable autonomy. Many in the Western left hoped that greater understanding might lead to a federal merger of the two States, preserving the best of each. That was not to be.

Two silent projects were present among German activists. For some, the objective was a lasting peace and friendly relations between the two Germanys. For others, most probably Egon Bahr and surely for Hans-Dietrich Genscher, Helmut Kohl's foreign minister, the objective was a takeover of the East by the West.

One way or another, the peace movement of 1983 was bringing the two Germanys together.

21.

Great Power Politics Takes Over

In the 1970s it had seemed to many that massive resistance to war and injustice could change the world for the better. In reality, the antimissile movement that peaked in 1983 was the last gasp of that movement, regardless of a few much smaller antiwar protests in decades to come. The expectation that popular movements might successfully intervene in Great Power policy making was fading. People proposed but power disposed.

Holding Hands

The image of little François Mitterrand and big Helmut Kohl solemnly holding hands in a Verdun cemetery on September 25, 1984, was adopted as an icon of peace and reconciliation. But the stories worth a thousand words told by a photograph do not necessarily tell the story.

Yes, the two leaders surely regretted the slaughter of nearly a million German and French soldiers in the battle of Verdun that lasted for most of the year 1916. Nobody sane could want to do that all over again. There can be no doubt that they were determined that never again should Germany and France wage war against each other.

But that was not the issue. Both nations had truly had enough of such mutual suicide. Alsace Lorraine was back in France, Germany didn't need it, and the rival colonial wars in Africa were over. There was absolutely no threat of a new Franco-German war to conjure away.

The real issue was altogether different. The issue for Mitterrand and Kohl was not to make peace with each other, but to make peace with Eastern Europe, with Russia, and to promote genuine disarmament and an end to threats of nuclear war. Their hand holding was at best an image of the status quo, of two European leaders firmly embedded in U.S.-controlled NATO, minor participants in the Cold War.

And even that was not the whole story. Mitterrand's gesture, holding out his hand to Kohl, was a gesture not of love but of political calculation. The wary Mitterrand had surely been among the first to sense the sea change in relations between the two Germanys brought about by the antimissile movement. He saw omens of a greatly enlarged and strengthened Germany, of a Germany recovering its sphere of influence in East Central Europe, or even turning toward economic partnership with Russia. Up to then, as the defeated power in World War II, Germany had been confined to the role of "political dwarf" in Europe, leaving France as the dominant political voice within the Western European community. But Germany was nevertheless already an economic giant. The hand stretched out to Germany was especially symbolic of Mitterrand's desire not to let giant Germany "get away," to become both the economic and political dominating power, leaving France behind.

Since images form public opinion, regardless of hidden reality, the Mitterrand-Kohl photo became the symbol of the "Franco-German couple." A genuine partnership had briefly existed between De Gaulle and Adenauer, both Catholics who spoke a common language; De Gaulle spoke fluent German. But the Bundestag quickly undercut their friendship treaty by making it subsidiary to United States "friendship." Later, a friendly working relationship developed between Valéry Giscard d'Estaing and Helmut Schmidt, both English-speaking liberal technocrats. But Mitterrand and Kohl had no common language (Mitterrand never saw any reason to speak any language but his own) and the two had nothing in common, least of all a political vision.

Fear of mounting German power was at the root of the strategy that dominated French foreign policy for the next decades: that of tying France and Germany tightly together by economic measures, and most decisively by the establishment of a common currency.

Already in 1979, the European Economic Community (forerunner of the European Union), had established a currency exchange mechanism called the European Currency Unit—whose acronym ECU was also the word for a seventeenth century silver coin, which sounded comforting to the French, who hoped to retain the word as the name for the future common currency. But on this point as on so many others, when it came to matters of money, French desires turned into German advantages. Mitterrand's policy of containing Germany turned into German containment of its European neighbors.

Subsequent history has shown the errors of Mitterrand's calculations, but at the time of his presidency, his strategy of "building Europe" around a common currency was adopted by almost the entire French political class, French media, French intellectuals and especially the French Socialist Party, where "Europe" replaced "socialism" as the great national goal of progress.

Making Peace

The significant meeting of the decade was, of course, the 1987 encounter between Ronald Reagan and Mikhail Gorbachev that ended the Cold War—or so it seemed at the time to most observers. And I think it fair to say that it seemed so especially to the two leaders who made it happen. These two totally contrasting human beings managed to come together on the grounds of normal human common sense.

On June 13, 1989, Mikhail Gorbachev and his wife Raisa paid a visit to Bonn. There was a huge popular welcome. The Russian leader, aglow with eager friendliness, shook a lot of hands. Mine was one of them. An extraordinarily warm, forceful handshake. Gorbachev was not an enigmatic leader. He was, perhaps, too transparent for his own good, sincere and ready to believe in the sincerity of flatterers such as Margaret Thatcher. Reagan, who as an actor was not quite so transparent, must have had a certain knack for judging people, and sensed more quickly than his advisors that Gorbachev was for real and that the two could make history together.

Gorbachev was surely pursuing a policy of radical détente which his predecessor, Yuri Andropov, had not lived to initiate. He was supported in this effort by the KGB, which tended to be relatively optimistic about East-West relations. Reagan had to ignore his bellicose neocon officials and depend on establishment advisors such as Paul Nitze to work out the Intermediate Range Nuclear Forces Treaty (INF) which removed the despised and feared Euromissiles.

The happy ending? Only purists such as Petra Kelly were dissatisfied. The treaty was incomplete, it did not move toward total nuclear disarmament, and British and French nuclear arms were untouched. Just about nobody was listening to her objections. But she was right.

Except for inveterate Cold Warriors, who saw every Russian peace gesture as a malicious trap, it was all over. Washington was left with no "evil empire" to oppose, no enemy to justify the lucrative arms race.

But the European peace movement was also left without a cause. It could consider that it contributed to the INF Treaty, which is no doubt true, but the Treaty was made over the heads of European governments which remained stuck in NATO, with no real peace policy of their own. Without the fear of nuclear Armageddon, the French arms buildup announced by President Mitterrand was unable to arouse significant indignation. The arms trade with Arab oil monarchies was lucrative and apparently relatively harmless, since nobody credited the Saudis with knowing how to make use of their expensive weapons. Moreover, since Germany was still restrained by its recent past, the arms industry was a field where France could make the most of its advance position.

The Fall of the Berlin Wall

By the mid-1980s, it was becoming clear that the two German States were going to be united, one way or another. The big question was HOW?

As with many emblematic historical events, the fall of the Berlin Wall was a spectacle playing out decisions that had been made backstage.

There had been a dress rehearsal. That was the Sopron picnic. It had a strong symbolic significance for sectors of the European elite because it was a vivid reminder of the Austro-Hungarian Empire, stage-managed by no less than its deposed heir, the Archduke Otto von Habsburg. A few years later, he began to be a familiar figure in my world, but he was always, I believe, much more influential than he appeared.

Sopron is an ancient town on a piece of Hungarian land jutting into neighboring Austria. After the Austro-Hungarian Empire was abolished by the victorious allies in World War I, a referendum was held to decide whether Sopron would belong to Austria or Hungary, and Hungary won. In 1989, as the Soviet Union was clearly loosening its hold on its East-Central European satellites, Hungary was discreetly affirming its independence. Thus Sopron was the ideal spot to initiate the dismantling of the Iron Curtain—iron fences actually—that separated the Soviet bloc from the West.

Hungarian and Austrian authorities agreed to permit a symbolic border opening at the end of a large picnic held on August 19 in the meadow between Sopron and the border with Austria. The occasion was organized by Otto von Habsburg as president of the Paneuropean Union, an elite organization dedicated to European unification along liberal lines (in opposition to the Nazi project of unifying Europe under German domination). It was decided that the border point would be temporarily opened for three hours to allow Hungarians and Austrians to fraternize. The Archduke's daughter Walpurga, secretary general of the Paneuropean Union, presided over the opening.

For Otto von Habsburg it must have seemed a strong omen of the restoration of some version of the Austro-Hungarian Empire, which was surely his deep, silent, long-term goal.

Now, many East Germans went to Hungary for their summer vacations, especially along the shores of Hungary's large Lake Balaton. Word went around, not by accident, to East Germans who wished to go West, so when the gate was opened, hundreds of East Germans poured across the border into Austria. The demonstration had been successful. From that point on, the division of Europe was clearly at an end.

The full spectacle took place three months later with the fall of the Berlin Wall. The world rejoiced. Not simply on behalf of the Germans who were no longer separated from each other but because this marked the end of the Cold War and a future of world peace. That is how the fall of the Berlin Wall was interpreted by millions of people. People rushed from Paris, Milan, Brussels to Berlin to be part of the great event. Pieces of the broken Wall become cherished trophies.

If I am not mistaken, the media played this up too much as "people voting with their feet," ignoring the backstage preparations for this inevitable spectacle. It was even portrayed as the triumph of the consumer society, as East Germans dropped everything for a long shopping spree on the Kurfurstendamm, until their money (and often their jobs) ran out.

It is up to serious historians to reach conclusions about the causes, outcome and long-term significance of the German reunification symbolized by the fall of the Berlin Wall on November 9, 1989. I was certainly in no position to follow this complicated process any more closely than any other external observer. But I do have a few general observations to make.

Not enough credit is given to Mikhail Gorbachev and to the 1980s peace movement. It is my view that the combination of the two played a decisive role in the (apparent) end of the Cold War in 1987-1991. The scope and passion of the peace movement certainly helped convince Gorbachev that the Western threat had subsided enough to dare seek a compromise. In fact, historically, the Soviet Union had always had doubts about the durability of the division of Germany. From the viewpoint of the East German communist leaders, Gorbachev sold them out. He was more interested in good relations with the West than with preserving control of East Germany. Gratitude and generosity have no place in power politics, least of all on the part of the "take no prisoners" imperial War Party in the United States. So the official U.S. line attributes the breakthrough entirely to the superiority of the American capitalist system and its overwhelming military power, with a nod toward Reagan and his team for daring to reap the benefits.

Mikhail Gorbachev was a naïve negotiator, foxed by the Americans. He seemed altogether too happy at being admitted to the club. In Washington, some still dispute the well-documented fact that U.S. officials orally promised Gorbachev not to extend NATO eastward beyond united Germany. This limit should have been formally written into a treaty to avoid all ambiguity. It seems that the Russian fear of German *revanchisme* stood in the way of their full recognition of the U.S. drive for world hegemony. NATO was even welcomed by some Russians as the way to "keep the Germans down." The Russians also seemed to take the ideological conflict too seriously, and thus to conclude that democratic reforms would put an end to Western hostility. A fatal error of judgment.

Valentin Falin, Moscow's highly respected ambassador to Bonn, who over the years had won the confidence of Willy Brandt, Egon Bahr and other influential members of the West German elite, tried to warn Gorbachev not to be so trusting. Falin developed projects for reunification, calling for according neutral status to both German States, or forming a Swiss-style confederation between the two, or finally allowing Germany to remain a NATO member but outside of its strategic command, as De Gaulle had accomplished for France. Never considered was the possibility that West Germany would simply annex East Germany, tear down its economy and allow NATO to expand eastward. But that is what happened.

Life in East Germany was not so terrible. Stasi spying, travel limits and shortage of Western consumer goods were the three most obvious complaints. On the other hand, from my travels in East Germany, I observed that stores seemed well-supplied with domestically produced and imported goods, not flashy but solid and utilitarian—in sharp contrast to the dismal aspect of Moscow department stores. There were no serious shortages in East Germany (there was talk of not enough bananas) and at the same time, jobs, housing, quality education and social welfare were guaranteed. The condition of working women was incomparably superior to that in West Germany. But certainly, the physical confinement within the Socialist bloc, the inability to come and go throughout all of Germany, was the greatest grievance.

The reunification did not take the form desired by many of those in East Germany—and even in West Germany—who worked for it. Asked about the possibility of reunification during the Green election campaign in 1983, Petra Kelly insisted that "we want reunification only if there is demilitarization." This was the consistent view of many leading peace activists in both East and West, who feared that a united Germany would again become a dangerously aggressive power. In the East, too, many of the protesters chanting *"Wir sind ein Volk"* ("we are one people") thought they were calling for a happy merger of the best of both systems, the personal freedom enjoyed in the West and social benefits enjoyed in the East, in a new, improved, peaceful Germany.

The total surrender of "real existing" communism in the East contributed to the defeat of the Western Left. It was commonplace for segments of the Western Left to claim that it was only the bad example of Soviet communism that stood in the way of the rise of "genuine" socialism in the West. On the contrary, the sharp distinction made by Western socialists between themselves and the defeated communists in the East produced no dividends. Western media and governments took the fall of the eastern bloc as an "unconditional surrender," proof of the total historic failure of socialism, and this message was delivered constantly to the public. This accelerated the Left's shift from social issues to the environment and human rights.

PART VII

The European Non-Parliament

22.

New World Order or New World Disorder?

The end of the eighties marked a turning point for the world, but it was not easy at the time to see exactly which way things were turning. Nineteen eighty-nine was a busy year. On January 20, Reagan completed his two mandates and President George H.W. Bush was sworn in as President (nobody used the "H.W." in those days because nobody imagined that a second President George Bush was waiting in the wings). In Washington, some didn't believe Gorbachev's peace moves. Others believed and decided to take advantage of them. That was the tendency that prevailed as the Bush administration hastened to accept every Russian concession. On December 2, encouraged by European leaders, Bush and Gorbachev met in Malta and declared an end to the Cold War. A violent storm obliged the two leaders to cancel their afternoon session.

Gorbachev had dreamed that all this would lead to "our common European home," with East-West convergence around some sort of social democracy. However, the Eurocommunism dear to Jimmy Weinstein was already defeated, and left parties were leaning toward accommodation with the neoliberal policies of Thatcher and Reagan. Italian friends were particularly dejected by their own domestic scene and told me outright that they didn't see how I could continue to report on "the left" when it was ceasing to exist.

That was worrying me, too. With all that was going on in the world, I found plenty to write about, for various outlets besides *In These Times*. And through all this, there were many conferences and discussions on problems of arms control and movements toward disarmament. But the varied journals I wrote for paid little or nothing and my main income still came from *In These Times,* often arriving late. From my visits to the ITT office in Chicago, I had the feeling that, except for Jimmy Weinstein, other staff members saw little point in subsidizing an American in Paris to write for a publication centered on domestic leftist and labor issues. As far as I could guess, my value to the paper was mainly that it attracted a certain number of contributions, notably from old lefties like the affluent veterans of the Lincoln Brigades, who were inevitably a vanishing constituency.

In that period, attention was focused on Eastern Europe. In April I spent a couple of weeks in Hungary, trying to understand its emerging Western-style democracy (with little success in a country about which I knew next to nothing and not a word of its language). Touring the Soviet Union was more interesting. In Leningrad (it was still Leningrad), in addition to the Hermitage museum and other artistic sites, it was still possible to visit the Lenin museum in the house where Lenin planned his seizure of power and the Museum of Religions and Atheism, with didactic displays illustrating the progression from religious to rational thinking. When I visited a few years later the Lenin museum was closed and the Museum of Religions and Atheism had been reconsecrated as the Orthodox Christian church it was in the first place.

With my very rudimentary long-forgotten Russian, I managed some simple conversations with people I met, for instance when I was invited to join a jolly wedding party in Leningrad where the prevailing viewpoint was that Gorbachev was too weak and that what was needed was a new Peter the Great. I found a similar outlook in chatting with a nuclear physicist on a bus in Kiev, in between his views on the effects of the 1986 Chernobyl nuclear power plant meltdown.

One result of that disaster was the surprise success of *les Verts,* the French Greens, who won twelve seats in the June 18, 1989 elections to the European Parliamentary (EP), the ostensible legislative branch of the European Community (EC) which later became the European Union (EU). This was the first electoral success of *les Verts,* due apparently to public reaction against the way French authorities (protective of France's own large nuclear power industry) had played down the spread of radiation from Chernobyl. This made the French Greens, with a dozen members, the largest of a European Parliament Green Group, relegating the German Greens to second place with only seven. This French success turned out to be very important for me personally.

In September, my friends the Pumphreys, who were then working for the *Grünen* in Bonn, informed me that the new Green Group in the European Parliament was looking for a press secretary. They had recommended me and thought I would be just right for the job. I was not so sure, but the job sounded just right for me, not least for providing a steady income. At that time, the Greens were widely seen as a rebirth of the left in a new form, based on the values of the environment, peace, feminism, and human rights. The members of these new parties came from contrasting political backgrounds and neither I nor anyone else could agree with all of them, considering their internal differences. But since my main issue was always opposition to aggressive war, I could relate to their commitment to peace.

After my first job interview in Brussels, I got word that the decision was held up by a deadlock in the group, between the Germans on one side and the Italians on the other. With support from the French, it was the stubborn blockage between Germans and Italians that finally led the Green Group to elect me as their press secretary on February 8, 1990, more than six months after their group was formed. As an American, I seemed neutral in regard to the conflicts between Europeans—a very profound lesson in how the United States has maintained almost total control of Western Europe. It's called "divide and rule," although in my case, they divided themselves, and I never ruled. Far from it. I did as I was told.

Who Were the European Greens?

The Green Group counted about 30 members (there was some coming and going from and to other Groups), from France, Germany, Italy, Belgium, and the Netherlands, in that order. The Belgians, who themselves were split between the Flemish Agalev and the Francophone Ecolo parties, tended to act as intermediaries, smoothing things out, appropriate for the host country.

The ideology of European unification is that we are all Europeans together, and national identity is a thing of the past. Close observation of the people's representatives in the Parliament showed quite the contrary.

The German Greens had already had seven members in the previous Parliament, as members of a Rainbow Group, which included a member of the Danish anti-Europe party. The June 1989 elections more than doubled the number of Greens elected and also shifted the balance from the Germanic north toward the Latin south of Europe. The northerners had been accustomed to the style of the extra-parliamentary movements of the 1970s and were skeptical of European institutions. The Italians, on the contrary, were mostly experienced politicians focused primarily on strengthening EC institutions.

The German-Italian discord finally led to a split in the job of secretary general, one for the Germans and one for the Italians. The Germans' choice was a holdover from the previous session, Juan

Behrend, who had grown up in Argentina as the son of Jewish Socialists who had fled Nazi Germany. From his background, Juan knew a great deal and was so familiar with several languages that he tended to mix them up. He was extraordinarily good-natured, which allowed certain German women MEPs to use him more as a comfort blanket than as a political advisor.

The Italian choice was Gianfranco Dell'Alba, who could not have been more different, as obscure and cryptic as Juan was candid and open. While Juan was clearly on the left, Gianfranco was less clearly on the right. The son of an admiral, with a degree in political science, Gianfranco was a leading personality in the Italian *Partito Radicale,* founded by Marco Pannella, whose mission was to undermine the traditional left, represented by trade unions and socialist parties, by the "radical" promotion of individual rights issues such as legalizing divorce, abortion, and recreational drugs, and promotion of human rights in non-Western countries. The flamboyant Pannella used these causes (however laudable in themselves) in ways calculated to upstage the Italian Communist Party, whose working-class base was often conservative on such issues.

In the EP, the *Partito Radicale* held its own secretive meetings and acted much like a sect, devising strategies and tactics to increase its influence. Dell'Alba drew his authority in the group from his ability to master all the complex rules of this opaque institution, and from his skill in wheeling and dealing, useful in obtaining desired committee posts for Group members.

My position as press secretary was not split in two, although it was evident that the *Radicali* wanted one of their own in the job. Instead, they managed to get the group to choose as my "assistant" (without consulting me) a young staff member whose main talent was being rather impertinently pretty. She had been the girlfriend of a *Radicale* MEP and worked for Emma Bonino, Pannella's successor at the head of the *Partito Radicale.* It was clear that she was put there less to "assist" me than to check up on me and even lead me into error. I had to take great care never to make a mistake.

I could count on support from Marie-Christine Aulas, who was familiar with my articles in *MERIP Report,* as well as from Solange Fernex, a gentle Christian pacifist from Alsace, and from the Belgians, especially the Group's co-president, Paul Lannoye.

In the 1989 elections, Greens scored highest in the United Kingdom with almost 15% of the vote, but due to the "first past the post" electoral system, none were elected. In compensation, the Green Group took on a British Green, Jean Lambert, as an official but non-voting member of the Group.

Among the Germans, the dominant personality was Claudia Roth, who drew on her background as a student of drama to project overwhelming righteous indignation over such matters as the fate of the Kurds. After years in the European Parliament, Claudia went back to Germany as a leader of the Bundestag Greens and a passionaria of human rights.

Unlike the Germans and French, who practiced rigorous male-female parity, the Italians were all male except for Adelaide Aglietta, who was a leading figure in the *Partito Radicale,* having served in the Italian Parliament and campaigned for prison reform, legalized divorce, and abortion. In the EP, she was firmly committed to promoting European federalism. In those days, the most enthusiastic partisans of European federalism were the Italians, perhaps both because they had scant respect for the Italian state and as a result of a very Italian affinity for international institutions, from the Roman Empire to the Roman Catholic Church.

Virginio Bettini, professor of urban geography at the University of Venice, was a pure "green," opposed to nuclear power and in favor of renewable sources of energy. The most sociable of the Italians, Bettini exercised his charm with the women in the group.

Eugenio Melandri was very different. A Catholic missionary and priest, with a degree in sociology from the University of Trento, center of the radical leftism that produced the Red Brigades, Melandri was mainly concerned with North-South issues, combating the arms trade, and non-violent resistance to involvement in military operations.

Marco Taradash, a member of the *Partito Radicale* and the Italian parliament, was a single issue militant for legalization of recreational drugs.

Alexander Langer stood apart from the other Italian MEPs. A journalist and academic, Langer had been active in the extra-parliamentary left group *Lotta continua* and in promoting reconciliation between German and Italian speakers in his native region, Alto Adige (now part of Italy) which as Sud Tyrol had been part of Austria. This reflected his background as son of an Austrian doctor and an Italian pharmacist.

This variety within the Italian delegation is only a sample of the considerable differences of orientation between members of the Green Group.

We traveled a lot. My work got started in the beginning of March with a long visit to Berlin to savor reunification and worry about the environment. I wrote my first communiqué about a trip we took to visit a trash dump in Ketzin, tsk tsking over East German pollution. In East Berlin we met "East German Greens" (who soon switched to some other party). Then we held a press conference. All this was harmless. There were lots of perks, such as the spring asparagus festival in Strasbourg, with music, white wine and all the asparagus you can eat in the presence of the Mayor of Strasbourg.

We were living in a glow of optimism, brought on by the end of the Cold War in general and by the unification of Germany in particular. During the Parliament's July 1990 session in Strasbourg, I attended an elegant sun-lit lunch organized by the West Germans to celebrate press freedom, with leading East German journalists as honored guests. I remember being impressed by the intelligence and eagerness of Thomas Silberstein, who was at the top of his profession in the German Democratic Republic and seemed happy to be welcomed by his Western colleagues. Little did he know: within months he would lose his job, as East German media were taken over by West Germans. This was the fate of most of the East German intellectual and business leaders. Their enterprises were either bought out or went bankrupt.

In the spirit of the times, the Group chose as its theme of the year Eastern Europe and concentrated on building contacts with Greens in former Soviet bloc countries. This was not wholly successful because the Estonian or Bulgarian "Greens" whom we contacted and encouraged tended to be shopping around for the most useful Western contact, and it was rarely us.

The First Bush War

But the Middle East was exploding again. On August 2, 1990, Iraq invaded Kuwait, annexing the territory a few days later. This led to a storm of media outrage against the dictator, Saddam Hussein, and his brutal aggression. As usual, things were not so simple. Saddam Hussein had reason to think he could get away with it. His invasion of Iran in 1980, which lasted until 1988 and caused over a million deaths, had been accepted and even aided by the United States. The United States, Saudi Arabia and Kuwait welcomed a conflict that bled the Islamic Republic. Iraq had also been drained by years of war and as an honest mercenary, the Iraqi strongman wanted to be rewarded by his sponsors for his costly services. But instead, he was left in the lurch, and the little sheikdom of Kuwait, instead of helping its big neighbor was pumping oil from underneath Iraqi soil. In the Iraqi view, Kuwait was a natural part of Iraq which owed its independent statehood solely to British imperialism. It is notorious that before invading Kuwait, Saddam Hussein had made his intentions known to the U.S. ambassador in Baghdad, who appeared not to object. But once he went ahead, the propaganda war took off. A young woman, later revealed to be the daughter of the Kuwaiti ambassador, shed tears before Congress claiming to have seen Iraqi invaders grab infants from incubators and throw them on the hard ground. This turned out to be a public relations stunt, but the effect was to undermine diplomatic efforts to find a peaceful solution, by portraying Saddam as a sadist with whom negotiation was not possible.

Five days after the Iraqi invasion of Kuwait, President George Bush ordered the organization of "Operation Desert Shield," in which U.S. forces would lead a large coalition to liberate Kuwait. U.S. troops poured into Saudi Arabia in preparation. For the next five months the Bush administration used its immense leverage to build up a coalition of 34 nations. In this interval, an opposition movement—since totally forgotten—tried to persuade Congress, European leaders, anybody, to allow negotiations that could permit Iraq to withdraw without another war. Such negotiations would surely have succeeded, since it was obvious that the full military force of the United States, even without its 33 coalition allies, could certainly drive Iraqi forces out of Kuwait. But it was all too clear that the Bush administration wanted this war, if only to demonstrate its capacity to act as international police force once the Cold War was over.

On September 11—a date that would become legendary exactly eleven years later—President George H.W. Bush drew the lessons of his action in an address to the U.S. Congress.

"Clearly," he announced, "no longer can a dictator count on East-West confrontation to stymie concerted United Nations action against aggression." In short, given its decisive influence on the United Nations and with no danger of a Russian veto, the United States henceforth had a free hand in the world.

The crisis in the Persian Gulf, he said, "offers a rare opportunity" to move toward "a new world order."

> Once again, Americans have stepped forward
> to share a tearful goodbye with their families before

> leaving for a strange and distant shore. At this very moment, they serve together with Arabs, Europeans, Asians and Africans in defense of principle and the dream of a new world order. That is why they sweat and toil in the sand and the heat and the sun.

Two days later, the two German States and the Allied Occupation Powers (the United States, the Soviet Union, Britain and France) signed the so-called "two plus four Treaty" authorizing German unification.

All this, according to President Bush, was leading to realization of humanity's eternal dream: "A world where the rule of law supplants the rule of the jungle. A world in which nations recognize the shared responsibility for freedom and justice. A world where the strong respect the rights of the weak."

On January 17, 1991, "Operation Desert Shield" turned into "Operation Desert Storm," with massive U.S. bombing of Iraq. The bombing was authorized by a U.N. ultimatum, and carried out in the name of a large coalition, but this was essentially a United States operation. The broad support served mainly to show that the United States could obtain broad support.

Despite considerable opposition, President Mitterrand decided that France should be part of the Desert Storm coalition, based on the notion that in order to have influence, one must join the club. The French National Assembly approved Mitterrand's war resolution by 523 to 43. Jean-Pierre Chevènement, who had returned to the government as Defense Minister, resigned in protest. On February 24, the "coalition" opened a ground offensive to liberate Kuwait, and on February 28, as U.S. air strikes massacred tens of thousands of retreating Iraqi soldiers, the war was "suspended"—meaning that Iraq would continue to be punished by sanctions and discriminatory measures.

The First Gulf War has gained the reputation of being just and sensible, especially in comparison with the Second Gulf War waged a decade later by the second President Bush. But like almost all U.S. wars, it was a war of choice, waged primarily to illustrate America's post-Cold War role as world policeman.

Gorbachev had been too optimistic to foresee the full implications of his international policy, and this is no doubt what incited a handful of Soviet military hardliners to kidnap him on August 19 in an attempted coup to save the Soviet Union. The coup backfired totally, enabling Moscow mayor Boris Yeltsin to take center stage as champion of… not the kidnapped Gorbachev but rather as champion of surrender to the West. Within days, the Communist Party of the Soviet Union was disempowered, the Baltic States were independent, and the USSR was disintegrating.

During my first year with the Greens, I was feeling neither particularly useful nor particularly welcome in a group torn by dissension. I even contemplated abandoning all this comfort, the annual asparagus, the monthly travel and the evening glass of *crémant d'Alsace,* in order to go to work for some peace research organization. That would have been a very foolish thing to do. But opposition to the first Gulf war momentarily united the Green Group—or most of it—in a common cause where for the first time I felt I belonged.

Alexander Langer and British Laborite Ken Coates co-chaired a "European Peace Initiative," calling for "regional reconciliation" among peoples of the Middle East, disarmament measures and "democratization of the United Nations" which was considered to have been abused by U.S. influence. The Green Group introduced a resolution calling for "immediate and concrete steps to halt the war," supported by a quarter of MEPs but rejected by the big Socialist and Christian Democrat Groups.

The group approved of my project to begin publishing a weekly antiwar newsletter, "Gulf Peace," a clearing house for information on antiwar initiatives, faxed to peace activists all over Europe. Paul Lannoye and Solange Fernex went to The Hague to ask the International Court of Justice to take up the question of the legality of the Gulf War. I helped arrange for two Green MEPs to attend the massive January 26 anti-war demonstration in Washington D.C. as guest speakers.

Even in this moment of unity, certain cracks appeared. Marco Taradash objected to the use of words criticizing the United States. Adelaide Aglietta, far more clever, illustrated a more subtle *Radicali* technique for avoiding any criticism of the United States by proposing two alternative resolutions: (1) for an international convention banning arms trafficking and (2) for abolition of the article which still exists in some European Community countries allowing the application of the death penalty in time of war.

All through the Gulf War, and even in its aftermath, Green MEPs kept raising issues concerning the legality of the war, the bombing of civilians, the ecological damage, the role of oil, the need for peace in the Middle East. It goes without saying that none of these efforts produced any noticeable results. But they showed good intentions.

23.

What Are We Doing Here?

Influential or not, the Greens were very welcome in the European Parliament because concern for the *environment* was an absolutely crucial argument in favor of European unity. The difficulty, or impossibility, of dealing with environmental problems on the national level has been a key argument for transfering national sovereignty to supranational institutions. The mere presence of an ecological party gave the comforting impression that the environment was being taken seriously. The Greens were immediately more "respectable" than the traditional leftist groups from which many of them had emerged.

Some MEPs from more established parties had been kicked upstairs into the European Parliament to get rid of them, and their primary ambition was to collect all their expenses on top of their huge salaries. Others were trying hard to give significance to their insignificant job, if only not to feel guilty about their high salaries and lavish perks. How was it possible to be so well paid for doing so little of importance? To put it another way, the MEPs were consoled for their powerlessness by all the money and privileges showered on them.

In a unique and probably illegal practice, the Green Group withheld a part of the salaries of their employees (including me) to finance Green parties. Elected Communists habitually kicked back part of their wages to their parties, to stay on the level of their working-class constituents. With the Greens it was different. The MEPs kept their full pay and only their staff had to contribute.

How It Worked

The main work of a modern parliament is not merely to *parler*, to talk, but to legislate. In the European Parliament, both these activities were strictly limited.

The real test of a democratic parliament is its authority to initiate legislation. The European Parliament does not have this right. Legislation originates in the totally bureaucratic, unelected European Commission, whose Commissioners are selected in order to give every Member State at least one post. They are, as one would suppose, besieged by lobbyists suggesting legislation that would favor their specific interests. The Commission proposes the laws and the Council, meaning the appropriate ministers of Member Governments, has the final decision. In between, the Parliament is consulted.

Legislation takes the form of Directives, which set out a general direction for matching legislation which the Member States are obliged to enact; and Regulations, which are directly applicable to the Member States. In between Commission and Council, the draft legislation (translated into umpteen languages) passes through the European Parliament to be tweaked by the appropriate committee. The tweaks are rarely significant and can be vetoed by the Council in most cases—according to complicated rules (which change from Treaty to Treaty).

The rules of procedure can differ according to the type of legislation, according to rules enshrined in the dozen treaties of succession ratified by the Member States. All this has created an obscure legalistic context that is impenetrable to common mortals.

It was touching to see the zeal with which our sincere MEPs threw themselves into the task of introducing a word here or a sentence there which might make the regulation in question more environmentally friendly. The problem was not that the Green MEPs failed to work hard, but rather that their hard work had very little practical effect.

My job was evidently to try to call media attention to these efforts. But it was soon all too clear that the media simply didn't care particularly what was going on in the European Parliament, nor what our well-intentioned MEPs had to say.

The only journalists assigned to the EP who showed real interest, and wrote real reports, were the Brits, because they were motivated. They were motivated, in fact, to deride the whole process of manufacturing intrusive Regulations that people didn't want or need. Coming from the Mother of Parliaments, they observed that this was no proper parliament, and they were right. It had no real powers and even the debates were not genuine debates between MEPs, as speakers were assigned minutes or seconds according to the size of their group, each making her quick point in her own language, with no give and take, no follow up—a sequence of short monologues.

The British led the frequent complaints about the monthly trips to and from Strasbourg where plenary sessions must be held according to treaties. Although the Parliament had its offices in Brussels, next to the European Commission and the European Council, the French had imposed Strasbourg—a historically disputed city in France just across the

Rhine from Germany—as symbolic of Franco-German reconciliation. But transport to this medium-sized town was time-consuming and inadequate, not to mention the expense of transferring MEPs, staff members, a mountain of documents in several languages and batteries of interpreters back and forth every month.

Some German media dutifully made stodgy reports about matters of little interest to the public, and Jean Quatremer, the permanent reporter for the French daily *Libération,* did all he could to propagate his fanatic adoration of European Construction. But in general, the European Parliament was wallowing in universal indifference.

Media interest could perk up when some particularly famous visitor came to call. There was great interest in the visit from Nelson Mandela. The visit by Boris Yeltsin aroused interest but was quite different. Yeltsin was scheduled to visit each Group in turn, but our turn was in the morning and he didn't make it. However, he held a press conference later in the day, which I attended. Yeltsin rambled on non-stop with platitudes delivered in a flat monotone. This was not a press conference, whether he realized it or not.

Multicultural Europe

To gain official privileges, a Group had to bring Members from diverse countries together under a political label. National groups would have contradicted the project of European unity. The British Conservatives managed to pretty much keep to themselves, with the occasional Dane. Everybody was supposed to be European first and foremost.

Despite all this obligatory mixing, what impressed me most from observing the day to day workings of the European Parliament was how much each individual reflected aspects of her own nation. Not that people of a particular nation were all alike—far from it—but their variations reflected something called national character, in its various forms. As an American outsider, I always found the differences between countries to be the greatest charm of this piece of the world. Yet the European Construction project aims at making them more and more alike—even Americanized, given the strong American cultural and political influences.

The importance of language is inescapable. In theory, English, French and German were the official languages. But in the plenary session, and even in the committee and group meetings, with the exception of a few polyglots, each MEP spoke in his or her national language. This meant that every room where MEPs got together was lined with interpreter booths, each booth equipped with two interpreters to relay each other. Interpreters are very well paid, and their transport and hotel bills had to be paid every time a Group took a trip to somewhere, which was about every month. The cost of multilingualism was enormous. But however much or little they may learn a variety of English as the contemporary lingua franca, people are stubbornly, passionately attached to their native tongue (as the separatist tendencies of Flemish speakers in Belgium and Catalan speakers in Spain make clear).

When I started working for the Green Group, the languages spoken in Group meetings were German, French, Italian, Dutch and English. Before I left, Spanish, Swedish and Finnish had been added to the mix. And still more were to come.

I was quick to observe, when I was able to listen to both the original and the translation, that however skilled the interpreters were, working very fast under intense pressure, they were rarely able to convey fully the tone, the nuance and sometimes even the sense of what was being said. This could cause dissension between Members who were already inclined to regard each other with suspicion, as between certain Italian and German members.

It could only get worse as more languages were added. I may have lost count, but as I figure, there are now twenty languages that must be spoken in EP meetings. Now, it is quite impossible for even the most gifted interpreter sitting in the German language booth to be able to translate into German from Greek, Portuguese, Dutch, Latvian, Bulgarian, Czech, Slovak, Slovenian, Maltese, Danish, Swedish and Finnish. So what happens is that, in the case of a language she does not master, the German interpreter has to tune into another interpreter who has translated to a different language. If the speaker is Hungarian, the Finnish translator may understand and translate it into Finnish, which the Swedish interpreter can translate, and the German interpreter, who knows Swedish, can put it into German. Meanwhile, the French interpreter is waiting for the German version to translate into French. And perhaps the Portuguese can pick it up from the French. There may be even more stops along the way. This process can entail long waits, before it gets to whichever language I am tuned into.

Stubborn cultural differences can also be observed. I remember well the occasion when famous actors such as Gérard Depardieu and directors such as Ettore Scola came to Strasbourg to argue in favor of the "cultural exception" to the Treaties, meaning to exempt works of art, in this case movies, from free trade provisions that could enable nations with a huge domestic audience (meaning the United States) to dump their products on the European market, squeezing out domestic production. What was interesting was that the defenders of European cinema came from France, Italy, Spain, Portugal and Greece. I believe Germans were sympathetic. But the initiative found no sympathy among northern Europeans, notably Scandinavians, who saw nothing wrong with having only American productions to watch.

Extra-Parliamentary Activities

The EP schedule went like this. Assuming four weeks to the month, two weeks were spent in Brussels, mostly on committee and group meetings. One week was devoted to the plenary session in Strasbourg, where legislation was adopted (or amended) and resolutions were passed. The fourth week was free for travel, all expenses paid. Each trip had some virtuous purpose related to the Group's work.

While I was with the Group, from 1990 to 1996, we traveled to Saint Petersburg and to the Cotentin peninsula in Normandy to inspect and deplore nuclear power plants. We traveled to Denmark to admire the huge "alternative energy" wind turbines that have since caused growing protests in France for cluttering up the landscape and killing birds. We traveled to Rome, Paris, London, Helsinki, Amsterdam, Madrid and Istanbul. We went to Berlin several times, to savor German reunification. We went to Ireland to disapprove of the armed border between Ulster and the Republic. We went to the Spanish Basque country to eat local ham and show sympathy for regional identities. We went to Sardinia, I can't remember why. We went to Sofia, capital of Bulgaria, meeting in a university that used to welcome Third World students, in the time of communism, but was now empty. The wine was excellent.

Our most ambitious trip took us to Rio de Janeiro in the spring of 1992 to hold a "Planetary Green Meeting" on the eve of the United Nations Conference on Environment and Development (UNCED), known as the Rio Earth Summit.

I flew to Rio a week before the others to make arrangements and also to look around. This gave me time to attend a meeting of "Green Press" in the beautiful city of Horizonte. While I was there, a colleague told me that before returning to Rio, I absolutely must rent a car and go see the colonial town of Ouro Preto (Black Gold). The gold mines of Ouro Preto made a big contribution to enriching Portugal, and for a moment in the eighteenth century Vila Rica, as it was known then, was the most populous city in Latin America, embellished by gold-lined baroque churches. Okay, I want to see that.

The drive through the Serra do Espinhaço mountains took longer than expected, so I was scarcely able to glance at the architectural points of interest in Ouro Preto before I had to turn around and drive back to the Belo Horizonte airport. I had not gone more than half way when a violent tropical storm broke out. My rented car was a pokey old FIAT with a single windshield wiper, which suddenly stopped wiping. Completely. The sky blackened and the rain was so intense that I could see absolutely nothing but the rear lights of the car some thirty yards in front of me. I could not see the steep precipice on my right but I knew it was there. I was terrified that I would fall so far behind the more powerful car in front of me that I would lose sight of it, my sole point of orientation. I returned to the airport exhausted and indignant at having been provided with a car in that condition. But I was unable to vent my wrath because the personnel at the car rental office claimed to understand not a word of English, or of Spanish, or of anything but Portuguese.

Anyway, I got back to Rio alive, in time to make arrangements for the First Planetary Green Meeting. I even had time to take a walk through the nearby favela, against the advice of every Brazilian I met. I saw nothing more dangerous than the man standing in front of an Evangelical Church, beckoning for me to come be saved. I reflected on the fact that the Vatican, by suppressing liberation theology, had managed to turn Brazilian Christianity over to the Evangelicals, linked in various ways to the United States and much more compatible with the far right than the Brazilian Catholic Church used to be.

The Planetary Green Meeting was based on the (correct) assumption that the official Earth Summit would produce no great benefits for either the environment or for development.

Therefore, the initiative was to present our own "Green Agenda" with 75 alternative proposals. The meeting was organized in collaboration with the Brazilian *Partido Verde,* which was then in its prime, represented by the popular singing star Gilberto Gil, which ensured local media attention.[26] Some 200 Greens from a score of countries attended,

---

26 As an ally of the Workers Party, Gilberto Gil became Minister of Culture after Lula was elected President in 2002. However, in 2014, the Partido Verde voted for impeachment of Lula's successor, Dilma Roussef. The party has

with representatives from Mali playing a leading role in discussions of development and debt relief for Africa. I hung out a bit in Rio with Suzanne Manley, an American Green from California.

Our second and final press conference in Rio on June first actually did attract a satisfying number of reporters. It was the occasion for an odd and revealing incident. While this was supposed to be a purely Green event, Gianfranco Dell'Alba was caught and reprimanded for distributing tracts advertising the *Partito Radicale Internazionale.*

1992: A Year of Tragedy

On August 10, I received word that my dear cousin David Johnstone had been shot in the back as he took a walk through the streets of San Francisco.

David was an editor for Macmillan publishers, and was in San Francisco to meet with writers and agents. He was the youngest of my three Johnstone cousins, and the one I was closest to, perhaps because he was the least "perfect" in his career path and most interested in new ideas. He had a wonderful wife, Tina Mantis, of Greek origin, and two young children living in an old farmhouse on Staten Island. They were Unitarians, and David had a strong social conscience, which led him to volunteer to teach courses in prisons.

David survived the shooting, but the bullets struck his spine and left him totally paralyzed in the lower part of his body. He was flown to New York for treatment, and Macmillan quickly began plans to redesign his office to accommodate his handicap. I was able to speak with him by telephone in the New York clinic where he was under treatment. He explained that he had sensed something strange behind him, but what could he have done? What I remember most vividly was his worry that people thought there was something wrong with his reactions. "Here they think it is strange that I'm not angry." He was simply not an angry person, and he tried to understand.

It was soon established that David had been shot by a 16-year-old black youth as initiation to join a gang. A committee was formed in San Francisco for the boy's defense.

David showed great spirit, accepting his handicap, eager for rehabilitation exercises. Everyone around him thought of how to adapt

---

remained small and politically ambiguous.

to this new situation. Then, on August 24, he died. The multiple injuries had taken their toll.

To me and others in the family, there was no feeling of wanting revenge or of anything else regarding the young murderer. He and David had no relation to each other. It was an accident, and yes, guns do kill people.

For the next few years, Tina devoted all her free time to the crusade for gun control, organizing protest demonstrations, speaking, writing. It was more than a decade later, when her children had grown up, that she withdrew from the hopeless cause and began a new life.

My daughter Elizabeth, her husband François Gaudu and their sons William, 4, and André, 2, happened to be visiting the United States when this tragedy occurred. They attended the funeral at the Unitarian Church in Staten Island, "the saddest day in the world."

In Brussels, life went on. The Group planned to go on a retreat in the Ardennes forest of Wallonia, and I bought a short wave radio in order to stay in touch with the world in our rustic setting. In my separate cabin, I turned on the radio early on the morning of October 20, 1992 and heard that Petra Kelly and Gert Bastian had been found dead in Petra's house in Bonn. It appeared that Gert had shot Petra through the head as she slept and then killed himself with the other bullet in his service revolver. It took weeks before the bodies were discovered.

There was no note, no warning. Everyone was free to imagine an explanation for this horror.

It was observed that Petra's intensity made her "a difficult person," and this had been hard on Gert. I shared Eva Quistorp's feeling that Petra had been marginalized by the Grünen, even as they "marched through the institutions," to use the old German leftist phrase. The couple's marginalization was indicated by the ghastly fact that it took weeks for the bodies to be discovered. In Germany, the up and coming Green was Joschka Fischer, the "realist" from Frankfurt. Petra and Gert were "fundamentalists" in that they were fundamentally committed to combating NATO, war, armaments. Petra was still famous and invited all over the world, but her impact in Germany had vanished. Her health was always fragile, and Gert was beginning to doubt whether he was physically able to keep caring for her. He was known to believe that the far right was gaining influence in Germany. To me, the only word that fits this tragedy is despair.

European Construction

During the 1989–1994 session, undoubtedly the most significant European institutional business was the Treaty on European Union, signed by Member States in the Dutch city of Maastricht on February 7, 1992. The Maastricht Treaty greatly expanded the areas covered by the European Economic Community, renamed the European Community—on its way to be further renamed the European Union. It established monetary union, leading to the common currency, the Euro, introduced ten years later.

As usual with European Construction, the Treaty was very long, obscure and tediously legalistic, certainly not meant to be read by the citizens whose lives it would impact. The Green Group was strongly opposed to its ratification, more so than other groups, and this opposition had its paradoxical side.

The Group's position was defined essentially by its members on the Institutional Committee, Bruno Boissière (France) and Adelaïde Aglietta. Both were committed European federalists, and for Aglietta, European federalism (that is, a centralized European State, on the model of the United States of America) was her guiding motivation for being there. But it was precisely these ardent federalists who opposed the Maastricht Treaty for its clumsy architecture, its ambiguities, precisely its failure to provide a clear basis for a (more or less) democratic Europe. Instead of greater powers and simpler procedures for the European Parliament itself, the new procedures, as the Group stated, were "so complicated and obscure that the Members themselves will have trouble understanding them, and the thick fog of decision-making procedures ensures that neither the press nor the public will know or care what is going on in the European Community's only democratic institution."

Three countries were required by their national constitutions to hold popular referendums to ratify the Treaty: France, Denmark and Ireland. In addition, the Italian, German and Belgian parliaments had vowed not to ratify the Treaty if it was rejected by the European Parliament. The European Parliament had only the right to an unbinding opinion, but the Green Group called on the Parliament to use the conditions of those three national parliaments to make its own rejection binding. However, in its unbinding vote, the European Parliament accepted the report presented by British Laborite David Martin and called on Member States to "ratify the Treaty without delay despite its inadequacies."

The Danes voted against it in their referendum, but some concessions were made to get them back in. The British also obtained specific adjustments applying only to themselves. In France, it was strongly opposed by Jean-Pierre Chevènement, who pointed out that in the future, 80% of French laws would originate in Brussels. But any criticism from the left was loudly discredited by the fact that Jean-Marie Le Pen was against the Treaty too. Still, it was adopted by a very narrow margin (50.7% to 49.3%).

At that time, the vision of "Europe," however blurred, had largely taken the place of whatever political goals and utopias used to inspire people. For many on the left, the totally unfounded idea prevailed that what we were unable to accomplish in our own country might be accomplished by a "social Europe."

But there was nothing "social" in the Maastricht Treaty.

Certainly, the Treaty was ghastly from an institutional point of view, but what particularly disturbed me were the economic provisions. Normally, a constitution sets out an institutional framework, suitable to accommodate whatever policies are subsequently decided. But the Maastricht Treaty (and its later versions) very precisely defined in advance not only the institutions but the economic policies that Member States are obliged to follow.

The "principles" were set out in Article 2:

> The Community shall have as its task, by establishing a common market and an economic and monetary union and by implementing the common policies or activities referred to in Articles 3 and 3a, to promote throughout the Community a harmonious and balanced development of economic activities, sustainable and non-inflationary growth respecting the environment, a high degree of convergence of economic performance, a high level of employment and of social protection, the raising of the standard of living and quality of life, and economic and social cohesion and solidarity among Member States.

The key here is "sustainable and non-inflationary growth," which is the watchword of the Germany Ordoliberals. Whether "growth" can be "non-inflationary" in all circumstances is highly debatable. "Sustainable" is a problematic term to qualify capitalist growth, which is characterized by dramatic ups and downs. Member States and the Community were required to act in accordance with the principle of "an open market with free competition"—free competition being rule number one in the European construction. This ultimately canceled the right of any Member State to protect its vital utilities, infrastructure and resources from takeover by the highest bidder from some other country.

The "primary objective" of the European Central Banks "shall be to maintain price stability." Combating inflation is all very well, but shouldn't banks be there to finance projects of public utility, such as infrastructure, energy sources, and large-scale industrial innovation?

Not under the Maastricht Treaty: "Overdraft facilities or any other type of credit facility with the ECB [European Central Bank] or with the central banks of the Member States in favor of Community institutions or bodies, central governments [...] or public undertakings of Member States *shall be prohibited* [...]." (My emphasis.)

Reading this, it suddenly struck me. The Maastricht Treaty ruled out Keynesianism—which, whatever its faults, has proven extremely effective in appropriate situations. It ruled out any national industrial policy.

Moreover, if States needed money, they must turn to commercial banks, with the interest rates set by the latter.

All of this gave vital decision-making power on the choice of investments to private financial institutions.

In practice, as has become clear twenty years later, the Maastricht criteria have not produced "a harmonious and balanced development of economic activities," or "sustainable and non-inflationary growth respecting the environment" (rather, lower growth rates than in the rest of the world, including in Switzerland and Norway, European countries not regulated by the Treaties); "a high degree of convergence of economic performance" (look at Greece); "a high level of employment and of social protection" (record unemployment and austerity measures nibbling away at European countries' social protection); the raising of the standard of living and quality of life" (well yes, for a privileged minority); and "economic and social cohesion and solidarity among Member States" (dissension and resentments continue to grow between Member States).

The Greens were absolutely right to oppose the Maastricht Treaty as an institutional monstrosity. But it was also an economic strait jacket, which was not their main concern.

Thursday in Strasbourg

Every Thursday of their monthly week in Strasbourg, MEPs can escape from the tedious work of approving amendments that will be ignored and enjoy a hearty session of giving moral lessons to the world. In this session, MEPs get to speak (within their allotted minutes or seconds) on "topical and urgent subjects of major importance." The debates culminate in what are called "urgent resolutions." Aside from occasional natural catastrophes, the urgent subjects concern human rights violations, usually in places MEPs had no reason to know much about. Their information came from specialized NGOs.

Who was listening to these virtuous mini-speeches? Aside from the latest busload of tourists trying out the simultaneous translation earphones in the gallery, virtually no one. The media echo is far from deafening. The urgent resolutions gain resonance with distance. In Bogota or Kuala Lumpur, the thought that their own national problems attracted the attention of the faraway European Parliament may appear significant. But these resolutions scarcely reflect genuine European concern.

The other function of the urgent resolutions is to enforce, among the MEPs themselves, the belief in "European values," the confidence that "Europe" is the world center of "human rights," with the duty and privilege of denouncing violations anywhere in the world. Like the generous salaries, the urgent resolutions give MEPs the reassuring impression that they are important, despite their powerlessness. Indeed, the basic purpose of the very existence of the European Parliament is to give the impression, primarily to Europeans themselves, that their institutions are democratic, with an elected Parliament.

The one instance where this virtuous exercise attracts media attention is the annual Sakharov prize, awarded for "freedom of thought" every October. Naming the prize after a famous Soviet dissident made it clear that this was not going to be politically neutral. Yes, there have been a few neutral choices (the first, Nelson Mandela), the Mothers of the Plaza de Mayo, and some humanitarians. But the "dissidents" are always chosen to illustrate that West is best. In twenty years the dissidents cited included two Russians, three Cubans, two Chinese, two Belarussians and, during the wars of Yugoslav disintegration, a leading Bosnian Muslim newspaper and two Kosovo Albanian nationalists.

Aside from making MEPs feel good about themselves, these prizes and urgent resolutions are intended to interfere in the political life of the countries involved. This exercise enforces the growing tendency in the Western political class toward "humanitarian intervention" and "regime change" justified by the superior "values" of our "democratic free market society," understood as the desirable model for all mankind.

24.

Lost in the Balkans

During the early nineties, the conflict in Bosnia, or rather the media portrayal of the conflict in Bosnia, was increasingly invading public consciousness, so that by the 1994 European Parliamentary elections it was widely considered the major issue in Europe, overshadowing all the rest.

I must admit that I was too busy with the stream of various issues dealt with by the Green Group in the European Parliament to give the Bosnian situation my full attention. The media presented it more as a series of repugnant atrocities than as a political issue (which would have aroused my analytic interest). I was worried and regretted that I was no longer free to investigate what was going on, but initially I did not suspect the extent of deception involved in the portrayal of the Bosnian drama.

Yugoslavia's Vulnerability

Yet I had reason to distrust the simplistic version being sold to the public. Back in 1984, on a visit to Belgrade, I had had long conversations with leaders of the internationally known Praxis group (a Marxist discussion group, which had many contacts with the British Labor Party). I spent hours with Professor Sveta Stojanovic, an internationally recognized scholar who had spent time at the Wilson Center in Washington, and his wife Andjelka Dotlic, my roommate in the Studenski Dom thirty years earlier.

Yugoslavia had suffered badly from the oil crises of the 1970s. The Iran-Iraq war had deprived Yugoslavia of Iraqi oil imports which it had already paid for in the form of important construction work there. As a result of debt and economic stagnation, the International Monetary Fund had moved in and was imposing unpopular austerity measures.

Tito had united the war-torn multiethnic country as it emerged from Nazi occupation by a socially and economically ambitious program of industrialization combined with popular worker self-management socialism. Yugoslavs enjoyed personal freedoms unknown in the Soviet bloc. But in a move to assuage an upsurge of Croatian nationalism in the 1970s, Tito had granted greater autonomy to the political leaders of Croatia and the other Republics and autonomous regions composing the Federation, often empowering political bureaucrats at the expense of worker self-management. After Tito's death in 1980, the country found itself with no strong central government able to deal with the IMF or impose positive policies on the Republics. The debt crisis fostered an "every man for himself" reflex among the Republics—let the others pay the debt. In such a multicultural nation, it was easy to find ethnic pretexts for these centrifugal movements.

The Praxis solution was to revive self-management by extending the possibilities for democratic choice upward from the workplace to where significant economic decisions were made—at the level of national (rather than local) investment.

In March 1984, Stojanovic called for democratization of the ruling party (the League of Communists of Yugoslavia) in order to foster democratic reform socialism. Stojanovic did not call for a multiparty system for two reasons: he wanted to make a practical proposal that the ruling party might accept; and political pluralism in multiethnic Yugoslavia would favor "re-Balkanization." That is, local ethnic rivalries risked being exploited by Great Powers—something that had notoriously happened in the past.

This background information should have enabled me to realize quickly that the ethnic conflicts which emerged dramatically in the early 1990s were influenced by complex economic problems. But Western media hastily attributed these conflicts to a simple spontaneous "rise of nationalism." Although it was only one among several, "Serbian nationalism" was compared to "the rise of Nazism" in the 1930s—a comparison with no relation to reality. But it caught the public ear. Later I learned that separatists in the Republics of Croatia and Bosnia had hired a U.S. public relations firm (Ruder Finn) precisely to develop that comparison, equating Serbs with Nazis, notably in Bosnia. But initially I was distracted and slow to put the pieces of the puzzle together.

Echoes of the First World War

There were many other significant factors which I ignored at the time and only learned years later, when I got around to systematic research.

From the vantage point of the European Parliament, a supremely relevant factor which I ignored at the time was the role of an association founded in Austria in 1978 called *Alpen-Adria,* building links between provinces of Austria, Italy and Yugoslavia, located between the Alps and the Adriatic Sea. All of these provinces, which in Yugoslavia included Slovenia and Croatia, had formerly belonged to the Austro-Hungarian Empire. Now it so happened that the most prominent sponsor of *Alpen-Adria* was Otto von Habsburg, the legitimate heir to that defunct Empire. Alpen-Adria had a strong ideological role, encouraging those former Habsburg provinces to consider themselves "more European" and thus culturally vastly superior to regions to their south, notably Serbia.

The Habsburgs had lost their centuries-old, powerful empire as a result of the First World War, or more precisely, as a result of the terms imposed by the Versailles treaties which had split the Empire between Germanic Austria itself, Hungary and surrounding states. This included creating Yugoslavia (south Slavs), an idea raised by Croatian patriots who hoped for greater independence by shifting their territory to the winning side, that is, by joining with the Kingdom of Serbia, then closely allied with France. Unfortunately, the Kingdom of the Serbs, Croats and Slovenians (later Yugoslavia) was marked from the start by tensions between the Catholic Croats and the Orthodox Christian Serbs, despite their common language. Such tensions could only warm the hearts of Habsburg loyalists who never accepted the loss of "their" Croatia to the Serbian enemy—whom they blamed for the assassination of the Archduke Francis Ferdinand in Sarajevo that led to the war and the dismantling of the Habsburg Empire.

And the leader of the Habsburg loyalists was, of course, none other than Otto von Habsburg. Otto von Habsburg was a Member of the European Parliament, elected from Bavaria on the conservative Christian Social Union list. He was also the most influential member of the European Parliament's foreign affairs committee.

It sometimes occurred to me that Otto von Habsburg was as good a Habsburg as any of his illustrious ancestors. I had occasion to share an elevator with him, chat in his presence at the bar over the evening *crémant d'Alsace,* watch him stroll casually down the rue Grétry on a Brussels evening. He had the aplomb of the true aristocrat, a command of German, Spanish and French which he used alternately in the Parliamentary debates and prided himself on following the Chinese adage: "Once you have a firm objective, time doesn't matter." Which objective might that be? What could be more natural than his aspiration to reconstruct the Empire of his forebears? In a new form perhaps, via European integration. I saw nothing at all shocking in this. What surprised me was that his EP colleagues never seemed to wonder how his unique background might influence his political motivations.

I remember one Strasbourg week when von Habsburg sponsored a special exhibit of photographs in the hall of the European Parliament designed to show that Croatia is "in the very heart of Europe," contrary to its Serbian neighbor. "Croatian culture" included relics of the Roman Empire, dating prior to the migration of the Southern Slavs into the Balkans. Most blatant was a pair of photos, one of an Austrian-style public building in Vukovar entitled "Croatian Culture" and the other, of the same building in ruins, entitled "Serbian culture." Nobody knew that Vukovar had been a mixed town when that building was constructed and that it was no more "Croatian" than "Serb," just as the civil war that devastated it was no more Serb than Croat. Indeed, the result of that conflict had been to expel from Croatia the Serb population that had lived there for centuries.

By the time of that exhibit, in early 1996, I had a clear idea of what was going on. But my early revelation took place on March 30, 1993, when the President of Yugoslavia, Dobrica Cosic (pronounced Dobritsa Chossich), appeared before the foreign affairs committee of the European Parliament.

It is necessary to explain this appearance. In what was left of disintegrating Yugoslavia, comprised only of Serbia and Montenegro, the power was in the hands of Slobodan Milosevic, the democratically elected President of Serbia. Milosevic chose Dobrica Cosic, Serbia's most distinguished novelist, for the symbolic role of President of Yugoslavia, no doubt precisely in an effort to establish dialogue with the rest of the world. Contrary to the media story, Milosevic was less concerned with the Bosnian war than with ending sanctions against Serbia. Bosnia was then independent, with a civil war being waged mainly between Bosnian Serbs fighting for their own autonomous territory (as *Republika Srpska*) and the Muslim party headed by Alijah Izetbegovic, fighting to unify Bosnia under its own domination. The international sanctions were imposed on Serbia in punishment for its presumed leading role in the Bosnian war. In reality, the Milosevic government of Serbia was strongly urging *Republika Srpska* to seek a settlement with the Muslim side, and even cut off aid when it refused to do so. (Eventually, U.S. envoy Richard Holbrooke used Milosevic's desire for peace to broker an end to the Bosnian war.)

Cosic had come to Brussels to plead for peaceful mediation. In fact, Cosic was such a strong advocate of compromise that he went so far as to propose voluntary partition of the Serbian province of Kosovo, to end strife with the province's Albanian population.

I attended the hearing in the European Parliament and found out that no one was hearing and no one was listening. The Yugoslav President scarcely had a chance to expose his ideas. Instead he faced a barrage of unanswerable hostile questions of the "when will you stop massacring civilians?" type. It was taken for granted that the Serbs were all guilty of "ethnic cleansing." The hostility was overwhelming, and the only perceptible motivation of the MEPs was to show each other how anti-Serb they were.

Behind all this was the persistent influence of Otto von Habsburg, who easily imposed his analysis of events on his colleagues who for the most part knew nothing at all about Serbia, Croatia, Albania and their history.

To my considerable surprise, Cosic was accompanied by my old friend Sveta Stojanovic, who acted as guide and interpreter. The morning after this futile hearing, I met Sveta at his hotel for a long conversation, which was the start of my effort to educate myself seriously.

But first of all, I was kept busy as the Greens prepared for the 1994 European Parliamentary elections.

There were changes in the Group. In particular, certain *Radicali* dropped their Green guise for more congenial surroundings. Marco Taradash, the champion of drug legalization, left the Greens for Berlusconi. For his part, the Italian co-Secretary General of the Green Group, Gianfranco Dell'Alba, got himself elected to the Parliament as a candidate on the Marco Pannella list (and again in 1999 on the Emma Bonino list who succeeded Pannella as leader of the *Partito Radicale*). In 1998 he became secretary general of "No Peace Without Justice," an organization devoted to demanding that Serbs be prosecuted for their alleged crimes in Yugoslav civil wars. Most significantly, in March 2009 Dell'Alba was named Representative of Confindustria—the Italian industrialists association—to the European Union in Brussels. In short, the revolving door took him from the Green Group to Italy's top business lobbying group. Despite all his institutional skill, in 2017 Dell'Alba fell for an email scam and transferred half a million euros of Confindustria money to the unidentified scammer, leading to the end of that phase of his career.

As for Emma Bonino, I last saw her around 2000 at a *Médecins du Monde* conference in Paris, where she joined with a top NATO general in extolling NATO as the best instrument for defense of human rights in the world.

In 1994, the version of the Bosnian conflict peddled by Christiane Amanpour on CNN and by Florence Hartmann in *Le Monde,* was leading to ever more emotional calls to "do something," especially by military means. In reality, that conflict had deep roots in history. Here I can only refer readers to my own 2002 book, *Fools' Crusade,* which covers much of the background. But this extremely complex situation was boiled down by leading media into a simple tale of Good versus Evil, identifying the Muslims with Good and the Serbs with Evil, and on that basis calling on the virtuous West to intervene on the side of Goodness.

The European Parliament had absolutely no power to do anything about this, but the habit of the urgent resolutions had encouraged the growing liberal tendency to give moral lessons to the world. In an age of neoliberalism when "the markets" make the big decisions, the very powerlessness of politicians, especially on the left, has contributed to making "humanitarian" advocacy appear to be the most important thing they can do, when they can't do much of anything else.

The vast "pro-Bosnia" campaign was based on several misrepresentations of the truth. The Presidency of Bosnia-Herzegovina was supposed to rotate between Muslims, Serbs and Croats, but once in office, the leader of the Muslim party, Alija Izetbegovic, had stayed there. Izetbegovic, who initially was not even all that popular among Muslims, publicly advocated introducing Islamic law wherever Muslims were a majority. This threat frightened the Serb inhabitants of Bosnia, whose ancestors had spent centuries as second-class citizens under Turkish Muslim rule. Their aim was simply to retain control of areas where they constituted a clear majority, but where to draw the lines was disputed. "Why should I be a minority in your country when you can be a minority in mine?" was the theme of the war over territory.

A huge propaganda campaign convinced the Western public that the Serbs had "invaded" Bosnia, just as Hitler invaded Poland, Belgium and France, in order to massacre defenseless Muslims. Since the Bosnian Serb forces were initially stronger than the Muslim forces, the Muslims were described as champions of "multiculturalism," innocent victims of Serbian nationalism. Supporters of the Muslims called for arming the Muslims, or as they put it, for creating "an even playing field." This sounds very fair in polo, but in war it can keep the conflict going indefinitely. What was not revealed at the time was that the UN arms embargo was being systematically violated, and the Muslim side was receiving not only arms but Mujahidin combatants from major Muslim countries, Afghanistan, Saudi Arabia and Iran, among others. And behind the "even playing field" slogan was the emerging call for NATO to go in on the Muslim side.

The identification of Bosnian Muslims with Jews during the Holocaust had great resonance, especially among Jewish intellectuals. At an international Green meeting in Paris, Joschka Fischer, alluding to Cohn-Bendit's Jewish origins, claimed that Dany could "sniff out these things" and had convinced him that the Serbs were a threat. The most spectacular champion of the Bosnian Muslims was Bernard-Henri Lévy, who put together a list of French candidates for the 1994 European Parliamentary elections called *L'Europe commence à Sarajevo* (Europe begins in Sarajevo), claiming that the future of multicultural Europe hung on the fate of "multicultural Sarajevo." The intellectuals on BHL's list seem to have confounded the messy situation in the Balkans with the Nazi conquest of Europe: Léon Schwartzenberg, André Glucksmann were the most prominent. There was support from Susan Sontag. The list was dropped before the election when BHL judged that it had served its purpose: made Bosnia the main issue. Bernard Kouchner, the one-time *Médecins sans frontières* doctor who has made a career of denouncing rather than curing, claimed that the idea was his own, because it promoted his pet idea of "the right to intervene."

BHL took part in outright deception, having himself filmed crouching against a wall in Sarajevo to avoid Serbian snipers, when full photos show people walking past casually, with no fear of snipers. United Nations peace-keeping officers on the spot (Canadian General MacKenzie, French General Morillon, et al) understood that the strategy of the Izetbegovic regime in Sarajevo was to use—or even manufacture—enemy attacks on civilians in order to goad NATO into intervention on the Muslim side. But that was not the media story.

The theme developed by a vast public relations campaign was "ethnic cleansing," a custom described as characteristically Serb, along with mass rape. As an example, the NGO *Médecins du Monde* covered France with billboards, featuring popular cinema stars Jane Birkin and Michel Piccoli, likening Milosevic to Hitler.

While all this was going on, Alexander Langer, at the time co-President of the Green Group alongside Claudia Roth, was the leading Green member of the Parliament's foreign policy committee and thus responsible for the Group's position on Bosnia and other Yugoslav conflicts. With his background as son of an Austrian father and Italian mother living in the contested territory of Alto Adige/Sud Tirol, Alex was particularly motivated to promote reconciliation. While everyone else was joining in the anti-Serb chorus, Alex worked with Austrians and Italians to found the Verona Forum, which organized meetings of representatives of the various nationalities in Yugoslavia with the aim of finding solutions. I followed his work eagerly. It was clear from these meetings that there were advocates of reconciliation in all ethnic groups and that the grounds for peaceful compromise existed. It was not as clear then as it later became that major NATO powers that did not want peaceful settlements: in fact, they wanted to use the human tragedy of Yugoslavia as an excuse to intervene.

As the cry for intervention rose, the Green Group retained a moderate position thanks to Alexander Langer's commitment to mediation rather than military threats.

Dany the Multicolored

I was very much surprised in those days by the sudden change of attitude among Germans concerning German involvement in wars. For years I had been hearing German Greens and Socialists repent of their country's past and vow to put an end to the *Feindbilder,* enemy stereotypes, applied to Slavic peoples that the Nazis had treated as dangerously inferior and in need of being invaded. All of a sudden, that taboo was lifted. In World War II, Germany had attacked Yugoslavia, absorbed Slovenia into the Reich, created an independent racist Croatia, and treated Serbs as the prime enemy. And now they were back at it, all with a clear conscience.

On April 8, 1993, the Constitutional Court in Karlsruhe ruled that despite the constitutional ban on Germany waging external wars, it was all right for German armed forces to take an active combat role in Bosnia, in the form of AWAKS flights. Four days later, NATO was flying in Bosnian skies. On April 26, the UN imposed total sanctions against Serbia, and on May 31, Cosic was ousted as President of Yugoslavia. His peace mission had failed. Nobody in the West wanted to hear a message of reconciliation from Serbia. The dominant mood was that Serbia was guilty and Serbs must be punished.

German involvement in military action was nevertheless highly controversial in Germany itself, strongly opposed by most German Greens. However, around this time an article appeared in the Berlin leftist daily, *Die Tageszeitung* (*"Die Taz"*), calling for German participation in NATO action against Bosnian Serbs, written by Dany Cohn-Bendit. The author had become famous as the emblematic figure in the May '68 disruptions, labeled by the media as "Dany the Red." Now he was a "Green." But he was never a "red" nor even ever a real "green." In reality, Daniel Cohn-Bendit was always a certain brand of anarchist. Not a leftwing anarchist. But a liberal-libertarian anarchist, a "let's break the rules for the fun of it" anarchist, in perfect sync with the economic theories of Milton Friedman.

In an exceptional move, I wrote to *Die Taz* with a response, actually contradicting a Green, pointing out that if anyone should *not* intervene militarily in Bosnia, it was surely the Germans, in light of their responsibility for the atrocities committed there in the 1940s. But that was only the beginning.

In the June 1994 elections, Daniel Cohn-Bendit was eighth on the list of the German Greens, as many in the party opposed him and hoped he wouldn't make it. But the Grünen did well enough for him to be elected.

The Grünen grew so rapidly that they were bound to attract opportunists who jumped on their bandwagon out of ambition rather than conviction. The prime example of this phenomenon was the tandem of Joschka Fischer and Dany Cohn-Bendit who together took control of the party in Frankfurt, under the banner of "realism." Neither showed any serious signs of ecological concern. Certainly, it was easy for them to abandon "fundamental principles" (the fault of those whom they branded "fundis") in favor of realistic pursuit of power.

Fischer had been a street fighter anarchist of modest origins, linked to groups that attacked nearby U.S. Army headquarters, who gave up his hell-raising for what was to become an extraordinarily successful political career. Cohn-Bendit came from a well-to-do Jewish family and never had to take a serious job—for him, everything seemed to be play. His parents sent him to a world-famous progressive boarding school near Frankfurt, the Odenwaldschule, whose slogan was "be who you are." Students and teachers mixed, calling each other by their first names. In 2015 the school was shut down following confirmed accusations of sexual abuse. But the "do whatever you want" attitude marked Dany Cohn-Bendit's role in May '68, centering on demands for mixed dormitories and sexual freedom at the University of Nanterre. After May '68, Dany pursued his anarchist course in Frankfurt as he ran an "anti-authoritarian" kindergarten. In his 1975 book *Le Grand Bazar,* he recounted playing sex games with pre-schoolers—an assertion he later explained as "verbal provocation" appropriate for the '70s but no longer acceptable.[27]

Watching Dany's behavior as Green MEP convinced me that he was fundamentally a lifelong spoiled brat. He would lounge back during meetings, as if in a vacation hammock. He would speak German without using the microphone, so that the interpreters could not hear him and those in the room who did not understand German had no idea what he was saying. That was characteristic of his cheerful indifference to everybody but himself.

The media loved him. While generally ignoring the more serious business of the Parliament, camera crews would follow Dany down corridors in hopes of an impertinent remark.

We were all invited to his fiftieth birthday party, in a Strasbourg restaurant, on April 4, 1995. The guests took places at tables, while Dany sat with his pal, Bernard Kouchner (the "humanitarian intervention" champion) facing us on a sort of stage, flanked by young women. The two heroes bragged jokingly about their great revolutionary past. When they began to sing the *Internationale* in a tone of mockery, Juan Behrend, with his Argentine experience, had to hide his revulsion at the contempt shown for people who had lived and died for their ideal. When the show was over, we realized we all had to pay for the expensive food and drink we had just consumed.

The End

On July 4, 1995, the Group was plunged into a state of shock. Word reached us that Alexander Langer's body had been found hanging from an apricot tree overlooking Florence. A note was found somewhere, stating simply, "I can't hack it any longer."

As in all such cases, tears mingled with disbelief. Magda Alvoet, a sensible Flemish Belgian, was chosen to replace Alex as Co-President of the Green Group alongside Claudia Roth. In January, Magda had organized a truly balanced symposium of experts on Rwanda, examining the background history of the massacres in April 1994, including the invasion from Uganda of Kagame's Tutsi army which initiated the conflict, culminating in massive slaughter of Tutsis as Kagame seized power. Magda displayed a capacity to seek to understand all sides of

---

27 "Daniel Cohn-Bendit scandaleux à Apostophe," The Museum of Cinema, dailymotion, https://www.dailymotion.com/video/x9kq78.

a complex, tragic situation—a capacity that was no doubt always rare and has been becoming rarer. It is a capacity vitally needed in efforts to mediate disputes and end conflicts.

A week later, on July 11, 1995, the town of Srebrenica[28] fell to Bosnian Serb forces. It took a while for rumors of massacres to emerge, and at the time we were all in mourning for Alex. In a press conference, Bosnian Foreign Minister Mohamed Sacirbey called for military support. As a highly educated American of Bosnian Muslim origin, Sacirbey made a good impression.

Dany Cohn-Bendit angrily attacked the Group's failure to "do something" to save people in Srebrenica. Claudia explained that we were too distracted by Alex's death. Cohn-Bendit demanded that the Group make a declaration: "We must either provide military means to Bosnia or defend Bosnia ourselves."

Austrian Green MEP Johannes Vogenhubber replied that "Powerless rage doesn't get rid of powerlessness. I have seen no explanation as to how military intervention would be successful. Instead let's use our resources to establish a constructive political position."

Events were moving fast. On August 4, Croatian forces, with U.S. backing, drove the Serbian population out of the borderline Krajina region—the biggest "ethnic cleansing" of the Yugoslav wars. Nobody in the West cared what happened to Serbs.

In the foreign affairs committee of the Parliament on July 26, Dany pounded the table in approval of calls by Marco Pannella and Otto von Habsburg to get tough with the Serbs. German MEP (CSU) Doris Pack rejected Belgrade's peace moves. She made the extravagant claim that in the Bosnian Serb capital of Banja Luka, "people are being tortured, Muslims there are the Jews of today." (There was no evidence for this.)

On August 28, a mortar killed 37 civilians in Sarajevo; the media (briefed by the Muslim side) instantly attributed the massacre to Serbs. This was questioned by U.N. military experts on the spot, but everyone who was not there knew who the "bad guys" were. The very next day the parliament in the Serb part of Bosnia ("Republika Srpska") voted to approve a U.S.-backed peace plan. But a day after that, on August

---

28 I have written at length about the Srebrenica massacres and have been strongly criticized for insisting that the killing of military-aged men in wartime, while sparing women, children and the aged in a single town, is a war crime but not "genocide." I cannot go through all that again here, but refer readers to my book, *Fools' Crusade.*

30, NATO carried out air strikes against Bosnian Serb forces. This was NATO's first act of non-defensive war, acting outside its defense treaty area, which it justified on humanitarian grounds.

Other conflicts were dividing the Group. There was a sharp split over the terms of the Maastricht Treaty. Vogenhubber and Frieder Otto Wolf, the most intellectual of the Grünen, were wary of European federalism. Frieder warned that European Monetary Union would be "a factor splitting the EU between the hard core and the periphery." (He turned out to be quite right.).

Dany Cohn-Bendit, in contrast, was viscerally opposed to the Nation State as such. He always favored drowning the nation in open border migration. "The nation state is a dangerous structure, if the wrong people come to power," he insisted. This reflected the Hitler obsession that has deformed political debate for decades. But wouldn't a federal Europe be even more dangerous "if the wrong people come to power"? And what about world government? What if "the wrong people" rule the whole world?

On October 24, 1995, the Group got around to deciding who would take Alex's place as leading Green delegate to the foreign affairs committee. There were two candidates. One was an East German Green, Elisabeth Schroedter, who was already active on the committee, focusing on foreign policy, in particular a common security concept with the Russian Federation. She wanted Europe's security policy to be diplomatic and non-military. She was the favored candidate of the majority of the German Greens.

Dany Cohn-Bendit found her too unknown. Who would listen to such a person? "Alex was known and listened to," said Dany. "Our position must be heard. I have a high profile and people listen to me. The Group must make full use of its resources"—meaning Dany's notoriety.

Dany casually admitted that he did not share the Group's position on all issues, and he might take their views into consideration or he might not.

Frieder Otto Wolf objected: "Green policy is not just a matter of personalities, it is a matter of content. I don't agree with Dany about drug legalization, for instance, but that is minor. Foreign policy is of major importance. We must stress the connection between ecology and peace. If not, we can do irreparable damage to the Green cause."

Dany was ready with an answer. "Damaging to the Greens? I'm invited all over Europe to help Greens. Next time I'll tell them, hey, take Frieder and see if that works better."

The vote was close, giving Elisabeth Schroedter 13 votes to Dany's 14.

After the vote I went to dinner with Johannes Vogenhubber who was as upset as I was. Something grave had just happened to the Greens. They had allowed mass media choice of star personalities to determine a major policy issue.

If the word soul has a meaning, and I believe it does, it designates a consistency, an adherence to the guiding principles of an individual or a Group. That evening, by a single vote, the Green Group lost its soul.

PART VIII

The Joint Criminal Enterprise

25.

The Scene of the Crimes

For six years, I had been wanting to go back to Yugoslavia. As long as I was working for the Green Group in the European Parliament, this was impossible, but I knew that as soon as I left the Group in June 1996, Yugoslavia would be my priority, and I began to prepare for it.

In *Le Monde diplomatique,* I read that there was a Paris-based review called "Dialogue" which had all the relevant documents on the background of the Yugoslav crisis, notably the then-notorious "Memorandum of the Serbian Academy of Arts and Sciences" which was constantly referred to by Western media as proof of Serbia's genocidal tendencies. I wanted to read it for myself, both in translation and in the original. So on November 3, 1995, I arranged to meet Bogoljub Kochovic, Dragan Pavlovic and the novelist Negovan Rajic, who edited this review dedicated to fostering rational dialogue among Yugoslavs of various political viewpoints and backgrounds. They provided me with all the documents I wanted, and soon even coopted me onto their editorial board, which included Croats, Slovenians, Bosnians and Serbs—all still considering themselves Yugoslav.

Had the commentators who cited "the Memorandum" actually read it? A French textbook for advanced high school students included this item:

> Ethnic cleansing: theory elaborated by members of the Serbian Academy of Sciences in Belgrade, which advocates ethnic homogenization of the territories of former Yugoslavia inhabited by Serbs, by using terror to drive out the other populations in order to enable the final annexation of these territories by Serbia.

This was totally false, from start to finish. In a school textbook!

The Memorandum was basically a critique of communist party rule, focusing on economic policies. A separate section, written by Professor Vasilije Krestic, blamed communist leadership for stigmatizing Serbia as the "oppressor nation" in Yugoslavia. This, he claimed, had encouraged the Albanians of Kosovo to drive Serbs out of Kosovo.

> Unless things change radically, in less than ten years' time there will no longer be any Serbs left in Kosovo, and an "ethically pure" Kosovo, that unambiguously stated goal of the Greater Albanian racists [...] will be achieved.
>
> The physical, political, legal and cultural genocide of the Serbian population in Kosovo is a worse defeat than any suffered in the liberation wars waged by Serbia... from 1804 to 1941.

The language may have been excessive (Professor Krestic later regretted having used the super-charged term "genocide"). But he was clearly not advocating "ethnic homogenization" but rather complaining that Serbs were its victims in Kosovo. The only explanation for this false interpretation of the Memorandum can be that journalists accepted without proof what they were told by interested parties, and textbook authors simply copied what they read in the newspapers (*Le Monde,* to be precise).

My reading of this and other documents was enough to make clear to me that the reality of Yugoslavia was hidden by a vast smokescreen of lies.

On a trip to New York in May 1996, Katrina van den Heuvel, who had written asking me to contribute to *The Nation,* received me kindly and said she would be delighted to have me contribute articles on Yugoslavia.

In September 1996, for the first time in many years, I set out in my little yellow Opel Corsa to see what I could see of what used to be Yugoslavia. Since I wanted the autonomy of driving my own car, I was basically limited to Slovenia and Croatia, the only parts of the shattered country covered by European auto insurance. The wars were over, but Serbia was still under sanctions.

On my way through Italy, I stopped with friends in Vicenza, where a vigorous campaign led by the Northern League was calling for secession of north-eastern Italy in a new state to be called Padania. The parallel was striking. Just as in northern Yugoslavia, the movement for secession was not inspired by political oppression but by the desire of the rich regions to secede from the poorer ones.

The Dalmatian coast is a marvel of bays and islands, with a great potential for harbors. Zadar, Split and Dubrovnik have all been important cities since antiquity. The coast backs up against a great wall of massive, rugged grey stone mountains, the Dinaric Alps, perhaps the most forbidding mountains in Europe. These mountains and their isolated valleys have been the setting for much of the most ferocious killing in recent wars. This magnificent natural setting is now Croatia's principal treasure—much appreciated by German vacationers.

In Split, the old port city built on the remains of the Roman Emperor Diocletian's palace, I stopped to interview several people. Top of my list was Nikola Viskovic, professor of philosophy of law at the University of Split and founder of the local Green Action Party. Over a long lunch of excellent fish and white wine, I took down notes as Professor Viskovic talked, but they had to remain off the record, as academic posts in Croatia were all having to be reconfirmed under the new nationalist regime. According to Nikola Viskovic:

> The Tudjman regime[29] is authoritarian, along the lines of the South American type of regime based on presidential power supported by the military. But in some ways it is even worse. I know whereof I speak as my mother is Chilean and I have lived in South America. What is worse than South America is the racist, neo-fascist element. In the army, the police and the party, but also in public opinion, the prevailing ideology and behavior reflect the extreme racist attitude of the Ustashe.[30]
>
> The first great massacre of the war was in Gospic, a mixed town in Croatia near the Serb Krajina.[31] At night, about 150 Serb men and women were taken in trucks and massacred. In Srebrenica the women and children were spared, but in Gospic the women were massacred too. Everybody knows that

29 Franjo Tudjman, a former communist and General in the Yugoslav Army, led Croatia's secession from Yugoslavia. He was President of the newly independent country until his death in 1999.

30 The Ustashe were a fascist party that ruled "The independent State of Croatia" under Nazi occupation of Yugoslavia in World War II, notorious for its mass murders of Serbs and Jews in pursuit of an ethnically pure Croatia.

31 Krajina (meaning borderland) is a region of southeastern Croatia traditionally inhabited by a large Serb population, brought there by the Habsburgs to defend the Empire from Muslim invasion.

> the killers were led by Tihomir Oleskovic who now has a restaurant near Zagreb. But the international media have shown no interest and the International Tribunal at The Hague ignores the matter.
>
> The international community is interested in human rights violations only in Bosnia, not in Croatia. Personally, I don't worry about men: they make the war. I worry for women and children. They are the ones who suffer from the Balkan logic of group responsibility...

During my travels, I avoided hotels. All along the coast, family houses of German size, solidity and cleanliness offer rooms to tourists. I invariably opened conversation in Serbo-Croatian, trying hard to give it a Croatian accent, and would then accept lapsing into German when the going got rough. The embarrassing thing about inadequate mastery of a language is that one can easily ask questions, but then fail to understand the answers.

Leaving Split in a driving rain, I followed a "Soba/Zimmer" sign to a very Catholic peasant home where I was fed on fried eggs, pork fat and an excellent ratatouille. This household was fiercely loyal to Tudjman's Croatia and the Mother of God. When the evening television broadcast concluded with scenes of marching naval officers, my hostess burst enthusiastically into the naval anthem. The atmosphere was heavy with patriotism and religion. They had not heard of Paris and seemed to think France was a dangerous place, finding it a bit suspect that I had ever dared live there.

Safely populated by a Pope-fearing, Virgin-worshipping, German-emulating population of tall blond Croats with no disorderly Southerners, the magnificent Dalmatian coast was an ideal Southern vacation spot for Northern Europeans. The toilets were clean, there were no beggars and theft seemed unlikely.

By now the rain had set in and seldom relented for the rest of my trip. I stopped in Ploce for lunch, buying the main Croatian daily *Vjesnik* and fruit: ripe yellow pears and grapes. The town was modern and was visibly prospering. No wonder: it was the center for smuggling weapons into Bosnia, in open violation of the international ban.

Bosnian Muslim leader Alija Iztbegovic had repeatedly asked for Ploce, a real port, to be attached to Bosnia-Hercegovina. But Tudjman had sewed up almost complete control of what was perhaps the greatest asset of former Yugoslavia, its Dalmatian coast, and was not likely to give it up.

Before reaching Dubrovnik, I stopped to admire the views in the village of Mali Ston, and as I walked around, a fine-looking old gentleman tending his vineyards asked me what on earth I was doing there as "we have wars and earthquakes." Looking for lodging in the neighboring village of Ston, I saw what he meant. The town was cordoned off by police, with an accumulation of trailer vans. At first I imagined some sort of festival. It was only between the church, with its steeple down, and the cracked town hall, that the word came to me: *potres!* Earthquake. The old town was roped off because of dangerous cracks in the houses, and the trailers were for townspeople to sleep in. And here I blundered in looking for a spare room!

I actually found a room for the night in the next town down the coast, Slano, which was the other major victim of the series of earthquakes then rocking the coast near Dubrovnik. I was awakened four times during the night by rather long, rolling but mild tremors. By this time I had shared cold cuts, cheese and home-made red wine with Niko Lobrovic and his wife and quite trusted them to alert me should evacuation be advisable. They were the most vivacious of my overnight hosts along the coast, and I was more relaxed. Having been helped in rebuilding their house and tourist business by faithful Belgian customers, they were kindly disposed to anyone arriving from Belgium.

Their house needed to be rebuilt because it had been burnt down by Serb soldiers while they had taken refuge elsewhere. When they came back, the rooming house they'd built and the restaurant they'd been building by the seaside were in ruins. So they went to work and rebuilt… with help from Belgian friends and an understandable grudge against soldiers who had burned down their house.

Geography explains what that destructive military activity was all about. Above Slano and again above the bay of Dubrovnik, the Croatian coast narrows to only a few kilometers. The hinterland has always been inhabited by Orthodox Serbs, who did not consider that the once independent city state of Dubrovnik should belong exclusively to Croatia. Thus in the early part of the war, Yugoslav forces attempted to surround and eventually capture Dubrovnik. This was a military failure but above all, like many Serb operations, a public relations disaster. The shelling of Dubrovnik itself, although relatively light (the assailants wanted to capture the pearl for themselves, not destroy it), was widely condemned as a barbarous attack on the cultural heritage of the civilized world.

Lobrovic was relieved that the war in Croatia was over for good but he was worried about two things: Islamic fundamentalism in Bosnia ("this is a problem for Europe") and the negative effects of capitalism on the environment and development of the Dalmatian coast. Small family pensions like theirs had to compete with huge modern hotels, which are "an industry." The couple had worked as cooks for the big German nudist colony on the outskirts of Slano and concluded that Germans lacked a sense of when to stop. "They say bathing nude is healthy, okay. But dining nude is a question of culture," he insisted.

On the outskirts of Slano, the sign marking the limits of the German nudist colony had clearly been used for target practice. Everything was still and deserted. The site was magnificent.

In the town of Slano, it was impossible to tell which ruins were due to the war, and which to the earthquake. The place was a shambles.

Glimpses of Bosnia-Hercegovina

My European auto insurance stopped at the Croatian border. I told border guards I wanted to proceed into Bosnia-Hercegovina but only if I could insure my vehicle. No problem: I produced DM 62 in exchange for a month's insurance, after an affirmative answer to my question as to whether the insurance was valid for the whole of Bosnia-Hercegovina.

Actually, it was not. But it was only much later, after I'd taken more risks than I realized, that I read the stipulation that it covered "only the Territory of the Croatian Republic of Herceg-Bosna"—which theoretically had ceased to exist.

I headed up the Neretva river toward the divided city of Mostar, whose emblematic Turkish bridge had been destroyed by Croatian forces in order to affirm the division between the Muslim left bank and the Croatian right bank of the river. As for the city's Serbs, they had been totally driven out—or if you prefer, "ethnically cleansed." Approaching Mostar, the sky was dark and sinister beyond the rows of charred trees lining the road.

In Mostar I walked around and took photographs (of buildings, not people), as unobtrusively as I could. The rain intensified. I was there primarily to gather visual impressions. I already knew quite a bit about the political stalemate, the spectacular failure of the European Union to unite the city after the war tore it apart. The Croat half flew Croatian flags and used the D-Mark while the Muslim part preferred U.S. dollars. The Croat part displayed campaign posters and graffiti extolling the Croat nationalist party, the HDZ, while the Muslim side was dominated by reminders of Izetbegovic's party, the SDA.

The Croat side was modern and sullen. The Muslim part was noticeably more animated. Despite heavy damage and bad weather, street and market life were being carried on with visible cheerfulness.

On a wall along the main left bank road, art students were painting a pretty fresco of people of all different nationalities dancing in happy harmony, a sort of Benetton ad. They had come all the way from Australia as ideological missionaries to promote harmonious multiculturalism.

Near the river, I was accosted by an old gentleman who thrust his umbrella over me and introduced himself as Professor Doctor Salih Rajkovic, son of a rich Muslim trader, author of the first historical and cultural guide to Mostar. I must be a professor doctor too, he surmised, and he thus had a duty to show the city to his "colleague." (I had encountered something similar in Cairo in 1977.) The fact was that I did not want to be taken in tow; I wanted to explore the town in my own way. But he was unshakable, answering questions I had not asked, telling me things I knew already or did not care to hear (which Austrian royal sponsored which public building during Habsburg rule). I fancy that visitors less jaded might find the gentleman absolutely charming. But I was irritated by his manner, both servile and self-aggrandizing, with his emphatically (and blatantly artificial) "oriental" courtesy, clinging tenaciously and preventing me from perhaps making more natural contacts with the local population. I also knew that this was going to cost me something beyond my tight budget. When I finally found a way to ditch him, he indeed asked for money and was dissatisfied with the amount I offered, considering "all the time" he had devoted to me. "My father was a very wealthy man, we had everything, but he taught me always to help those in need, because we are Muslims," he told me reproachfully. I doubled the ante, and thereby earned more unwelcome gestures of reverence.

I got a less friendly welcome the next day from Muslim policemen, who stopped my car on the main road, examined my papers suspiciously, told me I must obtain a permit from local authorities in order to take photographs and specifically warned me against photographing "military sites" under any circumstances. And just a few kilometers out of Mostar I passed a big military base on my left whose signs were all in

Arabic writing—totally alien to Bosnia. I did not take photographs, nor even stop for a closer look.

I was heading north, with the idea of proceeding to Sarajevo and from there to Jajce (whose waterfalls sent Rebecca West into raptures)[32] and on to Banja Luka, the capital of Republika Srpska, and from there to Zagreb. It would have been a great trip, but as I proceeded my misgivings grew.

The obviously Christian Orthodox village of Potoci was in ghastly ruins. Churches were destroyed, houses obliterated. Izetbegovic's party, the SDA, had painted its initials on the road to mark its territory. Groups of hitchhiking youths moved toward passing cars in a way that decided me to lock my car doors from the inside.

Rain fell. Clouds hung in the dark mountains rearing up ahead of me. Fog was gathering around the heights.

After emerging from a couple of tunnels, I was brought to a stop by a line of halted cars. Something was wrong with the road ahead, and cars, buses and trucks were lined up waiting for the military to take care of the problem. The war was over, but—was it a bombed-out bridge? Or what? There was no way to tell. I looked again at those great thundering mountains and glowering sky and remembered recent news reports of tough men with guns stopping (or shooting) foreigners for their cars (Mostar had been recently described as the stolen car capital of Europe). So I abruptly left the queue and drove ahead to find a wide space in which to turn around, where the IFOR[33] soldiers were standing. They were French, and when I explained my change of heart to the officer, he agreed that under the circumstances, "il vaut mieux faire demi-tour" (it's best to turn around). The enlisted men smiled and seemed to enjoy saying "bonjour." In this infernal setting, I was having my "ethnic identity" moment; how reassuring to hear French spoken and see friendly French faces.

This changed my plans entirely, so I returned to Mostar and from there set out in the opposite direction, on the right side of the Neretva, the Croat side, with the idea of visiting Medjugorje. The road was narrow and winding. On the upside, nothing but rocks poised to

---

32 Rebecca West, *Black Lamb and Grey Falcon* (New York: Viking Press, 1941)—a classic British account of travel in Yugoslavia between the two World Wars.

33 IFOR was a NATO-led "Implementation force" deployed in December 1995 in order to enforce the Dayton Peace Agreement which ended the 1992–1995 civil war in Bosnia.

fall onto the road. On the downside, nothing, period. No guard rail, just nothing.

Medjugorje (meaning between mountains) was a little village famous for apparitions of the Virgin Mary, recounted for some 15 years already by half a dozen local teenagers. Newspaper stories about this phenomenon always noted that the Catholic Church was skeptical and was not hastening to authenticate the miracle. That, of course, was the merest prudence, given the number of *miraculés* who could potentially wreck the whole show—which was apparently staged by the very strange Croatian Franciscan order, vehemently nationalist, and often in conflict with the rest of the Church. The visionaries must all grow up, live respectable lives and die before the Church can reasonably dare to validate their encounters with the Virgin Mary.

This was officially part of Bosnia, but there was not the slightest sign of any inhabitants other than Croats. A huge billboard of Pope Jean-Paul II welcomed visitors. Everywhere were Croatian flags. The post office sold only Croatia stamps. There was standing room only in the spanking new church where non-stop mass was being celebrated for the busloads of Americans, Austrians, Italians, even Asians. An outdoor auditorium was able to seat the multitude in good weather. Religious trinket shops, hotels and restaurants clearly provided a comfortable living to the inhabitants of this little boom town.

I stayed in a private home where, I was tearfully informed, everyone was suffering from some dreadful illness, with no help from the sacred environment.

In reality, Medjugorje was part of the "Croatian Republic of Herceg-Bosna," which had been officially dissolved when the United States ordered the Bosnian Muslims and Croats to stop fighting each other and form a "Croat-Bosniak (Muslim) Federation," the better to isolate the Serbs.

In theory, Bosnia-Hercegovina possesses some 10 to 15 kilometers of Adriatic coast, with the Croatian coastline on either side. But this bit of "Bosnian" coast, comprising only one town, Neum, was part of the unrecognized entity of Herceg-Bosna, under solid Croatian control. Tudjman pointedly chose Neum, a holiday resort, for conspicuous gatherings of his "Croatian Republic of Herceg-Bosna." The Croatian desire to live separate from the Muslims was every bit as strong as that of the Serbs, but was totally ignored by Western media.

Next I drove around inland Croatia, in precisely that border region, the Krajina, from which the Serb population had been driven out a little over a year ago. The road was empty on the way to Knin, the former capital of Serb Krajina. The town offered a striking silhouette of a fortress town in a dramatic valley. Close up, the scene was strangely empty of life. Knin was now a Croatian military outpost, seemingly inhabited exclusively by men. There was no hotel, no hospitality. On a corner in the center of town, two whole pigs were freshly roasted on skewers by men who seemed to be preparing a private feast. Something about the huge roasted porcine bodies stood upright on the corner of an empty street in the middle of town was strangely sinister. Croatian flags and slogans were much in evidence. The atmosphere was heavy and suspicious. I stopped to ask for directions, in a friendly and thoughtless way, and was answered in tones that seemed to be wrapped in layers of matting. I did not linger to take photographs. The road from Knin back toward the coast was particularly bad, filled with deep potholes, and the wrecked buildings occasionally bore ominous messages in English: "Fuck you stranger" and "mine."

Back on the Dalmatian coast, in Zadar, with its unselfconscious Roman ruins appropriated by cats, children at play and interesting weeds covered with snails, I saw the only Cyrillic[34] writing I encountered on the whole trip, hard to efface because in marble on the Serbian Orthodox Church. The church was loosely bolted shut, allowing a glimpse of the wrecked interior strewn with rubbish: articles of clothing, broken furniture. Zadar had been "ethnically cleansed" of its Serbs early in the war of Croatian secession. But the town seemed to have an irrepressible Mediterranean cheerfulness about it.

In my zigzagging, I decided that I wanted to see Gospic, which had been described to me as the scene of "the first massacre of the war" (although there were rivals for that distinction). The Gospic massacre took place from 16 to 18 October 1991, when Croatian militia drove well over a hundred Serb civilians from cellars where they had taken refuge during the state of alert that prevailed at that time. The particularity of the massacre which then took place was that the Serb victims were all non-combatant civilians, including women who had accepted a Croatian government invitation to return to their homes in Gospic from safer places.

The desolation of Gospic was indescribable. This had been a fairly large, mixed Serb-Croat town, and the Serb homes had all been

---

34 The Cyrillic alphabet was used only by Orthodox Christian Serbs, who also used the Roman alphabet.

blown up. Alone on the Eastern outskirts I encountered Bernarda Hardi, aged 73, living alone with her three fine white goats and some chickens. She came bounding across the road when she saw me stop to look around, and began to explain that her Serb neighbors had fled when their houses were blown up, and now the Croats had gone away too. She was eager to talk to me, all the more since her second husband died a few months ago, and she had no one to talk to but her goats. She warned me to stay away from the grain elevator just down the road—heavily mined, she said. At first I assumed she was Croatian, but after we had chatted for a while she told me that she was Magyar. Did that explain why she was left alone, intact, in the midst of all this desolation?

On the other side of town, there was an inhabited Croat part, but the only visible inhabitants were youths in the street throwing stones—at what I could not tell, and did not choose to find out.

That was the last place where I took photographs. I was ill at ease with the voyeurism of photographing the destruction of people's homes, and I began to say to myself cynically, "if you've seen one ruin, you've seen them all." The destruction went on, and on, and on. Village after village was in ruins. I put my camera away.

The formerly Serb Krajina region of Croatia had clearly been "ethnically cleansed," and once emptied of its original inhabitants, nobody was moving in to take their place. It is a harsh region, where survival required hard work. Everyone with whom I spoke in Croatia agreed that it was not safe for the Serbs to return, and that the Krajina region would remain largely deserted.

When I reached the Croatian capital, Zagreb, it was raining heavily, which obliged the drum majorettes to cut short the display of their art welcoming the German dignitaries opening "Bavarian Week." President Tudjman bestowed the Order of King Dmitri Zvonomir on Bavarian president Edmund Stoiber, who responded by vowing that Bavaria would intensify investment in Croatia and support its integration into the European Union.

Finding my way around was difficult. Maps were out of date. Street names had been changed from things like "Brotherhood and Unity" to the names of medieval Croat chieftains or of friendly cities in Germany.

Zagreb struck me as "naturally" rather than forcibly oppressive. Extreme nationalist feelings reigned, accompanied by kowtowing to Germans, without need for police terror. In the central bookshop, the most conspicuous spot before the cash register was surprisingly occupied by a new Croatian edition of "The Protocols of the Elders of Zion." Nearby was a handsome edition of the acts of a colloquium, "100 years of Ante Pavelic":[35] part of the "Ustasha revival," I was told.

In Zagreb, where the outside world that matters is either Germanic or American, where France was almost *terra incognita,* I was struck by the absurdity of French intellectual Alain Finkielkraut's gratuitous championing of this country in his book, *Comment peut-on être Croate?* You would search a long time to find a Croatian nationalist who gave a damn about the opinion of a Parisian intellectual, Jewish to boot. It's true that his book contributed to the massive demonization of Serbia in a country that was once Serbia's closest ally.

But it occurred to me that Finkielkraut's praise of Croatian nationalism was written neither for the benefit of the Croats nor to enlighten the French, but simply to provide an ideological alibi to Israel for its notorious military aid to Croatia, just in case an alibi was ever called for. Because, linked to the Germans and the Americans, Croatia has provided yet another market for particular Israeli know-how in fields which are not subject to a great deal of public scrutiny.

The lobby of a hotel like Panorama was frequented mainly by men, predominantly German and American, who looked like specialists in these fields. A hotel on the Zagreb ring road, assigned to the European Community Monitoring Mission, was even more strange. Guarded by police, off limits to ordinary mortals, this edifice bore all the earmarks of an intelligence agency "special operations" compound. The German television program "Monitor" had recently accused the head of the German mission there, Christoph von Bezold, of covering shipments of smuggled weapons to the Bosnian Muslims, on behalf of the *Bundesnachrichtensdienst* (BND), the German counterpart of the CIA.

The café behind the main theater used to be a hangout for intellectuals, but had been taken over by the new rich. A comic scene entertained me as I sipped my coffee and struggled to decipher the Croatian daily *Vjesnik.* Two squattish men sat down at the table opposite me in the large window recess. "Let's speak English so nobody can understand us," said the dark man in suit and tie to his seemingly less initiated companion. I did my best to look idly absorbed in the *Vjesnik* weather reports. "I do my own business," boasted man number one. Just what is it? "I do what others cannot do. What Clinton can't do, I get done." The

35 Pavelic was the leader of the Ustasha fascist movement that ruled the Nazi-sponsored Independent State of Croatia during World War II.

two laughed over "all those advisors" around Clinton. "I get things done. You want money, I get money, no problem. Why, I spent 47,000 DM in hotels just on my last trip to Germany." I waited in vain for details of his business. "I have a friend who wants to open a bank here," said man number two. "What kind of idiot wants to open a bank in this heap of shit?" retorted the man who knows how it's done. "No sensible banker will do business here, except the Austrians, who did all the business with former Yugoslavia. They've lost a lot. It was all done through the Jews. Tito was a Jew from Odessa, I have documents to prove it. So was Ceaucescu. It was part of the Jewish takeover of the communist movement..." His companion found this a bit much, but the man who knew how it's done was sure of his facts.

In Zagreb, I went to see Milorad Pupovac, one of three Serb representatives in the Croatian parliament, elected after Tudjman changed the law to reduce Serb seats from thirteen to three and to deny two provinces the regional autonomy legally guaranteed them. At the same time, the electoral law was changed to give ample representation to the Croatian diaspora, notably to residents of Herceg-Bosna. A nice-looking young man, tall and reserved, Pupovac spent his time receiving the remaining Serbs still living in Croatia and advising them on their problems. He was careful not to take sides. He stressed that both Serbia and Croatia had been adversely affected by the "peripheral nationalism" of the Serbs in Krajina and parts of Bosnia, and of the Croats in Herceg-Bosna. Panicked by the prospect of finding themselves in the position of oppressed minorities, leaders of these borderline communities pushed Zagreb and Belgrade toward more extreme positions.

In New Zagreb, a typical 1960s suburb of cement apartment blocks of modest flats, I stayed briefly with the mother of a Croatian peace activist whom I had met in Brussels. She was one of those people who cannot throw anything away, and every room including the bathroom was crammed full of what looked like junk. She told me that people who were not "pure Croats" had lost their jobs, or simply gone away without explanation. Nobody knew what had happened to them and nobody dared ask too closely.

By this time, the dampness had done its work and I was coming down with bronchitis. This first of my trips to postwar Yugoslavia had to end.

Pupovac told me that the tragic nature of the place was expressed by the Bosnian writer Mesa Silimovic in his novel *Death and the Dervish.* Death is asked, haven't you had enough? And the answer is, No, I need more.

26.

Serbia Alone

Serbian president Slobodan Milosevic had hesitated between trying to hold the Federation of Yugoslavia together and trying to ensure the safety of Serb minorities outside Serbia. He failed on both counts. As a result, he was denounced in Western media as an extreme nationalist dictator who was determined to "conquer" the rest of the country as it fell apart. In reality, Milosevic had joined American diplomat Richard Holbrooke in forcing the Bosnian Serbs to accept a compromise to end the war in Bosnia, as his main concern was to free Serbia from punishing sanctions. But even after facilitating peace in Bosnia, Serbia continued to be treated as the villain.

When I arrived in Belgrade in January 1997, Serbia was in political turmoil over the results of recent elections. The Serbian Socialist Party of Milosevic had lost several municipal elections, including in Belgrade itself, and other results were contested, requiring reruns. There were opposition street protests against certain election results. This was what might have been called "a vibrant democracy" if it hadn't been on the NATO hit list.

There were a lot of opinions to hear.

I was lodged by the parents of Dragan Pavlovic, Voya and Radmila, in their large apartment in central Belgrade. Their class origins were bourgeois by Yugoslav standards. However, the father, Voja, had done well as a lawyer, even so. Radmila, however, hated Milosevic with a passion, as bourgeois anywhere might hate a communist. She rejoiced to see street demonstrations against him—which were not all that rare. But Milosevic was no longer a communist, having left the League of Communists to form his own Serbian Socialist Party (SSP). The leaders of breakaway Slovenia and Croatia, Kucan and Tudjman, had also been members but turned to nationalism rather than socialism.

My first long conversation was with Dejan Popov, whom I had met in Strasbourg in 1991 at a meeting of Yugoslav Green Parties organized by Alexander Langer. He had given up politics altogether and was concentrating on completing his studies in trade law with a view to specializing in trade with China.

Dejan Popov called the election uproar a "very sad situation." He did not support the protests, objecting that the facts of the election were not at all as presented to the world. Yes, the governing SSP tried to use Serbia's very exacting electoral law to invalidate the opposition's victory in Belgrade, but they used the law, they did not break it, and they lost. Local elections were important for material reasons: allocation of flats and business connections.

On the national scale, Popov noted that the most flamboyant opposition leader, Vuk Draskovic, eagerly supported by Western media when he was in trouble with Milosevic, was far to his right, an heir to the Serbian nationalist Chetniks. His wife, Danica, violated the law by actually calling on people to take bombs and rifles to kill the President.

"Milosevic is referred to in the West as a dictator who has silenced the opposition press," I observed.

"I would say that the freedom of the press is greater here than in the United States," Dejan replied. "The largest circulation newspaper, a low-level tabloid called *Blic* (blitz), is owned by a German. It is totally anti-government. The opposition Democratic Party newspaper *Demokracija* is being sold all over. Every political group is publishing its own paper." (The Democratic Party was the leading pro-Western free market party.)

I asked about the result of sanctions.

"Catastrophic. Yugoslavia was the safest place on earth. Criminalization of society is the result of sanctions. Since things cannot be traded legally, they are traded illegally, and criminal gangs prosper."

"Is there a Serbian mafia trying to break the Albanian mafia hold on the drug trade?" I asked.

"An interesting question, but no. The Albanians with their clans are better organized. I haven't heard of any clashes between Serbian and Albanian criminal gangs; they work together," he replied.

It became clear to me that one result of sanctions is to "criminalize" the government itself, since one way or another, it will obtain what it needs. Under sanctions, the process necessarily involves confidential payments to intermediaries—in short, "corruption." So it follows that any government under sanctions will inevitably become vulnerable to accusations of "corruption," another opportunity for moral reprobation.

"Yugoslavia used to have a lot of trade with Europe. But now it's impossible: they are always making threats and demands. Milosevic was always trying to get along with the West. If I were in his place I'd be much stronger. The pressure is worse than expected. This government thought concessions to the West would bring good relations. They sacrificed a lot, and in return they get a slap in the face."

Popov told me that in 1991, the U.S. Secretary of State actually wrote a letter to Milosevic protesting because a butcher named Dejan Bulatovic had been beaten in prison after being arrested in a demonstration. According to Popov, anti-government demonstrators were brought in from other towns to throw stones and firecrackers at pro-government demonstrators. "They threw things at us from big expensive cars. They carried German and American flags," he recounted.

On a more personal note, I spent quite a bit of time with Ana Brujic, who had been one of my roommates in the Studentski Dom forty years earlier. She had had a lively career, working for the unions, then for the Board of Trade. She told me, "In 1990, when things were supposed to be changing, I became vice president of a new Chamber of Commerce. Then Yugoslavia broke up. My last job was as deputy director of the Yugoslav pavilion at Expo '92 in Seville. Stevan Stojanovic gave the opening speech on the theme of 'discovery', citing Nikola Tesla and other Serb scientists. That was on our opening day, April 16, 1992. On April 22 the Expo authorities shut down our pavilion saying that Yugoslavia didn't exist anymore. We opened a book in front of the pavilion and in two days, three thousand people signed saying they didn't want us to close. So we were allowed to open, but with no flag and with no exhibits either. It was terrible. The Spanish government brought in children, big children of 15 or 16 years old, from Croatia or Bosnia, who had lost parents in the war and came to tell us we were the enemy. I felt guilty although I had nothing to do with it."

Ana was critical of "social property," stemming from self-management socialism.

> I used to teach the workers about the virtues of self-management socialism, and I explained to Western leftists who came here admiringly. Now I'm ashamed. Maybe it could have worked in Sweden, but not anywhere else, certainly not here. The workers were not interested in managing anything, they didn't have to take the responsibility. They were paid regularly, but if their wages were low, then they'd work less. We have a saying: "You can't pay me as little as I can work."

Her son Darko, born in 1963, was terrified of being sent to war. In March 1991, he went on sit-down strike against the war in the middle of Belgrade. When he was in danger of being called to military service, Ana gave him her money and told him to leave. He was in New York studying computer science, with a Green Card thanks to marriage.

> Suddenly Slovenia attacked the Yugoslav Army. It was very surprising. How did Slovenia have such a powerful army that it could defeat the Yugoslav Army? Maybe the others didn't want to fight. Everything went too fast. Nobody explained what was happening.
>
> Today there was Yugoslavia, tomorrow there wasn't. Every week Milosevic, Tudjman, Izetbegovic and the other Republic leaders got together and said that everything would be all right. But actually it took five years for Yugoslavia to come apart. Step by step.

Ana hated Milosevic. Perhaps less for what he had done than for all that he had not done. Somehow he had let this happen.

Ana had gone to Sarajevo for her work in 1989 and was told by a member of Karadzic's Serbian Democratic Party that there would be a war between Muslims and Serbs. She refused to believe him and got quite angry. Now she was convinced that both sides started the war, after a noticeable rise of the Islamic religion in Bosnia. Our old roommate, Sefika, became a Muslim. "She said, 'I'm a Muslim.' We said, why? That's a religion. You can be a Turk, fine, or a Serb, or whatever. But a Muslim?! Because Tito said so." (Tito had ruled that "Muslim" was a "nationality," which gave self-declared Muslims a corresponding quota of posts in Bosnia.) "I think everyone is shedding crocodile tears for the Muslims, they don't really love Muslims. Why separate Muslims from Serbs?"

I spent the Serbian New Year's Eve with Ana, on January 13,[36] at the London restaurant on Belgrade's main pedestrian street.

> My first husband Petar was like a friend. I was already with him when you were here and he

---

36 Eastern Orthodox Christians use the Julian calendar; the year begins on January 14 according to the more recent Gregorian calendar.

> remembers you. He was and still is very handsome. We were together for 12 years. Petar didn't like children. The fourth time I was pregnant I refused to get an abortion and that was Darko. For me sleeping with him was like sleeping with a friend, nothing. Then came Moma, my great love, a TV journalist. It took just one day, or one evening to be precise. Great love. I hesitated to marry Moma because I sensed something was wrong. But then we got married. He loved drinking, carousing, women. He was very good with Darko, though. I hesitated to get a divorce because two divorces! But I did and was alone for seven years. Then I met Djura, a good man. But a sick man. He died six years ago.

The next evening I had dinner with Dejan Popov and Goran Kostic, who had remained the principal leader of the Serbian Greens. The conversation necessarily turned to Kosovo: that very day the Rector of Pristina University was victim of a car bomb attack by Albanian nationalists. A week earlier, two Albanians who had been elected on the Serbian Socialist Party list were murdered in front of their homes. This was a clear effort to frighten ethnic Albanians in Kosovo into supporting the secessionists, by eliminating those ready to cooperate with the government of Serbia.

Adem Demaçi (the Kosovo secessionist who won the European Parliament's 1991 Sakharov Prize) had been growing more insistent on having "Kosovo independence first and democratization later."

The majority of students at Pristina University were Albanians, and subjects were taught in both Serbian and Albanian, up until 1991–1992, when the ethnic Albanians left because they objected to some national history and literature courses. They formed their own private parallel university and schools. This was legal but complicated the problem of recognition of degrees. This reflected a tendency of Albanian students to prefer subjects, such as history and literature, that could glorify Albania, over scientific studies. Albanians were free to pursue their parallel activities, their schools were all allowed to function, and they published perhaps some thirty magazines and newspapers in Albanian.

Goran Kostic had the impression that while Americans officials in Kosovo claimed to be restraining Albanian nationalism, they were really encouraging it.

Our talk turned to agriculture. "Serbia is the biggest raspberry producer in Europe and produces the world's finest plums. We have high storage potential. But we lack connections and willingness in the West to deal with us. Through sanctions we lost our position in the European market to Chile."

The Western media's version of Serbian politics was that Slobodan Milosevic was a semi-dictator who rose to power by inciting extreme Serb nationalism. This was simply not true. The Serb minority in Kosovo province had been subject to harassment and persecution by the ethnic Albanian majority throughout the 1980s, a fact which was reported by mainstream Western newspapers at the time. Milosevic was accused of having aroused violent Serbian chauvinism during a visit to Kosovo in 1987. All he did was react to seeing Serb protesters who were being beaten by police by saying that they should not be beaten any more. That's all. Otherwise, Milosevic was a strong defender of multi-ethnic society.

There were truly nationalist politicians in Serbia, starting with Vojislav Seselj, leader of the Radical Party. Most other opposition party leaders were more "nationalist" than Milosevic. In reality, Milosevic's power base lay not in nationalist sentiments, but in what was left of Yugoslavia's socialist economy, which had come under strong Western pressure to "privatize."

This was acknowledged by the pro-Western Serbian journalist, Dejan Anastasjevic, who regularly spent part of his time receiving a virtual assembly line of foreign journalists sent there by their embassy information officers for briefings. This was because Anastasjevic, who worked for the Serbian version of *Time* (*Vreme*) as well as for the American *Time* magazine and the BBC, espoused an anti-Milosevic line which suited Western powers. After describing the various opposition political figures, he got to the point:

> The main issue here is the economy and privatization. Everybody says they are for it, but Milosevic has not privatized and cannot. He has not kept his promise to improve things. [Note: in short, Milosevic was a politician.] In 1987, Milosevic spoke of Swedish-style social democracy for Yugoslavia, but 90% of the economy still belongs to the State, although a so-called third sector, "Social Property" category is inherited from self-management socialism. The 1992

> Constitution says that Social Property must be treated the same as other types of property, so privatizing them could be unconstitutional. Social Property industries only produce losses. As this is Milosevic's real political base, he cannot privatize. Examples are the Smederevo steel works, the electrical industry in Nish, the communications industry.

Yugoslavia was under strong Western pressure to complete the dismantling of its socialist economy in violation of its own laws. What was wrong with Milosevic was that he couldn't go fast enough, blocked by domestic resistance and international sanctions.

"The Democratic Party has able economists, notably Miroljub Labus, who has tried to work out privatization arrangements with the United States," Anastasjevic told me. "The problem is that with Milosevic, this country is not going anywhere. Milosevic has failed to fulfill his social contract."

Anastasjevic dismissed worries about Kosovo. "As for Kosovo, it doesn't matter who is in Belgrade. The Albanian drug trade is traditional, based on the clan structure of society. But the Americans are sitting hard on Kosovo, to prevent an explosion."

He was wrong about that.

Milosevic and his Serbian Socialist Party won democratic elections, but never by a large enough majority to rule without forming a coalition with other parties. Sometimes he was obliged to accept a coalition with Seselj, but his permanent partner was a small party created by his own wife, Miryana Markovic.

It goes without saying that when a country's leader has an influential wife, she is inevitably condemned as the latest Lady Macbeth. Miryana was a lightning rod for hostility toward Slobodan, but she also had her fans—especially in the feminist intelligentsia, where she could be adored as Hillary Clinton came to be adored among American feminists. Miryana's party, JUL—the United Yugoslav Left—was the perfect partner for Slobodan's SSP. Between the two, they covered "the Left"—his was the working class left and hers was the politically correct leftist intelligentsia.

Goran Kostic advised me to interview Professor Vladimir Stambuk, President of the Committee for International Policy and Cooperation of JUL. He came to see me at the Pavlovic apartment for a long conversation. He was particularly ready to talk to me for lack of others to talk to. JUL, despite its ideal leftist program, was shunned by the entire Western left out of guilt by association… with demonized Milosevic, with Serbia.

Professor Stambuk made it clear from the outset that he was "Yugoslav and not Serb." (His Turkish name backed that up.)

"We have tried to make contact with the Democratic Party of the United States," he told me. "We invited them to a July 1995 conference on the Balkans… Our problem is the following: One can think whatever one wants about Yugoslavia, but we have organized a left ideological union covering all aspects of the renewed left, seeking a completely new strategy. We feel that the stubborn Western rejection of everyone except the nationalist politicians (Vuk Draskovic, Zoran Djindjic, etc.) makes no sense. We don't understand why the West is always trying to find a solution to nationalism by turning to extreme nationalists. It is just not understandable.

"JUL is seeking contacts with every democratic party. We think contacts and debate are basic everywhere. Because of the general blockade of Yugoslavia, we have not been able to do this. We think JUL has substantially influenced this country for democracy. We have sought contacts with Socialist parties but it seems that those responsible in the Socialist International are against any contacts. JUL is interested in normal civilized contacts, we think this country is coming out of a difficult time," Stambuk said.

I asked him whether the Left here see an alternative to Milosevic, given that he is the chief demon in the demonization of Serbia abroad.

His answer amounted to saying that all potential alternatives were to the right of Milosevic.

> The West does not understand that Milosevic in 1987 and 1988 prepared Yugoslavia to go toward the West. He supported a multi-party system and elections. This was seen by Serb nationalists as an opportunity to include the Serb part of Bosnia, and even in Croatia, in a Greater Serbia. In 1993 he had to make an agreement with the nationalists to prevent civil war. In plain fact he was never a nationalist. Milosevic has tried by peaceful means to transform society to conform to Western standards. People here have understood that. He was not for Greater Serbia but Yugoslav unity by overcoming bureaucracy.

> On the left, JUL is producing new ideas. Milosevic takes them over. His SPS is completely incompetent in that regard. JUL is the think tank of the left and the SPS has the foot soldiers." [JUL has 150,000 members and wins about 600,000 votes.]
>
> As for privatization, we call it "reshaping" the economy. We know our system must be compatible with what is happening in the world. We already had a market economy. What we want is equal treatment for all types of property, to be judged by market efficiency and not by category. Some collectively owned enterprises are very efficient economically, for example the "First of May" clothing manufacture in Pirot… We are in favor of joint ventures, because capital is brought in and invested in return for a share of ownership. We want to be able to live off wages.

All I heard from my interviews was so different from what I could read in the Western press that I asked Stambuk, "Who informs the international press here?"

"Starting in 1991," he replied, "a strange organization was formed: the International Journalists Club. Ten or fifteen people from the opposition, always the same, inform journalists at lunches and dinners. It's located on Knez Mihailova (Belgrade's central pedestrian street)…"

I interviewed many people in Belgrade.

Cedomir Antic, president of the board of Student Protest, vowed to keep protesting against the government.

The very pro-Western opposition politician, Vesna Pesic, slightly evaded the question as to whether the U.S. should employ sanctions. Sanctions hurt people, she said, "but there is a need for pressure."

I had a long interview with Miroljub Labus, the chief economist of the pro-Western Democratic Party of Serbia, who gave me a detailed description of the problems involved in privatization.

I also had long conversations with Vera Vratusa, a professor of sociology at Belgrade University whose Slovenian father was close to Tito and served as Yugoslav ambassador to the United Nations. A Marxist, Vera said she did not believe that Serbia had a national bourgeoisie ready to protect national interests: "This is a comprador bourgeoisie."

Through all this, I never encountered anything resembling the "rabid nationalism" which the foreign media attributed to Serbia. I never encountered anything resembling racism or hostility toward minorities. On the contrary, Serbs tended to identify with Jews as fellow victims of persecution during World War II and insisted on the need to "live together." This was the first of several trips to Serbia which all confirmed the same impressions. What was being said about Serbia in the West was nothing other than a Big Lie.

27.

The War NATO Needed

Contrary to the claims of Otto von Habsburg, the Serbs were as "European" as anyone else in the Balkans. Perhaps more so. Science was ardently esteemed and practiced (Nikola Tesla is the national hero). Their historic struggle for independence from the Ottoman Empire had inspired a particular devotion to British and French liberal ideas. They considered France their friend and protector. With British encouragement, they had rejected a 1941 non-aggression pact with Hitler, triggering a devastating German bombing and invasion. They had saved American pilots during World War II. They thought that was enough. They were sadly mistaken.

It is characteristic of contemporary "Western values" to care nothing for "Western values" as practiced in other nations. This may be because leaders, having adopted "Western values," tend to be self-confident and reluctant to be bossed around.

My impression in Belgrade was that most Serbs were simply unable to grasp the extent of the hate campaign being directed against them. It made no sense, and so they could not understand it. It was a bit like being hit by a terrible storm, something to put up with, laugh about, and wait for it to go away.

In August 1997, I rented a car in Belgrade in order to drive around Serbia, a land of gentle hills, well-kept orchards, and neat gardens. I visited some of the country's many medieval monasteries and historic places from the prehistoric site at Lepenski Vir on the Danube to the World War II museum in Kraljevo with photographs of the hostages—including women and adolescents—who had been executed by the Nazi occupiers in retaliation for attacks by resistance fighters.

In Nis (pronounced Neesh), in southern Serbia, there is a famous tower formed by the skulls of decapitated prisoners put on display by the Turkish rulers to show who was boss. The guardian of the Skull Tower was quite surprised when I showed up to see this historic reminder of a bloody past. Nobody came here anymore. In the 19th century, the French poet Alphonse de Lamartine had written a poem about this tower, paying tribute to the Serbian heroes who fought and died to liberate their people from Turkish rule. And now the West was taking sides against the Serbs on behalf of the protégés of the Turks.[37]

Serbia is ethnically mixed. The town of Novi Pazar (new bazaar) in southwestern Serbia, with its crowded Turkish markets, is a reminder of the past when the Ottoman Empire ruled the Balkans. Some who live there call themselves "Bosniak," a word used to denote a Muslim ethnic group whose population extends into regions beyond Bosnia, rather than to specific residents of Bosnia.

From Novi Pazar I drove into Kosovo, birthplace of the Serbian nation and now overwhelmingly populated by ethnic Albanians, some who have been there forever and many who immigrated over the mountains from neighboring Albania in recent decades, when the living was much easier in Yugoslavia than in Albania. The political leaders who called themselves "Kosovars" were in fact staunchly Albanian, aspiring to attach Kosovo to a "Greater Albania."

Driving on Kosovo's two-lane roads was an adventure in itself. There are a surprising number of dead dogs along the roadside. Even on a curve or approaching the top of a hill, drivers show their trust in fate by passing the car in front of them. This has its inevitable results, as I sampled while driving through the town of Zubin Potok: all traffic was halted while down the road police and ambulances sorted out the results of a head-on collision.

This obliged me to make a pleasant stop on the terrace of a roadside café where I reordered the delicious strawberry juice and got into conversation with the young man who was all alone running the place. He was a Serb named Milomir who liked to remember a pleasant time he had spent in Germany. He apologized for not being able to speak a word of English because his linguistic capacity had been absorbed by the need to learn Albanian in self-defense. He hoped speaking Albanian would help him avoid trouble. He used to commute to the University in Mitrovica and had to watch out, as he was occasionally beaten up by groups of Albanians. He was clearly afraid of them, which could account for his nostalgia for Germany. Zubin Potok was a Serb town so he was pretty safe there.

---

37 On May 16, 2019, the former head of the intelligence service of the Western-backed Kosovo Liberation Army, which profited from NATO bombing to seize control of Kosovo and proclaim it an independent State, Kadri Veseli, actually claimed that Nis had been an Albanian city centuries ago until Albanians were "forcibly expelled" by Serbs and demanded establishment of a tribunal for "Serbian crimes." The spirit of vendetta is eternal.

I stopped in the Kosovo capital, Pristina, in order to visit the headquarters of the Kosovar independence movement headed by Ibrahim Rugova. The headquarters were housed in the Writers Club, in a small building in the middle of town, operating freely without any restrictions imposed by the authorities they wanted to get rid of. There I was received by a spokesman who explained, in English, that the "Kosovars" were a persecuted people, oppressed by the Serbs. I had already met Rugova himself when he visited the European Parliament a couple of years earlier. With Green Group co-President Magda Aelvoet I attended a private meeting of EP leaders where he made the case for Kosovo's secession from Yugoslavia, slightly distorting the facts (he claimed that Milosevic had robbed Kosovo of more independence than it had ever had, without explaining the reasons, which were significant). Rugova was a mild-mannered, chain-smoking professor of French, whose main function was apparently to make a good impression on foreigners, since he exercised scant authority at home.

Regardless of who did what to whom over the last several centuries (which is disputed), there were undeniable cultural differences between Serbs and Albanians that probably constituted the root of the conflict. The Serbs had evolved into a resolutely modernizing people. They had emerged from centuries of submission to the Ottoman Empire determined to create a modern state. The Albanians of Kosovo, like their cousins in neighboring northern Albania, were still largely a clan society, refractory to any modern government, loyal to a tribal code of 1,262 rules laid down in the 15th century by an Albanian nobleman named Lekë Dukagnjini, called the Kanun. The key principle is that "blood must pay for blood," a principle that leads to lengthy feuds between clans as one threatens to take revenge against another. This clearly has nothing to do with modern legislation or police authority and favors development of mafia outlaw groups based on absolute clan loyalty (or omerta). Kosovo Albanians are notorious as traffickers in drugs, arms and sex slaves.

A culture that adheres to rules of blood revenge can be expected to bear grudges. And that is the case.

After my lesson in the Serbian repression of the Kosovars, I stopped in a nearby café and innocently asked for a coffee in Serbian. The waiter replied in English, "Why don't you learn Albanian?" I was too polite to reply that nobody other than an intimidated Serb was likely to take the trouble to learn such a linguistically isolated language. But the point of this incident was that Kosovo Albanians who refused to learn

Serbian could devote all their linguistic talents to learning English, the better to complain to foreigners about the Serbs.

Along the main street of Pristina, tree trunks were decorated with signs commemorating persons who had died recently, a custom in that part of the world. A photograph of the deceased was attached to a tree trunk. A color symbol indicated whether the man (women are not so honored) was Muslim, Christian or Communist. A significant number of Albanian names were identified as communists, the shared ideal that might have created the "unity and brotherhood" that was Yugoslavia's slogan. But communism was dead, leaving Albanian nationalism.

From Pristina I drove westward to revisit Peć after 43 years. I was thrilled to see the great mountains loom beyond the town, site of the medieval Serbian Orthodox Patriarchate. On my first visit, Peć had been a Serbian town. No more. Hotels, cafés, everything was Albanian.

The town had been electrified and was certainly more modern than before. But I was struck by the huge quantity of trash encumbering the clear waters of the mountain stream. There was trash everywhere. Albanians were extremely attached to maintaining their own homes, clean and hospitable, often built like fortresses to protect family members in case of blood feud. But their sense of civic responsibility was limited.

I stumbled on an old Serbian couple alone in their empty bookshop. Delighted to have someone to talk to, they spoke almost in whispers, although there was no one there to hear them.

The Milosevic government considered that the Yugoslav wars were over and was mainly concerned with getting the United States to lift sanctions as a reward to Milosevic for his contribution to ending the war in Bosnia. But in Kosovo, Albanian nationalists were turning to violence. An armed group calling itself the Kosovo Liberation Army (KLA) broke decisively with the nonviolence proclaimed by Rugova, who was increasingly shoved aside. In early 1998, the KLA undertook a campaign of killings, with the declared aim of detaching Kosovo from Serbia and attaching it to Albania. Not only Serbs were targeted. Albanians who accepted Serbian government rule, postmen and even politicians belonging to non-ethnic parties, were murdered, clearly in order to intimidate the entire Albanian population of Kosovo. In February 1998, Robert Gelbard, the U.S. representative to former Yugoslavia, declared that the Kosovo Liberation Army was "without any doubt a terrorist organization."

The principal result of this declaration was to assure Milosevic that the United States would understand the Serbian government's need to use force against the KLA. Which government in the world would not move to suppress a terrorist organization killing people on its own territory? Predictably, as the KLA attempted to turn the Drenica region of Kosovo into an armed stronghold, Yugoslav security forces moved to root it out.

The Serbian government offensive against the KLA was just beginning when I drove through Kosovo again in June 1998, this time accompanied by Linda Bullard, a close friend from the time when we were both working for the Green Group. Working with the agriculture staff, Linda had spearheaded a successful action to block the patenting of life forms, for example the Indian neem tree, by the Munich Patenting Agency. She had been invited to Subotica in northern Serbia for a meeting on environmental issues, and we met up in Belgrade where I again rented a car to drive to Kosovo.

The leading Serb historian of Kosovo was Dusan Batakovic, whom I had met at the defense of his doctoral thesis on "France and the Formation of Parliamentary Democracy in Serbia, 1830-1914" at the Sorbonne. Batakovic obtained the Serbian Orthodox Patriarch's "blessing" for Linda and me to be lodged for several nights in the Gracanica monastery, not far south of Pristina. Founded by Serbian King Stefan Milutin in 1321, the building is a UNESCO World Heritage Site. It is small and graceful, with domes and frescoes in the Byzantine tradition. The monastery has become a convent, cared for by nuns who tend the garden, raise chickens and earn a small amount of money from icons they paint and sell. Their beehives produced honey as well as wax from which they made the church candles. We were the only guests, and were able to dine with the nuns, enjoying their memorable omelet.

In nearby Pristina, I checked out the press center in the Park Hotel, a rather run-down modern structure where I had stayed before and preferred to avoid. The Serbian Ministry of Information had set up a press center open to all the foreign journalists who were converging on "the crisis zone." The situation was almost comic. All the amenities, from technical equipment to refreshments, were provided free by the Serbian authorities, whereas the foreign journalists totally ignored Serb briefings and wanted only to talk to "Kosovars." From what I could gather, the reporters were young, totally ignorant of the language, history or politics of the region and eager only to produce the story that would satisfy their editors in London or wherever. That would be a "Serb atrocity." Their favorite source was of course the Writers Club, where they could get the Albanian version. They were able to write that Kosovars were not allowed to use their own language, since they were unable to recognize that the kiosks were stacked with periodicals in Albanian.

On behalf of the Ministry, a young redhead named Snezana ran the center with a mixture of fatalism and irony. Like so many Serbs, she accepted the hostility of foreigners as if it were a form of bad weather. With a shrug. But one day, she had her small revenge.

That was when Christiane Amanpour arrived with her gear and her aura. For the Serbs, this was bad news: if Amanpour is here, something really bad is planned. The famous CNN star settled into the comfortable lounge without bothering to register. This was Snezana's chance. With an innocent air, she approached Christiane Amanpour and asked politely, "Excuse me, what is your name?"

Linda and I also drove around Kosovo. In Urosevac, we saw that a wedding was going on and invited ourselves into the Church to watch the Serbian Orthodox ceremony from the balcony. Afterwards, as people were leaving, the women in the wedding party were eager to talk with us, in the vain hope that we could get their message out to the world. Their theme was: "We are not leaving Urosevac, it is our town and we shall stay here forever." They complained of the trash that was littering the public garden "which used to be so neat." So, clearly, they had some negative thoughts about the growing Albanian population in the town. And the Albanians surely had negative thoughts about them. But the most aggressive expression of Serbian nationalism was the desire not to be driven out.

A year later, after NATO bombing had given Kosovo to the leaders of the Kosovo Liberation Army, the Serbs were in fact driven out of Urosevac which the Albanians call Ferizaj. The huge U.S. military base, Camp Bondsteel, is situated nearby.

From Urosevac we drove to Prizren, a traditional Albanian nationalist stronghold, observing what was left of a recently burnt down Orthodox monastery. From there we wanted to take a shorter road back toward Pristina but were stopped by a policeman who kindly advised us not to take that road, as it was dangerous. But so is any road in Kosovo. Driving on the two-lane Prizren-Urosevac road, around the curve ahead of me came two cars, one passing the other. To avoid collision, I slammed on the brakes and was immediately struck by the car following too closely behind. An incomprehensible altercation ensued, with the result that I ended up stopping again in Urosevac, this time to report the accident to the police. I had to manage this in Serbian as the officer in charge was again one of those Serbs who learned Albanian instead of

English. Informed of this occurrence, the car rental people in Belgrade immediately sent a substitute car, not because of the damages, which were slight, but because, they said, I had taken a risk in driving around Kosovo in a car with Belgrade license plates.

At the Gracanica convent, we had conversations with Sister Fotina, who had lived in New York and spoke perfect English. Her vocation had brought her back to Kosovo. She deplored the fact that the nuns had wanted to help the Albanians raise their children, who were often left to run loose, but "they only hate us." The town of Gracanica was a Serb enclave in an increasingly Albanian region. We visited a Serb family whose garden was so well cared for that there were even flowers between the two tracks of the driveway leading to the garage. The Djordjevic family had no intention of ever leaving, but a neighbor was preparing to take her son and move away. When I admired her teacup, she insisted on giving it to me. She would soon be leaving everything behind in any case. Albanian pressure to leave had been going on for decades but as Western threats against Belgrade merged with KLA attacks, more and more Serbs felt threatened.

On the plane flying back to Paris, a tall confident man sat down next to me and began to chat amiably. When I learned that he was a journalist, I said I had a low opinion of the journalists who reported from Yugoslavia. "You are absolutely right," he said. "*The Guardian* and *Le Monde* have a lot to answer for." Needless to say, they have never answered for it. The journalist was Renaud Girard, the leading foreign correspondent of the conservative French daily, *Le Figaro.*

Back in Belgrade, we saw Serb refugees from Kosovo camped in the park in front of the Parliament and visited a makeshift camp for refugees from Croatia and Bosnia in what had been a holiday camp site. There was never any international aid, or even recognition, for the thousands of "ethnically cleansed" Serbs. Instead, according to the media and above all to the International Tribunal for the Former Yugoslavia (ICTY), established by the United Nations but essentially run by NATO governments, "ethnic cleansing" was something done only by Serbs.

The ICTY had borrowed from U.S. criminal law the concept of "joint criminal enterprise" to apply to Serbian nationalism. This concept enabled the Tribunal, all judges and no jury, with no court of appeal except itself, to prosecute whichever Serb they chose, including those who never engaged in violence, as being part of said enterprise.

In July, U.S. emissary Richard Holbrooke was photographed sitting on the ground in a tent with KLA leaders. The "terrorists" had become allies.

Who was the real Joint Criminal Enterprise? I had no doubt. Basically, it was NATO, which was arranging to use the Kosovo problem as pretext to celebrate its 50th anniversary in 1999 by bombing Yugoslavia, thus initiating a new "humanitarian intervention" mission for the military alliance. With no more Soviet bloc to oppose, NATO found a new mission to perpetuate itself. It could turn into a human rights organization, defending populations allegedly threatened with "genocide" or overthrowing regimes that "kill their own people." Western mainstream media were reporting the story precisely in terms that would justify this aggression, by stereotyping Serbs as "ethnic cleansers" and the "Kosovars" as innocent victims.

What currently passed for the Left was more susceptible to war propaganda based on "humanitarian" arguments than the Right. The "center-left" mainstream media did most to prepare public opinion for the bombing of Serbia. But the "alternative" media were no better.

On the basis of my travels and research, in August I wrote two long analytical articles on Kosovo and submitted them to *In These Times*. James Weinstein welcomed them, but he was in semi-retirement, spending time in Oaxaca, and the paper was being run by "junior editors." To my shock, the junior editors refused to publish them.

For years, I had written for ITT about Europe, and I was offering an unusually well-informed, thorough analysis of a major world crisis. It wouldn't cost them anything as, since I started working for the European Parliament, my articles were all free. I wrote only when I thought I had something important to say, not expecting to be paid. On what basis did those inexperienced "junior editors" think they knew more about Yugoslavia than I did? From watching CNN? But *In These Times* was supposed to be an "alternative" news source.

This was an early taste of the self-censorship that overtook the Left as it became politically less and less significant but more and more pretentious morally. Once a cause was identified by the Western media-political establishment as "good," there was a herd-like rush to join it, to show that we are so good that we will not even listen to anyone who questions it, for fear of being identified with the Evil Ones.

A few years later, I accidentally discovered an internet exchange with one of those "junior editors," repeating a rumor that one "can't accept what Diana Johnstone writes about Yugoslavia because she is an old friend of Miryana Markovic," the wife of Slobodan Milosevic. As a point of fact, I have never met Miryana Markovic, and perhaps I should have. This brand of guilt by association assumes that if I knew her, she must be dictating my opinions. What is particularly disturbing in regard to journalistic quality is the fact that my considerable personal experience in Yugoslavia was not considered an asset but rather a disqualification.

I was not the only one. From *The New York Times* to the French communist newspaper *l'Humanité,* journalists with long experience of Yugoslavia were "taken off the story" if they deviated from the official NATO version.

When I submitted my Kosovo articles to *The Nation,* I never got an answer. In a telephone conversation concerning an earlier article, a friendly fact checker warned that there was opposition to my articles in the staff of *The Nation.* Apparently the vehemently anti-Serb line of Christopher Hitchens triumphed.

My articles on Yugoslavia were published elsewhere, notably in *Covert Action Quarterly,* run by my friends Ellen Ray and Bill Schaap. They did a good job, but the audience was much smaller and tended to be convinced already that NATO's war was criminal. I was excluded from media where I might have made a difference.

It always takes an obscure "incident" to start a war that should never be started. In January 1999, just in time for NATO's anniversary celebrations, the appropriate incident was duly discovered. On January 15, Serb forces pursued their elimination of "terrorists" by encircling a KLA base in the village of Racak, south of Urosevac. Several policemen had recently been killed nearby. The Serb raid killed a number of KLA fighters, as was announced by the government. The next day, this incident was transformed into the required casus belli by the dramatic performance of U.S. "diplomat" cum intelligence operative William Walker, whom the United States had connived to put in charge of the OSCE monitoring mission to Kosovo. Walker visited the scene and put on his act in front of reporters and photographers. "It's obvious people with no value for human life have done this," he proclaimed. "I do not have the words to describe my personal revulsion at the sight of what can only be described as an unspeakable atrocity. I have been in other war zones, and I have seen pretty horrendous acts, but this is beyond anything I have seen before." Walker's rich experience included running the U.S. show in El Salvador as right-wing death squads were murdering priests and nuns.

It must be said that Renaud Girard of *Le Figaro* attempted to correct the Walker story, and even persuaded his colleague in *Le Monde* to report the incident accurately. But it was no use. After the totally manipulated pretense of "negotiations" in a French chateau at Rambouillet, U.S. Secretary of State Madeleine Albright had the war she wanted. Her close assistant James Rubin made the dismissal of Rugova official by advertising his new friendship with KLA leader Hashim Thaqi, telling him he was so handsome he should be in movies. (Rubin and Christiane Amanpour were soon wed.)

The "Kosovo War" amounted to unilateral bombing of Serbia from March 24 to June 10, 1999. NATO troops never dared confront Serbian ground forces. NATO just bombed with impunity. The leading NATO governments waging that one-sided "war" were all "on the left": the Democrat, Bill Clinton, in Washington, the "new" Laborite, Tony Blair, in London. In France, although Chirac was President, Prime Minister Lionel Jospin was a Socialist and Germany was ruled by a coalition of the SPD and the Greens.

This was the culmination of the evolution of the Grünen from peace to war party whose beginnings I witnessed in 1995, when Dany Cohn-Bendit took over the foreign policy of the Green Group in the European Parliament, based on the simple fact that the media treated him as a star. As German foreign minister, Cohn-Bendit's "realo" chum Joschka Fischer provided the "humanitarian" spin to a war that killed thousands of civilians, destroyed Serbia's infrastructure, poisoned the earth with depleted uranium and turned Kosovo over to the group that a year earlier had been officially described as "terrorists." All with virtually no casualties on the NATO side.

There are always questions to be asked about the company Washington keeps in developing support groups within countries it has targeted for "improvement." There are also questions to be asked about the meteoric rise of Joschka Fischer, a high-school dropout whose youth was spent in ultra-left groups, some attacking U.S. military bases, and yet whose appointment in 1998 elicited from Richard Holbrooke the opinion that "Fischer will make a great foreign minister." As the ultimate outsider, with a CV like that, how did Fischer gain such sponsorship? How were U.S. policy-makers, who have their ways of vetting German leaders, so sure that a former anti-American street fighter would make "a great foreign minister"? What did they know about him that we didn't know?

In a tumultuous convention of the Grünen in Bielefeld on May 13, 1999, in the midst of the bombing, Fischer proved that Holbrooke had made the right choice. For much of the rank and file membership, Fischer's role as foreign minister leading an aggressive war was the total repudiation of everything the Greens stood for. An impassioned anti-war speech by trade unionist Annelie Buntenbach, calling for an unconditional end to the bombing, won applause, cheers and a standing ovation.

But Fischer, his face smudged with red paint thrown at him, saved his day thanks to his talent for slippery reasoning and demagogic oratory. This was the talent that had been spotted by political reporters at the start of his political career and made him a favorite of mainstream media.

"Sure," he retorted in response to Buntenbach, "you can call me a warmonger, and Milosevic will nominate you for the Nobel Peace Prize!" What's more, he warned his party comrades who introduced a resolution to end the bombing, "If you decide it I won't carry it out—let's make that clear."

In a 20-minute tirade, Fischer silenced the opposition by playing the war party's trump card: Auschwitz. He implicitly likened Albanians who had fled the bombing to neighboring countries to Jews deported by the Nazis. "I stand on three principles: Never again war! Never again Auschwitz! Never again Fascism!"

The mention of Auschwitz seemed then and now to rob some people of their ability to grasp what is wrong with declaring "Never again war!" in order to justify war.

As the air war continued, Fischer thereby won what media called his "ground war" in Bielefeld. Step by step, Cohn-Bendit and Fischer took over the German Green Party and changed its nature. The bombing continued, the most principled antiwar Greens sooner or later felt obliged to leave the party and die Grünen became Germany's leading champion of finding moral pretexts to justify war. This transformation ensured the party a long and prosperous life in the mainstream.

The NATO bombing began on March 24, with little public opposition. I joined a small demonstration in front of the Paris Opera, attended mostly by members of the large Serbian community in Paris, mostly professionals, engineers or medical personnel such as Dragan Pavlovic, an anesthetist who worked in an experimental laboratory in Bichat hospital in Paris. Until the last moment, many could not believe that Serbia's historic allies, France and the United States, would go through with it. Their thoughts went to relatives and friends in Serbia.

Dragan Pavlovic had lost his mother Radmila not long before and flew to Belgrade to find care for his aged father during the bombing. The young women who usually cared for him wanted to flee to the countryside. Because of the sanctions, telephone calls to Belgrade were wildly expensive, but nevertheless I called to hear his description of the bombing. He was trying to find ways to get information about what was really happening in Kosovo to the outside world. William Walker had ordered the OSCE monitors to leave Kosovo, and so there was no one there to verify or contradict the wild reports of Serb atrocities emanating from NATO governments, which tended to escalate the rhetoric as weeks passed and Serbia refused to capitulate. British and German government sources claimed "hundreds of thousands" of Albanian victims of an alleged campaign of expulsion and genocide. In reality, there was never any Serb plan, or even idea, to drive the huge Albanian population out of Kosovo. It was not practicable, it made no sense. Serbian policy had always been integration and protection of minorities. But picturesque photos of Albanians crossing the mountains into neighboring Albania or Macedonia were presented to the world as proof of "ethnic cleansing" when in reality those people were simply getting out of the way of the bombing. Serbs were also leaving Kosovo, with the difference that they never came back.

On May 20, NATO bombed the maternity ward of the Dragisa Misovic hospital center in Belgrade. Having returned to Paris, Dragan Pavlovic attempted to get his colleagues at the Bichat hospital in Paris to sign a statement condemning the bombing of hospitals. He was stunned when they declined. Did they really believe that Milosevic was "the new Hitler" bent on exterminating populations? Or were they afraid to go against the current of official self-congratulations at waging "humanitarian war"? For Dragan it was incomprehensible. At that moment, he decided to leave France. He looked for a job in Greece and ended up working in Germany. "We are used to having Germans as adversaries," some Serbs said. But France was the great historic friend and ally of Serbia. The betrayal was felt deeply by the Yugoslav diaspora in France.

Since the World War II bombing of Japan, U.S. strategy basically boils down to the implicit or explicit threat to wipe out the whole nation it is attacking. Since some NATO allied governments didn't want to go that far, and NATO generals didn't want to risk casualties in a ground war, the Clinton administration was obliged to agree to a compromise with Belgrade. Under the label of U.N. forces, NATO could occupy Kosovo, on conditions that were never respected. Without any authorization from anybody but itself, the Pentagon immediately grabbed a large piece of territory and started building a huge military base on it, named Camp Bondsteel.

A week after the Serbian government accepted a compromise (later violated by the Western powers) allowing NATO troops to occupy Kosovo, *Washington Post* correspondent Richard Cohen, wrote admiringly:

> The KLA had a simple but effective plan. It would kill Serbian policemen. The Serbs would retaliate, Balkan style, with widespread reprisals and the occasional massacre. The West would get more and more appalled, until finally it would, as it did in Bosnia, take action. In effect, the United States and much of Europe would go to war on the side of the KLA.
>
> It worked.

Yes, but the question is, was this essentially a "KLA plan"? What obliged the rulers in Washington, London and Berlin to go to war because a Balkan army was putting down a fairly weak armed rebellion? Would the KLA leaders, essentially gangsters involved in all sorts of illicit trafficking, have dared expose themselves to the vastly stronger Serbian forces without firm assurances from their Western allies that as a result, NATO would let them take over Kosovo?

The KLA amounted to very little in itself. It could neither conquer nor hold territory. It was just enough of an armed band to carry out assassinations and trigger reprisals. U.S. and German agencies were secretly arming the KLA, in cahoots with leaders in neighboring Albania. The little terror war by a band of Albanian nationalists was simply the trigger for the big terror war waged by NATO bombs and missiles.

No, this war was not the result of a clever plan by some ragtag Balkan clan leaders. This was a war deliberately planned and carried out by the real Joint Criminal Enterprise: NATO.

PART IX

The Age of Destruction

28.

From One War to Another

The Kosovo War marked a change in the attitude of the Left toward U.S. military intervention. An immense publicity campaign, playing on false analogies with World War II, succeeded in rallying much of the Left to the need to "do something"—and the only "something" available was NATO bombing.

This brought an abrupt end to my association with the European Green parties. I was back in France, where "humanitarian intervention" was ardently promoted by such star media personalities as Bernard Kouchner and Bernard Henri Lévy, whose claim to be "on the left" contributed to a degradation of the label.

Differences were so sharp that some friends were lost, and others were found. On May 16, in the middle of the NATO bombing, Jean Bricmont, professor of mathematical physics at the Catholic University of Louvain, came to see me in Paris. He had read my articles and wanted to talk with someone who shared his perspective. Although a scientist absorbed in issues of entropy and quantum mechanics, Jean had acquired a solid literary background thanks to his Jesuit education (despite his passionate rejection of their religious teachings). He was already controversial in France for having co-authored, with New York physicist Alan Sokal, a book which took to task certain French philosophers for trying to make their theories sound profound by citing scientific theories which they did not understand and which, far from clarifying their ideas, only made them more obscure.[38]

As time passed we became friends and collaborators, exchanging views and writing articles together. In 2005, Jean wrote *Impérialisme humanitaire* which I translated into English (although as a scientist, he was used to writing in English).

While NATO waged its illegal war, its special court criminalized the victims. On May 27, while the bombs were falling on his country,

---

38 Alan Sokal and Jean Bricmont, *Fashionable Nonsense: Postmodern Intellectuals' Abuse of Science* (New York: Picador USA, 1998). The British edition (1997) is titled *Intellectual Impostures* and the French is *Impostures Intellectuelles.*

President Milosevic was indicted for "war crimes" and for "crimes against humanity" by the Canadian chief prosecutor at the International Tribunal for former Yugoslavia (ICTY), Louise Arbor. These indictments were based solely on unsubstantiated rumors of mass killings, whereas NATO was quite openly killing people—mostly civilians since the Serbian military knew how to conceal itself; bombed "tanks" turned out to be cardboard decoys. ICTY's double standards made it clear that there was no legal recourse for the victims of Western bombing. NATO had judicial power sewed up too. The charges against Milosevic kept changing and were never proven, but Western mainstream media hastened to confirm its own verdict that he was guilty, thus justifying more and more bombing of his country. Here was a system with no separation of powers. The executive, the media and the judicial system all operated in perfect harmony. They were egged on by various privately-funded "human rights" organizations acting as unelected representatives of "civil society."

There was indeed opposition to the war within the far left, but it had no media voice. Even the relatively fair and balanced monthly, *Le Monde diplomatique,* had decided to leave interpretation of Yugoslavia to Catherine Samary, an important member of the Trotskyist *League Communiste Révolutionnaire* (LCR). She took the "neither-nor" line; we must "neither" support NATO "nor" support Milosevic. It is typical of such militant groups to approach conflicts in terms of which side they should "support." But there was no need to "support" anybody in order to condemn aggressive war. You do not have to "like" a person to oppose murdering him. There is no need to "support" a foreign leader in order to disapprove of bombing his country. But this notion that one must "take sides" has led radical leftist groups to condemn antiwar individuals on grounds that they must be "supporting" foreign leaders, invariably dubbed "dictators." The war is never against a country: it is always against a wicked leader, and you couldn't support *him.*

LCR leaders went further: they could support neither NATO nor Milosevic but they could support NATO's ally on the ground, the Kosovo Liberation Front.

Trotskyists tend to be on the lookout for signs of world revolution, and for some of them, the gangsterish KLA was seen as a "national liberation movement," no doubt because that was what they wanted to see. But this was not the Third World, and the Albanians of Kosovo were not fighting against a distant imperial power, but simply to take over a province of another country where they had grown into a majority. The implications of this are considerable for multicultural countries.

At the end of August, Jean managed to get me invited to take part in a round table at a big LCR meeting on the Balkans. The other speakers included Catherine Samary and the well-known journalist Edwy Plenel. As is common in France, Plenel's Trotskyist background proved to be excellent career preparation. At that time, he was an editor of *Le Monde* and a fervent supporter of the Kosovars. Surprisingly, the public at that meeting reacted with hostility to Plenel's enthusiasm for the KLA, whereas my remarks, stressing the complexities of the situation, were greeted with strong applause. This was a small sign among many of a split between leaders of leftist parties and their members.

At the beginning of October, I went home to Minnesota for what turned out to be the last time. There was still an active peace movement in the Twin Cities. I was greeted warmly by old friends and had many opportunities to speak about the Yugoslav wars in churches, colleges, the University. I was even interviewed by the *Minneapolis Tribune.* I took the occasion to drive to Saint Paul, hoping that the house of my Bonnell grandparents on Princeton Avenue, where I spent my early childhood, was still there. It was, and had been taken over by neighboring Macalester College for their "Russian house," inhabited by students learning Russian. That seemed to me fitting, and I like to hope this vocation has endured, but I fear it may have disappeared, as everything Russian has been demonized.

Later in October, on behalf of *Dialogue,* Dragan Pavlovic and I organized an international conference on "Justice and War," focusing especially on the legal aspects of the NATO aggression. Participants came from Belgium, Italy, Canada, Germany, Sweden, India and the United States.[39] We were able to hold our conference in the town hall of the 9th arrondissement of Paris, thanks to the generosity of the Gaullist mayor, Gabriel Kaspereit. The conference focused on the multiple abuses of international law by the NATO allies in relation to the conflicts of Yugoslav disintegration. Not a single media, not even the French news agency AFP, bothered to notice the event.

---

39 Participants included Brian Becker, Christopher Black, Gabriele Cerminara, Ramsey Clark, Olivier Corten, Barbara Delcourt, Domenico Gallo, R. K. Kent, Annie Lacroix-Riz, Jan Oberg, Cedomir Prlincevic, Catherine Samary, Elmar Schmähling, Zeljan Schuster, Raju G.C. Thomas, Siddarth Varadarajan, Roland Weyl.

Cedomir Prlincevic, the head of the small Jewish community of Pristina, missed the conference when his car broke down. But he sent a message, a personal account of what happened as NATO troops (called KFOR, Kosovo Force) and the KLA took over Kosovo

.

> ...I lived in a large complex of nice apartments inhabited by doctors, lawyers, university professors, managers of various institutions, the intellectual core of Pristina society. Right after KFOR arrived, the gangster elements attacked this section, called Milana. They moved up and down through the buildings, banging on doors, breaking them down, throwing tear gas into people's apartments, forcing them out on pain of death.
>
> ... For one thing the Albanians who attacked our apartment complex spoke a dialect that made it clear they were from Albania, not from Kosovo. ...
>
> ... Under these circumstances, who would stay? We lost everything, years of our lives—our lives and our community, the only place we can ever be at home—gone. Stolen.
>
> About 30,000 people were driven from this huge complex in Milana in a matter of days. I have had to flee to tiny quarters in Belgrade, I and my family, including my 81-year-old mother.
>
> The Jewish community in Pristina existed by fortuitous accident. During World War II the ethnic Albanian fascists in alliance with Italian and then German forces shot some local Jews. Then they arrested the rest and shipped them, in stages, to death camps. One large trainload of Jews took a wrong turn and got stalled several days at a train station and was liberated by the Russian Army. My family thus exists only by virtue of error; but my 81-year-old mother ... now has to face the destruction of her life, of all our lives. I personally was Chief Archivist in Pristina, and now at 61 years of age, what am I to do? What are any of us to do?

This was the sort of human interest story that might interest the media. But not when it went against the NATO narrative.

During research for my book on Yugoslavia, I discovered an excellent periodicals library tucked away in the basement of the futuristic headquarters designed by Oscar Niemeyer for the French Communist Party. Niemeyer's idea was to build for the masses, but by this time, the masses were gone and I had this library almost all to myself. There I met retired journalist Robert Décombe, who had been l'*Humanité* correspondent in Belgrade for years but whose opinions were no longer welcome. He was very helpful, giving me access to his own extensive files. He and a couple of colleagues urged me to write an article which they presented to *Humanité* editors for the Sunday edition, but it was no go. Georges Marchais was dead and PCF foreign policy was reduced to timid compensation for its past support for the Soviet Union.

It was early afternoon in Paris when a friend called and told me to turn on the television. This was September 11, 2001, and a plane had just run into one of the twin towers of the World Trade Center in New York. As I watched, a second plane ran into the second tower, so it was clear that this was not an accident.

That this was the work of Saudis retaliating against the United States for violating their sacred territory did not seem to me implausible. The United States had moved onto Saudi territory as a basis for attacking Iraq, as part of a broad aggression against the Middle East, so the idea that those being struck would strike back didn't seem totally inexplicable. I initially failed to grasp the implications.

The reactions of my friends George Pumphrey and Jean Bricmont were far more somber and astute. They saw right away that the United States was going to use this to wreak havoc all over the Middle East for years to come.

Four days after 9/11, Jean and I went into the Paris suburbs to the *Fête de l'Humanité,* staged annually by the French Communist Party. The huge Fête provides stands for various groups, national and foreign, discussions, an appetizing array of regional restaurants, a book fair and at the end, a big spectacle starring a popular singer of the day.

Walking around the fairgrounds, Jean was particularly shocked to see Communist Party posters calling for "Solidarity with the American people and the leaders they chose." With the American people, okay, but "the leaders they chose"? That meant George W. Bush and Dick Cheney—who were "chosen" by the Supreme Court only after some fooling around with the vote in Florida.

It didn't stop there. A major round table debate was organized on the 9/11 attacks, including "two minutes of silence in respect for the victims." The debate was already underway, but Jean managed to persuade the organizers that they should welcome to their round table "an American journalist"—me. They accepted, expecting something other than what they got. I asked rhetorically why the French Communist Party had not called for minutes of silence in respect for victims of U.S. bombing in Iraq, in Sudan, in Yugoslavia... The public applauded vigorously, far more than for the other speakers, to the embarrassment of the organizers.

This does not indicate that I am a great public speaker, which I am not. I don't enjoy public speaking and prefer to avoid it. Rather, this incident illustrated once more that even leaders of self-proclaimed "revolutionary" parties were enforcing the NATO line. Much or most of the public would have welcomed a contrary view, had they been allowed to hear it.

This 9/11 solidarity with the United States was soon required to take concrete form. The attacks on the World Trade Center and the Pentagon were huge crimes that called for intense police investigation and close cooperation with Interpol to track down foreign accomplices and have them extradited to the United States. This was certainly within the scope of America's international influence. But Washington quickly decided on a different approach. Why solve a crime when you can wage a war instead?

So it was decided that this was not a crime but "an attack on the United States," which evoked Article 5 of the NATO treaty specifying that an armed attack on one of the allies "shall be considered an attack against them all." The original notion behind NATO's collective security cause was that the United States would come to the defense of its much weaker European allies if they were attacked by the Soviet Union. But no, the only time Article 5 has been applied has been for the Allies to go to war in defense of the United States.

Defense from whom? The notion had always been defense from an aggressor nation. But there was no aggressor nation, as far as could be seen. No foreign power was accused, especially since those identified as the hijackers were mostly from Saudi Arabia, America's staunch ally and faithful arms purchaser. Saudi Arabian leaders were hastily spirited out of the country and back to Saudi Arabia, while Israeli Mossad agents spotted celebrating the Twin Tower disaster were also soon on their way home to Israel.

The culprit was rapidly identified as Osama bin Laden, a rich Saudi Arabian businessman of Yemeni origin, leader of the radical Islamic paramilitary organization al Qaeda. Back in the 1980s, bin Laden and United States were working together to drive Soviet occupiers out of Afghanistan. He had also helped recruit Mujahidin to fight for Izetbegovic's Muslim party in Bosnia. But the CIA is not fussy about the allies it needs in murky situations, and our former friend was now our worst enemy, reportedly hiding out in a remote part of remote Afghanistan. In Kabul, the ruling Islamic party, the Taliban, was reluctant to extradite him just like that, and kept demanding to see evidence. Washington was too impatient to fool around with diplomacy. The United States started bombing Afghanistan less than a month after the Twin Tower attacks, on October 7. The Taliban had begun to show signs of complying, but it was too late. The United States preferred to plunge into endless war.

At the time the bombing began, I happened to be in Ottawa for a conference, which gave me the opportunity to grasp the mood of the United States as presented on U.S. television. Panic and commercialism seemed to blend in curious ways. The detail that stuck in my mind was a broadcast explaining that eating ice cream was a good way to combat the stress caused by 9/11. I wondered how this compared with the reactions of peoples bombed by the U.S. Air Force in Vietnam, or Sudan, or Iraq, or Yugoslavia. There seemed to be an absence of the stoicism required for enduring a long war. But America's long wars happen somewhere else.

Although nobody even claimed that Afghanistan had launched the 9/11 attacks, it was assigned the role of enemy country that had to be invaded in order to defend America. That is how Washington's European NATO allies got drawn into an endless, hopeless war in a country known primarily for defeating foreign invaders. As it dragged along, this war was sold to the public as necessary to "liberate Afghan women"—which is something the Soviet Union had been trying to do when the United States armed the Islamists to throw the Russians out. What the invasion did accomplish was to free opium production from the restrictions enacted by the Taliban, thus ensuring Afghan farmers of a valuable cash crop and international drug dealers of a reliable source of supply for the heroin trade.

For me, the year 2002 was primarily devoted to finishing my book, *Fools' Crusade*. In Washington, the neoconservatives—Paul Wolfowitz as Undersecretary of Defense, along with Richard Perle,

Douglas Feith, Michael Ledeen, "Scooter" Libby, David Frum, Robert Kagan and others, with the crucial support of Vice President Dick Cheney—were taking full control of President George W. Bush's foreign policy. Indeed, when, in his January 2002 State of the Union message, President Bush condemned North Korea, Iran and Iraq as "the Axis of Evil," he was literally acting as spokesman for the neocons, as the speech was written by neocon David Frum.

This was also a year devoted to building up the myth of Saddam Hussein's arsenal of "weapons of mass destruction" as prelude to a massive attack on Iraq. These accusations were regarded with deep skepticism in France, Germany and Russia, nations with intelligence agencies of their own able to evaluate such reports. Any informed person knew that it made no sense to suggest that Saddam Hussein was going to give WMDs to al Qaeda, his mortal enemy. France in particular had good relations with Iraq, and President Chirac had no desire to see the country destroyed.

Everything came to a head in 2003. On January 22, Defense Secretary Donald Rumsfeld expressed scorn for "Old Europe," meaning those nations that wanted to avoid war. A week later, eight European leaders joined "New Europe" by expressing their support for the war that the United States was preparing to unleash on Iraq.

For the first time since De Gaulle, French leaders balked. At the February 2003 meeting of the U.N. Security Council meeting where U.S. Secretary of State Colin Powell brandished a fake vial of deadly anthrax to illustrate the Iraqi threat to humanity, France took the lead in expressing the widely felt skepticism that few dared admit. In an eloquent well-reasoned speech, Chirac's foreign minister Dominique de Villepin called for relying on further arms inspections before plunging into war. Give the inspectors time, he said. "No one can be sure today that taking the path of war will be shorter than the path of inspections. No one can be sure that it would lead to a world that is more secure, more just and more stable. War is always an acknowledgement of failure."

Refuting the claim that Iraq might arm terrorists, de Villepin noted: "In the present state of our information and research carried on in liaison with our allies, nothing allows us to establish such links." He warned that Western intervention might "risk aggravating the fractures between societies, cultures and peoples, fractures which favor terrorism."

Alluding to Rumsfeld's distinction between "old" and "new" Europe, the French foreign minister concluded: "It is an old nation, France, an old continent, Europe, that is speaking today, which has known wars, occupation, barbarism." Faithful to its values, he said, France wants to act steadfastly with all members of the international community, believing "in our capacity ensemble to build a better world."

In violation of the rules, the assembly broke into vigorous applause, and the Chinese delegation was observed to smile with satisfaction at the reference to "old nations."

I knew people who had watched the proceedings and called each other to express how thrilled they were by the speech of Dominique de Villepin. At last, a voice of peace! A suggestion that France would take the lead in bringing the world together rather than tearing it apart. Some people actually wept at the hope his words aroused.

The next day was marked by worldwide antiwar demonstrations, the last big antiwar demonstrations in the tradition of the movement against the war in Vietnam. In Paris, an American contingent joined the huge peace march from Denfert-Rochereau along the Boulevard St Michel to Chatelet.

Why did so many people oppose war against Iraq and not war against Yugoslavia? Because the invasion of Iraq lacked a "humanitarian" pretext, and public opinion, especially on the left, readily considered that any war in the Middle East must really be about oil.

In the United States the reaction to Dominique de Villepin's speech was angry and stupid. Congressmen took the grotesque measure of changing the name of "French fries" (which in France are simply called *frites* and are considered Belgian) to "Freedom fries." A propaganda campaign ensued reminiscent of American propaganda campaigns against de Gaulle in the 1960s.

But not all French politicians shared the independent vision of Dominique de Villepin. Many of his fellow conservatives were appalled by his disobedience to Washington. One of these was Nicolas Sarkozy, who connived to cause political embarrassment to Villepin while he was prime minister. Then, after being elected President of the Republic in 2007, Sarkozy rushed to the United States to ensure President George W. Bush of his loyalty. Although France stayed out of the Second Gulf War, the final upshot of its momentary revolt in 2003 was actually to tighten French obedience to NATO and to U.S. policy.

The Message in the Bottle

My book on the background of the Yugoslav war, *Fools' Crusade,* was published in late 2002 by Pluto Press in collaboration with *Monthly Review.* A book promotion tour was scheduled for March 2003, taking me to Philadelphia, New York, Chicago and, of course, Minnesota. However, at the end of a panel discussion at New York University, I underwent a strange interval of temporary amnesia—perhaps induced by a combination of stress brought on by public speaking and newly prescribed heart medicine that my system was not used to. I woke up in the hospital where I was kept for a week for tests which never produced any results other than a bill for $38,000. For Americans, that no doubt seems perfectly normal, but for Europeans such a huge sum is outlandish. I managed to negotiate a payment with my European insurance but decided never to return to the United States. It is too dangerous.

The other bad result was cancellation of my fairly modest book tour.

Many books are sold on the claim that they are "controversial." But when a book is *really* controversial, that is not how it works. It is more like sending a message across the sea in a bottle.

My book had a few good reviews in obscure journals but was totally ignored by mainstream media, which was no surprise. In April, Björn Ecklund, the managing editor of a magazine called *Ordfront* (meaning "word front"), came from Sweden to interview me in Paris. The magazine was the organ of a progressive network which had grown into the principal alternative left organization in Sweden. Björn Ecklund was impressed by my book, which challenged the unanimous mainstream view of a Manichean conflict between evil Serbs and their innocent victims. In August, Ordfront published a 9-page spread on "Yugoslavia lies" featuring my interview and excepts from *Fools' Crusade.*

It took three months for the counterattack to be launched. On November 3, 2003, the large circulation daily, *Dagens Nyheter,* published a hit piece by right-wing, pro-NATO attack dog Maciej Zaremba describing me as a "genocide denier." This was the line used from then on to discredit me personally and scare people away from reading what I wrote. The implication is that a "genocide denier" must be a horrible person who condones genocide (something that logically makes no sense). But what is wrong with denying a genocide that never took place? Indeed, in obscure circumstances, after Bosnian Serb forces captured the town of Srebrenica, an uncertain number of military-age men and boys were captured and executed. That is certainly a serious war crime. Muslim soldiers based in Srebrenica had carried out massacres in surrounding Serb villages, so the killings may have been part of a vicious cycle of revenge toward the end of a nasty civil war. But it is impossible to commit "genocide," extermination of a people, when women and children—the people's future—are spared. When they captured Srebrenica, the Serb forces made sure that women, children and the elderly were bused to safety. Many male prisoners were released later on.

However, the NATO-backed Tribunal found a sociologist who claimed that because the Muslims in Srebrenica were a patriarchal society, killing men amounted to "genocide" because the women would not return without them. This amounted to "genocide" in a single town—a novel definition with the potential to be widely applied in wartime. This strange interpretation was enough to qualify Srebrenica as "genocide" according to the ruling of an international court—making its denial a crime in some countries.

Those who attacked me for "denying that Srebrenica was a genocide" never argued with the facts and reasoning I presented.

Zaremba wrote: "*Ordfront* must be aware that, apart from the violation of press ethics, the article was a gross offence to all the victims of massacres and rapes in the Balkans, comparable in its impact on the survivors with denial of the Nazi Holocaust..." There we go! Opposing the NATO line is comparable to Holocaust denial. And why should survivors be devastated by refusal to use the word "genocide"?

There is an answer to that. The Muslim party in Bosnia, as well as NATO leaders and all the journalists who championed bombing Yugoslavia, have a vested influence in a label that justifies all they have said and done.

A very different view of *Fools' Crusade* was published in the much more obscure *Canadian Jewish Outlook* by York University law professor Michael Mandel—a serious scholar rather than an attack dog.

> Johnstone's analysis of the disgraceful behavior of the International Criminal Tribune for the 'former Yugoslavia' is so incisive for a non-lawyer as to make a lawyer blush ... *Fools' Crusade* is not only the definitive work on the Balkan Wars, it is also an inspiring example of how to rescue truth from the battlefield when it has become war's first casualty, an important lesson these days.

But in Sweden, other mainstream media joined the attack, without ever publishing my responses or arguing seriously with what I wrote. In fact, this "scandal" was not about me or about my book; it was about Sweden's increasingly close relation to NATO and obedience to U.S. foreign policy. Silencing a dissident voice was essential to wiping out the political heritage of Olof Palme and securing Sweden its place in the Western alliance, even though the nation did not formally join NATO.

As things developed, it became clear that the attack on me was primarily a pretext to bring *Ordfront* into line with the new Western ideology of "humanitarian intervention." Björn Eklund was soon under attack, leading to a complete change in the direction of the magazine. In fact the whole affair produced an upheaval in the organization and a putsch in the magazine, with Eklund fired and replaced by more NATO-compatible editors.

A major player in this coup was *Ordfront* chief editor Leif Ericsson, whose reasoning announced the triumph of conformity over critical analysis. In an essay entitled "Denying Guilt," Ericsson insisted on the establishment of a "common narrative" concerning the Balkan wars. "Such a narrative makes reconciliation possible. It becomes a common memory of mankind, which can help us understand ourselves and how we can avoid similar human catastrophes."[40]

The journalist was no longer asked to dig for new information and provide fresh analysis, but to contribute to the "common narrative." And, in this as in most cases, what is the origin of that narrative? NATO governments and the mainstream media.

Swedish friends had told me that the Swedish are particularly conformist in their ways. So are other peoples, but the "common narrative" struck me as a dangerously dogmatic demand for intellectual conformity, totally contrary to traditions of free expression, scientific enquiry and democratic pluralism. And this attitude has spread throughout the West, not only in Sweden.

Moreover, the "common narrative" was totally unsuited to "making reconciliation possible" because it was totally one-sided. The Serbs could never accept being labeled as the guilty party and the

---

40 Al Burke of Nordic News Network has written a superbly clear and accurate account of this whole *Ordfront* uproar, entitled "All Quieted on the Word Front," http://www.nnn.se/n-model/foreign/ordfront.htm. This is a most enlightening chapter in the decline of the critical left.

Muslim Party was determined to make the most of their official victim status. This refusal to hear both sides could only intensify and perpetuate mutual hostility.

To defend me against the Swedish media campaign, Edward S. Herman wrote a statement signed by Arundhati Roy, John Pilger, Noam Chomsky, Michael Albert, Tariq Ali and David Barsamian which defended my right to be heard and described *Fools' Crusade* as "an outstanding work, dissenting from the mainstream view but doing so by an appeal to fact and reason, in a great tradition."

Leading Swedish media refused to publish the statement. Nevertheless, the statement emerged a couple of years later in a leading British newspaper in a surprising way. On October 31, 2005, the *Guardian*—once the major voice of the British Left—published a hatchet job on Noam Chomsky which cited that statement in order to discredit him.

The hatchet wielder, Emma Brockes, employed a snide and superficial style which apparently had some fans. She opened her interview with a description of Chomsky's "nubby old jumper, big white trainers and a grandad jacket with pockets designed to accommodate a Thermos." After these fashion details came the intellectual description. Although recently voted the world's top intellectual (the peg for the story), Brockes echoed "suspicions over how he has managed to become an expert, seemingly, on every conflict since the second world war; it is assumed by his critics that he plugs the gaps in his knowledge with ideology."

But the main target of Brockes' insinuations was neither his dress code nor his intellect but rather his ethics, and this is where I came in. In 2003, a controversy flared up when "a journalist called Diane (sic) Johnstone" said the official number of victims of the Srebrenica massacre was exaggerated. (In reality, I explained the origins of those numbers, which were uncertain.)

> In the ensuing outcry, Chomsky lent his name to a letter praising Johnstone's "outstanding work." Does he regret it?
>
> "No," he says indignantly. "It is outstanding. My only regret is that I didn't do it strongly enough."

This exchange was used for the title of the Chomsky interview:

> **Q.** Do you regret supporting those who say the Srebrenica massacre was exaggerated?
>
> **A.** My only regret is that I didn't do it strongly enough.

Still, this went a bit better than the Swedish saga, because finally, thanks to the *Guardian* mediator and Seamus Milne, Chomsky and even I were allowed to get a word in against our attackers. And in Sweden, Björn Ecklund founded his own publishing house, daring to challenge common narratives…

29.

Globalizing France

In 2005, the Member States of the European Union were called upon to ratify a long and turgid document described as their new Constitution. A logical follow-up to the 1992 Maastricht Treaty, the "European Constitution" was presented to the public as the next inevitable step. In all 25 Member States, the political class was enthusiastic, but needed some device to demonstrate popular consent. Most governments chose parliamentary ratification, which was a cinch, but nine of them were confident enough to call a popular referendum giving citizens the opportunity to express their approval.

In France, the popular vote was set for May 29, 2005. Media poured out a torrent of propaganda informing citizens of their historic obligation to vote yes. It was a choice between peace versus war, prosperity versus decline, a brilliant future versus a return to an ugly past.

And yet, a large swath of the public studied the issues carefully, in order to decide for themselves. This turned out to be an extraordinarily intelligent exercise in grassroots democracy.

The "European Constitution" was neither fully European, nor was it what is normally considered a "constitution." It applied only to the Member States of the institutional framework which had evolved from the European Economic Community (EEC) to the European Community (EC) to the European Union, but which did not even include all of Europe. But it became normal to refer to that institutional framework as simply "Europe." Voters were admonished to vote "for Europe." How could they be against?

Nobody asked: Would the real historic, geographical and cultural Europe cease to exist if not held together by the institutions created since the 1950s?

Things would have been much clearer—too clear, in fact—if all this institution building had gone by the name of, let's say, Eastern Atlantica. That would have been more factually accurate than all the Euro-names.

Eastern Atlantica

Following the United States military victory and occupation of Western Europe in World War II, Washington took steps to perpetuate its domination of the countries it had occupied militarily by integrating them all into a new Atlantic Community, which had the United States and Canada as its Western branch. It started with the Organization for European Economic Cooperation, formed in 1948 to administer Marshall Plan aid, enabling war-ravaged economies to revive and provide markets for United States over-production. While the Soviet Union held together its occupied bloc by imposing client governments, the United States relied on economic interest and subtle co-optation to hold together its "community of values" more effectively and durably. The North Atlantic Treaty Organization (NATO) was founded in 1949, followed by the Atlantic Treaty Association in 1954, enlisting elites in support of NATO. In 1961, the U.S. State Department created the Atlantic Council, with branches in all of East and West Atlantica, coordinating efforts to promote public support for NATO "values." The Atlantic Council is linked by interlocking directorates to scores of elite organizations, institutes, and think tanks which develop policy consensus and help select and vet upcoming leaders in European countries.

This huge power configuration provided the real impetus for European unification, economic and military. Public emphasis, however, was on the idealistic side, the need to end war.

On the one hand, the disasters of two World Wars had naturally given rise to an ardent movement of European Federalists, who saw European Unification as an absolute necessity to ensure a peaceful future for the continent. This ideal has persisted to justify the "construction" process, even as it was led into a very different direction by the purely economic approach devised by Jean Monnet, in coordination with Washington.

French businessman Jean Monnet is portrayed as the main "founding father" (the term is American) of European unification. He was in fact totally Americanized and worked closely with senior U.S. officials throughout the process.

European Federalists dreamed of "the United States of Europe." However, Jean Monnet's goal was never to make of Europe an independent country like the United States. He even warned against "European nationalism," since he saw all nations as superfluous. Monnet concluded his Memoirs with this observation:

> Have I said clearly enough that the Community we have created is not an end in itself? It is a process of change, continuing that same process which in an earlier period of history produced our national forms of life. … The sovereign nations of the past can no longer solve the problems of the present: they cannot ensure their own progress or control their own future. And the Community itself is only a stage on the way to the organized world of tomorrow.[41]

In short, the project was never to create the political entity dreamed of by European Federalists (which was very likely impossible anyway, given the profound differences between European countries), but rather to destroy the decision-making power of nation states as a step toward world government. Given the overwhelming power of capitalism in the world today, this can only enable finance capital to fill the political vacuum. Whatever people think it is, East Atlantica amounts to a giant step toward Globalization.

Democracy Alive, Democracy Defeated

All of France's political and media leadership championed the European Constitution. As the star-studded campaign for voting "yes" got under way, a dissonant note came from the working class. On February 4, at a conference of France's largest trade union confederation, the CGT, called to endorse the Constitution, 82% of delegates voted against it. This was a sign of strong grassroots support for France's social model, threatened by the Constitution. As polls began to show the intention to vote "no" rising steadily, former Socialist culture minister Jack Lang trotted out his vast stable of celebrities to endorse the "yes" position by their charismatic presence. Jacques Delors warned of "cataclysm." Everything from the memory of Auschwitz to Paris's bid to host the Olympics was evoked as proof of the need to approve this Constitution. Everything but the text itself.

---

41 Jean Monnet, *Memoirs,* Introduction by George W. Ball, translated from the French by Richard Mayne (New York: Doubleday, 1978).

But contrary to all official expectations, ordinary citizens actually sat down and read the text, discussed it, and concluded that this was not for them.

The Treaty text was not an easy read. Many who had voted for the Maastricht Treaty without reading it, took the trouble this time, as some of the negative results of the earlier treaty began to be felt. The campaign brought to light the deep split between rulers and ruled.

It was an exciting period of living democracy, a quiet revolt against power infinitely more focused and significant than the May '68 upheavals.

All over France there was a proliferation of neighborhood meetings examining the text. In my own neighborhood alone, on the east side of the 18th arrondissement of Paris, I attended three different Treaty study groups within a few blocks of my home, all well attended with vigorous discussion.

To mention just a few things people found wrong with this Constitution:

- The text was approximately 500 pages long (depending on the language), in four main sections totaling 448 articles, plus an endless series of annexes and protocols. The language was often obscure. A normal democratic Constitution should limit itself to clear definition of an institutional structure, capable of accommodating policy changes. Instead, this endless, convoluted text set limits on what future policy could be. A "legal straitjacket," it was called.
- The principal objective of the Union was defined as "a highly competitive market economy" where "competition is free and undistorted." This meant that economic competition must be "undistorted" by State intervention on behalf of social equality. It was not clear then, but became clear later, that this overriding goal set member states competing against each other. It also enabled outside financial powers to "win" the competition.
- It perpetuated NATO. Article I-41, on the "common security and defense policy," specified that "commitments and cooperation in this area shall be consistent with commitments under the North Atlantic Treaty Organization." In short, it tied the European Union firmly to NATO for all time.
- Even more peculiar, the U.S. foreign policy doctrine of that period, the stress on combatting "terrorist attacks" (Article

> I-43) and on military contributions to the "fight against terrorism" (Article III-309), was written into the proposed European Constitution. This clearly implied dragging Europe into whatever "anti-terrorist" wars the United States chose to wage.

All this aroused strong criticism, but the primary focus of French citizens' revolt was defense of public services, understood as an essential factor of social cohesion and quality of life. Public services are the most egalitarian form of redistribution of wealth, as everyone benefits.

The Constitution's advocates lied outright by claiming that it would protect public services. The center of the *"non"* campaign was exposing this deception. The text never even mentioned "public services," and certainly no "right to public services." The Constitution took the "public" out of services, considering them only in terms of "economic interest" and profit—"income producing."

> Undertakings entrusted with the operation of services of general economic interest or having the character of an income-producing monopoly shall be subject to the provisions of the Constitution, in particular to the rules on competition, insofar as the application of such provisions does not obstruct the performance, in law or in fact, of the particular tasks assigned to them. The development of trade must not be affected to such an extent as would be contrary to the Union's interest.

This was a devious way of saying that the operation of any vital public utility, such as water, must be open to competition. Not just competition between national providers, but international competition. In short, a Member State's essential public services could end up totally owned by foreign operators with little concern for the needs of the domestic population as a whole.

The text went on to specify that "any aid granted by a Member State or through State resources in any form whatsoever which distorts or threatens to distort competition by favoring certain undertakings or the production of certain goods shall, insofar as it affects trade between Member States, be incompatible with the internal market." Meaning that the national government could *do nothing* that "distorts competition."

Even government aid to help maintain a vital private industry is ruled out.

While citizens studied the text, politicians and media bombarded them with trivial arguments. Television gave endless time to appearances of leaders of all major parties as well as every imaginable show biz celebrity, all warning that voting "against Europe" would lead to total disaster. Meanwhile, remarkably well-attended and enthusiastic meetings for "no" went unreported. On April 14, while President Jacques Chirac was warning a selected group of young people on an evening-long television show that if France rejected the Constitution she would be the "black sheep" of Europe, an enthusiastic crowd packed the big Zenith theater in Paris for a *"non de gauche"* meeting called by French Communist Party leader Marie George Buffet. Speakers included dissident Socialists and Greens, Trotskyists, Left Republicans, and a range of grass roots activists. A memorably forceful orator was Socialist Jean-Luc Mélenchon, who had voted for Maastricht, but this time broke with his party (as Jean-Pierre Chevènement had done long before). Mélenchon would re-emerge some ten years later as leader of an independent left movement.

Philosophy professor Marie-José Mondzain expressed the idealism that was still trying to resist the impetus toward neoliberalism. Most people reject a world where everything and everybody can be bought and sold, she said. They prefer to spend their lives giving and sharing. She had clearly struck the right note with the audience, which rose to its feet in a long standing ovation.

On a more practical level, the most active of the dissident Socialists, Henri Emmanuelli, pointed to a crucial difference between the European Union and its ideal model, the United States. At another huge rally in Paris on April 20, Emmanuelli noted that the United States pumps up its economy by massive deficit spending—pouring the money into the military. In contrast, the EU could have invested constructively in raising living standards in its new Member States—but this is prohibited by the rigid budget balancing rules already laid down in Maastricht. The ban on deficit spending has led to stagnation and tension between Member States.

In an effort to quell the rebellion in the ranks, Socialist Party General Secretary François Hollande hauled out the scarecrow, Jean-Marie Le Pen. If Le Pen was against it, all decent people must be for it. Dissident Socialists "were doing Le Pen's work for him." Hollande even went so far as to ask French television to invite Le Pen and other far right-wingers to come argue against the Constitution, in order to force leftists to vote for it.

The blackmail, "you agree with the National Front," did not work, and only deepened the bitter division among Socialists. For the Left, what mattered was what was happening: already, social benefits were being torn down in the name of "Europe," and the Constitution was designed to make it worse. Emmanuelli warned that such unregulated competition was what would lead to a revival of nationalism in Europe, not the speeches of Le Pen.

On May 29, the French went to the polls. With nearly 70% participation, the "no" votes won a clear majority of 54.68% against 45.32% in favor.

On June first, Dutch voters rejected the Constitution by an even larger margin: 61% to 39% with a turnout of 62%.

Since approval had to be unanimous, ratification of the Constitution was effectively blocked.

The president of the "alter-globalization" organization ATTAC,[42] Jacques Nikonoff, hailed the "no" votes as a salutary shock that would stimulate a real debate on basic economic issues that had been muffled for twenty years by "TINA"—Margaret Thatcher's famous argument that "there is no alternative" to neoliberalism. Nikonoff predicted that this popular victory would lead to radical transformation of the foundations of the EU—toward upwards social harmonization, the universal right to social services, a progressive industrial policy, opposition to all forms of neocolonialism, cancellation of Third World debt, dissolution of NATO, etc.

That is not at all what happened.

The term "constitution" was dropped, and the same text, with a few cosmetic changes, was revived as a treaty, and signed in Lisbon on December 13, 2007 by member states, including the French and Dutch governments. Since the French Constitutional Council ruled that certain provisions of the Lisbon Treaty were contrary to the French Constitution, the French Constitution was revised. At a special congress in Versailles in February 2008, these changes were approved by a parliamentary

42 The Association for the Taxation of financial Transactions and Citizen's Action (ATTAC) was founded in France in 1998 as a single-issue activist movement to promote a social tax on international financial transactions. With branches in several European countries, it criticizes without opposing globalization, advocating a "different" globalization, making ATTAC the leading "alter-globalization" movement.

vote of 560 to 181, totally disregarding the popular vote of May 2005. Parliamentary ratification followed rapidly.

Only the government of the Republic of Ireland dared submit the Lisbon Treaty to popular referendum. In a vote on June 12, 2008, the Irish rejected it. So, after some minor concessions and a torrent of "pro-Europe" propaganda, a second referendum was held on October 2, 2009 and the Irish duly complied. The Lisbon Treaty could thus enter into force on December 1, 2009.

The lesson was clear: in the European Union, if the people vote wrong, they are called on to vote again until they get it right, or else their vote is simply ignored.

The 2005 popular revolt against the "European Constitution" marked the last united struggle of the Left to preserve the French social model from the power of international finance. It was the last time that prominent Socialists (against their Party leadership) joined with Communists and a wide range of left groups and individuals on major issues of economic policy. They had done all they could, they had won, and the "political class" simply ignored the will of the majority. Rather than inspiring a lively discussion of basic issues, the referendum debacle took the breath out of the social movement. The Left began to splinter around other issues.

30.

The Bedouin and the Zionist

Dominique de Villepin's vision of France as champion of peace and disarmament never got beyond the rhetorical stage. The pro-American faction won the political infighting in the ruling conservative party, and in May 2007, Nicolas Sarkozy succeeded Jacques Chirac as President of the Republic. Six months later, the new president rushed to embrace George W. Bush in Washington, vowing that he wanted "to reconquer the heart of America." Speaking to the French American Business Council, Sarkozy said he "never could understand" why the two countries disagreed over Iraq. The "new France" had arrived.

Sarkozy felt very comfortable in the United States. When he was only four years old, his father Pal Sarkozy de Nagy-Bosca, an aristocratic immigrant from Hungary, left his wife to marry Christine Ganay in New York. Their son, Nicolas' half-brother, Pierre Olivier Sarkozy became an international banker. Nicolas' step-mother Christine left Pal and went on to marry Frank G. Wisner Jr., who among other things was sent in 2006 as a special State Department envoy to prepare the independence of Kosovo. His notorious father Frank Wisner Sr. had been chief of the OSS in the Balkans during World War II, head of CIA station in Albania, and organizer of the clandestine "Stay Behind" networks in East and West Europe. This included the notorious Gladio operation, whose agents were trained to subvert real or potential communist regimes; already in those days, Kosovo was spotted as having the potential to destabilize Yugoslavia. Of course, Nicolas Sarkozy had nothing to do with the elder Wisner, who had committed suicide in 1965, but in his American contacts he was close to a rather special milieu.

By the time Sarkozy arrived, the U.S. pretext for the 2003 invasion of Iraq was no longer defensible. Nobody believed any more in the "weapons of mass destruction" that Saddam Hussein was allegedly planning to turn over to his mortal enemies, al Qaeda terrorists. A strong ideological campaign was underway to establish a pretext for military intervention more generous-sounding than the "war against terrorism." The emphasis turned back to "human rights," which had been so hugely successful in gaining public support for the Kosovo War. An all-out effort was underway to establish a new international norm, "the Responsibility to Protect," or R2P, which would justify foreign intervention to protect a threatened population.

The U.N. General Assembly actually adopted R2P as a "recommendation" to the Security Council, which retained its right to approve military intervention (not that the United States ever really felt it needed its approval). A discussion of R2P was held in the United Nations in July 2009.

As author of *Humanitarian Imperialism,* Jean Bricmont was invited by United Nations General Assembly President Miguel d'Escoto Brockmann to take part in the discussion, along with R2P champion, former Australian foreign minister Gareth Evans, Noam Chomsky and others. Jean Bricmont made the following points:

- Although sometimes denigrated by R2P promoters as a "licence to kill," national sovereignty is the principal protection of weak states against strong ones.
- There is a long history of Western righteous indignation over violations of human rights, which they used to call "barbaric mores," justifying intervention and conquest. The promoters of R2P present it as the beginning of a new era when in fact it is the last gasp of an old one.
- The United Nations was founded to save humankind from "the scourge of war," precisely by strict respect for national sovereignty, in order to prevent Great Powers from intervening militarily against weaker ones. The United Nations needs to pursue its efforts to achieve its founding purpose before setting a new, supposedly humanitarian priority, which in reality can be used by the Great Powers to justify their future wars.

Of course, Jean was quite right, and less than two years later, the United States proved his point by citing R2P as the pretext for destroying Libya.

The Modernizing Bedouin

The dominant liberal ideology of multiculturalism has it that people of radically different cultures should all live together happily in a single State. But what about countries of radically different cultures living together in a single world? A planet of diversity? The same liberals who preach diversity at home support fitting culturally diverse nations into a single mold.

At the international level, the standards are double, triple, quadruple. Some States get a free pass despite their very exotic behavior, example Saudi Arabia. Others are considered unfit to belong to the world community, such as the Libya of Muammar Gaddafi. Gaddafi was a Bedouin, coming from a cultural background radically unfamiliar to Westerners, somewhere between Arab and African. He started out as an Arab nationalist revolutionary on the model of Egypt's Nasser, then, disillusioned with Arab leaders, turned to the cause of pan-African unity. He did not fit any mold. But neither did Libya, and his leadership had transformed this huge and sparsely populated land into a functioning State.

I was particularly outraged by the 2011 assault on Libya because I had actually been there and seen what it was like. Since Jean Bricmont was unable to attend an international symposium on the International Criminal Court (ICC) held in Tripoli in January 2007, he suggested to the organizers that they invite me, instead. The abuses of the "International Criminal Tribunal for Yugoslavia" had aroused my keen interest in the issue of international criminal "justice." I gladly prepared a paper and flew to Tripoli to discover Libya, or more precisely, the Great Socialist People's Libyan Arab Jamahiriya. This was a unique regime, attempting to merge modern socialism with moderate Islam and elements of direct democracy at the local level.

Like most foreign visitors, I stayed in a hotel overlooking a park with the Mediterranean in the background, and from there explored the city on foot. I was struck by the serenity and prosperity. Shops were well provided with quality goods, and in sharp contrast to Cairo (and even to Paris!) there was not a beggar or homeless person to be seen. Of course, Libya had an incomparably smaller population in relation to its size, and under Gaddafi, oil revenues ensured a decent standard of living for everyone. The 2010 UN Human Development Index placed

Libya well ahead of all other countries on the African continent.[43] In the traditional souk, no one tried to sell me anything, so that I was allowed to look around and shop tranquilly, with no bargaining and no baksheesh. In the park, I saw young couples sitting on benches and holding hands, girls sometimes with headscarves and sometimes not. Yet this was a Muslim country for sure; the Muezzin regularly sounded the hour of prayer, and no alcoholic beverages were available, but I replaced wine with sweet pastries. I never saw a glimpse of police maintaining this order.

Two political statements were immediately visible. There were wall posters—billboards really—with portraits of the Guide, Muammar Gaddafi. In his youth, when he took power in a bloodless coup of progressive modernizing officers, he had been strikingly handsome, but he had not aged well. He appeared strangely scruffy and distracted. And yet, as a young army officer, Gaddafi had succeeded in making a functioning state out of a tribal society, sharply raising economic and educational levels and attempting, with his *Green Book,* to articulate a modernizing form of Islam.

In the park next to the hotel, a large sign offered the following observation in Arabic, English and French: "Support of migration exporting countries is a way to limit the illegal migration." The French version was slightly more precise: *"La consolidation des économies des pays exportateurs d'immigrés est le moyen susceptible à mettre terme à l'immigration clandestine."*

This was a statement of a two-pronged policy which the Guide carried out scrupulously. To stop unauthorized immigrants from passing through Libya on their way to relatively nearby Italian ports, and from there to the rest of Europe, the government used both sticks and carrots: both repression of people smugglers and, more significantly, serious measures to raise incomes and living standards in sub-Saharan Africa. This included plans to use Libya's oil wealth to back creation of an African currency based on the gold standard, rather than on the French franc or other Western currencies. In Libya itself, sub-Saharan African workers were paid decent wages for their work. This policy of blocking mass migration was one of the factors ensuring good relations between Libya and Italy.

---

43 Its Human Development Index ranking sank from 64th place in the world in 2011 to 108th place in 2017. See "These countries are ranked highest—and lowest—for human development," World Economic Forum, https://www.weforum.org/agenda/2018/10/these-countries-are-ranked-highest-and-lowest-for-human-development/.

The two-day symposium on "The ICC: Ambition, Reality and Future Prospects" was held in the Academy of Graduate Studies on the edge of Tripoli. It was attended by about a hundred jurists from every continent. The keynote speaker was an eminent British professor of International and Comparative law, Jonathan Black-Branch. Over dinner in a Tripoli restaurant, I had the opportunity to converse with, or rather listen to, Bernard Lavigne, a French judge who at the time was working in the ICC prosecutor's office, and Kamel Rezag Bara, legal counsellor to the Algerian presidency.

As context, three days earlier, the United States had killed over fifty people in air strikes on Somalia, and the next day, President Bush ordered an additional 20,000 troops to Iraq.

At such a prestigious international symposium on such a politically sensitive subject, the total absence of the Guide seemed rather remarkable for a "harsh dictatorship." Most of the jurists present, including the Libyans, were far more favorable to the ICC than Gaddafi was known to be, or than I was. Gaddafi remained absent and silent. I think I may have been the person there who agreed with him most, since my point of criticism was that a proper justice system requires a police force, and that the only potential police force for the ICC was the world's foremost military power, that is, NATO. That meant that the court could only be very selective in its accusations, exempting NATO and its friends. This has certainly turned out to be the case.

This symposium was, I believe, part of Gaddafi's effort to overcome Libya's isolation and gain its acceptance as a "normal" country. From my contacts there, this normalization project enjoyed wide support among younger intellectuals, many of whom had studied in Britain or the United States. It appeared that Gaddafi was stepping back and allowing them to pursue their course.

Although I was an unqualified intruder, I was well received and able to have long conversations with a number of interesting people both during the symposium and in the days following. During our side trip to visit the extraordinary Roman ruins at Leptis Magna, I made friends with Zuhal Elamin from the Khartoum Law School who explained that most of the professors there were women, like herself.

Another woman lawyer whom I met was Azza Maghour, a clearly modern, bare-headed woman, who was on the defense team of Abdelbaset al-Megrahi, the Libyan found guilty of the Lockerbie bombing. I was particularly interested in the Lockerbie case, not only because my friend Bernt Carlsson had been a passenger on Pan Am flight 103 that exploded and crashed on the town of Lockerbie, Scotland, on December 21, 1988, but also because I had read a lot about the case. It bore all the signs of a CIA frame-up.

At the time of the disaster, it was widely assumed that the bomb had been placed by the Abu Nidal mercenary terrorist group hired by Iran to take revenge for the downing of an Iranian civilian airliner by a U.S. Navy cruiser over the Persian Gulf the previous July. Instead, the United States accused two Libyans of placing the fatal bomb with its timer in a suitcase on a flight from Malta to London via Frankfurt—an oddly circuitous route involving two baggage transfers. Blaming Gaddafi because "he does that sort of thing" was no doubt less embarrassing to Washington than calling attention to Iran's revenge scenario, and against Gaddafi, anything goes. After a few years, in the hope of getting the West to lift sanctions punishing Libya for Lockerbie, Gaddafi finally agreed to let two accused Libyans be put on trial by a special Scottish court meeting in the Netherlands. Under heavy U.S. pressure for a conviction, one Libyan was found guilty and the other was acquitted. The evidence was contrived and seriously discredited by testimony that emerged after the trial.

Azza Maghour agreed to receive me in her Tripoli office for an off-the-record briefing. Defense attorneys were looking forward to an appeal, convinced that proof of a frame-up was so compelling that it would lead to a second acquittal. Having read about this, I found her optimism totally justified.

Instead, complicated ways were found to avoid having to deal with clear evidence showing that U.S. agents had framed the Libyans. The decisive appeal was never heard. The convicted man, Abdelbaset al-Megrahi, ill with cancer, was persuaded to drop his appeal in order to be allowed to go home to his family.

But all that came later.

Back in Tripoli in 2007, I had a couple of long conversations with Omar el Badri, a retired Libyan lawyer and engineer who had served as secretary general of OPEC in 1970. He was critical of Gaddafi, less as a tyrant than as an embarrassment (rather milder than American liberals' outrage over Trump ten years later). El Badri was a great source of information about Libyan affairs and surprised me considerably by what he told me concerning the "Bulgarian nurses affair."

Five Bulgarian nurses and a Palestinian doctor had been sentenced to death for poisoning over 400 children found to be infected with HIV virus in the El Fatih children's hospital in Benghazi. The baffling epidemic was disclosed in 1999, causing an understandable public outcry and demand that the perpetrators be found and punished. Suspicion turned to nurses recruited to work in Benghazi for better wages than they would get in Bulgaria. This led to the arrests and conviction.

In Europe it was taken for granted that the charges were trumped up and false, and the assumption was that this was another criminal act by Muammar Gaddafi. In conversation with el Badri, I raised the subject expecting that he too would accuse his unloved Guide. To my great surprise, he did not grab this opportunity to blame Gaddafi but insisted that both he himself and the Libyan public in general were convinced that the Bulgarian nurses were indeed guilty. This assumption gained plausibility by analogy with other cases, unfamiliar to Westerners, in which Americans or Europeans had used Africans as unsuspecting guinea pigs in medical experiments.

Gradually, I began to piece together the whole story.

Clearly, the Libyan public firmly believed in the nurses' guilt. They were convicted and sentenced in Benghazi. Benghazi was the traditional stronghold of anti-Gaddafi resistance, based on loyalty to the overthrown monarchy and to traditional Islam. The context made it politically difficult to release the medical workers and allow them to go home, as European governments were demanding. The government found itself torn between the righteous indignation of the Europeans demanding that the nurses be freed and the righteous indignation of Libyans demanding that they be punished. Gaddafi's son, Saif al-Islam, had publicly criticized the trial and conviction of the nurses, so it was pretty clear that to the ruling family, this affair was an unwelcome obstacle to their policy of improving relations with the West. The problem was to satisfy the Europeans without enraging public opinion in Libya.

The solution was a scenario that is worth mentioning as evidence of how much the public is entertained by artificial events that conceal reality.

Six months after my trip to Libya, French President Nicolas Sarkozy's attractive (about to be ex-) wife Cecilia made a highly publicized trip to Libya to "rescue" the nurses from the Dictator. This performance provided glory for female powers of persuasion in Europe and an excuse for Gaddafi to get rid of the troublesome Bulgarians. Compensation was paid to families of the victims.

In 2012, a scandal broke in France alleging that Gaddafi had secretly transferred 50 million dollars to Sarkozy which he had used for his successful presidential campaign. The French press used this to claim that the Libyan dictator had "corrupted" the French president, without ever seriously explaining the motives for this largesse.

What did Gaddafi get in return? To me, there is an obvious answer. The mission of Cecilia, of course. With the hope that this would normalize Tripoli's relations with the West.

Then came the Arab spring. Large visible popular uprisings accompanied by violent repression broke out in Tunisia, Egypt, Bahrein, spreading to other countries in the region. In Libya, both the revolt and the repression were minor, but this was where Western powers decided to put R2P to the test.

The revolt occurred in Benghazi, where revolt was endemic, and not for economic reasons as in Tunisia. Taking their cue from the Tunisian and Egyptian uprisings, anti-Gaddafi militants decided to stage their own "day of rage" against the regime on February 17, 2011. The day was chosen in commemoration of fourteen people who died on the same day in 2006 in clashes between police and demonstrators protesting against disrespectful cartoons of the Prophet Muhammad. In short, the protesters were themselves anti-Western Islamists. And yet Western-educated Libyan officials easily convinced international human rights organizations that Gaddafi's repression threatened Benghazi with "genocide." All in the name of "responsibility to protect," the United Nations was quickly persuaded to impose a "no fly zone" on Libya, ostensibly to prevent the Libyan air force from exterminating its own people. In reality, a "no fly zone" means a zone where NATO rules the air space and can fly and bomb as much as it wants.

As the Security Council was deliberating, on March 17, 2011, I was in Brussels moderating a debate in the National Theater—not really a debate, but Noam Chomsky's appearance on stage to answer questions put to him by two admirers, Jean Bricmont and Canadian philosopher of education, Normand Baillargeon. After the performance, six of us went for a drink in the huge lounge of the nearby Hotel Metropole. At some point a loud cry went up at a table across the room, the sort of cry that accompanies soccer goals. A trio of excited middle-aged businessmen, Libyan as it turns out, soon came over to our table to "thank Chomsky." What for? The UN Security Council had just adopted the "no fly zone" resolution for Libya.

The reactions of our little group were varied. Most seemed to think that the Libyans were mocking Chomsky and that we should ignore them. I had to be restrained from saying what I thought of those parasites, who clearly looked forward to riding NATO coattails for their own personal advantage from what seemed clearly likely to be a "regime change." Chomsky said nothing at all.

We learned later that, a few days earlier, in an interview with the BBC, he had hailed the "liberation" of Benghazi as "wonderful." This is why the Libyan businessmen were congratulating him. Months later, Chomsky justified himself by making a distinction between the first five minutes, when NATO knocked out Libyan air power, which he said was legal according to UN Security Resolution 1973, and what he called "the second intervention." That was when NATO went on to bomb civilians, killing among others three of Gaddafi's grandchildren in their home in Tripoli, and to devastate the country, leaving it a shambles with no functioning government. In any case, Chomsky considered that Libya was "not a nice place."

I am not sure what he meant by that. As I saw it, for most of its inhabitants it was indeed a very nice place, where people lived well. I mention this with some misgivings, only to point out that nobody is perfect. Certainly, Noam Chomsky has made a unique contribution to critical analysis of U.S foreign policy. But even he might get something wrong. Paradoxically, I believe that even Noam, the co-author inter alia of *Manufacturing Consent,* tends to get most of his information from the very mainstream media he criticized. And also from "activists."

Chomsky had presented a critical analysis of the dangers of the "responsibility to protect" at the July 2009 U.N. conference where Bricmont also spoke. But he was more indulgent toward the concept.

> ...R2P can be a valuable tool, much as the Universal Declaration of Human Rights has been. Even though states do not adhere to the UD, and some formally reject much of it (crucially including the world's most powerful state), nonetheless *it serves as an ideal that activists can appeal to* in educational and organizing efforts, often effectively. (My emphasis.)

But which activists, and for what purpose? Chomsky was surely constantly besieged by "activists" of all sorts, groups of exiles recounting horror stories of the alleged atrocities being committed by the regime in their homeland. The sympathy of eminent figures such as Chomsky is extremely valuable to exiles seeking to justify U.S. intervention in favor of regime change in their homelands. The catch is that the well-intentioned humanitarians have no control over either the protection to be provided or the choice of situations in which it is applied; rather, this is in the hands of military forces, namely NATO, whose objectives may be very different.

There is a notable difference between activists from Middle East countries seeking U.S. intervention, and activists from Latin America seeking to end it. Americans are more likely to be sufficiently familiar with situations in Latin America to form a reasonable judgment, whereas American knowledge of the Middle East is extremely limited and heavily influenced by Israel. For those who get their impressions from media, Libya was *terra incognita,* reduced to the image of its "crazy dictator," Muammar Gaddafi.

Human rights organizations are prone to accept reports that provide fodder for their own denunciation campaigns. On February 2, Dr. Sliman Bouhuiguir, Secretary General of the Libyan League for Human Rights, told a meeting of pro-Western NGOs in Geneva that Gaddafi was planning to wipe out the people of Benghazi (accounting for about one tenth of Libya's population!). Solely on the word of their colleague, seventy such NGOs hastened to appeal to the United Nations, the European Union and the United States to take action against Libya. The pretext for overthrowing Gaddafi was only too welcome. Later, in a video interview[44] in Geneva with French journalist Julien Teil, Dr. Bouchuiguir, who was an expert on oil politics with close ties to the United States, acknowledged that he himself had no proof of his accusations.

Indeed, they were invented, but by the time eye-witness accounts established the truth, it was too late. It was not true that Gaddafi's "black African mercenaries" were committing atrocities. It was not true that Gaddafi had sent his air force to bomb Benghazi—the accusation justifying U.N. authorization of the "no fly zone," which in reality turned Libya into an unimpeded NATO bombing zone.

Once again, diplomacy was rejected in favor of war based on lies. African and South American governments were offering to mediate a solution, and Gaddafi himself was sending signals of his own willingness to negotiate retirement. But why bargain when you can bomb?

---

44 Julien Tiel, director, "Lies behind the "Humanitarian War" in Libya," Axis of Logic, http://axisoflogic.com/artman/publish/Article_63910.shtml.

BHL: France's Self-Appointed War Minister

There must be a number of unspoken motivations that drove NATO leaders to join with the most feudal Arab oil monarchies to eliminate Gaddafi. But two individuals proudly stand out as promoters of the enterprise. In the United States, the culprit was Hillary Clinton, famous for chortling happily over the news that the Libyan leader had been sadistically murdered.

In France, the polemic writer Bernard Henri Lévy (BHL) made a big show of persuading President Nicolas Sarkozy to turn against his erstwhile "friend" (although Sarkozy surely had his own reasons). BHL rushed to Benghazi to whisk a defecting Libyan official, Mahmoud el Jibril, off to Paris to convince French President Nicolas Sarkozy to support the "democratic revolution." With a Ph.D. in political science from the University of Pittsburgh, Jibril had been in charge of economic liberalization and privatization in the Libyan government. Now he presented himself as a leader of a transitional government.

Months later, Bernard-Henri Lévy boasted to the highly influential *Conseil Représentatif des Institutions juives de France* (CRIF) that it was "as a Jew" that he had intervened in Libya.[45] "I carried the banner of my loyalty to my name and my loyalty to Zionism and Israel" he declared at a CRIF conference on "Tomorrow the Jews of France."

> It is as a Jew that I participated in that political adventure, that I contributed to defining the militant fronts, that I contributed to elaborating a strategy and tactics for my country and for others. I wouldn't have done it if I hadn't been Jewish. What I say now, I said in Tripoli, in Benghazi, before crowds of Arabs…

In front of television cameras, BHL hotly denied that the revolt had anything to do with Islamists. "There are no Islamists in Benghazi" he declared flatly.

The BHL phenomenon is hard to explain, or even to understand. How did this vain, wealthy dilettante gain such influence? With his trademark unbuttoned white silk shirt and swept back coiffure, and

45 "BHL s'est engagé 'en tant que juif,'" *Le Figaro*, November 20, 2011. http://www.lefigaro.fr/flash-actu/2011/11/20/97001-20111120FILWWW00182-libye-bhl-s-est-engage-en-tant-que-juif.php.

his semi-hysterical diatribes, the man is a caricature of himself, and so far as I can gather, just about everyone in France considers him a very bad joke, a pretentious charlatan. How does he get away with it?

There is a lot about BHL to make people dislike him (as most do). He is a multimillionaire, having inherited his father's import-export company Becob, specializing in exotic wood extracted from Africa by underpaid workers living in minimal conditions. He ran it himself for a while and cashed in by selling it to his friend, billionaire François Pinault, who along with fellow billionaire Bernard Arnault own just about everything profitable in France, notably its luxury goods.

BHL wields an extraordinary influence on French publishing and media, where he can make or break careers.

He advises Presidents on foreign policy, always in the direction of what he takes to be U.S.-Israeli interests (although it could be argued that he gets this wrong).

He lives between New York, a lavish apartment in Paris' Saint Germain quarter, and an historic mansion in Marrakech. He recently put his Tangiers mansion up for sale because he "has too many" places to live. All this surplus housing enables him to win people over by inviting them for luxurious visits.

He carried on an open affair with a Guinness heiress despite his "perfect" marriage with third wife actress Arielle Dombasle, which is nothing compared to his early years when, as he has boasted to *Vanity Fair,* he sleeps only four hours, allowing him time to make out with three consecutive women the same night.

His devotion to libertinage inspired him to name his first child Justine Juliette, after the two heroines of the Marquis de Sade.

All this could make him disliked, envied or even admired (especially, it seems, in New York).

However, since he is labeled a "philosopher," I would like to analyze what it is in his voluminous writing that justifies the title. Aside from the influence of his money and influence, what has been the influence of his writing?

First of all, the main thing that his writings do not contain is a scrupulous regard for the facts. He has consistently distorted events in places that struck his interest: Afghanistan, Bosnia, Libya, Ukraine... but there his factual errors may have been intentional. In any case, admitting a mistake is as strange to him as taking the Metro or even driving his own limousine. When challenged, he usually lashes into a polemic or changes the subject.

Just as BHL's 2010 book *De la Guerre en Philosophie* was being lavishly praised by all his mainstream media friends, one reviewer, Aude Lancelin, actually read it and discovered this interesting detail. In support of his philosophical argument against Kant, BHL extensively cited the work of philosopher Jean-Baptiste Botul.

In reality, Botul, identified as founder of the philosophical school of "botulism," and author of "The Sex Life of Emmanuel Kant," was a hoax invented in the 90s by humorist writer Frédéric Pagès. One can wonder whether some anonymous ghost writer lost his job. But this exposure of BHL's research methods failed to damage his enormous influence, which seems untouchable.

The significant paradox is that the writer who has managed to acquire an international reputation as France's best-known philosopher has based his "philosophy" essentially on deep antipathy toward France.

In his 1981 book, *The French Ideology,*[46] BHL set out to demonstrate that France is essentially fascist and fascism is essentially French. Noble images of France are all deceptive lies. The author bravely undertook to face up to the real France, while holding back his "nausea faced with what I discovered and the vapors I had to breathe." To summarize pages of florid rhetoric, seeing the real France *makes him sick.*

Bernard-Henri Lévy was born in French Algeria in 1948, shortly before his family moved to France, where his father made his comfortable fortune. Neither he nor his family suffered under the Nazi Occupation. BHL read philosophy at the elite Ecole Normale Supérieure (where he was a favorite student of Althusser). As he tells it, he decidedly didn't like what he read, insofar as it was French.

His thesis is that the real homeland of fascism is neither Italy nor Germany, but rather France, where the ideas of fascism germinated. Germany emerges as relatively innocent. BHL does not attribute fascism to historic or economic factors but essentially to "ideas." His sources are French writers, of the right or of the left, who in the past expressed hostility toward the rule of money, the "plutocracy," the "200 families," corrupt politicians, the parliamentary regime which favored such corruption. There is no suggestion that certain factual realities might have incited such resentment against "the plutocracy." No, this can only be the deep hidden nature of France emerging from its sordid depths. A sentimental attachment to the sweet land of France, a sense of "belonging" are part of the litany of bad ideas condemned by BHL.

46 Bernard-Henri Lévy, *L'Idéologie française* (Grasset, 1981).

It is impossible not to recognize that when BHL speaks of "fascism," he is really speaking of anti-Semitism, which he associates with all the guilty thoughts he condemns.

Didn't France resist fascism as it rose throughout Europe? BHL acknowledges that "the pre-Pétain generation resisted the temptation." But France gets no credit for that. If the French failed to fall in love with German and Italian fascism, it was simply because these weren't French. France wanted a purely French fascism.

And for BHL, that's what they got with the Pétain regime: "… the most terrible, the most unbearable, is that, of that filthy scum, she [France] sniffed with delight the vilest odors. […] In a word, an authentic fascist revolution took place there, from 1940 to 1942, at least for thirty months, experienced in a sort of joy, jubilation and fervor."

That is how he describes France, shocked and humiliated, its northern half under German occupation and the south half still temporarily governed from the spa town of Vichy by Maréchal Pétain. The inevitable propaganda line of the Vichy government was to try to raise morale by trumpeting the opposite of the truth: that France was being "regenerated" under the slogan "Travail, Famille, Patrie." BHL portrayed the stunned passivity of much, probably most of the French population, too demoralized to do anything, as an exuberant revolution. The far right, to which Pétain belonged, used the Nazi victory to blame the progressive reforms of the Popular Front (1936-1938) for sapping patriotic morale and thus leading to France's defeat. This reactionary myth was the background for Pétain's conservative "regeneration." But for BHL, the French were overjoyed because they had their very own fascism.

In a critical review entitled "Provocation," Raymond Aron noted that BHL wrote "without the slightest understanding of the crises of conscience faced by countless good French citizens" devastated by their country's defeat. Aron, the most prestigious Jewish thinker of his generation, warned that through his own hysteria, BHL "will feed the hysteria of a segment of the Jewish community already prone to delusional words and acts."

Unfortunately, that is apparently precisely what happened. *L'Idéologie française* is the departure point of the long guilt trip on which BHL invited the French. The book is said to be his most influential, but who was influenced? The book inspired an uproar of refutations from left and right. Many objected that in his writings, Germany appears to be a rather innocent victim of French thoughts. But its influence was most surely felt where it could do the most harm: in the Jewish population of France, or more specifically, among those in the opinion-making section of the Jewish population most able to sustain and echo the book's deeply pessimistic message. BHL's condemnation of the French ideology surely contributed to the growing paranoia in the Jewish population, fed by constant reminders of the Holocaust, which BHL more or less openly blamed on French intellectual influence.

How could non-Jewish French people reassure their Jewish compatriots that they were not really in danger of extermination? The usual method, with strong government support, has taken the form of endless commemorations of "the Shoah" (an even more religiously connoted term than "Holocaust") on the dubious theory that constant reminders of past atrocities are the best way to prevent such atrocities in the future. There is no evidence for that theory. On the contrary, far from reassuring French Jews, constant reference to the Shoah appears only to have perpetuated and intensified Jewish fears. A vicious cycle is installed. The more one insists on "memory," supposedly to make sure "it can't happen again," the more Jewish children grow up fearing that it may happen again.

Cui bono? Only Israel could profitably exploit this fear by using it to incite French Jews to move to Israel. And indeed, the Israeli government openly exploits fear of "anti-Semitism in France" to recruit valuable new citizens.

In 2011, Moroccan-born French Jewish writer Jacob Cohen introduced the Hebrew word *sayanim* (singular *sayan*) in the title of his critical novel, entitled *Le printemps des Sayanim.* The word designates Jews of the diaspora who voluntarily act as informal agents of Israel out of devotion to the Jewish State. In this *roman à clés,* the chief *"sayan"* is a thinly veiled version of Bernard-Henri Lévy. In short, Cohen sees Lévy primarily as an agent of influence working on behalf of Israel.

It can be worth remarking that in all his condemnation of French "feelings of belonging," of attachment to the land, of devotion to "the French people," BHL shows no hint of awareness of a possible parallel with "the Jewish people" and their attachment to "the land of Israel."

31.

Black Humor Is No Joke

On December 1, 2003, the popular Franco-African comedian Dieudonné was a guest performer on a TV show called "You Can't Please Everybody." The show specialized in humorous parodies of current events. Dieudonné came on stage roughly disguised as "a convert to Zionist extremism," advising young people to "join the American-Israeli Axis of Good" if they wanted to get ahead. At a time of strong French disapproval of the U.S. invasion of Iraq, this allusion to George W. Bush's "Axis of Evil" was strongly applauded by the studio audience and fellow performers.

Jewish organizations chose to react to this sketch with extraordinary outrage, in particular to his concluding pronunciation of "Israel" as "Isra-heil." Although aimed against Israel, the performance was denounced as anti-Semitic. Dieudonné, confident that he had nothing against Jews per se, refused to beg for forgiveness. In an apparent effort to make an example of such impertinence, a campaign developed to have Dieudonné's shows banned.

In March 2004, Jean and I met Dieudonné in a restaurant in Brussels. Subsequently, after seeing his latest show, we would join him for conversation over his late dinner. This good-natured man, perceptive and curious about the world, never showed any sign of the "hate" of which he is accused. Like all the best humorists, he is fundamentally serious and thoughtful in every sense of the term, with a strong sense of the ironies of existence.

Dieudonné M'Bala M'Bala was born in 1966 in Fontenay-aux-Roses, a short distance south of Paris. His father was from Cameroun and his mother from Brittany. Before developing his successful one man show, he got his start in show business by joining up with his childhood friend, Élie Semoun, in a comedy duo where the big African and the small Jew played on ethnic stereotypes. On and off stage, Dieudonné campaigned against racism, even running unsuccessfully for office against the right-wing National Front in its stronghold of Dreux, sixty kilometers north of Paris. His considerable talent for imitating various ethnic accents and mannerisms was put to use in sometimes devastating sketches making fun of Africans, Chinese, Arabs, Americans—none of whom ever complained.

Dieudonné reacted to attack not by retreat but by upping the ante. His refusal to back down won both mounting condemnation and ever-increasing admiration. At a huge show on the day after Christmas 2008, he brought Holocaust revisionist Robert Faurisson on stage to award him a prize for being "insolent and unfit to associate with." Nothing was said to violate the Gayssot law, but after years of legal procedures, this bit of black humor cost him 10,000 euros in damages to Jewish organizations. Lawsuits piled up and police even raided his home on one early morning looking for something that wasn't there. But his popularity continued to rise.

Enter the Thought Police

One evening in November 2011, I went to an anarchist headquarters in the 20th arrondissement of Paris to hear what the author of a book called *La Galaxie Dieudonné* had to say. The book was an attack on everyone really or potentially associated with the "unfrequentable" and "insolent" Dieudonné, himself. The author, Michel Briganti, presented a long, unbroken monologue, designating people with whom he disagreed as *confusionnistes, complotistes* or anti-Semites. The campaign against Dieudonné had taken on the aspect of a witch hunt. Since Dieudonné was a strong opponent of the NATO attack on Libya (and is consistently pacifist), his guilty associates necessarily included people who had shared his opposition to that war.

As many as a hundred people, mostly young men, listened obediently. These were the foot soldiers of "Antifa." After an hour and a half of unbroken guilt by association, the audience was invited to ask questions. Silence. From the back of the hall, a man raised his hand to ask three little questions. Perhaps because he was the only black man present, he specified that he was French. First question, "Have you ever met Dieudonné?" Briganti's answer was simple: No. Second question: "Would you agree to debate with Dieudonné?" Instant answer, *"NO!* We don't debate with the enemy, we fight him!" Third question: "Since you know so much about Dieudonné, how many trials has he lost and how many has he won?" In the absence of a reply, the black Frenchman declared that "Debate is the basis of democracy" and left. Briganti called after him, "We don't debate with the enemy, we fight him!"

The refusal to debate adversaries is symptomatic of a dangerous tendency to reject reason in favor of imperious assertions, exclusion or violence. Such intolerance used to be the mark of Fascists but has increasingly become characteristic of those who call themselves anti-fascists, the Antifa. Refusal to debate implies that there is no point in arguing with members of particular population groups, since "they" are innately "like that" and will never change. Yet this exclusionary attitude has grown precisely in circles calling for inclusion and diversity.

Western Values?

Today European leaders harp incessantly on "Western values." But it has never been less certain what those values might be.

The allegorical figure of "Marianne" personifies official values of the French Republic: *liberté, égalité, fraternité.* It is customary to select a famous actress such as Brigitte Bardot or Catherine Deneuve as model for the latest image of Marianne reproduced on postage stamps.

In June 2013, French President François Hollande unveiled a surprising new concept of the Republic. The face chosen to adorn the new postage stamp was that of Inna Shevchenko, the Ukrainian leader of the militant group FEMEN, which had taken up residence in Paris a little over a year earlier. FEMEN were fighting against patriarchy, homophobia and religion by exhibiting rude slogans in English painted on their bare breasts. The choice of the Ukrainian activist as Marianne was hailed as a "symbolic message of equality, parity and mixing which for us are the essential values of today's France and the Republic."

Since the new Marianne did not speak French, she acknowledged the honor with a tweet in English: "From now on all the homophobes, extremists, fascists will have to lick my ass to send a letter."

What had Inna and the FEMEN done to deserve this? The Ukrainian women's hatred for Russia and love for the European Union might have something to do with it. In solidarity with the Russian anti-Putin exhibitionists Pussy Riot, a half dozen FEMEN sawed down a five-meter high Christian Cross in Kiev. In August 2012, Inna Shevchenko took her act to Paris where the authorities immediately provided her with a theater to use as an "international training center" for activists. Ordinary Ukrainians have a hard time getting papers to stay in France, but FEMEN moved right in. Their new home was located not far from where I live in the 18th arrondissement of Paris, the neighborhood with the heaviest concentration of Arabs and Africans in the city. How were they expected to react when the "new feminists" marched topless through these crowded streets, shouting "Muslims get naked!"? The local Muslims failed to take the bait and nothing happened.

In November 2012, FEMEN won support from women cabinet ministers in the Socialist government for disrupting a Catholic demonstration against "marriage for everyone" (the slogan used for gay marriage) by appearing topless with slogans in English: "Fuck God," "Fuck religion," "In Gay we trust" (who but an American could come up with that one?).

"If we show our boobs, they'll listen to us," the FEMEN declare. However, they have nothing to say. There is no reasoned argument, simply words intended to shock rather than to persuade. It is extremely doubtful that anyone was converted to support for gay marriage on the basis of that performance.

When several FEMEN covered with anti-Pope slogans invaded Notre Dame Cathedral in Paris in early 2013, Inna Shevchenko boasted of having swiped a bit of gold plating from one of the bells (then undergoing restoration). This led to arrests but in the end, the women were acquitted while the court imposed fines on the Cathedral guards for the way they expelled the intruders.

Their *chef d'œuvre* was reserved for the Eglise de la Madeleine in Paris during the 2013 Christmas season. FEMEN's leading French recruit, Eloïse Bouton, acted out "the abortion of Jesus," leaving a piece of calves' liver representing the fetus on the altar and announcing that "Christmas is cancelled."

On June 5, 2014, Russian President Putin arrived in France to take part in the fifty-year commemorations of the Normandy landing. To celebrate the occasion, FEMEN Yana Zhdanova entered the Musée Grévin (the Paris equivalent of London's Madame Tussauds), bared her breasts and acted out the murder of Vladimir Putin, with photographers immortalizing her fiendish glee as she repeatedly stabbed the wax figure.

Russia-hating FEMEN naturally supported the 2014 putsch that overthrew President Victor Yanukovich and installed a U.S. puppet government in Kiev. In Paris, five FEMEN peed on pictures of Yanukovich in front of the Ukrainian embassy. A FEMEN was photographed in Odessa showing her support for the neo-Nazi extremists as they set fire to the Labor Unions' House, killing 38 people opposed to the putsch.

So who are these harridans? Who funds them? Where did they come from? They are said to be funded by "businessmen" but details are unavailable. Strangest of all, the ideas for this "new feminism" opposed to "patriarchy" were provided by a man, Viktor Sviatski, their guru who manipulated what he called these "weak" young women.[47]

Body Language

The broad tolerance and even approval which greeted FEMEN's innovative "body language" did not extend to that of Dieudonné. The showman popularized a simple gesture, which he called the "quenelle," putting the right hand on top of the lowered left arm (or vice versa). Named after a fancy French dumpling, Dieudonné's quenelle is all too obviously a rude gesture ("up to here") roughly meaning "fed up." Or more precisely, "fed up with the system."

But in 2013, Alain Jakubowicz, President of LICRA (*Ligue internationale contre le racisme et l'antisémitisme*) declared that the quenelle was "a Nazi salute in reverse, signifying the sodomization of the victims of the Shoah." Dieudonné sued Jakubowicz for this morbidly extravagant fantasy but lost in court. Despite persistent denials, most of the political-media establishment has accepted the notion that the quenelle is really "a Nazi salute in reverse."

At this point both Socialist President Hollande and the leader of the conservative opposition party, Jean-François Copé, called for silencing the unmanageable entertainer. Editorialists disputed whether one should jail him for "incitement to racial hatred," close his shows on grounds of a potential "threat to public order," or put pressure on municipalities by threatening to cut cultural subsidies if they allow him to perform.

On January 6, 2014, French interior minister Manuel Valls sent a 3-page memo entitled "The struggle against racism and anti-Semitism" to police authorities all over France calling for "vigorous action" and authorizing police to shut down any event that might entail "a grave disturbance of public order." The government thereupon cancelled a Dieudonné show in Nantes at the last moment, sending ticket-holders home.

On January 10, as author of a book[48] against government censorship, Jean Bricmont was one of eight panelists invited to discuss "the Dieudonné affair" on the late evening television show, *Ce soir ou jamais.*

---

47 Quentin Girard, "Viktor Sviatski, un manipulateur dans l'ombre des Femen," *Libération,* September 4, 2013.

48 Jean Bricmont, *La République des censeurs* (Paris: L'Herne, 2013).

Bricmont tried to argue that Dieudonné should have the right to perform his shows and the public should have the right to see them, but he was constantly interrupted and drowned out by the other panelists. He was never again invited to debate on television. The University of Nice even cancelled Bricmont's invitations to speak on quantum mechanics, under pressure from "activists."

Politicians and media insisted that Dieudonné was finished. He was indefensible. To hear what they had to say, he was not funny, nobody laughed, nobody went to his shows, which were "Nazi rallies" that should be banned. As more and more theaters refused to book his shows, he was increasingly obliged to perform in places announced only at the last minute, sometimes on somebody's farm land. Yet Dieudonné continued to draw huge crowds of ardent fans. Indeed, the more he was attacked, the more his popularity skyrocketed. It cannot be denied that Dieudonné's lack of reverence for the religion of the Shoah struck a chord. That does not imply any denial of the historic facts. But any official doctrine ends up inciting opposition, and many people born decades after the events feel saturated with commemorations of the Shoah. The mere fact that one *must* believe in something can arouse doubts, or at least annoyance.

But Dieudonné would not be so popular if he were not the most talented humorist in France, the most intelligent, with a tragic dimension to his humor. He constantly addressed the most sensitive subjects, without inhibition, revealing the dark side of the human psyche but with a strong current of compassion. In his one-man shows at the Theatre de la Main d'Or (from which he was eventually expelled by its Israeli owners), he dared pursue the touching, the absurd, and the macabre, on such sensitive subjects as a bereaved war widow, corruption of African rulers, serial killers, pygmies, Alzheimer's—no subject was ever taboo. His was black humor in the full sense, which inspired a sort of "pity and sorrow" in his public, like Greek tragedy. But also enormous laughter.

But the campaign against Dieudonné has made many people afraid to go find out what he is like. Others will go wherever he is reduced to performing—as in a big bus.

Identity Politics can lead to conflict between groups concerning efforts to seek redress for historical wrongs. What happens when a society adopts concern for disparaged groups as the dominant virtue, but is adamantly and peculiarly selective as to which groups merit this concern? Dieudonné's request for subsidies to make a film on the African slave trade was turned down, whereas productions commemorating the Holocaust are countless. What if the group favored by law is extremely successful professionally even while claiming and enjoying unique victim status? In January 2014 a commentator observed:

> Especially among the "excluded," those who are "rejected by the system," there is bound to be a growing temptation to flout an imperative dogma erected by the government… When provocations by artists and FEMEN are indulgently tolerated, why ban provocations by youth from the [working class] suburbs? Because the Holocaust is "more sacred" than Christianity? Because the 'quenelle' is worse than pissing on the altar of a church? …
>
> Hostage of that downward spiral, the Jewish community of France, whether complicit, or deliberately, or against its will, has become a symbol of that State oppression. By designating the Jewish community as a sacred caste, the Gayssot law has made it a target. By giving it a separate status, it has made it the scapegoat for all the frustrations of France "at the bottom." The repression incites anti-Semitism, which in turn justifies another repressive turn of the screw, and so on…[49]

Not Funny

On January 7, 2015, two masked gunmen entered the Paris offices of the satirical weekly, *Charlie Hebdo,* and massacred a dozen people. Among them were several of France's best-known cartoonists.

Charlie Hebdo had built its notoriety by attacking religion, notably Christianity. But as Christians failed to react, Muslims proved to be a more sensitive target, protesting vehemently against insults to Islam. As Muslim outrage exploded over cartoons published in Denmark, *Charlie Hebdo* stepped up its own production of obscene cartoons deriding the Prophet Muhammad. This had led to death threats and special police protection, but police protection had been relaxed as the scandal seemed to have died down.

---

49 Matthieu Vasseur, "Les dangereuses métastases de la loi Gayssot," *Liberticides & Co,* January 14, 2014.

The two policemen still on guard were easily shot by the gunmen before entering the offices in the midst of an editorial meeting. Twelve people were slaughtered with automatic weapons, and eleven others wounded, some critically. As they left, one killer who came back to finish off a policeman who lay wounded in the street was heard to shout: "The Prophet is avenged!"

The killers fled toward the northeastern suburbs where they were eventually surrounded and killed by French security forces. They were identified as two brothers, Saïd and Sherif Kouachi, reportedly members of the Yemen branch of al Qaeda, which claimed responsibility.

Meanwhile their colleague, Amedy Coulibaly, on the East side of Paris, murdered a policewoman before taking hostages in a Kosher grocery store where he murdered four Jewish customers before being killed by police raiders.

This was the first in a series of deadly terrorist attacks in France by Islamic terrorists—usually petty criminals who had been converted to religious fanaticism while in prison or on trips to the Middle East. Coulibaly, of Malian origin, was one of these criminal converts.

On January 10, a million and a half people flooded Paris streets in the largest demonstration in modern French history, while hundreds of thousands demonstrated in other parts of the country. The "republican march" was intended to show that France was united against terrorism. An emotional declaration of solidarity soon caught on and was endlessly repeated: *"Je suis Charlie,"* I am Charlie. This did not mean that all those people identified with the publication, which had a small circulation and few readers. But the martyred weekly immediately became the symbol of freedom of expression.

In fact, its own editorial line was narrow. In 2008, another of *Charlie Hebdo's* famous cartoonists, Siné, was fired for anti-Semitism merely for remarking that President Sarkozy's son Jean "will go far, this lad" since he was reportedly converting to Judaism to marry the heiress of a prosperous appliance chain.

Officially and unofficially, France is an uncompromising champion of "laïcité," secularism, separation of State and Church—which historically meant the Catholic Church. It is also an ardent, unequivocal supporter of Israel. The Shoah has tended to replace Christianity as occasion for spiritual reflection. This is not something that goes down well with France's growing Arab population. Earlier Arab immigrants to France were not particularly religious, but in recent years, radical Islam has spread, especially among the younger generation.

The French government itself has aggravated the situation by its incoherent foreign policy. In Afghanistan, Mali and elsewhere, France sends forces to fight against al Qaeda or ISIS. But France *de facto* allied with those militants in its destruction of Libya and in its attempt to overthrow the secular government of Syria. When French converts to Jihad go off to Syria to join the Islamic State (Daesh), they are combating the same enemy as the French government: the Syrian government of Bashar al Assad. But Islamic State (Daesh) is considered by France to be the enemy.

Many Muslims can conclude that France is simply "against Muslims," whichever side they are on. As the funeral was being held in France for *Charlie's* editor Charb (Stéphane Charbonnier), riots broke out in front of French embassies in Muslim countries from Pakistan to Nigeria. Mobs burned French flags and rioted in Algiers. The *Charlie* uproar gave a trump card to the Islamist extremists against the forces of secularism in those countries.

At the same time, the so-called "Islamic State" or "Daesh," as well as "al Qaeda in Yemen" and associated fanatic Islamic groups were working hard to recruit fighters out of the Muslim communities in France and other European countries. Some 1,400 jihadists traveled to Syria from France to join the Holy War against Assad. They were lured by the heroic prospect of helping to "build the Caliphate"—which had some resemblances to an Israel for Muslims, a holy land restored.

The Middle East conflict is dangerously mirrored in France.

Israel is also recruiting, in its own much more respectable way. Tsahal holds annual support drives in Paris, and a number of French Jews do military service in Israel. Israel is deliberately and consistently doing all it can to excite fears among French Jews, in order to lure this desirable population into moving to Israel.

At the mass demonstration on January 10, foreign leaders came to Paris to show that they too were for *Charlie* and against terrorism. Without being invited, Israeli premier Benyamin Netanyahu forced his way into the front line of the VIPs in their private photo opportunity "march" and then visited a synagogue, where he informed French Jews that their only "home" was Israel. The line that France is "not safe for Jews" is vigorously echoed in U.S. media, raising fears in France of a boycott by American Jews, a potential economic and public relations disaster.

Both Sherif Kouachi and Amedy Coulibaly gave telephone interviews to BFMTV just hours before being killed by police raids.

Kouachi attributed his conversion to Jihad to the U.S. destruction of Iraq and seeing photos of Iraqis being tortured by Americans in Abu Ghraib.

The basic motive for the attack on *Charlie Hebdo* was quite possibly not so much to "avenge the Prophet" as to impress, inspire and recruit Muslims to join the great Jihad to restore the Caliphate in the Middle East.

In short, the *Charlie Hebdo* massacre may well have contributed both to recruitment of French Arabs to Daesh and to Netanyahu's efforts to lure French Jews to Israel.

The comedian Dieudonné was among the January 10 "I am Charlie" crowds. His own experience inspired an ironic reaction to this massive declaration of French devotion to freedom of expression. On his Facebook page he posted this sardonic comment:

> After this historic march, what can I say! Legendary! A magical instant equal to the Big Bang that created the universe!... or to a lesser extent (more local) comparable to the crowning of Vercingetorix. I am finally coming home. Know that this evening, so far as I am concerned, I feel like Charlie Coulibaly.

For this comment, after long court proceedings, Dieudonné was given a suspended sentence of two months in prison and fined 10,000 euros for "apologetics for terrorism."

32.

Wars and Elections

The second decade of the 21st century belonged to the war in Syria. In Syria, it all became clear—to those who were watching. All pretenses were exposed. The West was seen to be losing not only its material domination but also its moral supremacy and even more drastically, its perception of reality.

In Syria, Iran, Venezuela, the United States kept pursuing a failed effort to subvert the governments of other countries, ostensibly to impose Western-style democracy, while that democracy was being fatally subverted at home by the very same economic powers, both human and beyond human control. This self-destructive process was accompanied by a drastic intellectual decline that helped to ensure the continuing rise of that other part of the planet called the East, centered on China.

The Syrian Arab nationalist regime of Hafez al Assad had been in the sights of the Western politico-military machine for many years.[50] When, using the 2011 "Arab spring" as pretext, the NATO nuclear powers, Saudi Arabia and Israel, finally got around to carrying out their long-postponed plan to overthrow the secular government of Syria, the

---

50 "The dissolution of Syria and Iraq later on into ethnically or religiously unique areas such as in Lebanon, is Israel's primary target on the Eastern front in the long run, while the dissolution of the military power of those states serves as the primary short term target. Syria will fall apart, in accordance with its ethnic and religious structure, into several states..."—Oded Yinon, "A Strategy for Israel in the Nineteen Eighties," essay originally appearing in Hebrew in *KIVUNIM* (*Directions*), The World Zionist Organization Department of Publicity, 1982.

And there is the famous video of General Wesley Clark, on what he heard in the Pentagon in 2001: "So I came back to see him a few weeks later, and by that time we were bombing in Afghanistan. I said, 'Are we still going to war with Iraq?' And he said, 'Oh, it's worse than that.' He reached over on his desk. He picked up a piece of paper. And he said, 'I just got this down from upstairs'—meaning the Secretary of Defense's office—'today.' And he said, 'This is a memo that describes how we're going to take out seven countries in five years, starting with Iraq, and then Syria, Lebanon, Libya, Somalia, Sudan and, finishing off, Iran.'..." http://www.youtube.com/watch?v=bX7hMj2NKTc&feature=related.

country was no longer ruled by Hafez but rather by his gentle, reluctant heir, Bashar, who was off in London studying to be an eye doctor when his elder brother was killed in an accident, making him the family heir. Initially Bashar and his British wife, Asma, were praised by the media for their modern attitudes and desire to promote democratic reforms, but all that changed once the regime change plans got underway. It took only a few repressed demonstrations, whose origins are disputed, for Bashar al Assad to be suddenly promoted to the rank of the New Hitler, a brutal dictator reveling in the pleasure of murdering his own people.

The Illusion of People Protection

The full extent of the Libyan disaster was not yet apparent when, on January 18, 2012, United Nations Secretary General Ban Ki-moon addressed a New York conference hailing the success of R2P. He thanked his American audience for helping get him elected to a second term as United Nations Secretary General and from what he said, it was clear why they liked him so much.

> In 2011, history took a turn for the better. The responsibility to protect came of age; the principle was tested as never before. The results were uneven, but at the end of the day, tens of thousands of lives were saved. We gave hope to people long oppressed. In Libya, Côte d'Ivoire, South Sudan, Yemen and Syria, by our words and actions, we demonstrated that human protection is a defining purpose of the United Nations in the twenty-first century.

This illustrates just how far from reality Western-dominated international institutions had strayed. Leaving aside the Libyan catastrophe, and the murderous chaos prevailing in South Sudan and Yemen, it is enlightening to examine how R2P worked in Côte d'Ivoire (Ivory Coast).

In that West African former French colony, the December 2010 presidential election was disputed between the incumbent, Laurent Gbagbo, a member of the Socialist International, considered "nationalist" in the West, and his opponent, Alassane Ouattara, a graduate of the Wharton School of Economics at the University of Pennsylvania who had worked for the International Monetary Fund (IMF) for over thirty years. Although the Ivory Coast constitutional court validated

Gbagbo's re-election, the dispute dragged on for months leading to armed clashes between partisans of the two candidates. Western media described Gbagbo as a dictator illegally clinging to power and France imposed sanctions. In March 2011, a United Nations peace keeping force allowed pro-Ouattara forces, with French military aid, to take over the capital, arresting Gbagbo and his wife Simone and turning them over to the International Criminal Court (ICC), charged with "crimes against humanity." Ouattara took office, hailed by the Western media. In my African neighborhood of Paris, there were frequent protest marches in favor of Gbagbo.

The mixture of media demonization, internal subversion, sanctions, military intervention and criminal charges has become the standard recipe for regime change. When a population is divided, the West decides which side is "the people" who must be protected from their "dictator."

Since the International Criminal Court began its operations in The Hague in 2002, a lot has happened in the world that might be considered "crimes against humanity." But it is noteworthy that all 27 persons charged so far by the ICC are from Africa. Some are never captured but once in custody, they can expect to be convicted.

But in a unique development, on July 16, 2019, an ICC court actually acquitted Gbagbo of all charges against him. The Italian presiding judge, Cuno Tarfusser, noted that far from attacking his people as charged, President Gbagbo's guards had been on the defensive against attacks from "urban guerillas." For once, a Western-backed regime change plot was exposed. Gbagbo's exoneration went virtually unnoticed by the Western media that had played up all the accusations against him.

To return to January 2012, the U.N. Secretary General had no doubt that the "fundamental principle of human protection is here to stay." Considering "how to prepare ourselves for the next test of our common humanity," Ban declared: "We need not look far. That test is here—in Syria."

> Since the uprising began, I have spoken out, forcefully and directly. … Stop the violence, I told President Assad. The path of repression is a dead end. Listen to your people, I said repeatedly. Listen to your people's genuine aspirations.
>
> The world has embraced the responsibility to protect, not because it is easy, but because it is right.

> We therefore have a moral responsibility to push ahead.

But Ban Ki-moon concluded that there were "complexities": "At a time when unity is required, the Security Council is deeply divided."

Indeed. Unlike Ban, Russian and Chinese diplomats had seen all they wanted of R2P and its "no fly zone" in Libya and would not approve another resolution approving similar NATO action in Syria. The Western war against Assad could not be a repeat of the war against Gaddafi, complete with Security Council authorization. That forced it to be illegal and depending primarily on proxies.

Ban Ki-moon's remarks fit the standard regime change pattern: the sole cause of the troubles is the country's leader. He must be told to stop killing his people—or to go. Then what? The people will unanimously install democracy? In reality, the Syrian government was facing a complicated armed rebellion, aided from abroad, and supported by certain powers who did not seek "Syrian democracy" but rather the splintering of the country along ethno-religious lines. In reality, millions of Syrians—almost certainly a majority—supported a government that was fighting to hold the country together.

The Will to War

In the United States, anti-Assad Syrian exiles neutralized peace groups by horror stories incriminating their "dictator" (an English word with Hitlerian connotations). In France, closer to Syria, there were more Syrians who were still in contact with their country, who went back and forth, who supported Assad for his modernization, for his secular defense of religious diversity, and above all for preserving the nation. Even severe critics of particular government policies were obliged to support Assad against the terrifying prospect of being overrun by bands of fanatic Islamists, many of whom were not Syrian.

In Geneva, the Great Powers met, pretending to seek a political solution on the assumption that they knew best. For the West, the political solution had to start with Assad "stepping down," with no clear suggestion of what that would bring about.

Moscow was also urging Assad to make democratic reforms. In June 2014, the ruling Ba'ath party allowed its first multi-candidate presidential election, with Assad winning 89% of the vote, with 73 % of the electorate voting. The election could not be held in rebel areas but was held in Syrian embassies in countries with large Syrian refugee populations—except in France and other NATO and Arab Gulf states where Syrian embassies were closed. The U.S. Secretary of State dismissed the election as "a farce" before it took place. Ban Ki-moon—who had been calling for Assad to "listen to his own people"—said it was inappropriate to hold an election during a civil war.

In the forefront of Syrian regime change was French foreign minister Laurent Fabius. His term in office as Mitterrand's prime minister had been marred by two major scandals: the sinking of the Rainbow Warrior and failure to stop doctors from giving transfusions of blood infected by HIV to patients suffering from haemophilia. But now he was back in the government of François Hollande, calling for regime change in Syria.

In May 2012, Fabius declared that France would intervene against the Syrian regime. In December, Fabius insisted that the Al Nusra Front was "doing a good job on the ground" just as the Obama administration designated it a terrorist group.

On March 13, 2013, Fabius announced that France and Britain were going to deliver arms to the rebels.

Best of all, on August 17, 2012, Fabius declared that Syrian President Bashar el Assad "did not deserve to be alive on earth."

Some Israelis went even farther, implying that neither side deserved to be alive.

"This is a playoff situation in which you need both teams to lose, but at least you don't want one to win—we'll settle for a tie," said Alon Pinkas, a former Israeli consul general in New York, to the *The New York Times* in June 2013. "Let them both bleed, hemorrhage to death: that's the strategic thinking here."[51]

And yet, in late 2013 an historic opportunity to advance the cause of world peace was first seized and then thrown away.

The story began in August 2012 when President Obama, showing that he was tough despite his reluctance to lead the U.S. into a real war in Syria, said he had made it "very clear to the Assad regime that a red line for us is we start seeing a whole bunch of chemical weapons moving around or being utilized. That would change my calculus."

---

51 http://www.nytimes.com/2013/09/06/world/middleeast/israel-backs-limited-strike-against-syria.html?

One must imagine how that sounded to General Salim Idris, commander of the Western-backed rebels' Supreme Military Council. Idris like everyone knew that a semi-fictional massacre at Racak had been the pretext to bring NATO in on the side of Kosovo rebels fighting the Serbian government. Everyone knew that a totally fake genocide in Benghazi had succeed in giving NATO a welcome excuse to wipe out the Gaddafi regime, leaving the field to rival militias. General Idris was urging Washington to come to his aid by bombing the bejesus out of Syria. And Obama had announced the way to do it.

Just one year later, on August 21, 2013, deadly chemical weapons attacks took place on the Damascus suburbs of Ghouta. U.S. intelligence hastened to issue an "assessment" attributing the attacks to Bashar al Assad in person. The War Party in the White House fairly whooped for joy: Obama's "red line" had been crossed so now the Pentagon could go to it. Plans began for massive retaliation.

Seymour Hersh reported later what he was told by a former intelligence officer: "Under White House pressure, the US attack plan evolved into 'a monster strike'... The new target list was meant to 'completely eradicate any military capabilities Assad had', the former intelligence official said. The core targets included electric power grids, oil and gas depots, all known logistic and weapons depots, all known command and control facilities, and all known military and intelligence buildings." Britain and France were both to play a part.[52]

Such an attack was clearly intended to destroy not just a "regime," but a governable country, on the model of Libya.

Obama was in a difficult situation, under pressure to launch another "Operation Desert Storm" on what could be exposed as a false pretext. He had come to recognize that the attacks on Iraq and Libya did not turn out well.[53]

Obama had to know that the U.S. intelligence "assessment" that "Assad did it" was just as shaky as the infamous Iraqi WMD. Foreign intelligence services were warning that the evidence did not point to the Assad regime for the deadly sarin attack. In fact, everything pointed to a false flag attack by rebels. Even some Western newspapers said so. The British House of Commons actually voted against British participation in the planned punitive strikes.

---

52 Seymour M. Hersh, "The Red Line and the Rat Line", The London Review of Books, 17 April 2014. https://www.lrb.co.uk/v36/n08/seymour-m-hersh/the-red-line-and-the-rat-line

53 Jeffrey Goldberg, "The Obama Doctrine," *The Atlantic*, April 2016. http://www.theatlantic.com/magazine/archive/2016/04/the-obama-doctrine/471525/.

Then on August 30, Obama backed off and promised to study limited options to control chemical weapons.

The domestic War Party, his Middle Eastern allies and proxy rebels were all still calling for blood. Obama's own White House advisors, notably Susan Rice and Samantha Power, with an outside push from ex-Secretary of State Hillary Clinton, were all vehemently in favor of punishing Assad to save America's sacrosanct "credibility."

Secretary of State John Kerry was still favoring military strikes to demonstrate "our credibility"—meaning the credibility of threats. He put it like this: other countries "are watching to see if Syria can get away with it, because then maybe they too can put the world at greater risk."

At a September 9 press conference in London, when a reporter asked if there was anything Assad could do to prevent the bombing, Kerry replied: "Sure. He could turn over every single bit of his chemical weapons to the international community in the next week … But he isn't about to do it, and it can't be done, obviously."

At this crucial point Russian diplomacy came to the rescue.

The Russian response was "Oh yes we can." With amazing speed, foreign minister Sergei Lavrov brokered a deal by which Assad agreed to immediate internationally supervised destruction of his entire chemical weapons arsenal, which was actually carried out as promised.

This was an extraordinary signal that diplomacy could work, that together, Washington and Moscow could solve critical problems. Even promote world peace.

This was a lesson that the U.S. War Party absolutely refused to learn.

The story is worth repeating again and again, because it was so quickly covered over and forgotten, as if there were something shameful about it. The entire politico-media establishment continued to claim that Assad was responsible for the Ghouta attacks and that Obama had shown "weakness" by backing down. The success of the Syrian chemical weapons deal was rapidly forgotten. Though it no doubt contributed to the Nobel Peace Prize award to the Organization of the Prohibition of Chemical Weapons in December 2013 "for its extensive efforts to eliminate chemical weapons." That was very nice, but this mention of a technical organization was in reality a more or less subtle way of failing to recognize the political achievement of Obama and Putin.

Establishment politicians and media erased any recognition or memory of this missed opportunity. What should have been a lesson in how to use diplomacy in the cause of peace was turned into a lesson that has become steadily clearer: the Deep State does not welcome presidential interference in the projects of the War Party.

Meanwhile, U.S. diplomacy was busily creating a crisis in Ukraine that would lastingly poison U.S.-Russian relations. Hillary Clinton's former spokeswoman, Victoria Nuland, was handing out goodies to protesters in Kiev as moves were being made to enable the pro-Western, often extreme right opposition to stage a coup and overthrow a government that had tried to preserve good relations with both Russia and the European Union. The U.S. campaign to use Ukraine against Russia was already well underway.

Despite long and patient efforts, Russian diplomats had to conclude that genuine cooperation with the West to resolve the Syrian crisis was quite impossible. In September 2015, Russia accepted an official invitation from the legitimate government of Syria to come to its defense.

Between Scylla and Charybdis

Obama's designated successor appeared ready to correct Obama's 2013 mistake. Hillary Clinton as Secretary of State had wholly adopted the line of the War Party and as candidate was calling for exactly the sort of direct intervention in Syria that Obama had shied away from. Her extremely hostile attitude toward Putin, in addition to her expressed desire to install a "no-fly zone" in Syria, indicated an alarming willingness to risk war with the other major nuclear power in defense of an extremely dubious cause: the overthrow of a legitimate government with no alternative in sight.

Meanwhile, U.S.-Russian relations had sunk to Cold War levels over Ukraine. Most people in the West were totally unaware that the Crimean Peninsula was historically part of Russia, that it had been cavalierly "given" to Ukraine in 1954 by Khrushchev without consulting the people, and that since Ukraine gained independence through the breakup of the Soviet Union, most Crimeans would have preferred to belong to Russia. The Western public was also unconcerned over the danger to Russia of seeing its major naval base in Sebastopol (Crimea) fall under U.S. control should the new pro-Western leaders in Kiev succeed in joining NATO. The danger was removed by a referendum in which the overwhelming majority of Crimeans voted to return to Russia. The West called this return to Russia an invasion and a sign that Russia was threatening to invade its neighbors.

The same NATO governments that bombed Serbia in order to hand Kosovo over to a band of criminals went into throes of artificial indignation over this peaceful and incomparably more justifiable change of borders. The pretext of the Russian threat served to justify a NATO arms buildup worthy of such an opponent.

At about this time I decided to write a book about the foreign policy of Hillary Clinton, on the way to becoming President of the United States. She had demonstrated a murderous frivolity by her laughter at the news that the Libyan leader had been brutally murdered. She was blinded by a personal ambition which could lead to the worst catastrophes.This book, *Queen of Chaos,* was not meant as an election pamphlet inasmuch as I thought she was bound to win, considering that she enjoyed the full support of the establishment—Wall Street, Hollywood, the Military Industrial Complex, mainstream media. How could she possibly lose? I meant my book as a warning of what was to come with such a woman in charge, hoping vainly to awaken opposition to her dangerous inclinations.

The U.S. publisher imposed a silly subtitle, *the Misadventures of Hillary Clinton,* which I found embarrassingly cute. The French, German, Portuguese, Italian and Swedish publishers all found a subtitle that was more to the point.

To everyone's surprise, not least her own, Hillary lost the election. But not entirely. She lost, but neither she nor the establishment that supported her could acknowledge defeat to Donald Trump. The establishment did not have the power to reverse the election, but it did have enough influence to draw the nation into a prolonged period of hysterical denial of reality. The Clinton campaign's shabby attempt to link Trump to her pet enemy, Vladimir Putin, was transformed into an explanation for her otherwise clearly impossible defeat. There was no need for evidence; for the Clinton fanatics it was self-evident—only some malevolent outside power could account for the triumph of the most repugnant monster who ever emerged from our television screens.

Instead of celebrating "our first woman President," liberal America went into a frenzy of despising our first racist, sexist, homophobic, xenophobic, foreign-elected President, whose each and every word or gesture was worse than the one before. Rather than figure how to make the best of a bad deal, liberals simply wallowed in the horror show. However awful he was, might Trump at least be pushed to carry out his vaguely articulated desire to make peace here and there—not everywhere, but notably with Russia? Certainly not! If Trump was for it, all decent people must be against it. Anyone wanting peace with Russia was a Putin puppet.

This was a moment when expatriates were especially glad not to be in the United States.

Not that things were so wonderful over here.

The French Presidential election of 2017 was similar to that of the United States in two respects. In both cases, the electorate expressed dissatisfaction with establishment politicians. And in both cases, as voters were faced with two candidates they didn't like, the lesser evil was the sure winner.

Otherwise, the two elections were dead opposites. Trump was a bizarre outsider, elected largely as a fluke, against all the professionals. In contrast, Emmanuel Macron was the total insider, put in place by an extremely professional operation. Presented as a daring outsider, coming from nowhere with his exceptional "can do" vigor, Macron was a product of the deep establishment, the economic powers behind every throne.

The lineup of Macron supporters is truly impressive.

It starts with the amazing Jacques Attali, who has spent his life bringing the French political class into harmony with globalization. His private think tank, the Commission for Stimulating Economic Growth, was charged by President Sarkozy with drafting "300 Proposals to Change France"—a program for removing obstacles to the activities of financial capital. Co-opted into this elite group, the young Macron showed his stuff: eagerness to please the class to which he aspired but had not yet joined.

Attali took care of that, recommending him to the Rothschild Bank where Macron was able to earn his first millions and cement his loyalty to the banking class.

Newly elected, President Hollande took Macron onto his staff, where he studied the political scene closely, finding the Socialist President too wishy-washy in his pro-capitalist reforms. Then, as minister of Economy, Industry and Digital affairs, Macron approved the sale of France's critical energy corporation, Alstom, to General Electric. This sale effectively transferred control of France's nuclear power grid to an American company. It signaled total readiness to abandon any thought of national interest, or indeed of national security, in favor of "the markets." The decision was all the more scandalous in that it came in the wake of a brutal campaign by the U.S. government to use its extraterritorial clout, based on the use of the dollar as world currency, to ruin Alstom and force it to sell.[54]

Macron then went on revise French labor law to conform to the wishes of management but was slowed down by opposition from the Socialist Party's electoral base. Macron had shown his colors, and so when he resigned from the Hollande government in March 2016 to go his own way, billionaires were lined up to pay the fare.

The strategy was clear. In a two-round presidential election, the first step is to get into the second round. This meant getting rid of the front runner. That was former Prime Minister, François Fillon. He had won the Republican Party primary by a large margin and appeared certain to be the next President.

But at a crucial moment, the media suddenly dug up a scandal. Years before, Fillon had paid for more or less fictional work by his wife and children out of his parliamentary budget. This sort of thing is done by countless politicians and has no effect on the welfare of the nation. But blown into a major scandal, it threatened to send family man Fillon to jail, along with his wife.

What is truly disturbing in this story is the timely cooperation between two powers: the media and the judiciary. With unusual haste, judges rushed to press charges just at the moment when it was certain to sabotage the candidate's campaign.

Without that scandal, Fillon was on his way to being elected. A question arises: why did the super-rich go to the trouble of creating Macron when the leading candidate for the 2017 Presidential election was a fiscal conservative, ready to pursue an austerity policy? There are three reasons the globalist king-makers thought they could do better.

First, they were impatient with the leading parties for not enacting unpopular austerity measures fast enough, perhaps because the established parties were still in contact with ordinary people and sensitive to their objections. But with Macron, there was no troublesome political party, with its own demands, in the way. Macron created his own party, *"La République en Marche,"* whose only program was to follow the leader.

Second, Fillon's foreign policy was suspect. He retained traces of Gaullism, of concern for French independence. He strongly opposed French involvement in Syria, which threatened the very survival of the

54 See *Le piège américain* (*The American Trap*), by Frédéric Pierucci and Matthieu Aron, 2019.

Christian population, something that mattered to him. And he clearly objected to the imported American Russophobia, which was contrary to French interests and traditions, and was eager to restore normal relations with Moscow.

Finally, as a conservative Catholic, Fillon's personal outlook did not harmonize with the "anything goes" mores of the neoliberals. He could not be counted on to promote the societal reforms and fragmentation of public opinion promoted by Identity Politics.

With Fillon neutralized by scandal, Macron was on his way, with help from his friends. And what friends! Let's start with Bernard Arnault, the richest man in France and one of the richest in the world, who owns a huge swath of big name luxury items, as well as the daily tabloid, *Le Parisien,* and the economic daily, *Les Échos.*

Just about every major CEO in France supported Macron: Vincent Bolloré, tenth richest man in France, owner of the media conglomerate Vivendi; Thomas Enders, CEO of Airbus; and Pierre Gattaz, president of MEDEF, the employers' association. Then individuals such as the highly influential German-American art collector, Olivier Berggruen, who eagerly contributed to the Macron campaign.

And bankers galore. His old patron Rothschild of course, but even more zealously the former director general of asset management for France's largest bank, BNP-Paribas, Christian Dargnat, who took leave in April 2016 to organize Macron's campaign finances. This was done mainly by organizing very private cocktail parties where the rich were invited to come and make their contribution.

The crucial factor in creating Macron was, of course, the media. Mainstream media went all-out presenting Macron as the young hope of France, with the energy to get the stagnating country going again. He became a familiar face on magazine covers, often with his wife, Brigitte. The attractive then 64-year-old wife of a 39-year-old man was seen as a sure vote-getter among middle-aged women.

Macron's press lord friends included media magnate Arnaud Lagardère, whose group includes the popular weekly *Paris Match* (specializing in Emmanuel and Brigitte cover photos), the owners of *Le Monde,* and last but not least Patrick Drahi, the Casablanca-born Swiss-residing entrepreneur with triple citizenship (Israeli, French and Portuguese) who owns the daily *Libération,* the weekly *L'Express,* Radio Monte Carlo and BFMTV, the most watched continuous news channel in France.

Macron's support didn't stop there. Geographically, the greatest source of Macron donations after Paris was London. There was more financial support for the candidate in the United Kingdom than in the ten largest provincial cities in France. Macron could not raise as much money in Marseille, France's second largest city, as in Switzerland. Even Lebanese donors gave more than was raised in Bordeaux and Lille together.

So there could be no doubt about it. Emmanuel Macron was the choice of the billionaires, the banks, the globalizers and the "world cities" and certainly not "the people."

After sidelining Fillon, Macron beat leftist Jean-Luc Mélenchon to the second round where he faced National Front candidate Marine Le Pen. Although she had gained considerable working-class support thanks to a more "social" approach than her father Jean-Marie, the stigma of the Le Pen name was still enough to assure her opponent a landslide victory.

Voters were fed up with both main parties for doing more or less the same thing once in office. The huge paradox is that Macron disempowered and marginalized both of them by creating an unabashed neoliberal center, doing what they did only more so, while pretending to represent something new and different. With his hand-picked party controlling Parliament, and his opposition in disarray, Macron felt safe to be far more authoritarian and arrogant than his predecessors.

The losing candidates—Le Pen, Fillon, Jean-Luc Mélenchon—had all wanted to end the artificial U.S.-inspired hostility to Russia. Instead, Macron spoiled a promising visit by Vladimir Putin by using their joint press conference to launch an unjustified and inappropriate attack on the Russian-financed French news channel, RT France. Already during his campaign, Macron had banned accredited RT correspondents from attending his meetings and press conferences, a practice which has continued.

Even though he was a winner, Macron adopted the great political alibi initiated by the Clintonites after Hillary's dismal failure: attribute all unwelcome opinions to "Russian influence" and accuse the Russians of originating "fake news"—a transparent device meant to make mainstream media look good in comparison, despite public disaffection.

The Macron regime combines economic austerity policies targeting wages, pensions and public services with "societal" reforms meant to please the young urban population: broadened rights to medically assisted procreation, quotas for women, special attention to "visible minorities" (persons of color) and, of course, expressions of concern for the environment (with little in the way of concrete measures).

Concern for minorities mainly took the form of censorship, with tougher laws to criminalize "hate" speech—whatever that may be deemed to be.

All of this demonstrates that the so-called "center" can be just as authoritarian as the right or the left.

It may be pure accident, but Macron's leading political rivals have been subjected to disturbingly hostile judicial measures, relayed by the media to put them in a bad light. Marine Le Pen was accused of defrauding the European Parliament by having her staff members work for her party (now called the *Rassemblement National,* RN). Such practices are surely quite common in the European Parliament, but never before denounced. Based on this dubious offense, a legal trick was used to bankrupt Le Pen's political party. Courts applied a totally inappropriate law designed to freeze assets of major criminals such as drug traffickers while judgment is pending. This law was applied to Le Pen. The government dotation legally due her party based on its electoral score was confiscated. Half her parliamentary salary was also confiscated.

And that was not all. Marine Le Pen was angry when a TV interview likened her party to Daesh. To show the difference, she tweeted a message: "This is Daesh," illustrated by a photo of a beheading. For this, she was charged with offering an "apology for terrorism." A court even ordered her to undergo a psychiatric assessment to determine whether she was capable of understanding questions. The French Parliament revoked her parliamentary immunity. If found guilty, a political leader who won a third of the votes in the 2017 presidential election could face up to three years in prison and a fine of 75,000 euros—for a tweet.

Similar treatment was meted out to Macron's main opponent on the left. Jean-Luc Mélenchon had also been a Member of the European Parliament, and once again charges were trotted out that he had misused the vast funds available to MEPS. For obscure reasons, at 7 a.m. on October 16, 2018, police broke into Mélenchon's home and offices and took away all sorts of documents, professional and personal, including vacation photos. His communication director, Sophia Chikirou, was present in Mélenchon's home, a fact trumpeted by media as if there were something shocking about two unmarried persons being together. It is alleged that she was overpaid for her campaign work. The hot-tempered Mélenchon reacted angrily to the intrusions, and these reactions have been used to discredit him in the media. In fact, Mélenchon seemed to be seriously shaken by the incidents and has lost most of his political cutting edge since.

If this is the way his leading political opponents are treated, it should be no surprise to learn that when ordinary people go into the streets to protest against Macron, they are not treated with the most kindly consideration, as we shall see.

PART X

It Can't Go On Like This

33.

Phased Out

The future has been decided. By whom, or by what? By the financial markets, by technological advance, by international institutions—all unstoppable forces in their advance and inscrutable to those who feel it all sweeping past them. It is certainly not being decided by ordinary people, least of all those who are simply being phased out.

Emmanuel Macron is an eager instrument of the inevitable, of that future which is bound to happen because all those irresistible forces are pushing in that direction. In a word, it can be called "globalization"—*mondialisation* in French—turning the whole world into one place. Macron presents himself as speeding up the process. The name of the party he created, *La Republique en Marche,* expresses the idea, "let's get going!" We must hurry up and streamline the Republic on its way toward this future from which there can be no escape.

In this, Macron merely accelerated the changes initiated by his recent predecessors, but more blatantly. Like others in the Western world, a generation of French leaders let themselves be persuaded that they could sacrifice their industry, silence the demands of troublesome workers, and prosper on the basis of the West's intellectual advantage, specializing in financial transactions, innovation, communications, culture and various services. Such an advantage can only be temporary—unless one assumes that China, India and other nations earmarked for physical labor would be incapable of equaling and surpassing the West in intellectual achievements. By succumbing to this illusion, French leaders have allowed the nation's productive base to be reduced and endangered—with the notable exception of luxury goods, a precarious advantage.

The benefits of comparative advantage to investors and distributors are countered by the harm it does to millions of people dependent on activities which do not offer such an "advantage" but which kept whole regions alive and prosperous. The logic of "comparative advantage" makes each nation economically fragile, vulnerable to transport blockages, price fixing and even blackmail (think of the vulnerability to sanctions of oil-producing Venezuela).

Macron made his indifference to the people left behind in his race forward all too clear. His message to youth was essentially, "go create your own startup." You can't eat a startup, and startups are essentially dependent on some other self-supporting activity or on support from wealthy investors. Macron has all the arrogance of the self-made man: I did it, anyone who tries can succeed. But he had a lot of help along the way, help unavailable to the millions of his compatriots living in towns that thrived on industries whose activities have been outsourced, whose daily life is shaped by technological or bureaucratic requirements over which they have no control, whose farms operate at a loss, whose taxes rise as their incomes stagnate or recede, and whose daily environments become uglier and more polluted.

Then, in October 2018, the Government announced that it would raise the already heavy fuel tax by an additional 6.6 cents per liter for diesel and an additional 2.9 cents per liter for gasoline. For people of modest means dependent on getting around in their cars, this was the last straw. Moreover, the first protesters were informed that they should feel guilty for endangering the climate by driving their cars.

In May 2018, a 32-year-old cosmetician of French West Indian descent, Priscillia Ludosky, had already posted an on-line petition to Macron calling for lower taxes on essential goods and the establishment of a citizens' initiative referendum. When the gas tax was announced, the petition caught the attention of 34-year-old truck driver Eric Drouet, who lived in nearby Melun, 30 miles south of Paris, and on FaceBook the two of them called for holding a nationwide protest against fuel taxes on November 17.

Thanks to the internet, word got around. A week before the scheduled protest, 36-year-old repairman Ghislain Coutard in Narbonne had a bright idea which he posted in a video on FaceBook. "Each of us has a yellow vest," he said, holding one up as he sat in his car. "Put it where it's visible under the windshield. All week long until Saturday, to show you're with the movement."

Since 2008, every car must be equipped with a fluorescent yellow vest—*gilet jaune*—in case of emergency. If a driver has to get out on the highway because of an accident or breakdown, the yellow vest ensures visibility to avoid being run over. A fitting symbol.

Coutard's idea not only caught on, it was improved. On Saturday, November 17, all over France, hundreds of thousands of people came out actually wearing their *gilet jaune*. That was how it started.

All along, this has been a movement invented by ordinary working people themselves, without leaders and without trade unions or ideology. Immediately all those who think in terms of labels raised their key question: Are they on the left? Are they on the right? The leftist thought-police were suspicious: this must be "populism," meaning "extreme right." Groups of Antifa went to hunt down "fascists." But there were no fascists, indeed there were no labels that fit. These were just people, who were fed up with all political parties and did not want to be recuperated by any of them, even the marginal left or right parties not responsible for the policies they were protesting. Because whatever a party says, once it is elected… The *Gilets Jaunes* didn't ask each other whether they were on the left or on the right but simply talked about concrete issues. This independence helps account for the instant overwhelming public support for the movement: polls showed over 70% approval ratings.

Globalization is a network of World Cities, major centers actively participating in the world economy. Their residents can feel that they are citizens of the world, through trade, finance, communications, culture, and diversified immigration. In France that means Paris, with a nod to Marseilles, Lyons, Bordeaux. In between lies what has come to be called "the periphery,"[55] where the majority of French people have seen their incomes, social status and standard of living steadily deteriorate.

As rural France became increasingly a place to go through on your way to somewhere else (more and more trucks carrying goods from the Netherlands to Spain, for instance), the country has been endowed with up to 50,000 traffic circles, at a cost of about a million euros each. The *Gilets Jaunes* chose the grassy centers of these circles as places to meet, seek support from passing motorists, discuss their problems, and renew direct human contact impoverished by the closing of small-town cafés, churches, and schools. They blocked traffic, just enough to make their point. At the same time, thousands came to Paris to press their demands, made conspicuous by walking down the Champs Elysées in their yellow vests.

Sociologically, this revolt was the opposite of May '68. Instead of privileged students, imagining a non-existent working-class revolution

55 The geographer Christophe Guilluy, in his 2014 book *La France Périphérique,* called attention to the growing discrepancy between the rich cities and the forgotten small towns and rural areas where most people live, and where conditions have been steadily worsening. This could be likened to "flyover States" in the U.S.

in a time of prosperity, this was the working class itself, in hard times, not necessarily revolutionary, but with the French revolutionary history in mind, just in case.

They were men and women of working age or retired, of almost every possible trade or profession. In times of deindustrialization, many worked alone in transport, delivery, odd jobs. Overworked nurses were a significant element, illustrating the misery of public services. This was the emergence of the new post-industrial working class, underpaid, subcontracted, part-time, or precariously self-employed, without the solidarity of organized factory workers. This totally fragmented working class was nevertheless able to unite into a single movement all across the country.

Although it was soon lost in a flood of more general grievances and demands, the gas tax issue clearly illustrated the gap between big cities and the rest of the country. People living in Paris don't need cars. There is plenty of public transport. The greenish government of Paris has designated the automobile the enemy of the environment. Mayor Anne Hidalgo has done much more to rid Paris of cars than of rats, which are flourishing. Her anti-car policy seems popular with young "Bobos" (Bohemian bourgeois) fit enough to get around on bicycles or *trottinettes* (electric scooters). They can feel they are "doing something for the planet" by getting a bit of healthy exercise.

In "the periphery," it is another matter. People are being phased out by an economy that no longer needs production. Factories close, farmers hang themselves. Obliged by European Union directives, railroad service is being privatized and opened to international competition. With profit as the motive, rail transport ceases to be considered a public service, and small towns are abandoned. The high-speed trains between major cities are more profitable. To save money, small-town hospitals, schools, post-offices are also being closed and regrouped. Big chain commercial centers lodged near the new traffic circles have emptied villages of the shops that were a feature of sociability and a source of charm. All these changes oblige people to take to their cars.

Macron's latest "ecotax" looked all too much like an ecohoax. The proceeds were earmarked not to develop alternative energies but simply to reduce the government deficit, to show the Germans that France was "fiscally responsible" (they were not impressed). The tax was particularly steep on diesel fuel. This was infuriating to all those people who owned diesel vehicles because a few years ago, they were encouraged to prefer diesel as "better for the environment." Now they are told it's worse. And all these fuel taxes are clearly intended to compel car-owners to buy electric cars—which almost nobody can afford and which aren't even on the market yet.

To add to the exasperation, people who have to drive their cars are accused by politically correct television personalities of endangering the planet.

The gasoline tax soon became secondary as, from Saturday to Saturday, the weekly Yellow Vest demonstrations broadened their demands, expressing opposition to just about every current government policy. Rather than attempt to get everyone to agree to all that, the movement focused especially on the demand for legalization of a *Referendum d'initiative citoyenne* (RIC)—Citizens' Initiative Referendum—which would enable issues to be dealt with one by one as the people choose, with binding results. The referendum is an issue with deep resonance in France, due to bitterness over the politicians' total disdain for the results of the 2005 government-initiated referendum on the European Constitution. Etienne Chouard, a modest provincial professor who since 2005 has been trying to design constitutional reforms which would restore genuine democracy, has become the most influential thinker in a movement which does not seek advice from Paris intellectuals.

Insult and Injury

After scornfully ignoring the movement for three Saturdays, on December 10 Macron momentarily assumed a humble air to offer a few minor concessions—instantly and unanimously rejected as insufficient. That was that, and the Macron regime got back to violent repression while the calls, "Macron, resign!" grew stronger and more insistent.

French police forces are armed with the most formidable "crowd control" arsenal in Europe. Water cannon, tear gas grenade launchers, a range of heavy-duty truncheons and worst of all, the "less lethal" police "crowd control defensive" flash-ball launcher, the sinister LBD40, were all trotted out from the start. The LBD40 is extolled for its accuracy, which makes it all the more remarkable that so many of its rubber bullets have struck people in the face, causing serious injuries. Countless videos show police aiming their weapons straight at people's heads.

The Interior Ministry provides no figures, apologies or compensation concerning victims of police violence. After the first four Saturday demonstrations, activists compiled a list of over thirty serious injuries and mutilations, as well as the death in Marseilles of an 81-year-old Algerian woman who was killed by a teargas grenade as she moved to close her shutters. In the course of those first four protests, nine people had an eye shot out by rubber pellets from the LBD40, four people suffered loss of a hand, others had serious head or bodily injuries. Subsequent victims of grave injuries included a fireman, an off-duty soldier and even a 14-year-old Syrian refugee, who simply happened to be close to the action. Police have trapped crowds in a square or a stretch of avenue by blocking all exits and then drenching those who can't escape with tear gas. The fear of serious injury, especially the loss of an eye, has indeed discouraged many people from taking part, especially mothers of small children.

Such a level of police violence is unprecedented since the troubles caused by the war in Algeria. In May '68, police had orders not to cause serious injuries to students, and even during more recent episodes of violence in ethnically mixed suburbs, police were somewhat inhibited by fear that a racist incident could cause more violent flareups. No such restraint applied to the Yellow Vests.

Curiously, all this heavy-handed repression totally failed to prevent masked "Black Bloc" members from taking advantage of the opportunity to attack the police, set fires, break shop windows and occasionally do a bit of pillaging here and there. Police did nothing to prevent unidentified intruders from invading the ground floor of the Arc de Triomphe to smash up a statue of Marianne and otherwise leave their marks of vandalism.

It is noteworthy that almost all the seriously injured were peaceful Yellow Vest protesters, whereas the Black Blocs often got away unscathed.

Perhaps the Black Blocs believe they are fighting the system. Whatever their intentions, they have served as a useful auxiliary to government repression. Their depredations have been a key factor justifying police violence and enabling the media to turn part of the misinformed public against the Yellow Vests as a source of "aimless disorder." Fear of getting mixed up with the Black Blocs also scares people off.

Sometimes, the Yellow Vests fight back. The most famous is Christophe Dettinger, a French Rom, former light heavyweight boxing champion of France. He was there on January 5 when a squad of riot police violently attacked the *Gilets Jaunes* on a bridge over the Seine. Seeing a woman roughed up, the chivalrous Dettinger (a 37-years-old family man, father of three) surged from the crowd and beat back the heavily masked and shielded police with his bare fists. This made him a sort of folk hero and cost him a year in prison.

While the police used physical violence to crush the movement, Macron, his acolytes and mainstream media fired their verbal weapons. Based on the assumption that ordinary people are probably guilty of bad "populist" attitudes, their every word or gesture was scrutinized for confirmation.

Not that evidence was necessary.

In his 2019 New Year's message to the nation, President Macron feigned shock, declaring: "These days I have seen unthinkable things and heard the unacceptable." He was appalled to hear the Yellow Vests spread "hate speech" attacking "police forces, journalists, Jews, foreigners, homosexuals." This was a "negation of France."

Those who had actually been listening to the Yellow Vests had heard absolutely nothing negative about Jews, foreigners or homosexuals. True, some journalists were told off for their distorted reporting. About the police, well yes, under the circumstances, with people having their eyes shot out, bad feelings were inevitable. And yet, many protesters have approached the police as fellow victims of the system whom they seek to win over to supporting the movement—a far more revolutionary approach than shouting "everybody hates the police," since to succeed, every revolt must win over a part of the security forces. And in fact, while sadists in uniform may be enjoying themselves, there is great unhappiness in the ranks, with a policeman committing suicide every five days.

Mainstream media were on the lookout for the clue needed to brand the movement as "anti-Semitic"—the most damaging accusation of them all. In the Paris Metro late one Saturday evening, a reporter spotted three *Gilets Jaunes*, apparently heading home, in a jolly mood after a drink or two, singing and making the notorious Dieudonné gesture, the *quenelle*. According to the reporter, an aged Jewish woman tried to get them to stop by referring to Auschwitz but was ignored. Considering all that can happen in a Metro train late Saturday night, this was not a major drama, but it made headlines all over major newspapers. Aha, the *Gilets Jaunes* are anti-Semitic!

In another incident, the famous polemic writer, Alain Finkielkraut, member of the French Academy and known for his passionate devotion to Israel, emerged from a taxi on the edge of a GJ demo and was promptly recognized and verbally attacked for being a Zionist—which he unquestionably is. The person doing the insulting was clearly of Algerian origin. There was no physical violence. This incident was blown into a major scandal by media commentators who clearly found rude words hurled at a prominent Jewish intellectual more outrageous than young philosophy student Fiorina's loss of her left eye, about which they remained extremely discreet.

By the end of January, Macron had adopted the Clintonian alibi: the Russians did it. "It's Russia Today, Sputnik… on Internet, BFMTV is no longer the leader, it's Russia Today."

Indeed, more and more people watch the Russian-financed news broadcasts quite simply because they are more balanced than others. Frédéric Taddei, whose leading broadcast of free debate was gradually pushed off French government-financed TV screens, went over to RT France for a daily show in prime time, giving both sides of every possible issue.

RT reporters are among the very few who have gone out into Yellow Vest demonstrations with a microphone, cameramen and bodyguards (to protect from Antifa). The interviews make it clear that ordinary French people in Yellow Vests are capable of far more intelligent political analysis than most of the mainstream professionals. The French have a reputation of being "a political people," and the *Gilets Jaunes* confirm that traditions are not all dead.

Over the months, the Saturday demos thinned out. They may resurge, but other actions are undertaken. Conventions are being held in small towns to work out demands and methods. As an example, in July 2019, Yellow Vests carefully organized seizure of the largest autoroute toll station in the country, north of Paris. First, a small group of masked activists covered the cameras and removed the gates, without breaking anything. Then a crowd of Yellow Vests arrived to gesture motorists to go through without paying. This was a non-violent act with a clear political message: end privatization of public services. There is widespread resentment that the autoroutes, payed for by taxpayers, have been sold to private companies, which keep raising the tolls, when the profits could have gone to the public treasury.

Fundamentally, this is a movement aimed at restoring sovereignty to the people, a sovereignty that has been taken away and given to international institutions, banks, Trade Agreements and the European Union. How to wrest popular sovereignty back from such powerful institutions is a total quandary. The institution of the Citizens' Initiative Referendum is the most radical method proposed so far, a gentle attempt to revive democracy in a profoundly hostile institutional environment. Much more is needed.

However it turns out, the Yellow Vest challenge will have lasting effects. It has served as a political awakening.

Just a personal note of evaluation.

The *Gilets Jaunes* movement is profoundly French. It is deeply rooted in French history, legends, ethics, and practice. I cannot see anything quite the same happening in another country, and certainly not in the United States, which is too big, too diverse, too ideologically attached to individualism, too militarized, and whose difficulties may be related but are not at all the same. Still, assuming the *Gilets Jaunes* can't happen elsewhere, if they could manage to succeed in creating something positive at home, that might serve as an inspiration to different peoples to seek solutions more appropriate to themselves.

China is eliminating poverty and flourishing economically with what it calls "socialism with Chinese characteristics"—a system which its leaders are not seeking to spread to other countries. If France were not a prisoner of European Union Directives and obedience to America (celebrated every June at Normandy landing sites), people might develop a "social democracy with French characteristics": a mixed economy combining socialization of banks, key industries and public services with a large private sector. That was essentially the highly successful policy under De Gaulle.

Finally, the *Gilets Jaunes* are an argument for diversity between countries, for letting peoples follow their own historical inclinations rather than being forced into the uniform model of American-style capitalism, which preaches diversity within countries but not between them. The French will never make "good Americans." They should be allowed to be good French.

34.

Hubris and Humanity

The countries of the Western world are in a state of schizophrenic overconfidence and self-doubt. Their leaders persist in proclaiming "our values" as the model for the rest of humanity, while their own people are increasingly divided and disillusioned.

The eighteenth century was the century of the liberated mind. The nineteenth century was the century of Great Men. The twentieth century was the century of the common man. And the twenty-first century looks like it may become a negation of all of them. The century of nobody at all.

Irrationality and censorship restore chains to thought. Great Men are only statues to be demolished. The common man, once hailed as the hero of a radiant future, has been degraded to a superfluous nuisance, probably racist and homophobic. Ordinary folks have been reassigned from the glorious concept of "the people" to their derogatory redefinition under the rubric of "populism."

People are reduced to "consumers," while being told that by consuming, they are destroying the planet. Identity Politics has not only turned people against each other by group, but its late manifestation, Vegan speciesism, even turns people against people altogether, for being an overprivileged life form.

The West Against the World

The dominant Western ideology glorifies competition and personal success. Self-styled moral censors denounce "hate," while openly hating those they denounce. A mood of mutual hostility has swept over the United States. The mood is not (yet) so antagonistic in Europe, but competition is the official purpose of the European Union. Social purpose tied to the public interest is subtly outlawed as contrary to "fair competition" as sought by corporations. As for the losers, they lose. End of story.

The international scene is even much worse. American leaders are unable to view the world other than as a field for exercising U.S. "leadership," and all who balk are considered deadly enemies. America chronically needs enemies. The United States creates the needed stock of enemies by its project to dominate the whole world. Neither Russia nor China would be "enemies" if the United States did not force them to defend themselves. Washington's official creation of foreign enemies does not even serve the classical purpose of uniting the nation. All that is too far away, and the American people are fed up with military warfare, seemingly more absorbed in domestic political warfare against each other.

In military terms, the United States has shown itself adept in reducing "enemies" to ashes, but despite possessing an arsenal that defies the imagination, is quite inefficient in actually winning wars. After eighteen years of sending soldiers to kill and be killed in Afghanistan, the United States found itself obliged to try to make peace with the very same party it set out to overthrow, the Taliban. And yet Washington has continued to enlist the governments of Western Europe in its project of world domination, under various pretexts, and on the assumption that "globalization" is inevitable, while a "multipolar world" sounds sinister. American leaders sometimes put it this way: "If we don't rule the world, who will? Do you want it to be the Chinese?" Or, even less convincingly, "America is a light to the world, the last best hope of mankind." In reality, several decades of lost American wars, and the horrible devastation they have wrought, have transformed America into a dark shadow on the world and its greatest threat. To the question, "Why do they hate us?" there are as many answers as bombs dropped.

Throughout all this, the United States has maintained its hold on Europe through NATO on the ground and the Hollywood view of history in people's heads. The British ruling class has readily followed the U.S. lead under the impression that America is essentially an extension of the British Empire. Recent French leaders have considered that being in the good graces of Washington is necessary to maintain the status of France, such as it is. But even the French elite is sharply divided on this—more so every day—and the subservience to Washington is not widely popular, despite French addiction to American popular culture. As for Germany, Italy and Belgium, they have been U.S.-occupied countries since the end of World War II, and the nuclear weapons on their soil belong to the Pentagon, not to themselves. U.S. "occupation" takes many forms, not least thanks to the inability of the European Union to define an independent policy. But even there, discontent is rising. Forced hostility to Russia is contrary to European economic interests as well as to the facts of recent history, known to many.

U.S.-sponsored "globalization" is the last avatar of Western imperialist world domination. The great suspense and uncertainty concern how much damage its inevitable failure will do to the world.

The West Against Itself

A few decades ago, "the Left" was considered the center of opposition to imperialism, and champion of the right of peoples to self-determination. Today the most active section of the left considers that abstract principles of "human rights" should determine the fate of nations. People don't need national sovereignty as much as they need to get rid of their "dictators," and how this is done doesn't matter too much. The Left has the answer: when Third World countries are wrecked by conflicts instigated or exploited by the United States and its Saudi or Israeli allies, the short-term humanitarian impulse is to help refugees from devastated countries move to Europe or North America. The humanitarian impulse goes farther than that, losing the distinction between refugees and immigrants, welcoming them all.

For a while, increased immigration was considered by economic policymakers to be necessary to replace Europe's declining population, especially using the argument that young workers were necessary to pay the pensions of the retired. This argument has faded as unemployment persists, with no decent jobs for newcomers, while the social costs of immigration (free education, health care, etc.) increase, tending to outweigh any benefits.

Ironically, the Left has become the most zealous enforcer of the main tenet of globalization: open borders. The demand arose rather artificially in the United States due to opposition to Trump. In the European far left, the demand for fully open borders grew out of the defense of undocumented immigrants. It has tended to become more intransigent, on the tacit assumption that moving to the promised land of the West must be a happy ending for each individual, overlooking people's attachment to their native land or the problems they face as outsiders in a strange environment. A supposedly "generous" European immigration policy risks draining certain countries of the very people those countries need most for their own development. Those who stop to think of the practical consequences of truly open borders risk being labeled racist.

However, the demand for open borders will not be met so long as people can vote, because of its intense unpopularity. Why do leftist parties take such an unpopular position, when in the past, socialists were strongly opposed to unlimited immigration because it disunited the working class and brought down wages? "Open Borders" is a cause implicitly justified on the basis of a confused compensation for past sins: colonialism, racism and failure to welcome persecuted Jews in the early twentieth century. It also assumes a certain environmental determinism: people will become just like us once they are here. This attitude totally overlooks the strong psychological factor of human beings' attachment to the territories of their birth, to their own people (language, customs), which is nearly universal. Colonized peoples revolted because they wanted their space, their own development, not the imposition of ours.

"Open borders" expresses the extreme rejection of the Nation State, reduced to aggressive nationalism that leads to wars. A left fixated on 1933-1945 as universal paradigm identifies "nationalism" with Adolf Hitler, instead of with Ho Chi Minh, Amilcar Cabral, Mahatma Gandhi, Simon Bolivar, Patrick Henry, and a whole array of historic liberators. Historically, strict national boundaries were drawn (see the Treaty of Westphalia) precisely in order to end the religious wars that prevailed in their absence. Within the framework of the nation state, representative democracy was born. The state is capable of providing the social policies historically supported by the left, which would be quite impossible without it. Without the restraints of a defined state, supranational powers (at present, giant corporations and financial capitalism) would operate unimpeded in a chaotic world. It is precisely these restraints on capital and those social policies which are currently under attack in the West. All that is left unquestioned and untouched are the repressive forces, which are strengthened.

Open borders will never be a popular slogan.

Everything Is All Settled

A far more effective argument against national sovereignty is climate change. Global warming widely is seen as the greatest crisis not only in our time but in all of history. Since it affects the whole world, it must be a global question requiring global answers. The answers are far from clear, politically and above all practically, but the questions tend to relegate all other issues to the sidelines. On July 23, 2019, the French National Assembly was convened to vote on the Comprehensive and Economic Trade Agreement (CETA) between Canada and the European Union. Such international trade agreements greatly increase the volume of air transport and resulting CO2 emissions. This agreement risks having ruinous effects on ecologically sound agriculture in France and other European countries. It also introduces private arbitration tribunals allowing private corporations to overrule and fine governments—putting profits ahead of environmental protection. It is a perfect example of why "globalization" is bad for the environment.

That same day, 16-year-old climate crusader Greta Thunberg was at the French National Assembly, exhorting the legislators to grow up and do something now! Asked about CETA, she replied that she had no opinion. She had nothing to say about a trade agreement destined to augment trans-Atlantic air traffic, just as she was getting ready to set an example of ecological virtue by crossing the Atlantic by yacht.

The voyage on a yacht provided by the royal family of Monaco amounts to a caricature of environmental issues being reduced to life-style choices that are available to the rich but not, for example, to the *Gilets Jaunes.* Wealthy people who can afford an ecological lifestyle do not easily identify with people whose modest means leave them no choices at all. There are many environmental issues in need of vigorous public policy. There is urgent need for governments to regulate polluting industries, to take measures against manufacturers responsible for re-leasing tons of plastic wrapping into the environment, against the built-in obsolescence that destines most of currently produced goods to an early death on the scrapheap.

However, the massively sponsored and publicized crusade around the figurehead of Greta Thunberg focused almost exclusively on the demand for drastic reduction of CO2 emissions by shifting to renewable energies. That is already the official policy of most Western governments, of the United Nations, of the European Union, and above all, by leading financial and business interests. The main political re-sistance comes from the less advantaged sections of the population, who don't want to have to pay the taxes and submit to the cutbacks in pensions and social allocations that would finance "green" energy policy. The Greta Thunberg crusade is a powerful tool to overcome such popular resistance. It very quickly upstaged the *Gilets Jaunes* movement in mid-2019. Many consider social welfare or the threat of nuclear war to be minor issues compared to the imminent destruction of life on earth.

Some on the left see the current anti-CO2 movement to be a bold challenge to capitalism, above all to the fossil fuel industry. This overlooks the fact that those who control the fossil fuel industry can easily control the renewable energy industries—those such as the Rockefellers, who are deeply committed to the transformation. Those who profit from one can profit from the other, so long as government incentives are favorable.

In 2004, former US vice president Al Gore and David Blood, previously the head of Goldman Sachs Asset Management, joined together to create a firm, Generation Investment Analysis, designed to make "sustainable investment" profitable. Capitalism always needs new investment frontiers, and Blood and Gore saw possibilities to "create opportunities from climate change."

"Our objective in innovating with this new model was to focus on the best return for our clients, full stop," Al Gore told a business interviewer.[56] Now there is certainly nothing wrong with that—the job of investment advisors is to focus on their clients' returns. And there is every reason to believe in their best intentions toward the climate. When a former U.S. vice president and almost-successful Democratic Party candidate for the presidency combines with the investment manager of Goldman Sachs, there is a lot of clout there. But investment is a private choice of the privileged, like lifestyle. The hypothetical "oil lobby" is totally overshadowed today in comparison with the "green lobby" of financial institutions that see energy transition as the new frontier for a huge profitable business cycle.

The children's crusade is a fantastically successful public relations campaign to legitimize rigorous government measures favoring "green" investment, even at an uncalculated cost to the public.[57]

To save the planet, no sacrifice is too great. But a few crucial questions are neglected.

First of all, why not demand some sacrifices from the military-industrial complex? The Pentagon "carbon footprint" is colossal. Why not demand that the government shift spending from the military to ecological infrastructure reconstruction?

Some heavily subsidized energy sources are far from providing a substitute for fossil fuels—such as the windmills that deface the countryside with huge objects that don't get the job done. Energy transition

56 Lenny T. Mendonca and Jeremy Oppenheim, "Investing in sustainability: An interview with Al Gore and David Blood, May 2007. https://www.mckinsey.com/business-functions/sustainability/our-insights/investing-in-sustainability-an-interview-with-al-gore-and-david-blood.

57 See "The Manufacturing of Greta Thunberg—For Consent: The Behavioural Change Project 'To Change Everything'": http://www.wrongkindofgreen.org/2019/09/18/the-manufacturing-of-greta-thunberg-for-consent-the-behavioural-change-project-to-change-everything-volume-ii-act-v/.

cannot go faster than the technological means to do it. A truly effective energy transition would require not simply subsidies but the sort of public industrial policy which is virtually impossible under European Union rules enforcing private sector competition. The search for profit can lead into many a dead end, especially when subsidized by the taxpayer.

In any case, the contribution by Europe and the United States to carbon emissions is declining and insignificant compared to those of China and other developing nations.

The Thunberg message is that there is no harm in skipping school since "the science is settled." There is nothing more to learn. But is the "science" really settled? Indeed, is science ever "settled"? Science advances by eternal questioning, and hundreds, even thousands of serious scientists are not so sure that this matter is settled. What is meant by that slogan is that all that may be needed to be understood about the extremely vast subject of climate, whose study involves a broad range of specialized knowledge, has been decided by the IPCC.

The official role of the U.N.-sponsored Intergovernmental Panel on Climate Change (IPCC) is "to assess on a comprehensive, objective, open and transparent basis the scientific, technical and socio-economic information relevant to understanding the scientific basis of risk of *human-induced climate change,* its potential impacts and options for adaptation and mitigation." (My emphasis) It is also specified that: "Since the IPCC is an intergovernmental body, review of IPCC documents should involve both peer review by experts and review by governments."

This clearly means that the IPCC works with a built-in bias, enforced by *government* review, to relate climate change to human causes. Other causes are neglected. The mandate obliges the IPCC—which does not do its own research—to sponsor studies of human-generated CO2 emissions, rather than of solar radiation or other atmospheric conditions. Certainly, concerning such an important issue, all aspects should be studied in a true scientific spirit: open mindedness and free exchange of viewpoints.

The treatment of the climate issue as "settled" is characteristic of contemporary liberal authoritarianism. The early 21st century is a strange period in which anyone who challenges, or simply casts doubt on the "common narrative," whether about the climate, or immigration, or gender, or regime change wars, can be denounced as a "denier" or "conspiracy theorist" or "racist" or "apologist for dictators." The pressure to conform has increased tremendously, with growing censorship of opinions characterized as "hate" or "conspiratorial." This has an intimidating effect on public discussion.

The mainstream media have moved farther and farther away from informing the public and nearer to instructing them in what they should think and do. Opinion managers assume that the masses are not mature enough to judge complex matters. Climate, like other complex technical subjects, is considered beyond the public's ability to comprehend. This assumption underlies the rejection of debate, which could only "mislead" the public on questions that need to be left to experts.

Unfortunately, there is a degree of truth in this. The issue of expertise raises what is perhaps the greatest of all contemporary challenges to "government by the people": the extreme, overwhelming difficulty of understanding our bafflingly complex high technology world. People are constantly having "technological progress" imposed on them, whether they like it or not, because experts have decided it is good for them.

A generation so uncertain and so avid for certainty needs to be reminded of John Stuart Mill's principle that the credibility of our beliefs results from their ability to stand up to constant attempts to refute them. Our most cherished convictions "have no safeguard to rest on, but a standing invitation to the whole world to prove them unfounded."[58]

A powerful communications industry linked to dominant economic interests is there to provide relatively simple but emotionally charged answers to such a difficult problem as climate change. Obviously, crusading school children didn't figure it out; they were taught this lesson then took it into the streets. Their sincerity is not in doubt. But rather than the public picking up these lessons second hand from kids skipping school, it would be more promising to allow and encourage conflictual public debate among scientists, hoping that knowledge can advance, as it always has, from the confrontation of opposing opinions.

---

58 "If even the Newtonian philosophy were not permitted to be questioned, mankind could not feel as complete assurance of its truth as they now do. The beliefs which we have most warrant for have no safeguard to rest on, but a standing invitation to the whole world to prove them unfounded." -John Stuart Mill, *On Liberty,* 1859.

The People Against Themselves

Identity Politics has been cynically exploited by the Clintonian Democrats as a way to develop electoral clienteles. (This recalls the typical manipulation of ethnic groups by the Democratic political machines in major cities.) The method involves spectacular promotion of token women, blacks, Latinos, to "represent" populations in purely symbolic fashion. It thrives on a post-socialist, moralizing ideology which has simultaneously promoted multicultural diversity and identity chauvinism, oblivious to their contradictions. This combination can only lead to trouble as each group finds itself in moral status competition with others. There are more and more speeches and laws condemning "hate," but hate does not appear to be diminishing. Indeed, the more "hate" is condemned, the more it flourishes.

When individuals are bunched into groups assigned intrinsic qualities—from victimhood to racism—normal human ties of mutual concern, shared purpose, comprehension and compassion are severed. In a grotesque development, new "gender" identities are invented, whose "cause" overshadows the real problems of genuinely disadvantaged minorities. Economic issues are forgotten as groups mobilize solely to police "attitudes." Billionaires prosper more than ever before, while down below people bicker over safe spaces and toilet use.

Identity politics and political correctness are sometimes called "neo-Marxist." In reality, these practices are the total reversal of the Marxist view of society, in which conflict did not arise from intrinsic qualities, but from a class structure determined by the organization of the means of production. The idea behind the class struggle was not that the working class should "hate" the bourgeoisie, but rather that the dispossessed should get together to analyze and change the social relationships related to the production and use of wealth. The plays of Bertolt Brecht illustrate this point: the capitalist does not oppress the worker because he is a bad guy, but because capitalism forces him to compete with others in pushing down wages in order to survive, or his business will go under. Whatever is or was wrong with Marxism, it projected a view of humanity far kinder and gentler than what prevails in the United States today, with its spillover throughout the West.

Much of the far left sees its villains in purely moral rather than politico-economic terms. People on "the right" are simply bad people with bad attitudes. For the Antifa in particular, people on the "extreme right" (for them, a broad category) must be opposed by censorship or violence, not by rational argument.

The great social advantage of the Christian religion (and of others, I assume) was to regard each individual as a soul, a "spark of the divine." A rational spirituality could still accept the concept of soul as a precious spark of life. The soul demands respect. This mutual respect is visibly evaporating in much of the West. Instead, a society dominated by selfish competition sees people in terms of "winners" and "losers," inciting many "losers" to despair. Millions of men and women sacrifice their minds and bodies to drugs. Americans are so distrustful of each other that many feel they must be fully armed. Since people are so dissatisfied with themselves, let technology fix it. Sex change is the spearhead of this trend. Children are being taught at an early age that the sex they were born with can be discarded for another. Brain inserts will come next to make people "smarter"—what does that mean? More like the robots designed to replace them? The "transhumanists" are preparing to phase out humanity in favor of new improved versions. These transformations are being pursued by the private sector, with support from public authorities but outside of democratic control. They are presented as inevitable progress because if technology can, it will. It will, because finance capital is forever on the outlook for some profitable social upheaval.

The contemporary West combines a mood of "anything goes" with a new sort of nameless tyranny. The term "fascism" is misleading. Fascism historically involved a strong charismatic leader of a disciplined, armed party, imposing unity and order on the basis of a clear (however erroneous) program commanding mass support. Today, whatever leadership there is lies behind the scenes, promoting chaos and disorder. Today's strange tyranny is something new, without a name of its own. In the "information society," it has no clear doctrine but rather a fluid and often contradictory set of beliefs circulated by the information industry. This is a media-message tyranny, and it is significant that the most important instance of government repression has concerned not some act of violent rebellion but the peaceful revelation of facts that the public was not supposed to know. Treated by U.S leaders as Enemy Number One, Julian Assange was not building bombs to attack Washington but was simply conveying significant information to the public.

Yet the government rarely censors. Censorship is privatized. Free discussion is increasingly restricted by the informal imposition of a "common discourse" on a range of key issues—Russia, Middle East "dictators," immigration, climate, gender—imposed not by direct repression but by social conformism. Correct opinion is dictated by mainstream media and their publicized commentators, Hollywood, propaganda NGOs (of which the most egregious is Avaaz, which has recently been calling for volunteers to denounce and silence politically incorrect websites in Europe), more ominously by social media, and even by militant groups calling themselves "antifascist."

Today's "charismatic dictator" is the information and entertainment industry. This industry creates its own simulation of reality. The artificial reality can include "both sides" to issues which miss the crucial point and manipulate would-be rebels.

We have reached a point where most significant division in Western society may well be the sharp break between those whose view of reality is guided by the "common discourse" and those who see it as false. We see friendships being destroyed by this rupture in belief. The non-believers don't agree among themselves. But at least they are alike in attempting to revive free critical thinking.

The fight for truth is the most critical battle in our emerging civil wars. So long as people fail to distinguish between manipulation and honesty, between truth and falsehood, they can neither define correctly what is wrong nor find solutions.

35.

Truth

The most obvious lesson to draw from a long life of observing public events is that the spirit of the times can change drastically from one period to another. In many respects, there was more optimism in the depths of the Depression than in our age of consumer abundance. Today's technical means of communication should be used to spread knowledge and mutual understanding. Instead, they have been used to deceive the public, spreading lies to gain support for unjustifiable wars—Yugoslavia, Afghanistan, Iraq, Libya, Syria….

The practice of deceit reached an extravagant new peak of danger with the campaign of calumny against Russia. In reality motivated by Vladimir Putin's 2007 declared rejection of a "unipolar world" dominated by the United States, the hostility has been fed by a crescendo of falsehoods. Russia was stigmatized as an aggressor for its defensive reaction to the Western-provoked crisis in Ukraine in 2014. Then, the electoral upset of Hillary Clinton in 2016 set off an operation to arouse chauvinist hostility based on the preposterous assertion that her defeat was caused by "Russian interference." The enormity of this lie has not prevented it from gaining overwhelming acceptance in the United States—accompanied by unprecedented U.S. military provocation against two nuclear powers, Russia and China.

The need to combat official deception has never been more urgent.

What we have observed over the past twenty years is an increasing growth of the sort of propaganda appropriate to wartime. This is part of the frantic effort of U.S. leaders to maintain a global hegemony that is increasingly rejected—perhaps even, finally, in the European satellites. Rejection of U.S. hegemony has become the National Liberation Struggle of our times.

For around two centuries, the "Left" was the term designating the most forward-looking, creative political forces in our societies. The Left fought for the independence of Vietnam and other colonized Third World countries. Now it is absent from the whole international movement to restore national sovereignty, condemned as "extreme right."

The Left is sabotaged from within by dogmatism. When "left" is reduced to a catechism, it cuts itself off from the real world and serves only as a means to denounce or punish deviations from the creed. Especially in the United States, but with European branches, the militant sect of Antifa has set itself up as the Torquemada of true leftism. It does not restrict itself to physical attacks on white supremacists in Portland, Oregon, but takes it upon itself to issue fatwas against humble writers trying to find the needle of truth in the haystack of lies served up by the authoritarian neoliberal center.

Oddly enough, I first heard of Caitlin Johnstone in the summer of 2017 when her writing was the object of a barrage of attacks on CounterPunch. That was indeed the start of Caitlin's rise to great prominence in anti-war circles and the beginning of CounterPunch's decline from "fearless muckraking" to snide sniping at the genuine heirs to the independent spirit of the founder, Alexander Cockburn.

The gist of the CounterPunch attacks on the Australian Johnstone were that she dared say she would join even with someone on the right against war. That is simple good sense, but it was picked up by the Antifa purification squad as proof of tendencies toward fascism. When I saw them coming after Caitlin, I figured they'd be coming after me, and that my association with CounterPunch was soon coming to an end.

The specialty of the Antifa is to situate the threat of tyranny on the powerless margins of society—from isolated groups of costume party neo-Nazis to outspoken persons on the left accused of "red-brown" tendencies. This amounts to keeping the Left herded into its sheep pen, while the wolves roam freely. For tyranny is not to be found among such eccentrics, but smack in the center of society, the authoritarian center represented politically by the Clintonian Democratic Party, mainstream media, the military industrial complex and globalized neoliberal finance capital. In practice, the Antifa are working to maintain what they call "the Left" as a powerless support group to the authoritarian center, by protecting it from "the extreme right" or from an alleged "red-brown" coalition. A marginal left fighting a marginal right keeps the respectable "center" in power forever.

If anything, Antifa exclusionism can only promote the far right as the only viable opposition to a system which includes Antifa.

Antifa attacked me, I believe, for the fact that I give priority to telling the truth and opposing war to just about anything else. Their pretext was the fact that, in my articles on the 2017 French elections, I noted similarities between the views of left candidate Jean-Luc Mélenchon and National Front candidate Marine LePen, notably on improving relations with Russia, adding that they could not get together because of opposing views on immigration. Nobody who knows anything about French politics could deny that. But for the Antifa, mentioning Marine LePen without raving against her "fascism" meant that I was "shilling" for her. As an Israeli Antifa, self-appointed gate-keeper of the Left, put it on his blog, I am a "rat" trying to infiltrate the Left to move it toward fascism. Considering how long I've been around, I have been making very slow progress in that project.

If Antifa is "the Left," they can have it. I have never fought to show that I am "on the left," but to tell the truth and to understand what is happening. Also, to be fair and factual, even about my adversaries. If I must claim a label, it would be that of an independent truth-seeker.

In many ways, the world as I have observed it has gotten worse over the decades. I am encouraged by two things. One is the presence of a new generation of truth seekers. The truth is alive, however marginalized.

The other is a simple fact learned from experience. Life is full of surprises. Things never turn out exactly as planned or foreseen. The future looks grim, but we haven't seen it. It is surely full of surprises, and they can't all be bad.

Index

Made in the USA
Las Vegas, NV
22 March 2024